Contents

1052

NEW EDITION

Biology

Mary Jones and Geoff Jones

HAMPTON
SCHOOL

Name	Form	State	Date	Initials
Richard Coshie	5G	N	8/9/05	RJD
Simon Blythe	3A	A	6/9/06	M I J
Max Barford	3F			
Robert Morey	3A	C-	7/9/15	GJR (Mr Ryan)

State   N New   A Good   B Fair   C Poor

CAMBRIDGE
UNIVERSITY PRESS

PUBLISHED BY THE PRESS SYNDICATE OF THE UNIVERSITY OF CAMBRIDGE
The Pitt Building, Trumpington Street, Cambridge, United Kingdom

CAMBRIDGE UNIVERSITY PRESS
The Edinburgh Building, Cambridge CB2 2RU, UK
40 West 20th Street, New York, NY 10011–4211, USA
477 Williamstown Road, Port Melbourne, VIC 3207, Australia
Ruiz de Alarcón 13, 28014 Madrid, Spain
Dock House, The Waterfront, Cape Town 8001, South Africa

http://www.cambridge.org

First published 1984
Fourth printing 1986
Second edition 1987
Eighth printing 1993
Third edition 1995
Eleventh printing 2004

Prepared for publication by Stenton Associates

Printed in Italy by G. Canale & C. S.p.A.

A catalogue record for this book is available from the British Library

ISBN 0 521 45618 5 paperback

Notice to teachers

Acknowledgements

3l, Bruce Iverson/SPL; 3r, 16, 38, 51, 82, 84l, 88, 89, 92b, 93, 103, 163, 166, 173r, 174, 211, 228, 229, 265, 273, Biophoto Associates; 17, 195, 220, 248, 294, Michael Brooke; 20, Hattie Young/SPL; 25, NHPA/A.N.T.; 52, Andrew Syred/SPL; 73, Guatti/Colorsport; 84r, Professor P. Motta, Dept of Anatomy, University 'La Sapienza', Rome/SPL; 92t, Centre for Cell & Tissue Research, York; 97, Dr Jeremy Burgess/SPL; 108, courtesy of Dr R.H.F. Hunter; 115, Roy Shaw; 116, Paul Franklin/Oxford Scientific Films; 122, Mrs J.M. Bebb; 156, Mike Birkhead/Oxford Scientific Films; 165, courtesy of J.A. Chapman; 170, Science Photo Library; 173tl, Chris Bjornberg/SPL; 173bl, 202, 271b, 286, 290t, C. James Webb; 181, courtesy of John Crothers, Field Studies Council at Nettlecombe Court, Taunton; 183, Eleanor Jones; 189, John Shaw/NHPA; 191, Bryan & Cherry Alexander; 193t, Ronald Toms/Oxford Scientific Films; 193b, J. Allan Cash; 194, R. Thompson/Frank Lane Photographic Agency; 198t, Michael Jones/AZ Botanical Collection; 198b, David Woodfall/NHPA; 199l, 223, 253b, Nigel Cattlin/Holt Studios International; 199r, G. Behrens/Ardea, London; 201, Heather Angel; 203t, Ardea, London; 203b, courtesy of Dr A.J. Pontin; 210, NASA, GSFC/SPL; 214t, Sean Sprague/Panos; 214b, Martin Bond/SPL; 216l, Michael Harvey/Panos; 216r, Brian Rogers/Biofotos; 218, 219, WWF/R.C.V. Jeffery; 221, Tick Ahearn; 224l, IHR (Littlehampton); 224r, Glasshouse Crops Research Institute Index; 225, Kathie Atkinson/Oxford Scientific Films; 227, Paul Richards/Life File; 230, Cystic Fibrosis Trust; 239, Hutchison Library; 242, David Parker/SPL; 245t, NHPA/Agence Nature; 245b, Geoff Jones; 246t, by courtesy of the National Portrait Gallery, London; 246b, L. Lee Rue/Frank Lane Picture Agency; 250, Stephen Dalton/NHPA; 253t, Primrose Peacock/Holt Studios International; 259, Barnaby's Picture Library; 260, Maurice Nimmo/AZ Botanical Collection; 262, D.P. Wilson/Frank Lane Picture Agency; 268, A. Neil/Panos; 271t, Ron Giling/Panos; 276, Liba Taylor/Panos; 277l, Philippe Plailly/SPL; 277r, courtesy of Professor Richard Begent; 278, Barry Bomzer/Tony Stone Images; 279, Professor P. Motta/G. Macchiarelli/University 'La Sapienza', Rome/SPL; 281, David Hoffman; 290b, courtesy of Adnams Sole Bay Brewery/photo by Steve Wolfenden; 291, Fergus Smith/Life File; 292, Abbie Enock/Travel Ink/Life File; 293, courtesy of HP Foods Ltd, Aston Cross, Birmingham; 297, Geoff Tompkinson/SPL

NHPA = Natural History Photographic Agency
SPL = Science Photo Library

The 'facts' that appear on pages 33, 49, 81, 87, 109, 110, 115, 117, 118, 133, 154, 175, 177, 268 and 284 are reproduced by kind permission of the Guinness Book of Records 1995 Copyright © Guinness Publishing Limited 1994.

The following illustrations were drawn by Alasdair Jones: 6.9, 7.34, 8.35, 8.37, 8.50, 9.1, 9.23, 10.1, 10.9, 10.10, 11.11, 11.18(b), 12.5(part), 12.8, 12.9, 12.10, 12.15, 13.6, 13.22, 13.23(part), 13.24, 13.25, 13.26, 13.27, 14.4, 14.6, 14.24, 15.12, 16.13, 18.2, 18.3, 18.13, 18.19, 19.2.

Front cover: Bengal tiger, Tony Stone; Back cover: pink orchid cactus flower, Tony Stone; flamingo, Telegraph Colour Library

1   The organisation of living things

1.1   All living things have certain characteristics.

Biology is the study of living things, which are often called **organisms**. Living organisms have several features or **characteristics** which make them different from objects which are not alive.

1 They **reproduce**.
2 They **feed**.
3 They **respire** – that is, they release energy from their food, often by combining it with oxygen.
4 They **grow**.
5 They **excrete** – that is, they get rid of substances which they do not want. These have been made by some of the chemical reactions going on inside them.
6 They **move**.
7 They are **sensitive** – that is, they can sense and respond to changes in their surroundings.
8 They are made of **cells**.

Cell structure

1.2   Microscopes are used to study cells.

All living things are made of cells. Cells are very small, so large organisms contain millions of cells.

To see cells clearly, you need to use a microscope. The kind of microscope used in a school laboratory is called a **light microscope** because it shines light through the piece of animal or plant you are looking at. It uses glass lenses to magnify and focus the image. A very good light microscope can magnify about 1500 times, and can show all the structures in Figs 1.1 and 1.2.

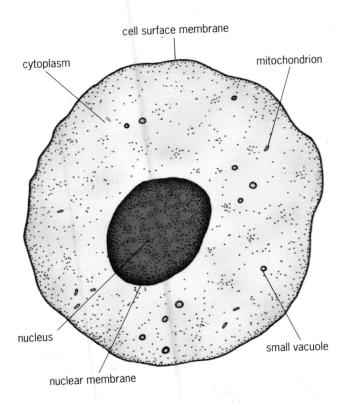

1.1   A typical animal cell as seen with a light microscope

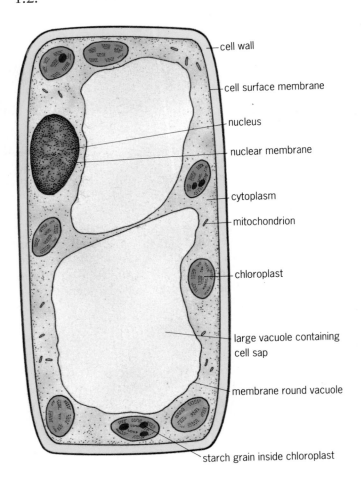

1.2   A typical plant cell as seen with a light microscope

1

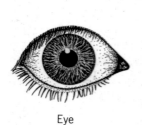

Eye

Hand lens magnifies x 10

light microscope magnifies x 400

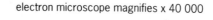

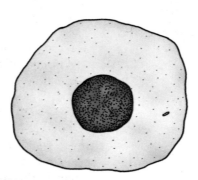

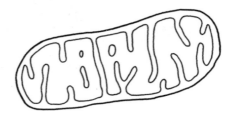

electron microscope magnifies x 40 000

The human eye cannot see most cells

Using a hand lens, a cell can be seen as a dot.

With a light microscope, you can see some of the structures inside a cell, such as a mitochondrion.

With an electron microscope, the internal structures of a mitochondrion can be seen.

To see even smaller things inside a cell, an **electron microscope** is used. This uses a beam of electrons instead of light, and can magnify up to 500 000 times. This means that a lot more detail can be seen inside a cell, as shown in Fig 1.5.

Questions

1 List the characteristics of living things.
2 How many times can a good light microscope magnify?
3 How many times can an electron microscope magnify?

1.3 All cells have a cell membrane.

Whatever sort of animal or plant they come from, all cells have a **cell membrane** around the outside. Inside it is a jelly-like substance called **cytoplasm**, in which are found many small structures called **organelles**. The most obvious of these organelles is usually the **nucleus**. The whole content of the cell is called **protoplasm**.

1.4 Plant cells have a cell wall.

All plant cells are surrounded by a **cell wall** made of **cellulose**. Paper, which is made from cell walls, is also made of cellulose. Animal cells never have cell walls made of cellulose. Cellulose belongs to a group of substances called **polysaccharides**, which are described in Section 4.8. It forms fibres, which criss-cross over one another to form a very strong covering to the cell (Fig 1.6). This helps to protect and support the cell.

Because of the spaces between the fibres, even very large molecules are able to go through the cellulose cell wall. It is therefore said to be **fully permeable**.

2

1.5 Cell membranes are partially permeable.

All cells have a membrane surrounding the cell. It is called the **cell surface membrane**. In a plant cell, it is very difficult to see, because it is right against the cell wall.

The cell surface membrane is a very thin layer of protein and fat. It is very important to the cell because it controls what goes in and out of it. It is said to be **partially permeable**, which means that it will let some substances through but not others.

1.6 Cytoplasm is a complex solution.

Cytoplasm is a clear jelly. It is nearly all water; about 70% is water in many cells. It contains many substances dissolved in it, especially proteins.

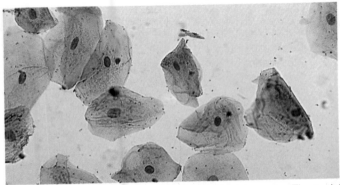

1.4 Human cheek cells seen through a light microscope. The nuclei are stained a deeper colour than the cytoplasm.

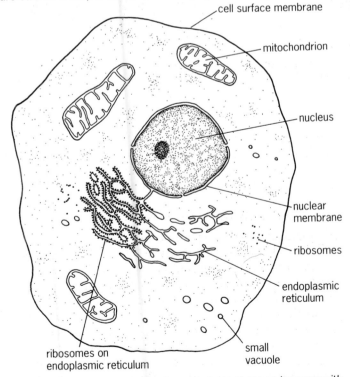

cell surface membrane

mitochondrion

nucleus

nuclear membrane

ribosomes

endoplasmic reticulum

ribosomes on endoplasmic reticulum

small vacuole

1.5 A typical animal cell, showing structures that can be seen with an electron microscope

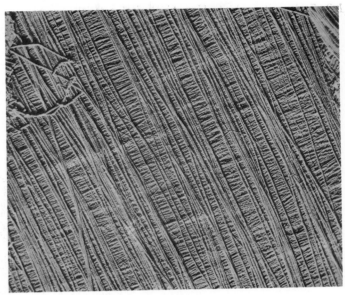

1.6 Cellulose fibres in a plant cell wall

1.7 Most cells contain vacuoles.

A vacuole is a space in a cell, surrounded by a membrane, and containing a solution. Plant cells have very large vacuoles, which contain a solution of sugars and other substances called **cell sap**.

Animal cells have much smaller vacuoles, which may contain food or water.

1.8 Endoplasmic reticulum is a membrane network.

Endoplasmic reticulum is a maze of membranes which runs all through the cytoplasm. They are assembly lines for making fats and proteins out of smaller molecules in the cell. Endoplasmic reticulum is found in all cells.

1.9 Chloroplasts trap the energy of sunlight.

Chloroplasts are never found in animal cells, but most of the cells in the green parts of plants have them. They contain the green colouring or pigment called **chlorophyll**. Chlorophyll absorbs sunlight, and the energy of sunlight is then used for making food for the plant by **photosynthesis** (Chapter 5).

Chloroplasts often contain starch grains, which have been made by photosynthesis. Animal cells never contain starch grains.

1.10 Mitochondria release energy from food.

Most cells have mitochondria, because it is here that the cell releases energy from food. The energy is needed to help it move and grow. Mitochondria are sometimes called the 'powerhouses' of the cell. The energy is released by combining food with oxygen, in a process called **aerobic respiration**. The more active a cell, the more mitochondria it has.

3

1.11 Ribosomes make proteins.

Ribosomes are very tiny, round objects, often attached to the endoplasmic reticulum. It is here that proteins are made, by joining together smaller molecules called **amino acids**. To get the amino acids in the right order, the ribosomes follow instructions from the nucleus. This process is described in Chapter 15.

Practical 1.1 Looking at animal cells

The easiest place to find animal cells is on yourself. If you colour or **stain** the cells they are quite easy to see using a light microscope (Fig 1.7).

1 Using a clean fingernail, or section lifter, gently rub off a little of the lining from the inside of your cheek.
2 Put your cells onto the middle of a clean microscope slide, and gently spread them out. You will probably not be able to see anything at all at this stage.
3 Put on a few drops of **methylene blue**.
4 Gently lower a coverslip over the stained cells, trying not to trap any air bubbles.
5 Use filter paper or blotting paper to clean up the slide, and then look at it under the low power of a microscope.
6 Make a labelled drawing of a few cells.

Questions

1 Which part of the cell stained the darkest blue?
2 Name two structures which you could not see in your cells, but which you would have been able to see if you were using an electron microscope.

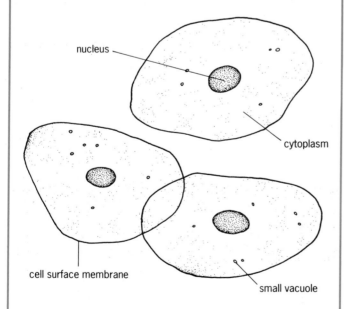

1.7 Human cheek cells seen through a light microscope

Practical 1.2 Looking at plant cells

To be able to see cells clearly under a microscope, you need a very thin layer. It is best if it is only one cell thick. An easy place to find such a layer is inside an onion bulb.

1 Cut a small piece from an onion bulb, and use forceps to peel a small piece of thin skin, called epidermis, from the inside of it. Do not let it get dry.
2 Put a drop or two of water onto the centre of a clean microscope slide. Put the piece of epidermis into it, and spread it flat.
3 Gently lower a coverslip onto it.
4 Use filter paper or blotting paper to clean up the slide, and then look at it under the low power of a microscope.
5 Make a labelled drawing of a few cells.

Questions

1 Name two structures which you can see in these cells, but which you could not see in the cheek cells.
2 Most plant cells have chloroplasts, but these do not. Suggest a reason for this.

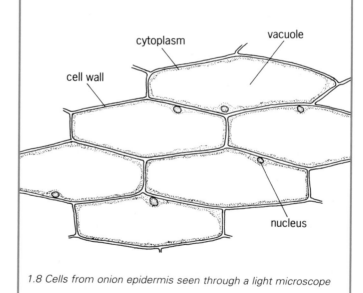

1.8 Cells from onion epidermis seen through a light microscope

1.12 The nucleus stores inherited information.

The nucleus is where the information is stored which helps the ribosomes to make the right sort of proteins. The information is kept on the **chromosomes**, which are inherited from the organism's parents.

Chromosomes are very long, but so thin that they cannot easily be seen even by the electron microscope. However, when the cell is dividing, they become short and thick, and can be seen with a good light microscope.

Table 1.1 A comparison between animal and plant cells

Similarities

1 Both have a cell surface membrane surrounding the cell.
2 Both have cytoplasm.
3 Both contain a nucleus.
4 Both contain mitochondria.
5 Both contain endoplasmic reticulum.
6 Both contain ribosomes.

Differences

Plant cells	Animal cells
1 Have a cellulose cell wall outside cell surface membrane	No cell wall
2 Often have chloroplasts containing chlorophyll	No chloroplasts
3 Often have very large vacuoles, containing cell sap	Only have small vacuoles
4 Often have starch granules	Never have starch granules; sometimes have glycogen granules
5 Often regular in shape	Often irregular in shape

Animal and plant cells obtain their food in different ways. Plants make their own food, so their cells contain chloroplasts. Starch granules store some of the food they make. Animals often have to move to find their food. This is made easier if their cells do not have a rigid wall.

Questions

1 What sort of cells are surrounded by a cell surface membrane?
2 What are plant cell walls made of?
3 What does fully permeable mean?
4 What does partially permeable mean?
5 What is the main constituent of cytoplasm?
6 What is a vacuole?
7 What is cell sap?
8 Chloroplasts contain chlorophyll. What does chlorophyll do?
9 What happens inside mitochondria?
10 Where are proteins made?
11 What is stored in the nucleus?
12 Why can chromosomes be seen only when a cell is dividing?

Cells and organisms

1.13 There is division of labour between cells.

A large organism such as yourself may contain many millions of cells, but not all the cells are alike. Almost all of them can carry out the activities which are characteristic of living things (Section 1.1), but many of them specialise in doing some of these better than other cells do. Muscle cells, for example, are specially adapted for movement. Cells in the leaf of a plant are specially adapted for making food by photosynthesis.

1.14 Similar cells are grouped to form tissues.

Often, cells which specialise in the same activity will be found together. A group of cells like this is called a **tissue**. An example of a tissue is the layer of cells lining your stomach. These cells make enzymes to help to digest your food (Fig 1.9).

The stomach also contains other tissues. For example, there is a layer of muscle in the stomach wall, made of cells which can move. This muscle tissue makes the wall of the stomach move in and out, churning the food and mixing it up with the enzymes.

1.15 An organ contains tissues working together.

All the tissues in the stomach work together, although they each have their own job to do. A group of tissues like this makes up an **organ**. The stomach is an organ. Other organs include the heart, the kidneys and the lungs.

1.16 A system contains organs working together.

The stomach is only one of the organs which help in the digestion of food. The mouth, the intestines and the stomach are all part of the **digestive system**. The heart is part of the circulatory system, while each kidney is part of the excretory system.

The way in which organisms are built up can be summarised like this:

Organelles make up **cells** which make up **tissues** which make up **organs** which make up **systems** which make up **organisms**.

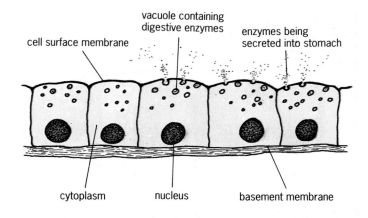

1.9 Cells lining the stomach; an example of a tissue

Chapter revision questions

1 Make a list of the parts of a cell which can be seen:
(a) in the light microscope as well as the electron microscope;
(b) only in the electron microscope.

2 Arrange these structures in order of size, beginning with the smallest.
stomach, mitochondrion, starch grain, cheek cell, nucleus, ribosome

3 For each of the following, state whether it is an organelle, a cell, a tissue, an organ, a system, or an organism.
(a) heart (b) chloroplast (c) nucleus (d) cheek cell
(e) onion epidermis (f) onion bulb (g) onion plant
(h) mitochondrion (i) human being (j) lung.

4 State which part of a plant cell:
(a) makes food by photosynthesis
(b) releases energy from food
(c) controls what goes in and out of the cell
(d) stores information about making proteins
(e) contains cell sap
(f) protects the outside of the cell.

5 A tree is a living organism, but a bicycle is not. Using these as examples, explain the differences between living and non-living things.

6 With the aid of large labelled diagrams, make a comparison of a typical plant cell and a typical animal cell. Whenever possible, explain the reasons for their differences and similarities.

7 Use the index to find out about the *structure* and *functions* of each of the following kinds of cells. For each one, explain how its structure helps it carry out its function.
palisade cell, root hair cell, guard cell, xylem cell, phloem sieve cell, sperm cell, ovum, neurone.

8 Use the index to find information about each of the following systems in humans. For each system:
(a) list the main organs which make up the system
(b) outline the main functions of the system.
nervous system, circulation (blood) system, breathing (gas exchange) system, urinary system, male and female reproductive systems.

2 Diffusion, osmosis and active transport

2.1 Diffusion results from random movement.

Atoms, molecules and ions are always moving. The higher the temperature, the faster they move. In a solid substance the molecules cannot move very far, because they are held together by forces between them. In a liquid they can move more freely, knocking into one another and rebounding. In a gas they are freer still. Molecules and ions can also move freely when they are in solution.

When they can move freely, molecules tend to spread themselves out as evenly as they can. This happens with gases, solutions, and mixtures of liquids. Imagine, for example, a rotten egg in one corner of a room, giving off hydrogen sulphide gas. To begin with, there will be a very high concentration of the gas near the egg, but none in the rest of the room. However, before long the hydrogen sulphide molecules have spread throughout the air in the room. Soon, you will not be able to tell where the smell first came from – the whole room will smell of hydrogen sulphide.

The hydrogen sulphide molecules have spread out or **diffused** through the air. Diffusion is the movement of particles from a place where they are in a high concentration, to a place where they are in a lower concentration. Diffusion evens out the particles.

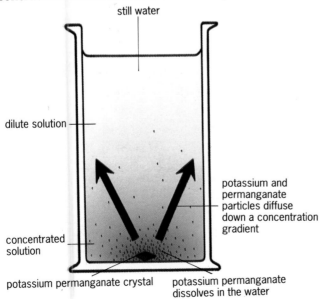

2.1 Apparatus to demonstrate diffusion

still water

dilute solution

concentrated solution

potassium permanganate crystal

potassium and permanganate particles diffuse down a concentration gradient

potassium permanganate dissolves in the water

Practical 2.1 To show diffusion in a solution

1 Fill a gas jar with water. Leave for several hours to let it become completely still.
2 Drop a small crystal of potassium permanganate into the water.
3 Make a labelled drawing of the gas jar to show how the colour is distributed.
4 Leave the gas jar completely undisturbed for several days.
5 Make a second drawing to show how the colour is distributed.
6 You can try this with other salts as well, such as copper sulphate or potassium dichromate.

Questions

1 Why was it important to leave the water to become completely still before the crystal was put in?
2 Why had the colour spread through the water at the end of your experiment?

2.2 Diffusion is important to living organisms.

Living organisms obtain many of their requirements by diffusion. They also get rid of many of their waste products in this way. For example, plants need carbon dioxide for photosynthesis. This diffuses from the air into the leaves, through the stomata. It does this because there is a lower concentration of carbon dioxide inside the leaf. This is because the cells are using it up. Outside the leaf in the air, there is a higher concentration. Carbon dioxide molecules therefore diffuse into the leaf, down this concentration gradient.

Oxygen, which is a waste product of photosynthesis, diffuses out in the same way. There is a higher concentration of oxygen inside the leaf, because it is being made there. Oxygen therefore diffuses out through the stomata into the air.

Diffusion is also important in gas exchange for respiration in animals and plants. Some of the products of digestion are absorbed from the ileum of mammals by diffusion.

1 What effect does temperature have on the movement of atoms, molecules and ions?
2 What is diffusion?
3 List three examples of diffusion which occur in living organisms.

2.3 In osmosis, water diffuses through a membrane.

Figure 2.2 illustrates a concentrated sugar solution, separated from a dilute sugar solution by a membrane. The membrane has holes or **pores** in it which are very small. An example of a membrane like this is visking tubing.

Water molecules are very small. Each one is made of two hydrogen atoms and one oxygen atom. Sugar molecules are many times larger than this. In visking tubing, the holes are big enough to let the water molecules through, but not the sugar molecules. It is called a **partially permeable membrane** because it will let some molecules through but not others.

There is a higher concentration of sugar molecules on the right-hand side of the membrane in Fig 2.2, than on the left-hand side. If the membrane was not there, the sugar molecules would diffuse from the concentrated solution into the dilute one until they were evenly spread out. However, they cannot do this because the pores in the membrane are too small for them to get through.

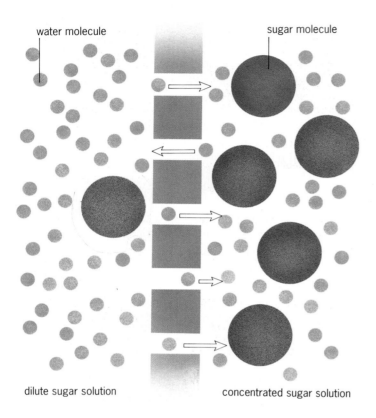

water molecule

sugar molecule

dilute sugar solution

concentrated sugar solution

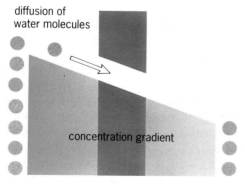

partially permeable membrane

diffusion of water molecules

concentration gradient

2.2 Osmosis

There are more water molecules on the left-hand side of the membrane than the right, so there is a concentration gradient for water molecules. They travel down the gradient, from left to right.

Is there a concentration gradient for sugar molecules? Why don't they travel down it?

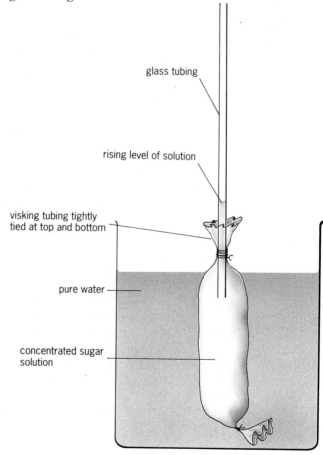

glass tubing

rising level of solution

visking tubing tightly tied at top and bottom

pure water

concentrated sugar solution

2.3 Apparatus to demonstrate osmosis. Water diffuses from the pure water into the sugar solution, down its concentration gradient. Sugar molecules cannot diffuse out, because the pores in the visking tubing are too small for them. Therefore, the level of the sugar solution rises, as it is diluted by the water diffusing into it by osmosis.

There is also a concentration gradient for the water molecules. On the left-hand side of the membrane, there is a high concentration of water molecules. On the right-hand side, the concentration of water molecules is lower because a lot of the space is taken up by sugar molecules. The water molecules therefore diffuse from the left-hand side into the right-hand side. They can do this because the pores in the membrane are large enough for them to get through.

What is the result of this? Water has diffused from the dilute solution, through the partially permeable membrane, into the concentrated solution. The concentrated solution will become more dilute, because of the extra water molecules coming into it.

This process is called **osmosis**. Osmosis is the diffusion of water molecules from a place where they are in a higher concentration (such as a dilute sugar solution), to a place where the water molecules are in a lower concentration (such as a concentrated sugar solution) through a partially permeable membrane.

Questions

1 Which is larger – a water molecule or a sugar molecule?
2 What is meant by a partially permeable membrane?
3 Give an example of an artificial partially permeable membrane.
4 How would you describe a solution which has a high concentration of water molecules?
5 What is osmosis?

2.4 Cell membranes are partially permeable.

Cell membranes behave very like visking tubing. They will let some substances pass through them, but not others. They are partially permeable membranes.

There is always cytoplasm on one side of any cell membrane. Cytoplasm is a solution of proteins and other substances in water. There is usually a solution on the other side of the membrane, too. Inside large animals, cells are surrounded by tissue fluid (Section 7.22). In the soil, the roots of plants are often surrounded by a film of water. Single-celled organisms such as *Amoeba* are also surrounded by water.

So, cell membranes often separate two different solutions – the cytoplasm, and the solution around the cell. If the solutions are of different concentrations, then osmosis will occur.

2.5 Osmosis and animal cells.

Animal cells burst in pure water Fig 2.4 illustrates an animal cell in pure water. The cytoplasm inside the cell is a fairly concentrated solution. The proteins and many other substances dissolved in it are too large to

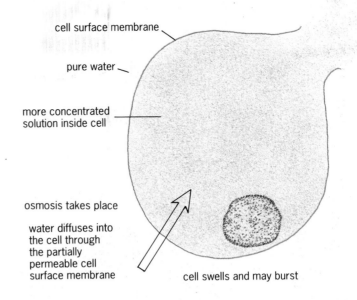

2.4 *An animal cell in pure water*

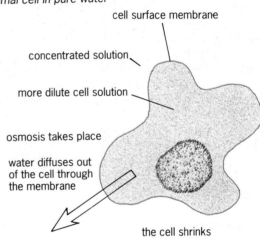

2.5 *An animal cell in a concentrated solution*

get through the cell membrane. Water molecules, though, can get through.

If you compare this situation with Fig 2.2, you will see that they are similar. The dilute solution in Fig 2.2 and the pure water in Fig 2.4 are each separated from a concentrated solution by a partially permeable membrane. In Fig 2.4 the concentrated solution is the cytoplasm and the partially permeable membrane is the cell membrane. Therefore osmosis will occur.

Water molecules will diffuse from the dilute solution into the concentrated solution. What happens to the cell? As more and more water enters it, it swells. The cell membrane has to stretch as the cell gets bigger, until eventually the strain is too much, and the cell bursts.

Animal cells shrink in concentrated solutions Fig 2.5 illustrates an animal cell in a concentrated solution. If this solution is more concentrated than the cytoplasm, then the water molecules will diffuse out of the cell. Look at Fig 2.2 to see why.

As the water molecules go out through the cell membrane, the cytoplasm shrinks. The cell shrivels up.

2.6 Osmosis and plant cells.

Plant cells do not burst in pure water Fig 2.6 illustrates a plant cell in pure water. Plant cells are surrounded by a cell wall. This is fully permeable, which means it will let any molecules go through it, so osmosis will not occur across it.

Although it is not easy to see, a plant cell also has a cell membrane just like an animal cell. The cell membrane is partially permeable. A plant cell in pure water will take in water by osmosis through its partially permeable cell membrane in the same way as an animal cell. As the water goes in, the cytoplasm and vacuole will swell.

However, the plant cell has a very strong cell wall around it. The cell wall is much stronger than the cell membrane and it stops the plant cell from bursting. The cytoplasm presses out against the cell wall, but the cell wall resists and presses back on the contents.

A plant cell in this state is rather like a blown-up tyre – tight and firm. It is said to be **turgid**. The turgidity of its cells helps a plant that has no wood in it to stay upright, and keeps the leaves firm. Plant cells are usually turgid.

Plant cells plasmolyse in concentrated solutions Fig 2.7 illustrates a plant cell in a concentrated solution. Like the animal cell in Fig 2.5, it will lose water by osmosis. The cytoplasm and the vacuole will shrink. As the cytoplasm shrinks, it stops pushing outwards on the cell wall. Like a tyre when some of the air has leaked out, the cell becomes floppy. It is said to be **flaccid**. If the cells in a plant become flaccid, then the plant loses its firmness and begins to wilt.

If the solution is very concentrated, then a lot of water will diffuse out of the cell. The cytoplasm and vacuole go on shrinking. The cell wall, though, is too stiff to be able to shrink much. As the cytoplasm shrinks further and further into the centre of the cell, the cell wall gets left behind. The cell membrane, surrounding the cytoplasm, tears away from the cell wall (Fig 2.7).

A cell like this is said to be **plasmolysed**. This does not normally happen because plant cells are not usually surrounded by very strong solutions. However, you can make cells become plasmolysed if you do Practical 2.2. Plasmolysis usually kills a plant cell because the cell membrane is damaged as it tears away from the cell wall.

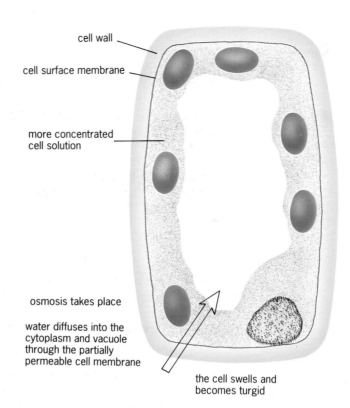

cell wall

cell surface membrane

more concentrated cell solution

osmosis takes place

water diffuses into the cytoplasm and vacuole through the partially permeable cell membrane

the cell swells and becomes turgid

2.6 A plant cell in pure water

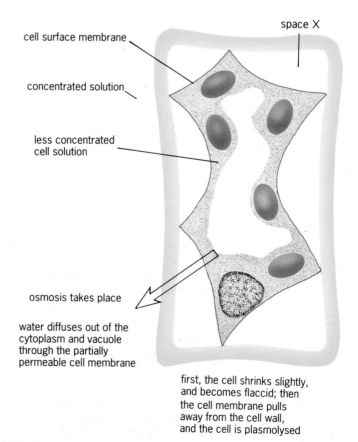

space X

cell surface membrane

concentrated solution

less concentrated cell solution

osmosis takes place

water diffuses out of the cytoplasm and vacuole through the partially permeable cell membrane

first, the cell shrinks slightly, and becomes flaccid; then the cell membrane pulls away from the cell wall, and the cell is plasmolysed

2.7 A plant cell in a concentrated solution

Questions

1 What happens to an animal cell in pure water?
2 Explain why this does not happen to a plant cell in pure water.
3 Which part of a plant cell is (a) fully permeable and (b) partially permeable?
4 What is meant by a turgid cell?
5 What is plasmolysis?
6 How can plasmolysis be brought about?
7 In Fig 2.7, what fills space X? Explain your answer.

Practical 2.2 To find the effects of different solutions on plant cells

1 Set up a microscope.
2 Take three clean microscope slides. Label them A, B and C.
3 Put a drop of distilled water onto the centre of slide A.
4 Put a drop of medium strength sugar solution onto slide B.
5 Put a drop of concentrated sugar solution onto slide C.
6 Peel off a very thin layer of the red epidermis from a rhubarb petiole (leaf stalk). To get good results, it should be as thin as possible (only one cell thick).
7 Cut three squares of this epidermis, each with sides about 5 mm long.
8 Put one square into the drop of solution on each of your three slides.
9 Carefully cover each one with a coverslip. Clean excess liquid from your slides with filter paper.
10 Look at each of your slides under the microscope. Make a labelled drawing of a few cells from each one.

Questions

1 Which part of the cell is coloured red?
2 What has happened to the cells in pure water? Explain your answer.
3 What has happened to the cells in medium strength sugar solution? Explain your answer.
4 What has happened to the cells in concentrated sugar solution? Explain your answer.

Fact!

Pumpkin-growers can make their prize specimens even larger by injecting a strong sugar solution into the pumpkin. The increase in size can be dramatic. Can you explain why?

Practical 2.3 To demonstrate osmosis using eggs

Beneath the shell of a hen's egg is a thin, partially permeable membrane. If you can dissolve away the shell, you will expose this membrane.

1 Take two fresh hen's eggs. Put each into a beaker and cover them with dilute hydrochloric acid. Leave them for several hours, until all the shell has dissolved.
2 Take the eggs out of the acid, and wash them gently.
3 Label two clean beakers A and B. Put an egg into each.
4 Cover egg A with distilled water. Cover egg B with concentrated salt solution. Leave the eggs in these solutions for a few days.
5 Make a labelled drawing of each egg in its solution.
6 Remove the eggs from their solutions, and examine them. Note down any differences between them.

Questions

1 What happened to egg A? Explain your answer.
2 What happened to egg B? Explain your answer.
3 Hen's eggs are not usually immersed in salt solution or water. What substances do you think normally diffuse through the membrane around the egg?

Practical 2.4 To demonstrate osmosis using potatoes

1 Label four petri dishes A, B, C and D.
2 Cook a small potato, with its peel still on, in boiling water for five minutes.
3 Meanwhile, cut a raw potato in half. Peel part of each half (Fig 2.8) and cut out a hollow in the centre. Do *not* cut right through it.

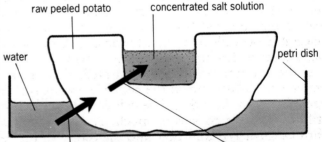

raw peeled potato   concentrated salt solution

water   petri dish

Osmosis takes place; water diffuses into potato cells, because the cell solution is more concentrated than water. The water level falls.

Osmosis takes place; water diffuses into the concentrated salt solution, because the salt solution is more concentrated than the cell solution. The well fills up.

2.8 Experiment to demonstrate osmosis using potatoes

4 Put one half into dish A and the other into dish B.
5 Do the same with the boiled potato. Put one half into dish C and the other into dish D.

— continued —

6 Pour distilled water into dishes A and C and into the hollows in potatoes B and D.

7 Pour concentrated salt solution into dishes B and D and into the hollows in potatoes A and C.

8 Make labelled drawings of all your potatoes and dishes. Leave them for a day or so.

9 Examine your potatoes and make labelled drawings of your results.

Questions

1 What has happened in potato A? Explain your answer.

2 What has happened in potato B? Explain your answer.

3 When potatoes C and D were boiled, the cell membranes were destroyed. Explain your results for these two potatoes.

4 Why is it very important not to cut right through the potatoes when you are making the hollows?

2.7 Active transport.

There are many occasions when cells need to take in substances which are only present in small quantities around them. Root hair cells, for example, take in nitrate ions from the soil. Very often, the concentration of nitrate ions inside the root hair cell is higher than the concentration in the soil. The diffusion gradient for the nitrate ions is *out* of the root hair, and into the soil.

Despite this, the root hair cells are still able to take nitrate ions in. They do it by a process called **active transport**. Fig 2.9 shows how active transport takes place.

In the cell membrane of the root hair cells are special **carrier proteins**. Carrier proteins pick up nitrate ions from outside the cell, and then change shape in such a way that they push the nitrate ions through the cell membrane and into the cytoplasm of the cell.

As its name suggests, active transport uses energy. The energy is provided by respiration inside the root hair cells. This produces the energy-rich substance ATP. (You can find out about respiration and ATP in Chapter 6.) Energy from ATP is needed to produce the shape change in the carrier protein.

Most other cells are also able to carry out active transport. In the human small intestine, for example, glucose can be actively transported from the lumen of the intestine into the cells of the villi.

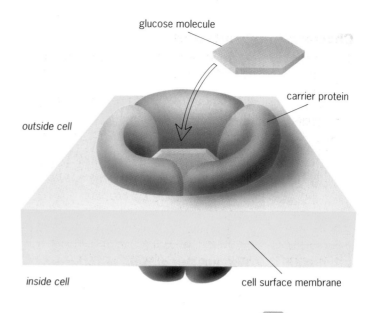

glucose molecule

carrier protein

outside cell

inside cell

cell surface membrane

1. The glucose molecule enters the carrier protein.

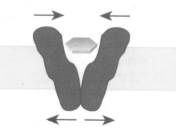

2. The carrier protein changes shape. The energy needed for it to do this comes from ATP, produced by respiration in the cell.

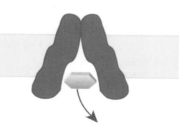

3. The change of shape of the carrier protein pushes the glucose molecule into the cell.

2.9 Active transport

Chapter revision questions

1   Which of these is an example of (a) diffusion, (b) osmosis, or (c) neither? Explain your answer in each case.

(i) Water moves from a dilute solution in the soil into the cells in a plant's roots.

(ii) Saliva flows out of the salivary glands into your mouth.

(iii) A spot of blue ink dropped into a glass of still water quickly colours all the water blue.

(iv) Carbon dioxide goes into a plant's leaves when it is photosynthesising.

2   An experiment is set up as shown in Fig 2.10. Starch molecules are too big to go through visking tubing. Water molecules and iodine molecules can go through.

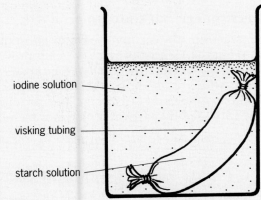

iodine solution

visking tubing

starch solution

2.10

(a) In which direction will the iodine molecules diffuse? Explain your answer.

(b) In which direction will the water molecules diffuse? Explain your answer.

(c) Draw and label a diagram to show what the apparatus would look like after an hour. Label the colours of the two solutions.

3 Enzymes

3.1 Enzymes are biological catalysts.

Many chemical reactions can be speeded up by substances called **catalysts**. A catalyst alters the rate of a chemical reaction, without being changed itself.

Within any living organism, chemical reactions take place all the time. They are sometimes called **metabolic reactions**. Almost every metabolic reaction is controlled by catalysts called **enzymes**.

For example, inside the alimentary canal, large molecules are broken down to smaller ones in the process of digestion. These reactions are speeded up by enzymes. A different enzyme is needed for each kind of food. For example, starch is digested to the sugar maltose by an enzyme called **amylase**. Protein is digested to amino acids by **protease**. These enzymes are also found in plants, for example in germinating seeds, where they digest the food stores for the growing seedling.

Another enzyme which speeds up the breakdown of a substance is **catalase**. Catalase, however, does not work in the alimentary canal. It works *inside* the cells of living organisms – both animals and plants – for example in liver cells or potato cells. It breaks down hydrogen peroxide to water and oxygen. This is necessary because hydrogen peroxide is produced by many of the chemical reactions which take place inside

cells. Hydrogen peroxide is a very dangerous substance, and must be immediately broken down.

Not all enzymes help to break things down. Many enzymes help to make large molecules from small ones. One example of this kind of enzyme is **starch phosphorylase**, which builds starch molecules from glucose molecules inside plant cells. You can find out more about starch phosphorylase if you do Practical 5.2.

3.2 Enzymes change substrates to products.

A chemical reaction always involves one substance changing into another. The substance which is present at the beginning of the reaction is called the **substrate**. The substance which is made by the reaction is the **product**. Some examples of substrates and products for reactions catalysed by particular enzymes include:

substrate	product	enzyme
starch	maltose	amylase
glucose	starch	starch phosphorylase
hydrogen peroxide	water and oxygen	catalase

3.3 Enzymes have active sites.

Figure 3.1 shows how an enzyme works. Enzymes are proteins. Their molecules have a very precise

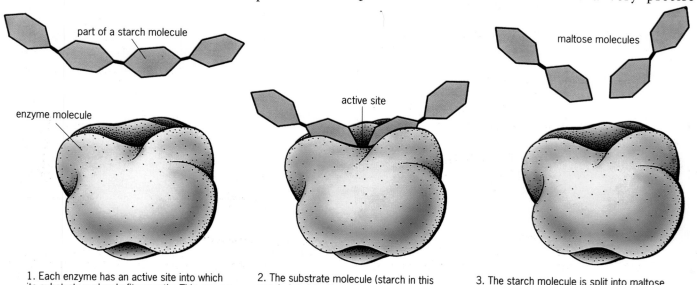

1. Each enzyme has an active site into which its substrate molecule fits exactly. This enzyme is amylase, and its active site is just the right size and shape for a starch molecule.

2. The substrate molecule (starch in this case) slots into the active site.

3. The starch molecule is split into maltose molecules. The enzyme is unaltered, and ready to accept another part of the starch molecule.

3.1 How an enzyme works

three-dimensional shape. This shape includes a 'dent', which is exactly the right size and shape for a molecule of the enzyme's substrate to fit into. This 'dent' is called the **active site**.

When a substrate molecule slots into the active site, the enzyme 'tweaks' the substrate molecule, pulling it out of shape and making it split into product molecules. The product molecules then leave the active site, which is now ready to do the same to another substrate molecule.

3.4 All enzymes have certain properties.

All enzymes are proteins They have molecules with a very precise three-dimensional shape, containing an active site.

Enzymes are catalysts They are unchanged by the reaction they catalyse. Each enzyme molecule can be used over and over again. This means that a small amount of enzyme can catalyse the conversion of a lot of substrate into a lot of product.

Enzymes are made inactive by high temperatures This is because they are proteins, which are damaged by temperatures above about 40 °C.

Enzymes work best at a particular pH Most enzymes work best at a pH of about 7. This is also because they are proteins, which are damaged by very acid or very alkaline conditions.

Enzymes are specific Each enzyme can only convert one kind of substrate molecule into one kind of product molecule. This is because the active site of the enzyme molecule has to be exactly the right shape to allow a substrate molecule to fit into it.

3.5 How temperature affects enzyme-catalysed reactions.

Most chemical reactions happen faster when the temperature is higher. At higher temperatures molecules move around faster, which makes it easier for them to react together. Usually, a rise of 10 °C will double the rate of a chemical reaction (Fig 3.2(a)).

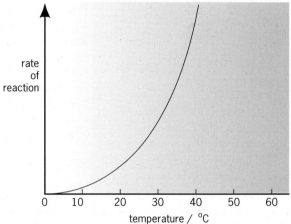

(a) No enzyme involved
The rate of reaction doubles with every 10 °C rise in temperature. This is because the molecules which are reacting move faster and have more energy at higher temperatures.

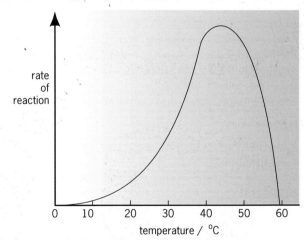

(a) Enzyme-catalysed reaction.
Between 0 - 40 °C, the rate of reaction rises in just the same way as in graph (a) for just the same reasons. But at 40 °C, the enzyme begins to be damaged, so the reaction slows down. By 60 °C, the enzyme is completely destroyed. 40 °C is the **optimum** temperature for this enzyme - the temperature at which the rate of reaction is greatest.

3.2 How temperature affects chemical reactions

Practical 3.1 The effect of catalase on hydrogen peroxide

Catalase is found in almost any kind of living cell. It catalyses this reaction:

$$\text{hydrogen peroxide} \xrightarrow{\text{catalase}} \text{water + oxygen}$$

1 Read through the instructions. Decide what you will need to observe and measure, and draw a suitable results table.
2 Measure 10 cm³ of hydrogen peroxide into each of 5 test tubes or boiling tubes. TAKE CARE – wear safety goggles. (Hydrogen peroxide is a powerful bleach – wash it off with plenty of water if you get it onto your skin.)
3 To each tube, add **one** of the following substances.
   (a) some chopped raw potato
   (b) some chopped boiled potato
   (c) some fruit juice
   (d) a small piece of liver
   (e) some yeast suspension
4 Light a wooden splint, and then blow it out so that it is glowing. Gently push the glowing splint down through the bubbles on your tubes.
5 Record your observations, and explain them as fully as you can.

Most of the chemical reactions happening inside a living organism are controlled or catalysed by enzymes. Enzymes are very sensitive to high temperature. Once the temperature gets to about 40 °C, they begin to be damaged. When this happens to an enzyme, it cannot catalyse its reaction so well, so the reaction slows down. At higher temperatures, the reaction will stop completely because the enzymes are destroyed (Fig 3.2(b)).

Questions

1 Why do chemical reactions happen faster at high temperatures?
2 What is meant by optimum temperature?
3 Why is the optimum temperature for many enzyme controlled reactions about 40 °C?

Practical 3.2 Investigating the effect of temperature on enzyme activity

Amylase is an enzyme in saliva. It breaks down starch to maltose.

1 Draw a suitable results table.
2 Put 2 cm³ of starch solution into each of four test tubes. Label them A, B, C and D.
3 Put tube A into a refrigerator. Record the temperature of the refrigerator.
4 Put tube B into a test tube rack on your bench. Record the room temperature.
5 Put tube C into a water bath at about 35 °C. Record the temperature of the water bath.
6 Put tube D into a water bath at about 80 °C. Record the temperature of the water bath.
7 Collect about 5 cm³ of amylase solution in a clean boiling tube. Dilute it with an approximately equal amount of distilled water, and mix thoroughly.
8 Put a drop of iodine solution into each of the cavities on a spotting tile.
9 Add 2 cm³ of amylase solution to each of the four tubes. Record the time at which amylase solution was added to each tube.
10 Stir each one with its own glass rod.
11 At two minute intervals, check each tube to see if it still contains starch. Do this by dipping the glass rod into the tube, and then into a spot of iodine solution on the spotting tile. If it turns black, there is still starch there. If it stays brown, the starch has gone.
12 Stop the experiment after 30 minutes.

Questions

1 In which tubes did the starch disappear by the end of the experiment?
2 What had happened to the starch in these tubes?
3 How could you check what the starch had been turned into?
4 Why must each tube have the same amounts of starch, and the same amounts of amylase solution?
5 Why did each tube have its own glass rod?
6 At which temperature did this enzyme seem to work best? Can you explain why?
7 At which temperature did this enzyme seem to work most slowly? Can you explain why?

Making use of enzymes

3.6 Enzymes are used in biological washing powders.

Biological washing powders contain enzymes, as well as detergents. The detergents help greasy dirt to mix with water, so that it can be washed away. The enzymes help to break down other kinds of substances which can stain clothes. They are especially good at removing dirt which contains coloured substances from animals or plants, like blood or egg stains.

Some of the enzymes are **proteases**, which catalyse the breakdown of protein molecules. This helps with the removal of stains caused by proteins, such as blood stains. Blood contains the red protein haemoglobin. The proteases in biological washing powders break the haemoglobin molecules into smaller molecules, which are not coloured, and which dissolve easily in water and can be washed away.

3.3 The green areas in this hot spring are photosynthetic bacteria. Their enzymes are able to function efficiently at the high temperatures of the water.

Some of the enzymes are **lipases**, which catalyse the breakdown of fats to fatty acids and glycerol. This is good for removing greasy stains.

The first biological washing powders only worked in warm, rather than hot, water, because the proteases in them had optimum temperatures of about 40 °C. However, proteases have now been developed which can work at much higher temperatures. These proteases have often come from bacteria which naturally live in hot water, in hot springs. This is useful, because the other components of washing powders – which get rid of grease and other kinds of dirt – work best at these higher temperatures.

3.4 *Fruit juice is naturally cloudy. To make a clear juice, the enzyme pectinase may be used during the production of the juice.*

Practical 3.3 Investigating biological washing powders

Design and carry out an experiment to test one or more of the following hypotheses:

(a) A biological washing powder removes egg stains from fabric better than a non-biological washing powder.

(b) Biological washing powders work best at lower temperatures than non-biological washing powders.

(c) Some kinds of protease are better than others for use in biological washing powders. (Your teacher will tell you what kinds of protease are available for you to test.)

(d) Lipases – enzymes which digest grease – help to remove grease stains from fabrics.

(e) Lipases, like all enzymes, are proteins. If a washing powder contains a mixture of lipase and protease, the proteases break down the lipases, making them less effective.

If you want to test the protease-containing powders on fabrics, you could first stain the fabrics with a protein-containing stain such as egg. Alternatively, you could use pieces of exposed, developed photographic film. This contains the protein gelatin; if the gelatin is broken down by a protease, then the picture disappears.

You could make grease stains using a fat such as lard or butter, mixed up with a little of a red stain called Sudan III. Don't put too much grease on – give the washing powders and enzymes a fighting chance!

Your teacher will suggest suitable amounts of enzymes or washing powders to use.

Whichever methods you use, do not let the enzymes come into contact with your hands any more than necessary. Remember, you contain a lot of protein and fat! The enzymes used in commercially available washing powders are in tiny particles each wrapped in a layer of wax, which keeps them from damaging the skin of anyone who handles them. The enzymes you will be using may not be in this form, so you need to take care.

3.7 Enzymes are often used in the food industry.

Fruit juices are extracted using an enzyme called **pectinase**. Pectin is a substance which helps to stick plant cells together. A fruit such as an apple or orange contains a lot of pectin. If the pectin is broken down, it can be much easier to squeeze juice from the fruit. Pectinase is widely used commercially both in the extraction of juice from fruit, and in making the juice clear rather than cloudy.

Enzymes are sometimes used when making baby foods. Some high-protein foods are treated with **proteases**, to break down the proteins to polypeptides and amino acids. This makes it easier for young babies to absorb the food.

There is a great demand for sugar in the food industry. Not only is it used in making many sweet foods, but it can also be used as a food for microorganisms used in making food substances. (You can read about some of these in Chapter 19.) As well as getting sugar directly from sugar cane and sugar beet, it can be made from starch. This is done by crushing starch-containing materials – perhaps potatoes or grain – with water, and then adding **amylase**. The amylase digests the starch to maltose, making a syrup.

Some sugars are sweeter than others. Fructose, for example – a sugar found in fruits – is sweeter than most other sugars. People who really like sweet things, but are worried about eating too much sugar, may prefer to eat fructose rather than glucose or sucrose, because they can get just as much sweet taste with less sugar. However, most of the sugar we get from plants is either glucose or sucrose. An enzyme called **isomerase** can be used to convert glucose into fructose.

17

Practical 3.4 Investigating the use of pectinase in making fruit juice

Design and carry out an experiment to test one or more of the following hypotheses:

(a) You can extract more juice if you add pectinase to the fruit than if you do not.

(b) Juice is extracted more quickly if pectinase is added to the fruit than if it is not.

(c) The effect of pectinase varies on different kinds of fruit, e.g. apples and pears.

(d) Pectinase has a greater effect on the amount of juice extracted from old fruit than from freshly-picked fruit.

(e) It is more difficult to extract juice, even when using pectinase, from Golden Delicious apples than other varieties.

(f) People cannot tell the difference in the appearance of juice extracted using pectinase and juice extracted without it.

(g) Pectinase added to the extracted juice can make it clear.

(h) Pectinase has an optimum temperature.

(i) Bought fruit juice contains pectinase.

You will find it best to pulp your fruit before trying to extract juice from it. If you are using apples, you can do this by chopping them up roughly, and then blending them with some distilled water in a food processor or other blender. You may then like to heat the blended apple to about 40 °C for around 15 minutes, as this speeds up the juice extraction. You can extract the juice by placing the crushed apple in a funnel lined with filter paper, and collect the juice which drips through.

Your teacher will suggest suitable amounts of pectinase to use.

Since you are doing this investigation in a laboratory, and since the pectinase you use may not be food grade, you must not taste the fruit juice you make.

3.8 Enzymes are often immobilised when used in industry.

If you did Practical 3.4, you will realise that the fruit juice you extracted also contained the pectinase which you used. This is not good for two reasons:

1 People want to drink fruit juice, not enzymes!

2 The enzyme has been wasted. Remember that enzymes can work over and over again – they are not 'used up' when they catalyse their reaction. If the

enzyme could be saved, it could be used again to extract more fruit juice.

These two problems can be solved by attaching the enzymes to something, so that they do not get mixed up in the product they are making. This is called **immobilising** the enzymes. There are many ways of doing this. One way is to stick them to little beads made of a substance called alginate. This is a bit like the agar jelly you may have used for growing bacteria.

If you stuck the pectinase enzymes to alginate beads, then only the apple juice would drip through the filter paper. The enzymes would stay behind. You could mix up the enzyme-beads with more apple pulp, and use them again to make more fruit juice.

Practical 3.5 Using immobilised lactase to make glucose from milk

Milk contains a sugar called lactose. Lactose is a disaccharide. It can be broken down by the enzyme lactase to form glucose and galactose.

$$\text{lactose} \xrightarrow{\text{lactase}} \text{glucose} + \text{galactose}$$

This is done commercially on a large scale. One reason for doing it is that, when cheese is made from milk, there is a lot of liquid waste called whey. (You can read about this in Section 19.11.) The whey contains lactose. If the lactose is changed to glucose and galactose, then it can be used for making sweets.

1 Measure 8 cm³ of sodium alginate solution into a small beaker.

2 Add 2 cm³ of lactase solution to the sodium alginate, and mix them carefully.

3 Take a second clean beaker. Pour some calcium chloride solution into it.

4 Now you are going to make some sodium alginate/lactase beads. Take up some of the sodium alginate/lactase solution into a small syringe. Very carefully add some of the solution, drop by drop, to the calcium chloride solution. (Don't let the tip of your syringe touch the calcium chloride solution – just drop the liquid from somewhere roughly level with the top of the beaker.) You should see your drops forming little beads. The beads are formed by the sodium alginate, and they have lactase trapped in them.

5 Let the beads harden for a minute or two. Then wash your beads by tipping the calcium chloride solution with the beads in it into a sieve or tea strainer, and gently running clean (preferably distilled) water over them.

6 Take a clean syringe barrel, and put a small piece of nylon gauze at the bottom of it. Fill it with the washed beads, as shown in Fig 3.5. Shake them gently so that they settle in and pack closely together. Don't push them!

— continued —

Fact!

In 1860, the first commercial enzyme extract was sold as an aid to digestion. It contained amylase and protease.

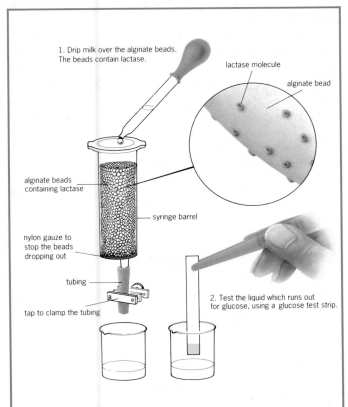

1. Drip milk over the alginate beads. The beads contain lactase.

lactase molecule

alginate bead

alginate beads containing lactase

syringe barrel

nylon gauze to stop the beads dropping out

tubing

tap to clamp the tubing

2. Test the liquid which runs out for glucose, using a glucose test strip.

3.5 Apparatus for Practical 3.5

7 Now you can try out your immobilised enzymes. Take some milk, and pour it gently over the beads in the syringe. Make sure you have something to catch it in as it drips out.

8 Dip a glucose test strip into some of the milk. Dip another glucose test strip into the liquid which drips out of the immobilised enzyme column. Record your results.

Questions

1 Suggest why you needed to wash the beads before putting them into the syringe barrel.

2 What was the purpose of the piece of nylon gauze in the syringe barrel?

3 How quickly did the liquid move through the immobilised enzymes? Could you speed it up? Might this affect your yield of glucose? (If you have time, you could test several different arrangements, to see how to get the fastest, highest yield of glucose.)

3.9 Biosensors use enzymes.

A relatively new development in medicine is the use of **biosensors**. A biosensor is a device which uses enzymes

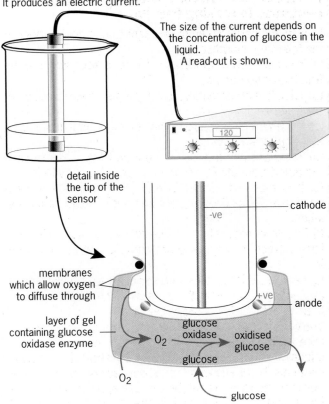

The sensor is dipped into the liquid to be tested. It produces an electric current.

The size of the current depends on the concentration of glucose in the liquid.
A read-out is shown.

120

detail inside the tip of the sensor

-ve

cathode

membranes which allow oxygen to diffuse through

layer of gel containing glucose oxidase enzyme

+ve

anode

O_2

glucose oxidase

oxidised glucose

glucose

O_2

glucose

Glucose from the liquid being tested diffuses into the gel. The enzyme catalyses its breakdown, using up oxygen in the process. So oxygen diffuses out from the area around the anode and cathode. This causes a change in the current flowing between them.

3.6 A biosensor which can be used to test glucose concentrations in blood or urine

to detect the levels of something, such as the levels of glucose in a person's blood.

Figure 3.6 shows one kind of biosensor used for testing glucose levels in blood or urine. It might be used by someone with diabetes. You can read about diabetes in Section 10.15.

The enzyme used in this biosensor is called **glucose oxidase**. It is immobilised, so that it will not wash away when put into blood or urine. This enzyme catalyses the conversion of glucose to an acid and hydrogen peroxide.

$$\text{glucose} + \text{oxygen} \xrightarrow{\text{glucose oxidase}} \text{gluconic acid} + \text{hydrogen peroxide}$$

So, if the biosensor is put into some urine which contains glucose, oxygen is used up.

This change in oxygen levels is detected by another part of the biosensor. This responds to the change in oxygen by producing an electric signal. It is called a

19

3.7 A girl with diabetes uses a biosensor to find out the glucose concentration in her blood. She puts a drop of her blood onto a strip coated with glucose oxidase. This activates the digital display, giving her an immediate readout.

however, deposits of various chemicals tend to build up over the immobilised enzyme, stopping it from getting at its substrate. All the same, this kind of biosensor for glucose can go on working for well over a month.

It is now becoming possible to use glucose biosensors to give diabetics just the right amount of insulin exactly when they need it. The enzyme-containing part of the biosensor is fixed into a blood vessel. When glucose levels are high, the transducer responds by sending a signal to a device containing insulin, and insulin is automatically injected into the patient's blood. The larger the amount of glucose in the blood, the larger the signal, and the larger the amount of insulin injected.

transducer. The size of the electrical signal which the transducer produces depends on the size of the oxygen change. So the biosensor can tell you not only whether or not there is glucose in the urine, but also how much.

Many different kinds of biosensors are being developed, using different enzymes to detect different substances. The enzymes do not always produce changes in oxygen levels; any change which can be detected by the transducer will work.

Why are biosensors useful? One reason is that they are very **specific**. Each kind of enzyme only catalyses one reaction with one substrate, so the biosensor will react only to this substrate, and not to anything else. The glucose biosensor, for example, would not respond to sucrose or any other kind of sugar.

Another reason is that they can be very **sensitive**. Quite small amounts of glucose produce a large enough change in oxygen levels to be detected by the transducer.

A third reason is that they can **last** for quite a long time. The enzymes in the biosensor are immobilised, and, of course, do not get used up in the reactions they catalyse. So the biosensor can be used over and over again. In theory, it could be used forever! In practice,

4 How animals feed

Nutrition

4.1 All organisms feed.

All living organisms need to take many different substances into their bodies. Some of these may be used to make new parts, or repair old parts. Others may be used to release energy.

Taking in useful substances is called feeding, or **nutrition**.

4.2 Green plants turn simple chemicals into complex ones.

Green plants take in simple substances, which they get from the air and soil. They use carbon dioxide, water and minerals, which are simple **inorganic** substances. The plant builds them into more complex materials, such as sugars. Sugars are **organic** materials. Organic substances are ones which have been made by living things.

The way in which plants feed is called **autotrophic nutrition**. 'Auto' means self, and 'trophic' means feeding. Therefore 'autotrophic' means that the plant feeds itself, and does not rely on other living things to make its food for it. Autotrophic nutrition is described in Chapter 5.

4.3 Animals take complex substances from plants.

Animals cannot make their own food. They feed on organic substances which have originally been made by plants. This is called **heterotrophic nutrition**. 'Hetero' means other, so 'heterotrophic' means that an animal feeds on substances made by other organisms. Some animals eat other animals, but all the substances passing from one animal to another were first made by plants.

4.4 Your diet is the food you eat each day.

The food which an animal eats every day is called its **diet**. Most animals need seven kinds of food in their diet. These are:

carbohydrates	minerals
proteins	water
fats	roughage
vitamins	

A diet which contains all of these things, in the correct amounts and proportions, is called a balanced diet (Section 4.18).

Carbohydrates

4.5 Starch and sugars are carbohydrates.

Carbohydrates include starches and sugars. Their molecules contain three kinds of atom – carbon (C), hydrogen (H), and oxygen (O). A carbohydrate molecule has about twice as many hydrogen atoms as carbon or oxygen atoms.

4.6 Glucose is a simple sugar.

The simplest kinds of carbohydrate are the simple sugars or **monosaccharides**. **Glucose** is a simple sugar. A glucose molecule is made of six atoms in a ring, with other atoms pointing out from and into the ring (Fig 4.2).

The molecule contains six carbon atoms, twelve hydrogen atoms, and six oxygen atoms. To show this, its **molecular formula** can be written $C_6H_{12}O_6$. This formula stands for one molecule of a simple sugar, and tells you which atoms it contains, and how many of each kind.

Although they contain many atoms, simple sugar molecules are very small. They are soluble, and they taste sweet.

4.7 Sucrose is a complex sugar.

If two simple sugar molecules join together, a large molecule called a complex sugar or **disaccharide** is made (Fig 4.1b). Two examples of complex sugars are **sucrose** (the sugar you use on the table) and **maltose** (malt sugar). Like simple sugars, they are soluble and they taste sweet.

4.8 Starch is a polysaccharide.

If many simple sugars join together, a very large molecule called a **polysaccharide** is made. Some polysaccharide molecules contain thousands of sugar molecules joined together in a long line. The **cellulose** of plant cell walls is a polysaccharide and so is **starch**, which is often found inside plant cells (Fig 4.1c).

Most polysaccharides are insoluble, and they do not taste sweet.

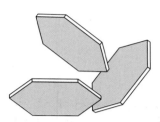

(a) Simple sugar molecules e.g. glucose

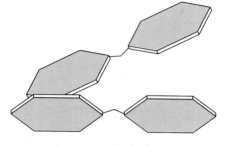

(b) Complex sugar molecules e.g. maltose

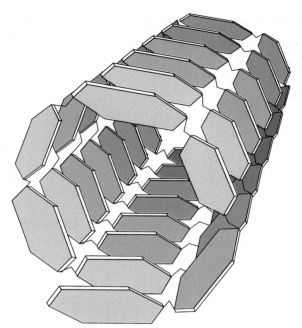

(c) Part of a polysaccharide molecule e.g. starch

4.1 Carbohydrate molecules

Practical 4.1 Testing food for carbohydrates

Whenever you are doing any kind of food tests, there are certain procedures you should always follow.

Always do a standard test first. For example, if you are testing foods for simple sugars, begin by testing a known simple sugar, such as glucose. Keep the result of this test, so that you can compare your other results with it.

Keep foods completely separate from each other. This means using clean tubes, spatulas and knives for each kind of food.

Use the same amount of reagents for each test.

To test for simple sugars

1 Draw a results chart.
2 Cut or grind a little of the food into very small pieces. Put these into a test tube. Add some water, and shake it up to try to dissolve it.
3 Add some **Benedict's solution**. Benedict's solution is blue, because it contains copper salts.
4 Boil it. If there is any simple sugar in the food, the Benedict's solution will turn orange red.

This test works because the simple sugar reduces the blue copper salts to a red compound. Sugars which do this are called **reducing sugars**. All simple sugars are reducing sugars, and so are some complex sugars.

To test for non-reducing sugars

Some complex sugars, such as sucrose, are not reducing sugars, so they will not turn Benedict's solution red. To test for them, you first have to break them down to simple sugars. Then you must do the Benedict's test.

1 Draw a results chart.
2 Make a solution of the food to be tested.
3 Do the simple sugar test, to check that there is no reducing sugar in the food.
4 Boil a fresh tube of food solution with hydrochloric acid. This breaks apart each complex sugar molecule into two simple sugar molecules.
5 Add sodium hydrogencarbonate solution until the contents stop fizzing, to neutralise any left-over hydrochloric acid in the tube.
6 Now add Benedict's solution and boil. A red colour shows that there is now reducing sugar in the food, which was produced from non-reducing sugar.

To test for starch

There is no need to dissolve the food for this test.
1 Draw a results chart.
2 Put a small piece of the food onto a white tile.
3 Add a drop or two of **iodine solution**. Iodine solution is brown, but it turns bluish black if there is starch in the food.

Questions

1 Why should you cut food into small pieces and try to dissolve it before you do a food test?
2 If you test a food, and find that it contains a simple sugar, there is no point in doing the non-reducing sugar test. Why not?
3 How could you test a solution to see if it contained iodine?

4.9 Animals get energy from carbohydrates.

Carbohydrates are needed for energy. One gram of carbohydrate releases 17kJ (kilojoules) of energy in the body. The energy is released by respiration (Chapter 6).

Questions

1 Which three elements are contained in all carbohydrates?
2 The molecular formula for glucose is $C_6H_{12}O_6$. What does this tell you about a glucose molecule?
3 To which group of carbohydrates do each of these substances belong: (a) glucose, (b) starch, (c) sucrose?
4 Why do animals need carbohydrates?

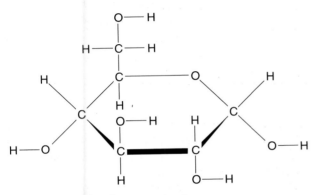

4.2 The structure of a glucose molecule

CARBOHYDRATES ARE NEEDED FOR ENERGY.

4.3 Carbohydrate foods

Proteins

4.10 Proteins are long chains of amino acids.

Protein molecules contain some kinds of atoms which carbohydrates do not. As well as carbon, hydrogen and oxygen, they also contain nitrogen (N) and small amounts of sulphur (S).

Like polysaccharides, protein molecules are made of long chains of smaller molecules joined end to end. These smaller molecules are called **amino acids**. There are about twenty different kinds of amino acid. Any of these twenty can be joined together in any order to make a protein molecule (Fig 4.5). Each protein is made of molecules with amino acids in a precise order. Even a small difference in the order of amino acids makes a different protein, so there are millions of different proteins which could be made.

Some proteins are soluble, such as haemoglobin, the red pigment in blood. Others are insoluble, such as keratin. Hair and fingernails are made of keratin.

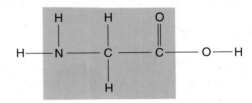

4.4 The structure of an amino acid molecule

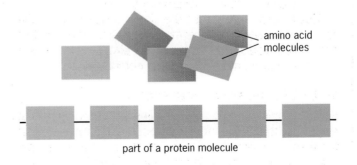

amino acid molecules

part of a protein molecule

4.5 Protein and amino acid molecules

23

4.11 Proteins are used for growth and repair.

Unlike carbohydrates, proteins are not always used to provide energy. Many of the proteins in the food you eat are used for making new cells. New cells are needed for growing, and for repairing damaged parts of the body. In particular, **cell membranes** and **cytoplasm** contain a lot of protein.

Proteins are also needed to make **antibodies**. These fight bacteria and viruses inside the body. **Enzymes** are also proteins.

Fact!

The largest animal in the world, the blue whale, is a filter feeder. It feeds on tiny shrimp-like animals called krill.

PROTEINS ARE NEEDED FOR GROWTH, REPAIR AND FIGHTING DISEASE.

4.6 Protein foods

Fats

4.12 Fats are made of glycerol and fatty acids.

Like carbohydrates, fats contain only three kinds of atom – carbon, hydrogen and oxygen. A fat molecule is made of four molecules joined together. One of these is **glycerol**. Attached to the glycerol are three long molecules called **fatty acids** (Fig 4.7).

Fats are insoluble in water.

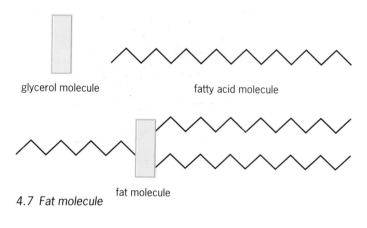

glycerol molecule

fatty acid molecule

fat molecule

4.7 Fat molecule

4.9 Animals which live in very cold places, such as these minke whales, may have thick layers of blubber under their skin to keep in body heat

FATS ARE NEEDED FOR ENERGY AND FOR KEEPING WARM.

4.8 Fatty foods

4.13 Animals store energy in fat.

Like carbohydrates, fats can be used in a cell to release energy. A gram of fat gives about 39kJ of energy. This is more than twice as much energy as that released by a gram of carbohydrate. However, the chemical reactions which have to take place to release the energy from the fat are quite long and complicated. This means that a cell tends to use carbohydrates first when it needs energy, and only uses fats when all the available carbohydrates have been used.

The extra energy which they contain makes fats very useful for storing energy. Some cells, particularly ones underneath the skin, become filled with large drops of

Table 4.1 Carbohydrates, fats and proteins

	Carbohydrates	Proteins	Fats
Elements which they contain	C, H, O	C, H, O, S, N	C, H, O
Smaller molecules of which they are made	Simple sugars (monosaccharides)	Amino acids	Fatty acids and glycerol
Solubility in water	Sugars are soluble; polysaccharides are not very soluble, often completely insoluble	Some are soluble, some insoluble	Insoluble
Why animals need them	Easily available energy (17kJ/g)	Making cells, antibodies, enzymes; only used for energy when all other stores have run out (17kJ/g)	Storage of energy (39kJ/g), insulation
Some foods which contain them	Bread, cakes, potatoes, rice	Meat, fish, eggs, milk, cheese, peas, beans	Butter, lard, margarine, oil, fat meat, peanuts

25

Table 4.2 Vitamins

Vitamin	Foods which contain them	Why they are needed	Deficiency disease
A	Butter, egg yolk, cod liver oil, carrots	To keep the cells lining the respiratory system healthy; to make a pigment in the rod cells in the retina of the eye, needed for seeing in dim light	Infections of cells lining respiratory system, night blindness
B (There are at least twelve different B vitamins, but they usually occur together.)	Wholemeal bread, yeast extract, liver, brown rice	Involved in many chemical reactions in the body, for example respiration	**Beri-beri**, which can occur where polished (not brown) rice is the staple diet; this disease causes muscular weakness and paralysis
C	Oranges, lemons, blackcurrants, raw vegetables, potatoes	Keeps tissues in good repair	**Scurvy**, which causes pains in joints and muscles, and bleeding from gums and other places; this used to be a common disease of sailors, who had no fresh vegetables on long voyages
D	Butter, egg yolk; can be made by the skin when sunlight shines on it	Helps calcium and phosphate to be used for making bones	**Rickets**, which causes bones to become soft and deformed; this disease was common among young children in industrial areas, who rarely got out into sunshine

fat or oils. These stores can be used to release energy when needed. This layer of cells is called **adipose tissue**. It also helps to keep heat inside the body – that is, it insulates the body. Animals which live in very cold places, such as seals and some whales, often have especially thick layers of adipose tissue, called blubber.

Questions

1 Which three elements are contained in all fats?
2 List two reasons why animals need fats in their diet.

4.14 Vitamins are needed in small amounts.

Vitamins are organic substances, which are only needed in tiny amounts. If you do not have enough of a vitamin, you may get a deficiency disease. Table 4.2 shows some of the most important ones.

Practical 4.4 Testing foods for vitamin C

Vitamin C is found in many foods which come from plants. Fruit juices, potatoes and many green vegetables contain quite large amounts of vitamin C.

The test for vitamin C is described below. Use this test to investigate one or more of the following hypotheses.

— continued —

(a) Freshly squeezed lemon juice contains more vitamin C per cm^3 than other types of lemon juice.
(b) Raw potato contains more vitamin C per g than boiled or baked potato.
(c) Freezing vegetables or fruit juices reduces their vitamin C content.
(d) Storing vegetables in a refrigerator retains more vitamin C than storing them at room temperature.
(e) Chopped raw apple left exposed to the air loses vitamin C faster than boiled apple treated in the same way.

When you have tried the basic test described below, you may like to modify it. For example, you may be able to find a better way of measuring exactly how much liquid you add to the DCPIP. You could also use a solution containing a known concentration of vitamin C as a 'standard', and then calculate the concentration of vitamin C in the liquids you are testing.

The DCPIP test for vitamin C

DCPIP is a dark blue liquid. Vitamin C causes DCPIP to lose its colour.
1 Measure 2 cm^3 of DCPIP into a clean test tube.
2 Use a dropper pipette to add the juice you are testing to the DCPIP. Do this drop by drop, and count the number of drops you need to add to make the DCPIP lose its blue colour.

The *fewer* drops of juice you need to add, the *more* vitamin C there is in the juice.

4.15 Minerals are needed in small amounts.

Minerals are inorganic substances. Only small amounts of them are needed in a diet. Table 4.3 shows some of the most important ones.

4.16 Water dissolves substances in cells.

Inside every living organism, chemical reactions are going on all the time. These reactions are called metabolism. Metabolic reactions can only take place if the chemicals which are reacting are dissolved in water. This is one reason why water is so important to living organisms. If their cells dry out, the reactions stop, and the organism dies.

Water is also needed for other reasons. For example, plasma, the liquid part of blood, must contain a lot of water, so that substances like glucose can dissolve in it. Dissolved substances are transported around the body.

4.17 Roughage keeps the alimentary canal moving.

Roughage, or fibre, is food which cannot be digested. It goes right through the digestive system from one end to the other, and is egested in the faeces (Section 4.43).

Roughage helps to keep the alimentary canal working properly. Food moves through the alimentary canal because the muscles contract and relax to squeeze it along. This is called peristalsis (Fig 4.20). The muscles are stimulated to do this when there is food in the alimentary canal. Soft foods do not stimulate the muscles very much. The muscles work more when there is harder, less digestible food, like roughage, in the alimentary canal. Roughage keeps the digestive system in good working order, and helps to prevent constipation.

All plant food, such as fruit and vegetables, contains roughage. This is because the plant cells have cellulose cell walls. Some plants also contain lignin. Humans cannot digest cellulose or lignin.

One common form of roughage is the outer husk of cereal grains, such as oats, wheat and barley. This is called bran. Some of this husk is also found in wholemeal bread. Brown, or unpolished, rice is also a good source of roughage.

Questions

1 Which vitamin prevents rickets?
2 Why do you need iron in your diet?
3 What is metabolism?
4 Why do organisms die if they do not have enough water?
5 Describe how food is moved along the alimentary canal.
6 Plant foods contain a lot of roughage. Explain.

Balanced diet

4.18 Diets should provide the right amount of energy.

Every day, a person uses up energy. The amount you use partly depends on how old you are, which sex you are and what job you do. A few examples are shown in Fig 4.10.

The energy you use each day comes from the food you eat. If you eat too much food, some of the extra will probably be stored as fat. If you eat too little, you may not be able to obtain as much energy as you need. This will make you feel tired.

All food contains some energy. Scientists have worked out how much energy there is in a particular kind of food. You can look up this information in

Table 4.3 Minerals

Mineral element	Foods which contain it	Why it is needed	Deficiency disease
Calcium (Ca)	Milk, cheese, bread	For bones and teeth	Brittle bones and teeth
Phosphorus (P)	Milk	For bones and teeth	Brittle bones and teeth
Fluorine (F)	Fluoride toothpaste, fluoridated water	Makes tooth enamel resistant to decay	Bad teeth
Iodine (I)	Seafood, table salt	For making hormone thyroxin	Goitre, a swelling in the neck; slow metabolic rate
Iron (Fe)	Liver, egg yolk	For making haemoglobin, the red pigment in blood which carries oxygen	Anaemia – not enough red blood cells, so the tissues are short of oxygen and cannot release energy

In food the minerals are present in the form of ions. For example, phosphorus is not present as the element (which burns in air!), but as phosphate ions.

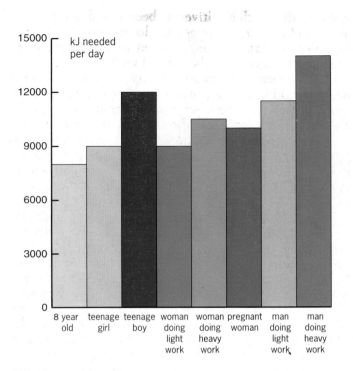

4.10 Daily energy requirements

Table 4.4 Energy content of some different kinds of food

Food	kJ/100g	Food	kJ/100g
Breakfast foods		rice	1536
cornflakes	1567	spaghetti	1612
oatmeal	1698		
boiled egg	612	**Desserts**	
brown bread	948	apples	196
white bread	991	bananas	326
whole milk	272	melon	96
sugar	1680	oranges	150
butter	3041	canned peaches	373
low fat spread	1506	strawberries	109
marmalade	315	double cream	1841
		apple pie	1179
Main meals		currant bun	1385
stewed steak	932	trifle	674
roast chicken	599	ice cream	698
ham	1119	custard	496
roast lamb	1209		
fried liver	1016	**Snacks**	
grilled chop	1380	chocolate	2214
grilled sausage	1500	fruit yoghurt	405
steak and kidney pie	1195	crisps	2224
fish fingers	749	plain biscuits	1925
sardines	906	chocolate biscuits	2197
cheddar cheese	1682	roast peanuts	2364
cottage cheese	402		
baked beans	270	**Drinks**	
cabbage	66	unsweetened	
carrots	98	fruit juice	143
lettuce	36	coffee	12
peas	161	tea	0
boiled potatoes	339	Coca-cola	168
chips	1065	wine	284
tomatoes	60	orange squash	15

reference books. A few examples are given in Table 4.4. One gram of fat contains twice as much energy as one gram of protein or carbohydrate. This is why fried foods should be avoided if you are worried about putting on weight.

4.19 Diets should contain a variety of food.

As well as providing you with energy, food is needed for many other reasons. To make sure that you eat a balanced diet you must eat food containing carbohydrate, fat and protein. You also need each kind of vitamin and mineral, roughage and water. If you miss out any of these things, your body will not be able to work properly.

The staple foods of many countries are carbohydrate foods. Rice, the staple food of China, is largely a carbohydrate food. So are potatoes, the staple food for much of Europe. These foods also contain plenty of fibre and some vitamins and minerals. However, they may not contain very much protein.

4.20 Too much saturated fat increases the risk of heart disease.

The kind of fat found in animal foods is called **saturated fat**. These foods also contain **cholesterol**. Some research suggests that people who eat a lot of saturated fat and cholesterol are more likely to get heart disease than people who do not. This is because fat deposits build up on the inside of arteries, making them stiffer and narrower. If this happens in the arteries supplying the heart muscle with blood, then not enough blood can get through. The heart muscles run short of oxygen and cannot work properly. The deposits can also cause a blood clot to be formed which results in a heart attack.

Dairy products such as milk, cream, butter and cheese contain a lot of saturated fat. So do red meat and eggs. But vegetable oils are usually **unsaturated fats**. These do not cause heart disease. So it is sensible to use these instead of animal fats wherever possible. Vegetable oil can be used for frying instead of butter or lard. Polyunsaturated spreads can be used instead of butter.

Fish and white meat such as chicken do not contain much saturated fat, so eating more of these and less red meat may help to cut down the risk of heart disease.

4.21 Obesity causes health problems.

People who take in more kilojoules than they use up get fat. Being very fat is called **obesity**. Obesity is dangerous to health. Obese people are more likely to get heart disease, strokes, diabetes and many other problems.

Most people can control their weight by eating normal, well-balanced meals and taking regular exercise. Crash diets are not a good idea, except for someone who is very overweight. Although you may manage to lose a lot of weight quickly, you will almost certainly put it on again once you stop dieting.

A much more successful way of losing weight is to make changes in your diet which you think you will *always* be able to stick to. Spread your meals out evenly during the day – don't go for hours without eating and then have a 'binge'. Eat foods containing plenty of fibre, but low in saturated fat and salt. There is no need to ban any foods completely, so long as the diet is balanced overall.

4.22 Starvation and malnutrition.

In many countries in the world, there is no danger of people suffering from obesity. In some parts of Africa, for example, several years of drought have meant that the harvests have not provided enough food to feed all the people. Despite help from developed countries, many people have died from starvation.

Even if there is enough food to keep people alive, they may suffer from **malnutrition**. Malnutrition is caused by not eating a balanced diet. One common form of malnutrition is **kwashiorkor**. This is caused by a lack of protein in the diet. It is commonest in children between the ages of 9 months and 2 years, after they have stopped feeding on breast milk.

Kwashiorkor is often caused by poverty, because the child's mother does not have any high-protein food to give to it. But sometimes it is caused by a lack of knowledge about the right kinds of food that should be eaten.

Children suffering from kwashiorkor are always underweight for their age. But they may often look quite fat, because their diet may contain a lot of carbohydrate. If they are put onto a high-protein diet, they usually begin to grow normally again.

Questions

1 How many kilojoules a day are needed by:
   (a) a teenage girl,
   (b) a man doing heavy work?
2 Which kinds of food contain saturated fat, and why should they be avoided?
3 Explain the difference between starvation and malnutrition.

4.23 Food additives and labelling.

A food additive is something which is added to the food for reasons other than nutrition. The main kinds of food additives, and the reasons for adding them to food, are listed in Table 4.5.

In Europe, each permitted food additive is given an E number. This was meant to reassure people, because it shows that each additive has been tested and passed as safe. However, many people do not like the idea of anything 'unnatural' being added to food, and so E numbers have come to be viewed with suspicion.

In some cases, this suspicion may be justified. The orange food colouring tartrazine, for example, does appear to cause behavioural problems in some children. Food colourings do not improve the food in any way. However, many food additives are really very good for us. Ascorbic acid, for example, added to many foods to help it to keep well and not go brown, is vitamin C. And without preservatives, there would be many more cases of food poisoning each year.

The labels on food packaging tell you a lot about the contents of the food. There are usually two sets of information. The **nutritional information** tells you how much energy, and which nutrients (protein, carbohydrate etc.) the food contains. This is listed both for 100 g of the food, and also for a typical portion. You can use this information to help you to decide whether the food has any ingredients which you would like to avoid, for example a lot of saturated fat; and also whether it contains plenty of the things which you would like to eat more of, for example fibre. The list of **ingredients** tells you exactly what there is in the food, including all the additives. In the UK, the order of the ingredients on the label is in the order of the amount present.

Question

This label appeared on the packaging for a frozen pizza.

Ingredients

Wheatflour, tomato, water, cheese, mushroom, tomato puree, yeast, hydrogenated vegetable oils, thickener (modified starch), onion, salt, garlic, sugar, oregano, flour improver (soya flour, ascorbic acid), malt flour, black pepper.

Nutritional information (typical values)

	per 100 g	per slice
energy	707 kJ	745 kJ
protein	7.9 g	8.3 g
carbohydrate	26.9 g	28.3 g

4.11 Food label

(a) Which ingredient is present in the largest amount?
(b) Why has modified starch been used in making the pizza?
(c) Which of the ingredients are additives?
(d) A 15-year-old girl needs about 9 600 kJ per day. What percentage of her daily energy needs would be supplied by one slice of pizza?
(e) Look at labels on pizza which is sold unfrozen. What differences are there between the ingredients of the frozen and unfrozen pizzas? Suggest explanations for these differences.

Table 4.5 Some examples of food additives

Type of additive	Example	E number	Types of food	Function of additive	Notes
Flavourings	Monosodium glutamate	E621	Soups, stock cubes, many convenience foods	Enhances the flavour of savoury foods	An amino acid which occurs naturally in many foods; has been used in Chinese cooking for centuries
	Vanillin		Desserts, cakes, chocolate	Gives vanilla taste	Natural vanillin comes from the pods of the vanilla orchid; but most is now made artificially
Colourings	Tartrazine	E102	Sweets, drinks	Gives yellow or orange colour	Tartrazine can cause hyperactivity in some children
	Caramel	E120	Sweets, drinks, soups	Gives brown colour	Caramel is made by heating sugar
Preservatives	Sulphur dioxide	E219	Fruit juice, dried fruit	Kills bacteria and preserves the vitamin C content of the food	
	Sodium nitrite	E250	Meat products, for example sausages	Stops growth of harmful bacteria	There is some evidence that large amounts of nitrate in the diet may increase risk of cancer
	Ascorbic acid	E300	Fruits, meat	Stops browning - it is an anti-oxidant	Ascorbic acid is vitamin C; it is also used as a flour improver, as it helps bread dough to rise
Emulsifiers	Lecithin	E322	Powdered milk	Stops oil and water separating out into layers	

Digestion

4.24 Digestion makes food easier to absorb.

An animal's alimentary canal is a long tube running from one end of its body to the other (Fig 4.12). Before food can be of any use to the animal, it has to get out of the alimentary canal and into the bloodstream. This is called **absorption**. To be absorbed, molecules of food have to get through the walls of the alimentary canal. They need to be quite small to be able to do this.

The food you eat usually contains some large molecules. Before they can be absorbed, they must be broken down into small ones. This is called **digestion**.

4.25 Not all foods need digesting.

Large carbohydrate molecules, such as polysaccharides, have to be broken down to simple sugars.

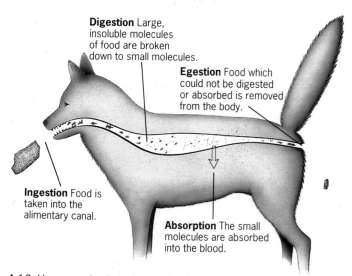

Digestion Large, insoluble molecules of food are broken down to small molecules.

Egestion Food which could not be digested or absorbed is removed from the body.

Ingestion Food is taken into the alimentary canal.

Absorption The small molecules are absorbed into the blood.

4.12 How an animal deals with food

30

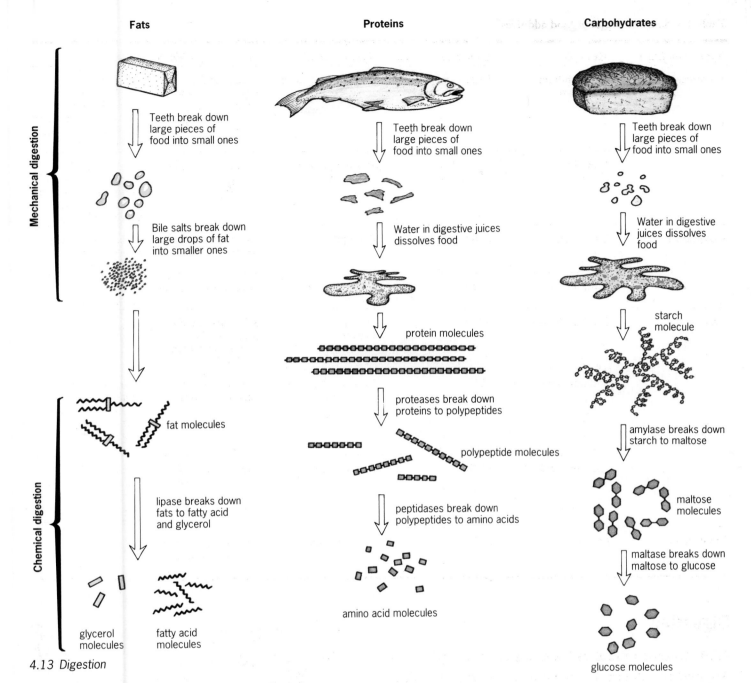

Fats	Proteins	Carbohydrates

Mechanical digestion

Fats: Teeth break down large pieces of food into small ones

Bile salts break down large drops of fat into smaller ones

Proteins: Teeth break down large pieces of food into small ones

Water in digestive juices dissolves food

protein molecules

Carbohydrates: Teeth break down large pieces of food into small ones

Water in digestive juices dissolves food

starch molecule

Chemical digestion

fat molecules

lipase breaks down fats to fatty acid and glycerol

glycerol molecules

fatty acid molecules

proteases break down proteins to polypeptides

polypeptide molecules

peptidases break down polypeptides to amino acids

amino acid molecules

amylase breaks down starch to maltose

maltose molecules

maltase breaks down maltose to glucose

glucose molecules

4.13 Digestion

Proteins are broken down to amino acids. Fats are broken down to fatty acids and glycerol (Fig 4.13).

Simple sugars, water, vitamins and minerals are small molecules, and can be absorbed just as they are.

4.26 Digestion may be mechanical and chemical.

Often the food an animal eats is in quite large pieces. These need to be broken up by teeth, and by the churning movements of the alimentary canal. This is called **mechanical digestion.**

Once any pieces of food have been ground up, the large molecules present are then broken down into small ones. This is called **chemical digestion.** It involves a chemical change from one sort of molecule to another. Enzymes are involved in this process.

Questions

1 What is digestion?
2 Name two groups of food which do not need to be digested.
3 What does digestion change each of these kinds of food into: (a) polysaccharides, (b) proteins, (c) fats?
4 What is meant by chemical digestion?

Digestion in humans – teeth

4.27 Human beings feed holozoically.

Like all animals, mammals eat organic food. This may be plants, or it may be other animals which themselves have eaten plants. This is called heterotrophic nutrition. Mammals feed by taking in, or ingesting, pieces of food which they digest inside their alimentary canal. This is a particular sort of heterotrophic nutrition, called **holozoic nutrition**. Humans are mammals. They feed holozoically.

4.28 The structure of a tooth.

Teeth help with the ingestion and mechanical digestion of food. They can be used to bite off pieces of food. They then chop, crush or grind them into smaller pieces. This gives the food a larger surface area, which makes it easier for the enzymes to work. It also helps to dissolve soluble parts of the food.

The structure of a tooth is shown in Fig 4.15. The part of the tooth which is embedded in the gum is called the **root**. The part which can be seen is the **crown**. The crown is covered with **enamel**. Enamel is the hardest substance made by animals. It is very difficult to break or chip it. However, it can be dissolved by acids. Bacteria will feed on sweet foods left on the teeth. This makes acids, which dissolve the enamel and decay then sets in.

Under the enamel is a layer of **dentine**, which is rather like bone. This is also quite hard, but not as hard as enamel. It has channels in it which contain living cytoplasm.

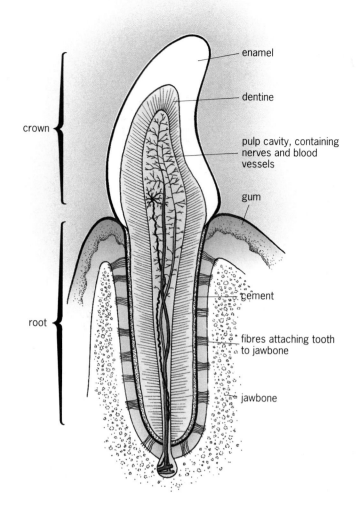

4.15 Longitudinal section through an incisor tooth

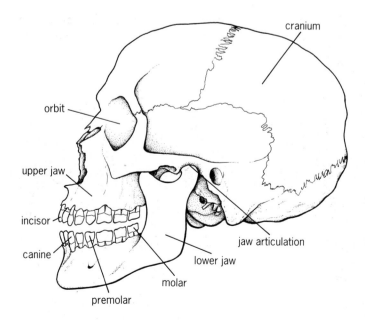

4.14 A human skull

In the middle of the tooth is the **pulp cavity**. It contains nerves and blood vessels. These supply the cytoplasm in the dentine with food and oxygen.

The root of the tooth is covered with **cement**. This has fibres growing out of it. These attach the tooth to the jawbone, but allow it to move slightly when biting or chewing.

4.29 Mammals have different types of teeth.

One of the ways in which mammals differ from other animals is that they have different kinds of teeth. Most mammals have four kinds (Figs 4.14, 4.16). **Incisors** are the sharp-edged, chisel-shaped teeth at the front of the mouth. They are used for biting off pieces of food. **Canines** are the more pointed teeth at either side of the incisors. **Premolars** and **molars** are the large teeth towards the back of the mouth. They are used for chewing food. The molars right at the back are sometimes called wisdom teeth. They do not grow until much later than the others.

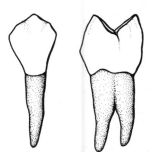

front view side view

Incisors are chisel shaped, for biting off pieces of food.

Canines are very similar to incisors in humans.

Premolars have wide surfaces, for grinding food.

Molars, like premolars, are used for grinding food.

4.16 Types of human teeth

4.30 Mammals have two sets of teeth in their life.

Mammals also differ from other animals in having two sets of teeth. The first set is called the **milk teeth** or deciduous teeth. In humans, these start to grow through the gum, one or two at a time, when a child is about five months old. By the age of eighteen or twenty months, most children have a set of 20 teeth.

The milk teeth begin to fall out when the child is about seven years old. They are all replaced by new ones, and twelve new teeth also grow, making up the complete set of **permanent teeth**. There are 32 altogether. Most people have all their permanent teeth by about seventeen years of age.

4.31 Plaque causes tooth decay.

Tooth decay and gum disease are common problems. Both are caused by **bacteria**. You have large numbers of bacteria living in your mouth, most of which are harmless. However, some of these bacteria, together with substances from your saliva, form a sticky film over your teeth, especially next to the gums and in between the teeth. This is called **plaque**.

Plaque is soft and easy to remove at first, but if it is left it hardens to form tartar, which cannot be removed by brushing.

Gum disease If plaque is not removed, the bacteria in it may infect the gums. The gums swell, become inflamed, and may bleed when you brush your teeth. This is usually quite painless, but if the bacteria are allowed to spread they may work down around the root of the tooth. The tooth becomes loose, and may have to be removed (Fig 4.17).

Tooth decay If sugar is left on the teeth, bacteria in the plaque will feed on it, changing it into **acid**. The

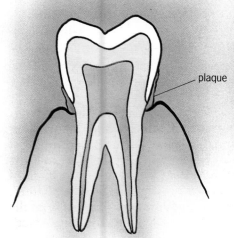

1. Plaque builds up around the edges of teeth and gums.

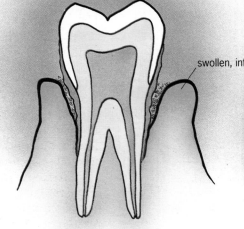

2. If the plaque is not removed, the bacteria may work down around the roots of the tooth.

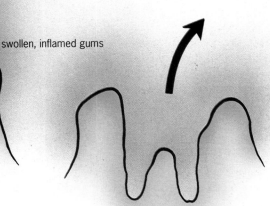

3. The tooth is loosened, and may fall out or have to be removed.

4.17 Gum disease

33

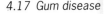

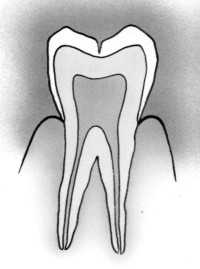

1. Particles of sugary foods get trapped in cracks in the teeth.

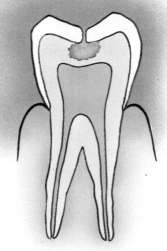

2. Bacteria feeding on the sugar form acids, which dissolve a hole in the enamel and dentine.

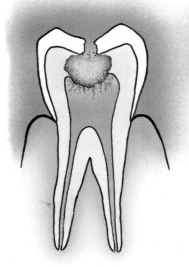

3. There are nerves in the pulp cavity, so the tooth becomes very painful if the infection gets this far.

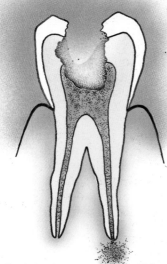

4. The infection can spread rapidly through the pulp cavity, and may form an abscess at the root of the tooth.

4.18 Tooth decay

acid gradually dissolves the enamel covering the tooth, and works its way into the dentine (Fig 4.18). Dentine is dissolved away more rapidly than the enamel. If nothing is done about it, the tooth will eventually have to be taken out.

4.32 Tooth decay and gum disease can be prevented.

There are several easy things which you can do to keep your teeth and gums healthy and free from pain.

1 Don't eat too much sugar If you never eat any sugar, you will not have tooth decay. But nearly everyone enjoys sweet foods, and if you are careful you can still eat them without damaging your teeth. The rule is to eat sweet things only once or twice a day, preferably with your meals. The worst thing you can do it to suck or chew sweet things all day long. And don't forget that many drinks also contain a lot of sugar.

2 Use a fluoride toothpaste regularly Fluoride makes your teeth more resistant to decay. Drinking water which contains fluoride, or brushing teeth with a fluoride toothpaste makes it much less likely that you will have to have teeth filled or extracted.

Regular and thorough brushing also helps to remove plaque, which will prevent gum disease and reduce decay.

3 Make regular visits to a dentist Regular dental check ups will make sure that any gum disease or tooth decay is stopped before it really gets a hold.

Questions

1 What is holozoic nutrition?
2 What are incisors, and what are they used for?
3 Describe two ways in which mammals' teeth differ from those of other animals.
4 What is plaque?
5 Explain how plaque can cause
   (a) gum disease,
   (b) tooth decay.

Digestion in humans – the alimentary canal

4.33 The alimentary canal is a muscular tube.

The alimentary canal (Fig 4.19) is a long tube which runs from the mouth to the anus. The wall of the tube contains muscles, which contract and relax to make food move along. This movement is called **peristalsis** (Fig 4.20).

Sometimes, it is necessary to keep the food in one part of the alimentary canal for a while, before it is allowed to move into the next part. Special muscles can close the tube completely in certain places. They are called **sphincter muscles**.

To help the food to slide easily through the alimentary canal, it is lubricated with **mucus**. Mucus is made in goblet cells which occur all along the alimentary canal.

Each part of the alimentary canal has its own part to play in the digestion, absorption and egestion of food.

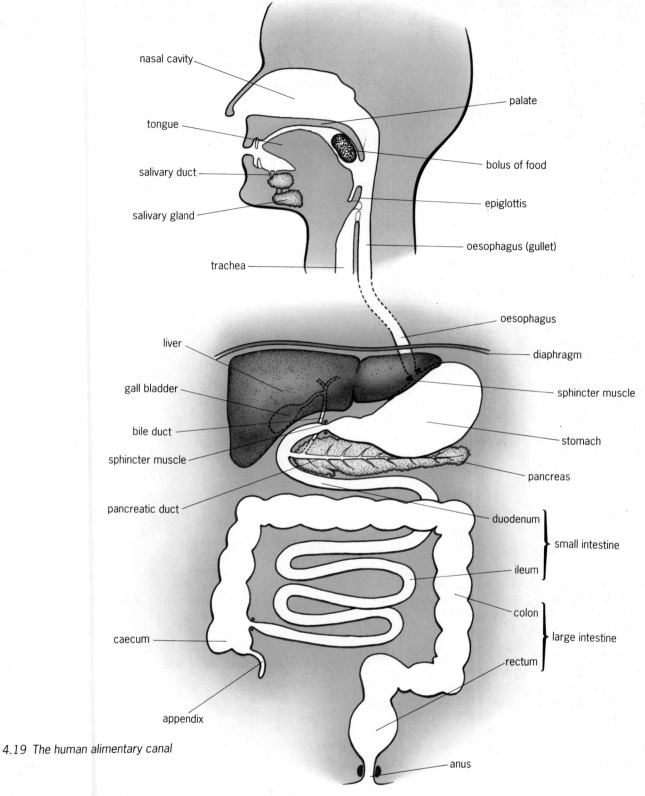

nasal cavity

tongue

salivary duct

salivary gland

trachea

palate

bolus of food

epiglottis

oesophagus (gullet)

oesophagus

liver

gall bladder

bile duct

sphincter muscle

pancreatic duct

diaphragm

sphincter muscle

stomach

pancreas

duodenum

small intestine

ileum

colon

large intestine

rectum

caecum

appendix

anus

4.19 The human alimentary canal

4.34 In the mouth, food is mixed with saliva.

Food is ingested using the teeth, lips and tongue. The teeth then bite or grind the food into smaller pieces. The tongue mixes the food with saliva, and forms it into a **bolus**. The bolus is then swallowed.

Saliva is made in the **salivary glands**. It is a mixture of water, mucus and the enzyme amylase. Amylase begins to digest starch in the food to maltose. Usually, it does not have time to finish this because the food is not kept in the mouth for very long.

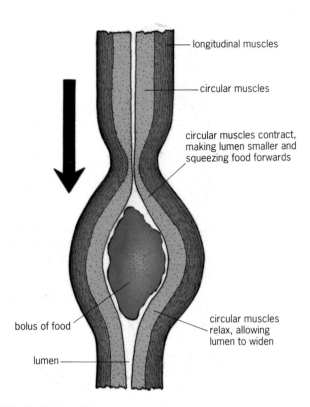

longitudinal muscles

circular muscles

circular muscles contract, making lumen smaller and squeezing food forwards

circular muscles relax, allowing lumen to widen

bolus of food

lumen

4.20 Peristalsis

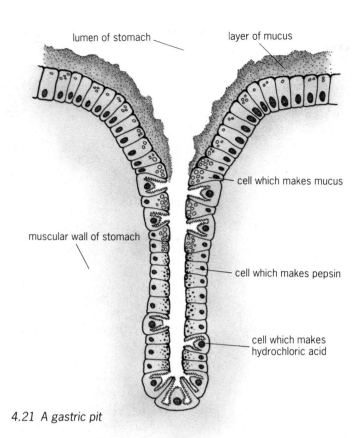

lumen of stomach

layer of mucus

cell which makes mucus

muscular wall of stomach

cell which makes pepsin

cell which makes hydrochloric acid

4.21 A gastric pit

4.35 The oesophagus carries food to the stomach.

There are two tubes leading down from the back of the mouth. The one in front is the **trachea** or windpipe, which takes air down to the lungs. Behind the trachea is the **oesophagus**, which takes food down to the stomach.

When you swallow, a piece of cartilage covers the entrance to the trachea. It is called the **epiglottis**, and it stops food from going down into the lungs.

A sphincter muscle at the bottom of the oesophagus opens to let the food into the stomach.

4.36 The stomach stores food and digests proteins.

The stomach has strong, muscular walls. The muscles contract and relax to churn the food and mix it with the enzymes and mucus. The mixture is called **chyme**.

Like all parts of the alimentary canal, the stomach wall contains goblet cells which secrete mucus. It also contains other cells which produce an enzyme called **pepsin**, and others which make **hydrochloric acid**. These are situated in pits in the stomach wall called **gastric pits** (Fig 4.21).

Pepsin is a protease. It begins to digest proteins by breaking them down into polypeptides. Pepsin works best in acid conditions. The acid also helps to kill any bacteria in the food.

The stomach can store food for quite a long time. After one or two hours, the sphincter at the bottom of the stomach opens and lets the chyme into the duodenum.

4.37 The small intestine is very long.

The small intestine is the part of the alimentary canal between the stomach and the colon. It is about 5 m long. It is called the small intestine because it is quite narrow.

Different parts of the small intestine have different names. The part nearest to the stomach is the **duodenum**. The part nearest to the colon is the **ileum**.

4.38 Pancreatic juice flows into the duodenum.

Several enzymes are secreted into the duodenum. They are made in the **pancreas**, which is a cream coloured gland, lying just underneath the stomach. A tube called the pancreatic duct leads from the pancreas into the duodenum. Pancreatic juice, which is a fluid made by the pancreas, flows along this tube.

This fluid contains many enzymes. One is **amylase**, which breaks down starch to maltose. Another is **trypsin**, which is a protease and breaks down proteins and polypeptides to amino acids. Another is **lipase**, which breaks down fats to fatty acids and glycerol.

These enzymes do not work well in acid environments, but the chyme which has come from the stomach contains hydrochloric acid. Pancreatic juice contains **sodium hydrogencarbonate** which neutralises the acid.

4.39 Bile helps to digest fats.

As well as pancreatic juice, another fluid flows into the duodenum. It is called **bile**. Bile is a yellowish green, watery liquid. It is made in the liver, and then stored in the gall bladder. It flows to the duodenum along the bile duct.

Bile does not contain any enzymes. It does, however, help to digest fats. It does this by breaking up the large drops of fat into very small ones, making it easier for the lipase in pancreatic juice to digest them. This is called **emulsification**, and it is done by salts in the bile called bile salts.

Bile also contains yellowish pigments. These are made by the liver when it breaks down old red blood cells. The pigments are made from the haemoglobin. They are not needed by the body, so they are eventually excreted in the faeces.

4.40 Digestion is completed in the small intestine.

As well as receiving enzymes made in the pancreas, the small intestine makes some enzymes itself. They are made by cells in its walls.

The inner wall of the small intestine – the duodenum and ileum – is covered with millions of tiny projections. They are called **villi**. Each villus is about 1 mm long. It is the cells covering the villi which make the enzymes. The enzymes do not come out into the lumen of the small intestine. They stay attached to the cell surface membranes of the cells lining the small intestine. These enzymes complete the digestion of food.

Maltase breaks down maltose to glucose. **Sucrase** breaks down sucrose to glucose and fructose. **Lactase** breaks down lactose to glucose and galactose. These three enzymes are all carbohydrases. There are also

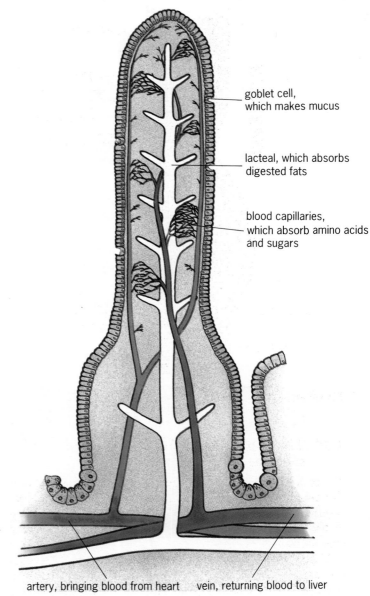

goblet cell, which makes mucus

lacteal, which absorbs digested fats

blood capillaries, which absorb amino acids and sugars

artery, bringing blood from heart   vein, returning blood to liver

4.22 Longitudinal section through a villus

Table 4.6 How the small intestine is adapted for absorbing digested food

Feature	How this helps absorption to take place
1 It is very long, about 5 m in an adult.	This gives plenty of time for digestion to be completed, and for digested food to be absorbed as it passes through.
2 It has villi. Each villus is covered with cells which have even smaller projections on them, called microvilli.	This gives the inner surface of the small intestine a very large surface area. The larger the surface area, the faster food can be absorbed.
3 Villi contain blood capillaries.	Digested food passes into the blood, to be taken to the liver and then round the body.
4 Villi contain lacteals, which are part of the lymphatic system.	Fats are absorbed into the lacteals.
5 Villi have walls only one cell thick.	The digested food can easily cross the wall to reach the blood capillaries and lacteals.

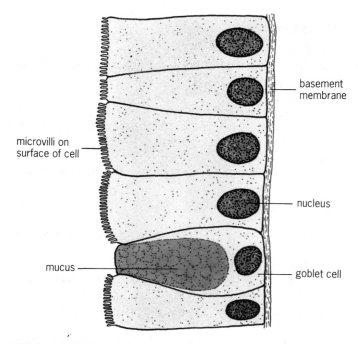

4.23 Detail of villus surface

labels: basement membrane; microvilli on surface of cell; nucleus; mucus; goblet cell

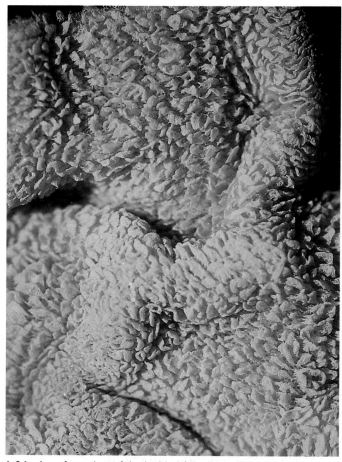

4.24 A surface view of the inside of the ileum. You can see that the surface is folded. The tiny 'flaps' are villi. Both the folds and the villi help to increase the surface area, to speed up absorption.

proteases, which finish breaking down any polypeptides into amino acids. **Lipase** completes the breakdown of fats to fatty acids and glycerol.

4.41 Digested food is absorbed in the small intestine.

By now, most carbohydrates have been broken down to simple sugars, proteins to amino acids, and fats to fatty acids and glycerol.

These molecules are small enough to pass through the wall of the small intestine and into the blood. They pass through by diffusion and active transport. This is called absorption. The small intestine is especially adapted to allow absorption to take place very efficiently. Some of its features are listed in Table 4.6.

4.42 The colon absorbs water.

Not all the food that is eaten can be digested, and this undigested food cannot be absorbed in the small intestine. It travels on, through the caecum, past the appendix and into the colon. In humans, the caecum and appendix have no function. In the colon, water and salt are absorbed.

The colon and rectum are sometimes called the **large intestine**, because they are wider tubes than the duodenum and ileum.

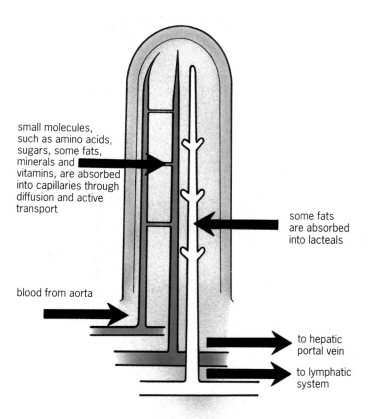

labels: small molecules, such as amino acids, sugars, some fats, minerals and vitamins, are absorbed into capillaries through diffusion and active transport; some fats are absorbed into lacteals; blood from aorta; to hepatic portal vein; to lymphatic system

4.25 Diagrammatic section through a villus to show how food is absorbed

4.43 The rectum temporarily stores undigested food.

By the time the food reaches the rectum, most of the substances which can be absorbed have gone into the blood. All that remains is undigestible food (roughage), bacteria and some dead cells from the inside of the alimentary canal. This mixture forms the **faeces**, which are passed out at intervals through the anus. The anus has a circular sphincter muscle.

4.44 All absorbed food goes straight to the liver.

After it has been absorbed into the blood, the food is taken to the liver, in the **hepatic portal vein** (Fig 4.26). The liver processes some of it, before it goes any further. Some of the food can be broken down, some converted into other substances, some stored and the remainder left unchanged.

The food, dissolved in the blood plasma, is then taken to other parts of the body where it may become **assimilated** as part of the cells.

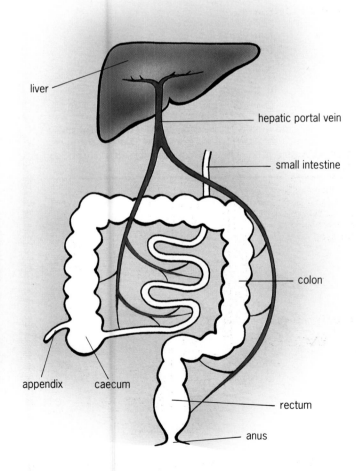

4.26 The hepatic portal vein

Questions

1 What is a sphincter muscle?
2 Name two places in the alimentary canal where sphincter muscles are found.
3 In which parts of the alimentary canal is mucus secreted? Explain why.
4 Name two parts of the alimentary canal where amylase is secreted. What does it do?
5 What is the epiglottis?
6 Why do the walls of the stomach secrete hydrochloric acid?
7 Which two parts of the alimentary canal make up the small intestine?
8 Which two digestive juices are secreted into the duodenum?
9 How do bile salts help in digestion?
10 Name three enzymes made by the cells covering the villi in the small intestine and explain what they do.
11 (a) In which part of the alimentary canal is digested food absorbed?
   (b) Describe three ways in which this part is adapted for absorption.
12 In which part of the alimentary canal is water absorbed?
13 What do faeces contain?

Digestion in other mammals

4.45 Herbivores eat plants; carnivores eat animals.

Humans eat a very wide variety of food. They are **omnivores**. The human alimentary canal is designed to cope with a diet containing both plant and animal material. However, many animals have a much more restricted diet than this. Some, such as sheep, eat only plants. They are called **herbivores**. Others, such as cats, eat only animal material. They are called **carnivores**.

Plant material is much more difficult to digest than animal material. This is because each plant cell is surrounded by a tough cellulose cell wall (Section 1.4). This makes it difficult for the digestive enzymes to reach the food material inside plant cells. Very few types of animal can make an enzyme which can digest cellulose. Animal cells do not contain cellulose, so they are much easier to digest.

The alimentary canals of herbivores and carnivores, therefore, are very different from one another.

Fact!

Dried twisted gut is still used for stringing tennis rackets.

39

Table 4.7 Summary of chemical digestion in the human alimentary canal

Part of canal	Juices secreted	Where made	Enzymes in juice	Substrate	Product	Other substances in juice	Function of other substances in juice
Mouth	Saliva	Salivary glands	Amylase	Starch	Maltose		
Oesophagus	None						
Stomach	Gastric juice	In pits in wall of stomach	Protease (pepsin)	Proteins	Polypeptides	Hydrochloric acid	Acid environment for pepsin; kills bacteria
Duodenum	Pancreatic juice	Pancreas	Amylase	Starch	Maltose	Sodium hydrogen-carbonate (NaHCO₃)	Neutralises acidity of chyme, to make an alkaline environment for enzymes
			Protease (trypsin)	Proteins and polypeptides	Amino acids		
			Lipase	Emulsified fats	Fatty acids and glycerol		
	Bile	Liver, stored in gall bladder	None			Bile salts	Emulsify fats
						Bile pigments	Excretory products
Ileum	No juice secreted; enzymes remain in or on the cells covering the villi	By cells covering the villi	Maltase	Maltose	Glucose		
			Sucrase	Sucrose	Glucose and fructose		
			Lactase	Lactose	Glucose and galactose		
			Peptidase	Polypeptides	Amino acids		
			Lipase	Emulsified fats	Fatty acids and glycerol		

All of the digestive juices also contain **water**. Water is used in splitting the large food molecules. It also acts as a solvent for the enzymes, substrates and products. The juices also contain **mucus**, which is a lubricant, and helps to protect the walls of the alimentary canal from being digested by the enzymes. The colon and rectum play no part in digestion. They are concerned with absorption and egestion. They are not included in this table.

4.46 Different diets need different kinds of teeth.

Sheep use their teeth for cropping grass. They then grind it as thoroughly as possible, to break down the cellulose cell walls. Cats use their teeth for killing their prey, and cutting meat into pieces small enough to swallow.

Incisors   The incisors of a sheep, which are found only on the lower jaw, are long and chisel-shaped. They cut against a hard pad on the top jaw to chop off pieces of grass (Fig 4.27). A cat, however, has much smaller incisors. They are peg-shaped, and are used for gripping food (Fig 4.28).

Canines   A sheep has no canines. A cat has long pointed canines, which it uses for killing its prey.

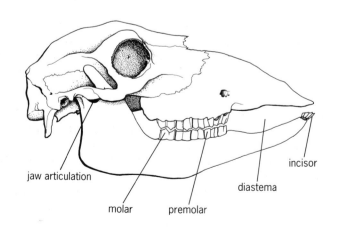

4.27 A sheep skull

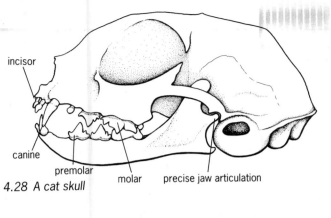

4.28 A cat skull

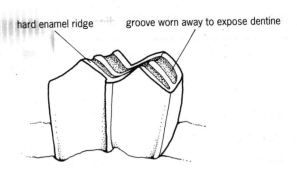

hard enamel ridge   groove worn away to expose dentine

4.29 A sheep's molar tooth showing the surface ridges

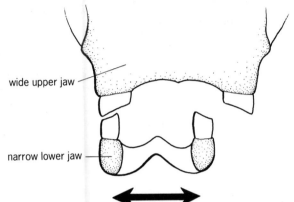

wide upper jaw

narrow lower jaw

teeth move sideways over one another, to grind food

4.30 Vertical section through a sheep's jaws, looking from the front

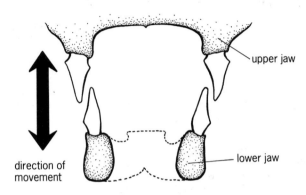

upper jaw

direction of movement

lower jaw

teeth slice past one another, cutting food into pieces

4.31 Vertical section through a cat's jaws, looking from the front

A sheep has a long, toothless gap between its incisors and its premolars. This is called a **diastema**. The diastema is used for manipulating the grass in the sheep's mouth, as it is repeatedly turned around to be chewed from different angles.

Premolars and molars A sheep's premolars and molars have broad, ridged surfaces. The ridges on the top teeth fit into the grooves on the bottom ones. They are moved in a circular, sideways motion, grinding the grass between them (Figs 4.29 and 4.30).

A cat's premolars and molars have sharp, cutting edges. The largest ones are called **carnassial** teeth. As the jaw moves up and down, the top and bottom teeth cut past one another like scissor blades, chopping the food into pieces (Fig 4.31).

Pulp cavity Sheep chew their food for a long time, and so their teeth are always being worn away by grinding the cellulose in the grass they eat. To make up for this wear, their teeth continue to grow all their lives. The pulp cavity is large, and has a wide opening at the bottom which does not restrict the blood supply. This helps to provide the substances needed to make the tooth grow.

Cats, however, keep their food in their mouths for only a short time. Their teeth do not get worn down so fast, and there is no need for them to grow continuously. The pulp cavities of a cat's teeth are smaller than those of a sheep, allowing in only enough food and oxygen to keep the tooth alive.

4.47 Herbivores have loosely linked jaws.

Sheep move their jaws from side to side, as well as up and down in order to grind their food as thoroughly as possible. This means that the lower jaw must be quite loosely linked, or **articulated**, with the upper jaw. Cats, on the other hand, need a crisp, sharp chopping movement to deal with their food. The lower jaw is articulated precisely with the upper jaw, allowing only a very slight side to side movement.

Questions
1 Why is plant material more difficult to digest than animal material?
2 What is a diastema?
3 Explain how (a) a sheep, and (b) a cat, use their premolars and molars.
4 Sheep have large pulp cavities, but cats have only small ones. Explain why.

41

Table 4.8 Summary of the differences between the alimentary canals of a sheep and a cat

Sheep, a herbivore	Cat, a carnivore
Lower jaw loosely articulated, allowing side to side and up and down movement	Jaw precisely articulated, allowing only up and down movement
Incisors long, chisel-shaped, forward-pointing, for cropping grass	Incisors short, peg-shaped, backward-pointing, for holding prey
No canines	Canines long and pointed for killing prey
Diastema for manipulating grass	No diastema
Broad, ridged, premolars and molars for grinding grass	Sharp-edged premolars and molars for cutting meat
Open roots allow teeth to grow continuously	Constricted openings in roots do not allow growth of teeth

Heterotrophic nutrition – *Amoeba*

4.48 *Amoeba* feeds by phagocytosis.

Amoeba (Fig 4.32) is a microscopic organism which consists of only one cell – it is unicellular. It belongs to the kingdom Protoctista (Chapter 17).

Amoeba lives in ponds and slow-moving streams. It moves slowly over the bottom, or over the surface of dead leaves, using its **pseudopodia** (false feet). There are many other protoctists in the water which are smaller than *Amoeba*. *Amoeba* feeds on these.

It has no special sense organs, but the surface of the cell is sensitive to chemicals in the water. This is rather like the human sense of smell. All living organisms release chemical substances and *Amoeba* can therefore sense where its potential prey is. It slowly moves towards it, travelling up a chemical gradient – that is, moving towards the place where the chemical is most concentrated.

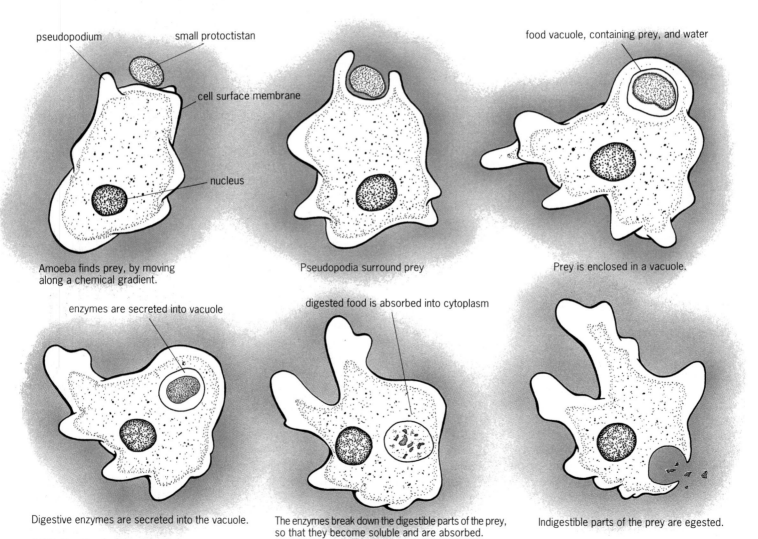

pseudopodium — small protoctistan — cell surface membrane — nucleus

Amoeba finds prey, by moving along a chemical gradient.

Pseudopodia surround prey

food vacuole, containing prey, and water

Prey is enclosed in a vacuole.

enzymes are secreted into vacuole

Digestive enzymes are secreted into the vacuole.

digested food is absorbed into cytoplasm

The enzymes break down the digestible parts of the prey, so that they become soluble and are absorbed.

Indigestible parts of the prey are egested.

4.32 Feeding in Amoeba

42

When a small protoctist has been found, *Amoeba* puts out pseudopodia around it. The pseudopodia completely surround the protoctist, and join up around it. It is now enclosed in a food vacuole inside the cell, in a drop of water. This process is called **phagocytosis** ('cell feeding').

The protoctist must now be digested. Enzymes are secreted into the food vacuole, which digest the protoctist in a similar way to the digestion of food in your alimentary canal. The digested, soluble food is then absorbed into the cytoplasm of *Amoeba*.

Some of the protoctist may not have been digested. These indigestible remains stay in *Amoeba* for some time, but periodically they are passed out.

Human white blood cells, called phagocytes, can take in and digest bacteria in just the same way that *Amoeba* feeds.

4.49 *Amoeba* digests food intracellularly.

Amoeba takes its food into its cell, and then secretes enzymes onto it to digest it. This is called **intracellular** digestion, because it takes place inside a cell ('intra' means inside).

Mammals digest their food inside their alimentary canal. The food is not inside the cells, and so this is called **extracellular** digestion, because it takes place outside a cell ('extra' means outside).

Questions

1 What does unicellular mean?
2 How does *Amoeba* find its food?
3 What is phagocytosis?
4 Explain the difference between intracellular and extracellular digestion.

Heterotrophic nutrition – insects

4.50 Houseflies and mosquitoes suck up their food.

Houseflies feed on almost any kind of organic matter. Saliva flows along a proboscis onto their food. Enzymes in the saliva digest the food, making a solution. The dissolved food is then sucked up through the proboscis, using powerful muscles (Fig 4.33).

Houseflies may contain harmful bacteria in their saliva, or on their feet. If you eat food which a housefly has fed on, you may get a disease. You can find out more about this on page 45.

Mosquitoes feed by piercing and sucking. Female mosquitoes feed on blood. They first pierce a hole through the skin of an animal, for example a human,

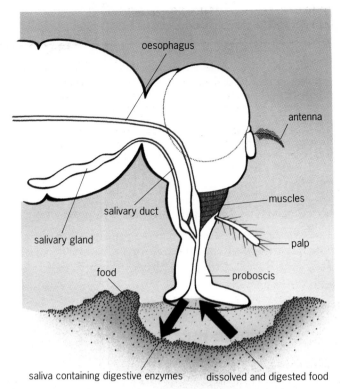

4.33 Feeding in a housefly

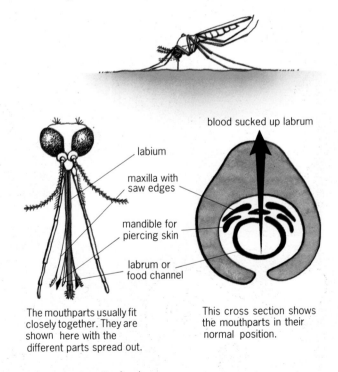

The mouthparts usually fit closely together. They are shown here with the different parts spread out.

This cross section shows the mouthparts in their normal position.

4.34 How a mosquito feeds

and inject saliva. The saliva contains a substance which stops the blood from clotting. They then suck up the blood (Fig 4.34).

In some parts of the world – but not in Britain – mosquitoes carry disease-causing organisms in their

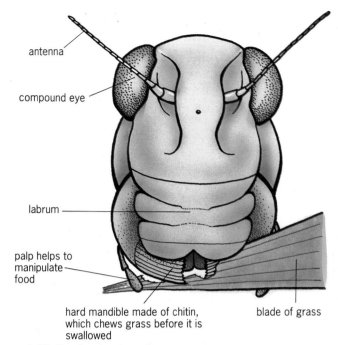

saliva. When they inject saliva into a person's body, they may pass on a disease, such as malaria or yellow fever. You can find out more about this on page 268.

4.51 Locusts have jaws to bite their food.

Locusts feed in a similar way to mammals in that they bite off pieces of food using hard jaws made of **chitin** (Fig 4.35). The food is then digested inside their alimentary canal.

4.35 Feeding in a locust

Heterotrophic nutrition – filter feeding

4.52 Many whales are filter feeders.

Some animals which live in water feed by passing water through some sort of 'sieve'. Tiny floating organisms, called plankton, are trapped in the sieve and then swallowed.

Figure 4.36 shows a baleen whale. This enormous animal feeds by swimming forward, so that water passes through the baleen plates. Tiny planktonic organisms, many of them too small to be seen with the naked eye, are trapped in enormous quantities. The whale licks them off the plates with its tongue, and swallows them.

4.36 How a humpback whale feeds. The whale swims forward rapidly with its mouth open, and pushes a huge gulp of water into its mouth. It then closes its mouth and pushes the water out. The baleen fringes hanging from the roof of the mouth trap the plankton.

Heterotrophic nutrition – saprophytes

4.53 Fungi feed saprophytically.

Moulds and mushrooms belong to the kingdom Fungi (Chapter 17). A common mould is the bread mould *Mucor* (Fig 4.37). *Mucor* grows on many kinds of non-living organic material, such as bread. It consists of threads or **hyphae**, which make up a **mycelium**.

Mucor feeds on the substances on which it grows. The tips of the hyphae secrete enzymes, which digest the bread. The starch is broken down to glucose, which is soluble, and diffuses into the hyphae. Proteins in the bread are broken down to amino acids, and fats to fatty acids and glycerol. All of these are absorbed by the hyphae. The hyphae then grow forward into the space made by the dissolved bread (Fig 4.38).

This type of nutrition is called **saprophytism**. All fungi feed in this way, and so do many bacteria. It is the way in which dead organisms are decayed, and is very important because it helps to release nutrients from them which would not otherwise be available.

4.54 Some saprophytes are harmful.

Saprophytic fungi and bacteria can be a real nuisance. They may grow in and feed on our food. As well as digesting the food, they often produce unpleasant substances which make the food taste and smell bad. Sometimes they produce dangerous substances called **toxins**, which can cause food poisoning.

However, some saprophytes make changes to food which we enjoy. We use bacteria and fungi to make cheese, yoghurt and other foods. You can find out more about this in Chapter 19.

4.55 *Salmonella* causes food poisoning.

One common cause of food poisoning is the bacterium *Salmonella*. You can become infected with *Salmonella* if you eat food containing a lot of these bacteria.

Raw meat often contains *Salmonella*. When the meat is cooked, the bacteria are killed. However, if the raw meat touches another food which is *not* going to be cooked, and the bacteria have time to multiply, then you may swallow a large dose of bacteria when you eat this uncooked food.

Another way in which you may become infected with *Salmonella* is by eating food which has not been properly cooked. Raw chicken often contains *Salmonella*. If a frozen chicken is put into the oven without first being completely thawed, then the outer layers may cook perfectly while the inside only gets warm. The *Salmonella* can stay alive in these warm parts, and may breed quickly. When you eat the chicken – especially if it has been allowed to cool slowly, giving the bacteria extra time to breed – you may get food poisoning.

Salmonella food poisoning is not usually dangerous. You feel very ill, get diarrhoea, and are sick, but most people recover in a few days. However, an old, weak person, or someone who is already ill, may die.

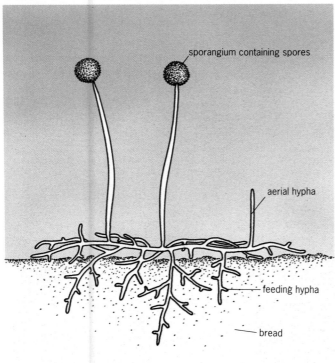

4.37 Mucor. *The network of hyphae is called a mycelium*

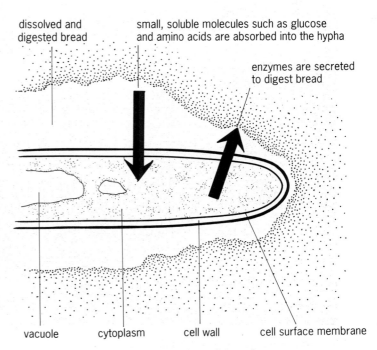

4.38 *The tip of a hypha growing through bread*

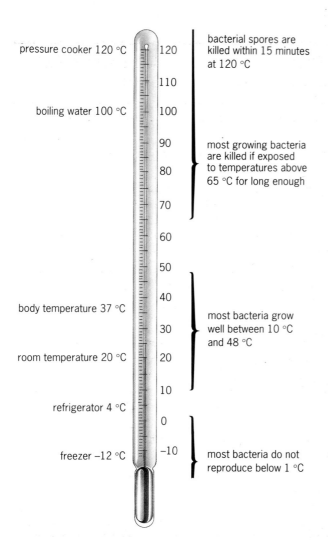

pressure cooker 120 °C — 120 — bacterial spores are killed within 15 minutes at 120 °C

— 110

boiling water 100 °C — 100

— 90

— 80 — most growing bacteria are killed if exposed to temperatures above 65 °C for long enough

— 70

— 60

— 50

— 40

body temperature 37 °C

— 30 — most bacteria grow well between 10 °C and 48 °C

room temperature 20 °C — 20

— 10

refrigerator 4 °C — 0

freezer −12 °C — −10 — most bacteria do not reproduce below 1 °C

4.39 How temperature affects bacteria

4.56 Good hygiene prevents food poisoning.

If you observe certain rules when preparing food, then neither you nor anyone else eating your food should ever need to worry about food poisoning.

1 Keep your own germs off the food Wash your hands before cooking, and after handling any raw meat. Keep your hair out of the food. Don't cough, sneeze or smoke over it.

2 Keep animals away from food Even the cleanest pets may carry dangerous germs, so keep them away from human food. Cover food to stop flies walking on it, as their feet and saliva carry bacteria.

3 Keep raw meat away from other food Wash your hands and all utensils and work-surfaces that have been in contact with raw meat before you use them for other foods. Keep raw meat on the lower shelves of the refrigerator, well away from other foods to be eaten without cooking, so that no blood can drip on them.

4 Cook food thoroughly Thaw frozen meat thoroughly before cooking, so that the inside will cook properly. (This isn't necessary when using a microwave cooker, because the food cooks as fast on the inside as it does on the outside.)

5 Avoid reheating cooked food The cooling-down and heating-up process gives any bacteria in the food a warm temperature in which to-breed. If you *must* reheat, then cool quickly and reheat quickly to a high temperature. Most bacteria will be killed if the food is made really hot. However, there are some bacteria which produce toxins which are *not* destroyed by heat, so even properly cooked food can produce food poisoning if these bacteria have previously been given a chance to breed.

6 Do not refreeze frozen foods that have thawed As the food thaws, bacteria may begin to breed in it. When refrozen, these bacteria are only inactivated, not killed. When the food is thawed the second time, these bacteria may breed again.

4.57 Food preservation stops unwanted microbial growth.

Many kinds of bacteria and fungi will live and feed on human food if they get the chance. Although many of them are not dangerous, they often spoil the food, making it unfit to eat.

Food can be kept for short periods of time by putting it into a refrigerator. The temperature inside is usually about 4 °C. Bacteria and fungi only grow slowly at this temperature, so it takes longer for food to go bad.

To keep food for longer periods of time, something more drastic needs to be done to it. Some of the methods we use for doing this are listed in Table 4.9.

4.58 Irradiated foods keep longer.

In the 1990s, a new method of food preservation was introduced into some countries. It uses gamma radiation to kill bacteria in the food. This makes the food keep longer. Irradiation is, at the moment, the only method which can make chicken completely *Salmonella*-free.

There are some problems with the use of irradiation. One problem is that many people simply do not like the idea of eating food which has been treated in this way, because they are afraid of radioactivity. In fact, no radioactivity remains in the food, so it is perfectly safe in this respect.

Irradiation has other effects on the food, apart from killing bacteria. Some methods of irradiation have a

Table 4.9 Some methods of food preservation

Method	How the food is treated	Why the method works	Examples of suitable foods
Freezing	Rapidly cooled to –15 °C. Wrapped to prevent dehydration.	Microorganisms cannot grow at –15 °C.	Almost all
Drying	Air-dried or oven-dried until water content is very low.	Microorganisms cannot grow without water.	Flour, fruit, vegetables
Freeze-drying	Dehydrated quickly at low temperature. Once dried, it can be stored at room temperature.	Microorganisms cannot grow without water. Rapid drying at low temperatures preserves flavour.	Instant coffee
Smoking	Exposed to smoke, or to chemical treatment.	This dries the food, and coats it with a film of chemicals which stops micro-organisms growing.	Meat, fish
Salting	Soaked in concentrated salt (sodium chloride) solution.	Microorganisms cannot grow in concentrated salt solutions.	Meat, vegetables
Pickling	Soaked in acids such as vinegar (acetic (ethanoic) acid)).	Few microorganisms can grow in highly acidic conditions.	Onions, eggs
Jam making	Boiled with added sugar.	Few microorganisms can grow in concentrated sugar.	Fruit
Vacuum packing	Food is sterilised, then air is removed and the food is sealed in airtight plastic.	Growth of some microorganisms is reduced by lack of air. Packaging prevents entry of microorganisms.	Bacon
Canning	Boiled and sealed in cans.	Boiling kills microorganisms. Can prevents entry of microorganisms.	Vegetables, meat, fruit
Pasteurisation	Heated to 63 °C for 30 mins, or higher temperatures for shorter time.	Kills disease-causing microorganisms and reduces the numbers of others, without spoiling the flavour.	Milk
Ultra heat treatment – UHT	Steam at 160 °C blown through the liquid food	Kills microorganisms	Milk
Irradiation	Irradiated with gamma radiation	Kills microorganisms	Chicken, shellfish, vegetables

similar effect on the nutrients in the food as heating does, for example destroying some vitamins. However, it is possible to irradiate food without causing any loss of nutrients.

A big problem with irradiation is that, although it destroys all the bacteria in the food, it does not destroy any toxins which they may already have produced. When food inspectors test food to make sure that it is safe, they usually test for the presence of bacteria, but not for toxins. So they might declare an irradiated food safe to eat – because it contains no bacteria – while it is really *not* safe – because it contains toxins. It is therefore very important that food is only irradiated *before* there is any opportunity for toxins to build up in it.

Questions

1 What is saprophytic nutrition?
2 Name two ways in which saprophytes can be useful, and one way in which they can be harmful.
3 Why is it important to keep raw meat away from cooked foods?
4 Why should frozen chickens be thawed thoroughly before cooking?

Chapter revision questions

1   With the aid of examples wherever possible, explain the differences between each of the following pairs of terms
    (a) autotrophic; heterotrophic
    (b) monosaccharide; disaccharide
    (c) inorganic; organic
    (d) enamel; dentine
    (e) digestion; absorption
    (f) herbivore; carnivore
    (g) intracellular digestion; extracellular digestion
    (h) cellulose; cellulase

2   (a) What is meant by a balanced diet?
    (b) Using Table 4.4 and Fig 4.10, plan menus for one day which would provide a balanced diet for (i) a teenage boy, and (ii) a pregnant woman. For each food you include, state how much energy, and which types of nutrients it contains.

3   Some of the things that a healthy diet should contain include:
    (a) the right number of kilojoules – not too few or too many;
    (b) plenty of roughage (fibre);
    (c) polyunsaturated fats instead of saturated fats;
    (d) not too many sugary foods.
    Explain how each of these can help to keep a person healthy.

4   For each of these digestive juices, state (a) where it is made, (b) where it works, and (c) what it does.
    (i) pancreatic juice
    (ii) saliva
    (iii) bile
    (iv) gastric juice

5   Describe what would happen to a piece of steak, containing only protein, and a chip, containing starch and fat, as they passed through your alimentary canal.

6   The function of the stomach is to store food, and to begin to digest it. The small intestine, however, first completes the digestion of food, and then absorbs it. In the form of a table, keeping equivalent points opposite one another, make a comparison between these two organs, bearing in mind their different functions.

5 How green plants feed

5.1 Green plants feed autotrophically.

Green plants make their food by using inorganic substances to build up organic substances. This is called **autotrophic nutrition**. The inorganic substances which a green plant uses are carbon dioxide, water and a variety of minerals. Using these simple substances, the plant makes all the carbohydrates, fats, proteins and vitamins which it needs.

5.2 Plants make glucose from carbon dioxide and water.

To make carbohydrates, green plants combine carbon dioxide and water. The carbohydrate which is made is **glucose**. At the same time, oxygen molecules are produced.

carbon dioxide + water $\longrightarrow$ glucose + oxygen

However, if you mixed together carbon dioxide and water, they would not combine to make glucose and oxygen. They have to be given energy to make them combine. The energy which green plants use for this is **sunlight** energy. The reaction is therefore called **photosynthesis** ('photo' means light, and 'synthesis' means manufacture).

5.3 Chlorophyll absorbs sunlight.

However, sunlight shining onto water and carbon dioxide still will not make them react together in this way. The sunlight energy has to be trapped, and then used in the reaction. Green plants have a substance which does this. It is called **chlorophyll**.

Chlorophyll is the pigment which makes plants look green. It is kept inside the chloroplasts of plant cells, arranged on a series of membranes (Fig 5.8). Spread out like this, it can trap the maximum amount of sunlight.

When sunlight falls on a chlorophyll molecule, the energy is absorbed. The chlorophyll molecule then releases the energy. The energy makes carbon dioxide combine with water, with the help of enzymes inside the chloroplast.

5.4 Photosynthesis is a chemical process.

The full equation for photosynthesis is written like this

$$\text{carbon dioxide + water} \xrightarrow[\text{chlorophyll}]{\text{sunlight}} \text{glucose + oxygen}$$

To show the number of molecules involved in the reaction, a balanced equation needs to be written. Carbon dioxide contains two atoms of oxygen, and one of carbon, so its molecular formula is CO_2. Water has the formula H_2O. Glucose has the formula $C_6H_{12}O_6$. Oxygen molecules contain two atoms of oxygen, and so they are written O_2.

The balanced equation for photosynthesis is this

$$6CO_2 + 6H_2O \xrightarrow[\text{chlorophyll}]{\text{sunlight}} C_6H_{12}O_6 + 6O_2$$

Questions

1 Which inorganic substances does a plant use to make food?
2 What kind of energy does a plant use to make carbon dioxide combine with water?
3 What is chlorophyll?
4 What happens when sunlight falls on a chlorophyll molecule?
5 What does a balanced equation show?

Leaves

5.5 Plant leaves are food factories.

Photosynthesis happens inside chloroplasts. This is where the enzymes and chlorophyll are which catalyse and supply energy to the reaction. In a typical plant, most chloroplasts are in the cells in the leaves. A leaf is a factory for making carbohydrates.

Leaves are therefore specially adapted to allow photosynthesis to take place as quickly and efficiently as possible.

Fact!

The largest leaves of any plant belong to the raffia palm, which grows on the Mascarene Islands in the Indian Ocean, and also the Amazonian bamboo palm. They both have leaves up to 19.8m long.

5.6 The structure of leaves.

A leaf consists of a broad, flat part called the **lamina** (Fig 5.1), which is joined to the rest of the plant by a leaf stalk or **petiole**. Running through the petiole are vascular bundles (Section 7.29), which then form the **veins** in the leaf. These contain tubes which carry substances to and from the leaf.

Although a leaf looks thin, it is in fact made up of several layers of cells. You can see these if you look at a transverse section (TS) of a leaf under a microscope (Fig 5.2).

The top and bottom of the leaf are covered with a layer of closely fitting cells called the **epidermis** (Fig 5.4). These cells do not contain chloroplasts. Their function is to protect the inner layers of cells in the leaf. The cells of the upper epidermis often secrete a waxy substance, which lies on top of them. It is called the **cuticle**, and it helps to stop water evaporating from the leaf. There is sometimes a cuticle on the underside of a leaf as well.

In the lower epidermis, there are small holes called **stomata** (singular: **stoma**). Each stoma is surrounded by a pair of sausage shaped **guard cells** (Fig 5.4) which can open or close the hole. Guard cells, unlike the other cells in the epidermis, do contain chloroplasts.

The middle layers of the leaf are called the **mesophyll** ('meso' means middle, and 'phyll' means leaf). These cells all contain chloroplasts. The cells nearer to the top of the leaf are arranged like a fence or palisade, and they form the **palisade layer**. The cells beneath them are rounder, and arranged quite loosely, with large air spaces between them. They form the **spongy layer**.

Running through the mesophyll are veins. Each vein contains large, thick-walled **xylem vessels** (Section 7.27) for carrying water, and smaller, thin-walled **phloem tubes** (Section 7.28) for carrying away food which the leaf has made.

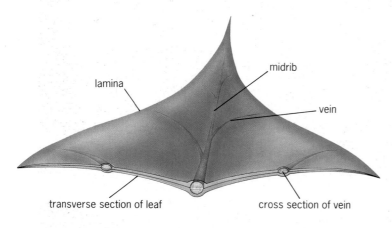

5.1 The structure of a leaf

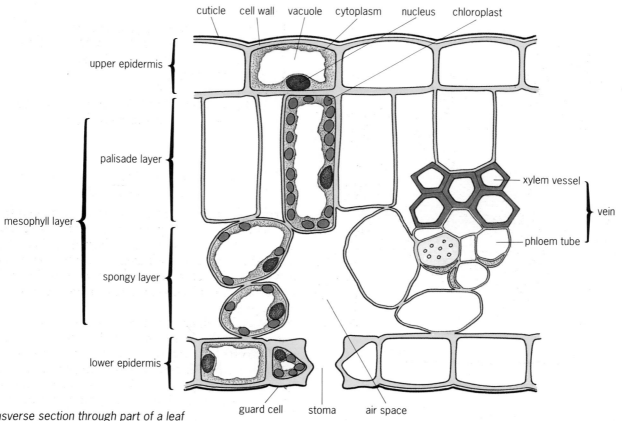

5.2 Transverse section through part of a leaf

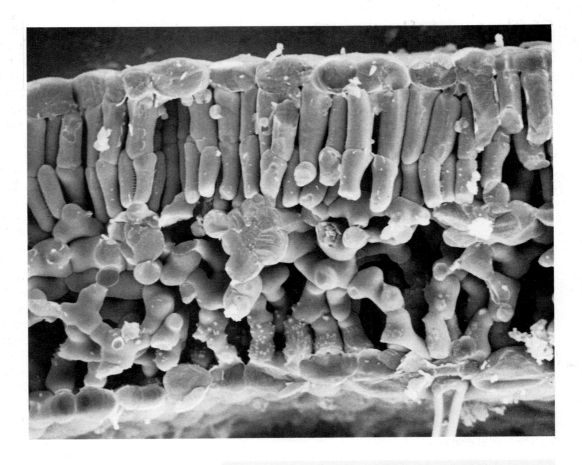

5.3 A scanning electronmicrograph of a section through a lupin leaf. Compare this with Fig 5.2, and see if you can identify all the different layers.

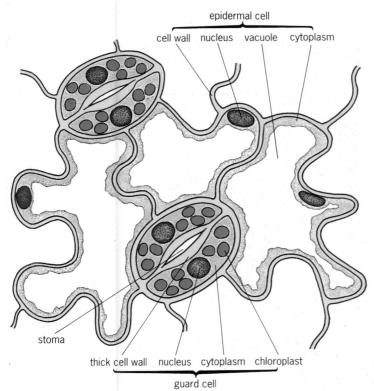

epidermal cell

cell wall   nucleus   vacuole   cytoplasm

stoma

thick cell wall   nucleus   cytoplasm   chloroplast

guard cell

5.4 Surface view of the lower epidermis of a leaf

Questions

1. What is another name for a leaf stalk?
2. Which kind of cells make the cuticle on a leaf?
3. What is the function of the cuticle?
4. What are stomata?
5. What are guard cells?
6. List three kinds of cells in a leaf which contain chloroplasts, and one kind which does not.

5.7 Leaves are adapted to obtain carbon dioxide, water and sunlight.

Carbon dioxide   Carbon dioxide is obtained from the air. There is not very much available, because only about 0.03% of the air is carbon dioxide. Therefore the leaf must be very efficient at absorbing it. The leaf is held out into the air by the stem and the leaf stalk, and its large surface area helps to expose it to as much air as possible.

The cells which need the carbon dioxide are the mesophyll cells, inside the leaf. The carbon dioxide can get into the leaf through the stomata. It does this by diffusion, which is described in Chapter 2. Behind each stoma is an air space (Fig 5.2) which connects up with other air spaces between the spongy mesophyll cells. The carbon dioxide can therefore diffuse to all the cells

51

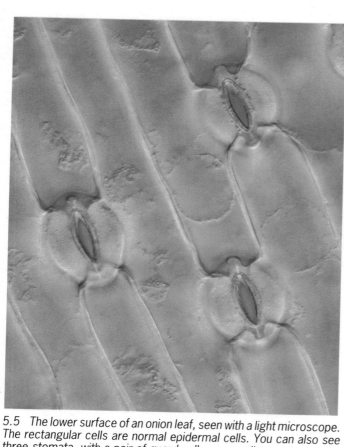

in the leaf. It can then diffuse through the cell wall and cell membrane of each cell, and into the chloroplasts.

Water Water is obtained from the soil. It is absorbed by the root hairs (Section 7.38), and carried up to the leaf in the xylem vessels. It then travels from the xylem vessels to the mesophyll cells by osmosis, which is described in Chapter 2. The path it takes is shown in Figs 5.6 and 5.7.

Sunlight The position of a leaf and its broad, flat, surface help it to obtain as much sunlight as possible. If you look up through the branches of a tree, you will see that the leaves are arranged so that they do not cut off light from one another more than necessary. Plants which live in shady places often have particularly big leaves.

5.5 The lower surface of an onion leaf, seen with a light microscope. The rectangular cells are normal epidermal cells. You can also see three stomata, with a pair of guard cells surrounding each one.

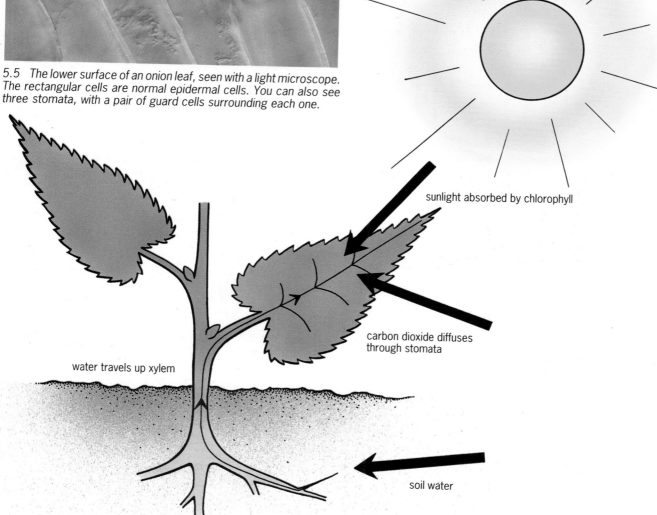

sunlight absorbed by chlorophyll

carbon dioxide diffuses through stomata

water travels up xylem

soil water

5.6 How the materials for photosynthesis get into a leaf

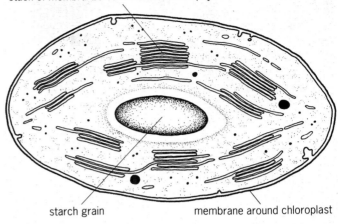

stack of membranes covered with chlorophyll

starch grain

membrane around chloroplast

5.8 The structure of a chloroplast

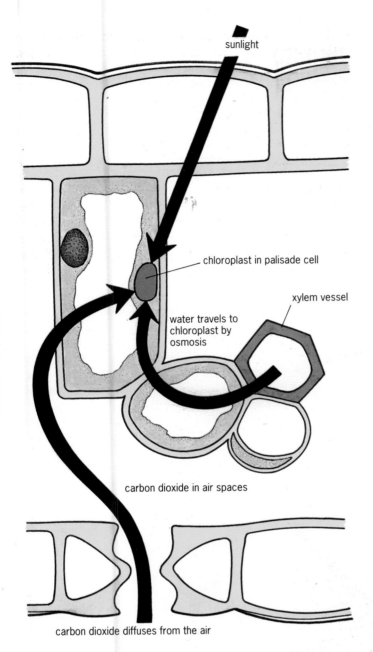

sunlight

chloroplast in palisade cell

xylem vessel

water travels to chloroplast by osmosis

carbon dioxide in air spaces

carbon dioxide diffuses from the air

5.7 How the raw materials for photosynthesis get to a palisade cell

Table 5.1 **Adaptations of leaves for photosynthesis**

Adaptation	Function
Supported by stem and petiole	To expose as much of it as possible to sunlight and air
Large surface area	To expose as much of it as possible to sunlight and air
Thin	To allow sunlight to penetrate to all cells; to allow CO_2 to diffuse in and O_2 to diffuse out as quickly as possible
Stomata in lower epidermis	To allow CO_2 and O_2 to diffuse in and out
Air spaces in spongy mesophyll	To allow CO_2 and O_2 to diffuse to and from all cells
No chloroplasts in epidermis	To allow sunlight to penetrate to mesophyll layer
Chloroplasts containing chlorophyll present in mesophyll layer	To absorb sunlight, to provide energy to combine CO_2 and H_2O
Palisade cells arranged end on	To keep as few cell walls as possible between sunlight and chloroplasts
Chloroplasts in palisade cells arranged broadside on, especially in dim light	To expose as much chlorophyll as possible to sunlight
Chlorophyll arranged on flat membranes inside chloroplast	To expose as much chlorophyll as possible to sunlight
Xylem vessels within short distance of every mesophyll cell	To supply water to chloroplasts for photosynthesis
Phloem tubes within short distance of every mesophyll cell	To take away organic products of photosynthesis

The cells which need the sunlight are the mesophyll cells. The thinness of the leaf allows the sunlight to penetrate right through it, and reach all the cells. To help this the epidermal cells are transparent, with no chloroplasts.

In the mesophyll cells, the chloroplasts are arranged to get as much sunlight as possible, particularly those in the palisade cells. They can lie broadside on to do this, but in strong sunlight, they often arrange themselves end on. This reduces the amount of light absorbed. Inside them, the chlorophyll is arranged on flat membranes (Fig 5.8) to expose as much as possible to the sunlight.

Practical 5.1 Looking at the epidermis of a leaf

Using a piece of epidermis

1 Using forceps, carefully peel a small piece of epidermis from the underside of a leaf.
2 Put the piece of epidermis into a drop of water on a microscope slide.
3 Spread it out carefully, trying not to let any part of it fold over. Cover it with a cover slip.
4 Look at your slide under the microscope, and make a labelled drawing of a few cells.

Making a nail varnish impression

1 Paint the underside of a leaf with transparent nail varnish. Leave to dry thoroughly.
2 Peel off part of the nail varnish, and mount it in a drop of water on a microscope slide.
3 Spread it out carefully, and cover with a coverslip.
4 Look at your slide under the microscope, and make a labelled drawing of the impressions made by a few cells.
5 Repeat with the upper surface of a leaf.

Questions

1 On which surface of the leaf did you find most stomata?
2 Which of these two techniques for examining the epidermis of a leaf do you consider (a) is easiest, and (b) gives you the best results?
3 There are two kinds of cell in the lower epidermis of a leaf. What are they, and what are their functions?

5.8 Glucose is used in different ways.

One of the first carbohydrates to be made in photosynthesis is **glucose**. There are several things which may then happen to it.

Energy may be released from glucose in the leaf All cells need energy, which they obtain by the process of respiration (Section 6.4). Some of the glucose which a leaf makes will be broken down by respiration, to release energy.

Glucose may be turned into starch and stored in the leaf Glucose is a simple sugar. It is soluble, and quite a reactive substance. It is not, therefore, a very good storage molecule. Firstly, being reactive, it might get involved in chemical reactions where it was not wanted. Secondly, it would dissolve in the water in and around the plant cells, and might be lost from the cell. Thirdly, when dissolved, it would increase the strength of the solution in the cell, which could damage the cell.

The glucose is therefore converted into **starch** to be stored. Starch is a polysaccharide, made of many glucose molecules joined together. Being such a large molecule, it is not very reactive, and not very soluble. It can be made into granules which can be easily stored inside the chloroplasts.

Glucose may be used to make other organic substances The plant can use glucose as a starting point for making all the other organic substances it needs. These include the carbohydrates sucrose and cellulose. Plants also make **oils** (liquid fats).

With the addition of minerals containing nitrogen and sulphur, amino acids can be made. These are then joined together to make **proteins.** The plant also makes other substances such as chlorophyll and vitamins.

The mineral substances required are all obtained from the soil. They are absorbed through the root hairs. Some of the most important ones are listed in Table 5.2. Water culture experiments (Fig 5.10) can show which minerals a plant needs, and what happens to it if it does not have them.

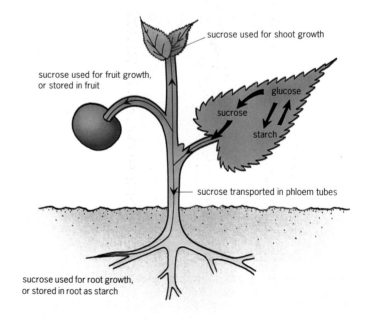

5.9 *The products of photosynthesis*

Glucose may be transported to other parts of the plant
A molecule has to be small and soluble to be transported easily. Glucose has both of these properties, but it is also rather reactive. It is therefore converted to the complex sugar sucrose to be transported to other parts of the plant. Sucrose molecules are also quite small and soluble, but less reactive than glucose. They dissolve in the sap in the phloem tubes, and can be distributed to whichever parts of the plant need them (Fig 5.9).

The sucrose may later be turned back into glucose again, to be broken down to release energy, or turned into starch and stored, or used to make other substances which are needed for growth.

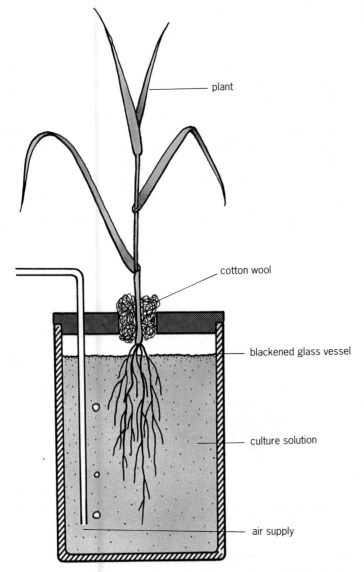

5.10 *Apparatus for water culture experiments. Several plants are grown like this, in identical conditions. Some, the controls, are given a culture solution containing all the minerals needed by plants. Others have a solution from which one mineral is missing. By comparing each plant with the control plants, the effects of a lack of each mineral can be seen. You can perform similar experiments with the small floating plant duckweed, in petri dishes containing different solutions.*

Practical 5.2 Using starch phosphorylase to make starch

The first carbohydrates made in photosynthesis are sugars, such as glucose. Plants change some of the sugars into starch for storage. The enzyme which catalyses this reaction is called starch phosphorylase. Potatoes contain quite a lot of this enzyme.

1 Peel a small potato, chop it roughly, and then liquidise in a food processor with some distilled water.
2 Pour the liquid through some muslin, to filter out any large pieces of potato.
3 Pour some of the filtrate into a centrifuge tube. Label your tube. Put your tube into a centrifuge. Make sure that the centrifuge is balanced, with approximately equal amounts of liquid in all of the tubes. Spin the tubes for about 4 minutes. This will pull all the bits of cells to the bottom of the tube, and leave a clear liquid at the top. The starch phosphorylase will be in the clear liquid.
4 Using a dropper pipette, carefully take the clear liquid from the top of the tube, without disturbing the sediment at the bottom. Add a drop of the liquid to a drop of iodine solution, to check that it does not contain any starch. If it does, put it back in the centrifuge and spin it for a few more minutes before retesting.
   When your liquid is free from starch, you can test it to see if it can change glucose into starch. You need to use glucose which has combined with phosphate, called glucose-1-phosphate.
5 Share out your liquid into two clean test tubes. To one of them, add 2 cm^3 of glucose-1-phosphate solution. To the other, add 2 cm^3 of distilled water. Leave both tubes in a warm place for about 10 minutes.
6 Test the contents of each tube for starch, using iodine solution.

Questions
1 Starch phosphorylase is found inside potato cells. Explain why you needed to break up the potato in a food processor to do this experiment.
2 Why did you need to check that the liquid from the potato did not contain any starch, in step 4?
3 Why did you need to leave your tubes in a warm place?
4 Suggest why potato cells need starch phosphorylase.

Fact!

Honey is made of nectar from flowers by bees. It usually contains a lot of glucose and is in the form of a supersaturated solution. The glucose crystallises out slowly in all untreated honeys, eventually making the honey solid.

Table 5.2 Mineral salts required by plants

Element	Mineral salt	Why it is needed	Deficiency disease
Nitrogen	Nitrates or as organic compounds from nitrogen-fixing bacteria	To make proteins	Poor growth, yellow leaves
Sulphur	Sulphates	To make proteins	Poor growth, yellow leaves
Phosphorus	Phosphates	To make ATP (see Section 6.5)	Poor growth, especially of roots
Magnesium	Magnesium salts	To make chlorophyll	Yellowing between veins of leaves
Iron	Iron salts	To make chlorophyll; iron is not contained in chlorophyll, but is needed for its manufacture	Yellowing in young leaves
Potassium	Potassium salts	To keep correct salt balance for cells	Mottled leaves

All of these minerals are obtained from the soil. They are absorbed in solution through the root hairs.

Questions

1 Why is glucose not very good for storing in a leaf?
2 What substances does a plant need to be able to convert glucose into proteins?
3 Why do plants need iron?
4 How do parts of the plant such as the roots, which cannot photosynthesise, obtain food?

Photosynthesis experiments

5.9 Experiments need controls.

If you do Practicals 5.4, 5.5 and 5.6, you can find out for yourself which substances a plant needs for photosynthesis. In each experiment, the plant is given everything it needs, except for one substance. Another plant is used at the same time. This is a **control**. The control plant is given everything it needs, including the substance being tested for.

Both plants are then treated in exactly the same way. Any differences between them at the end of the experiment, therefore, must be because of the substance being tested.

At the end of the experiment, test a leaf from your experimental plant and your control to see if they have made starch. By comparing them, you can find out which substances are necessary for photosynthesis.

5.10 Plants for photosynthesis experiments must be destarched.

It is very important that the leaves you are testing should not have any starch in them at the beginning of the experiment. If they did, and you found that the leaves contained starch at the end of the experiment, you could not be sure that they had been photosynthesising. The starch might have been made before the experiment began.

So, before doing any of these experiments, you must destarch the plants. The easiest way to do this is to leave them in a dark cupboard for at least 24 hours. The plants cannot photosynthesise while they are in the cupboard because there is no light. Therefore they use up their stores of starch. To be certain that they are thoroughly destarched, test a leaf for starch before you begin your experiment.

5.11 Iodine solution can stain starch in leaves.

Iodine solution is used to test for starch. A bluish black colour shows that starch is present. However, if you put iodine solution onto a leaf which contains starch, it will not immediately turn black. This is because the starch is right inside the cells, inside the chloroplasts (Fig 5.8). The iodine solution cannot get through the cell membranes to reach the starch and react with it. Another difficulty is that the green colour of the leaf and the brown iodine solution can look black together.

Therefore before testing a leaf for starch, you must break down the cell membranes, and get rid of the green colour (chlorophyll). The way this is done is described in Practical 5.3. The cell membranes are first broken down by boiling water, and then the chlorophyll is removed by dissolving it out with alcohol.

Practical 5.3 Testing a leaf for starch

1 Take a leaf from a healthy plant, and drop it into boiling water in a water bath. Leave it for about 30 seconds. (The length of time needed varies for different types of leaves. 30 s is about right for geranium leaves.)
2 Remove the leaf, which will be very soft, and drop it into a tube of alcohol in the water bath (Fig 5.11). Leave it until all the chlorophyll has been dissolved out of the leaf.
3 The leaf will now be brittle. Remove it from the alcohol, and dip it into water again to soften it.
4 Spread out the leaf on a white tile, and cover it with iodine solution. A black colour shows that the leaf contains starch.

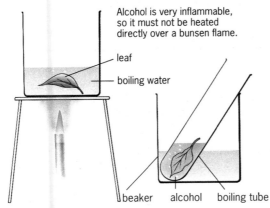

Alcohol is very inflammable, so it must not be heated directly over a bunsen flame.

leaf

boiling water

beaker   alcohol   boiling tube

5.11 Testing a leaf for starch

Questions

1 Why was the leaf put into boiling water?
2 Why did the alcohol become green?
3 Why was the leaf put into alcohol *after* being put into boiling water?

Practical 5.4 To see if light is necessary for photosynthesis

1 Take a healthy geranium plant, growing in a pot. Leave it in a cupboard for a few days, to destarch it.
2 Test one of its leaves for starch, to check that it does not contain any.
3 Using a folded piece of black paper or aluminium foil, a little larger than a leaf, cut out a shape (Fig 5.12). Fasten the paper or foil firmly over both sides of a leaf on your plant, making sure that the edges are held firmly together. Don't take the leaf off the plant!
4 Leave the plant near a warm, sunny window for a few days.
5 Remove the cover from your leaf, and test it for starch.
6 Make a labelled drawing of the appearance of your leaf after testing for starch.

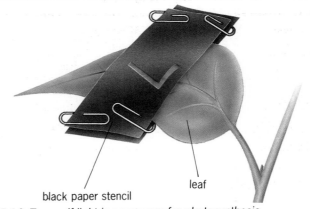

black paper stencil   leaf

5.12 To see if light is necessary for photosynthesis

Questions

1 Why was the plant destarched before the beginning of the experiment?
2 Why was part of the leaf left uncovered?
3 What do your results tell you about light and photosynthesis?

Practical 5.5 To see if carbon dioxide is necessary for photosynthesis

1 Destarch a plant.
2 Set up your apparatus as shown in Fig 5.13. Take special care that no air can get into the flasks. Leave the plant in a warm sunny window for a few days.
3 Test each treated leaf for starch.

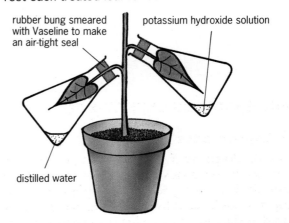

rubber bung smeared with Vaseline to make an air-tight seal   potassium hydroxide solution

distilled water

5.13 To see if carbon dioxide is necessary for photosynthesis

Questions

1 Why was potassium hydroxide put in with one leaf, and water with the other?
2 Which was the control?
3 Why was Vaseline put around the tops of the flasks?
4 What do your results suggest about carbon dioxide and photosynthesis?

—— continued ——

Practical 5.6 To see if chlorophyll is necessary for photosynthesis

1. Destarch a plant with variegated (green and white) leaves.
2. Leave your plant in a warm, sunny spot for a few days.
3. Test one of the leaves for starch.
4. Make a drawing of your leaf before and after testing.

Questions

1. What was the control in this experiment?
2. What do your results tell you about chlorophyll and photosynthesis?

Practical 5.7 To show that oxygen is produced during photosynthesis

1. Set up the apparatus as shown in Fig 5.14. Make sure that the test tube is completely full of water.
2. Leave the apparatus near a warm, sunny window for a few days.
3. Carefully remove the test tube from the top of the funnel, allowing the water to run out, but not allowing the gas to escape.
4. Light a wooden splint, and then blow it out so that it is just glowing. Carefully put it into the gas in the test tube. If it bursts into flame, then the gas is oxygen.

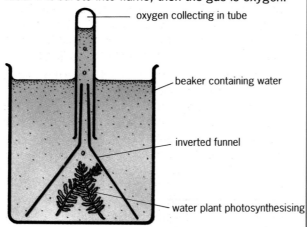

5.14 To show that oxygen is produced during photosynthesis

Questions

1. Why was this experiment done under water?
2. This experiment has no control. Try to design one.

5.12 Many factors affect rate of photosynthesis.

If a plant is given plenty of sunlight, carbon dioxide and water, the limit on the rate at which it can photosynthesise is its own ability to absorb these materials, and make them react. However, quite often plants do not have unlimited supplies of these materials, and so their rate of photosynthesis is not as high as it might be.

Sunlight In the dark, a plant cannot photosynthesise at all. In dim light, it can photosynthesise slowly. As light intensity increases, the rate of photosynthesis will increase, until the plant is photosynthesising as fast as it can. At this point, even if the light becomes brighter, the plant cannot photosynthesise any faster (Fig 5.15a).

Over the first part of the curve, in Fig 5.15a, between A and B, light is a **limiting factor**. The plant is limited in how fast it can photosynthesise because it does not have enough light. You can show this because when the plant is given more light it photosynthesises faster. Between B and C, however, light is not a limiting factor. You can show this because, even if more light is shone on the plant, it still cannot photosynthesise any faster. It already has as much light as it can use.

Carbon dioxide Carbon dioxide can also be a limiting factor (Fig 5.15b). The more carbon dioxide a plant is given, the faster it can photosynthesise up to a point, but then a maximum is reached.

Temperature The chemical reactions of photosynthesis will only take place very slowly at low temperatures, so a plant can photosynthesise faster on a warm day than a cold one.

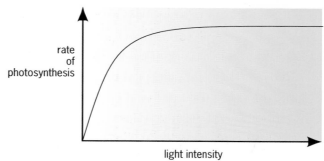

(a) Light intensity and rate of photosynthesis

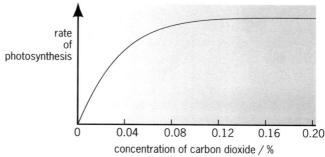

(b) Carbon dioxide concentration and rate of photosynthesis at high light intensity

5.15 Some factors affecting the rate of photosynthesis

Stomata The carbon dioxide which a plant uses passes into the leaf through the stomata. If the stomata are closed, then photosynthesis cannot take place. Stomata often close if the weather is very hot and sunny, to prevent too much water being lost. On a really hot day, therefore, photosynthesis may slow down or stop for a time.

Questions

1 What is meant by a limiting factor?
2 Name two factors which may limit the rate of photo-synthesis of a healthy plant.
3 Why do plants sometimes stop photosynthesising on a very hot, dry day?

Chapter revision questions

1 Copy and complete this table.

	obtained from	used for
nitrates	soil, through root hairs	making proteins
water		
magnesium		
carbon dioxide		

2 Explain the following
(a) There is an air space behind each stoma.
(b) The epidermal cells of a leaf do not have chloro-plasts.
(c) Leaves have a large surface area.
(d) The veins in a leaf branch repeatedly.
(e) A leaf containing starch does not turn black imme-diately when you put iodine solution onto it.
(f) Chloroplasts have many membranes in them.
3 Which carbohydrate does a plant use for each of these purposes? Explain why.
(a) transport
(b) storage
4 Describe how a carbon atom in a carbon dioxide molecule in the air could become part of a starch molecule in a carrot root. Mention all the structures it would pass through, and what would happen to it at each stage.
5 Read the following passage carefully, then answer the questions, using both the information in the passage and your own knowledge.

White light is made up of all the colours of the rainbow. Sea water acts as a light filter which screens off some of the light energy, starting at the red end of the spectrum. As sunlight travels downwards through the water, first the red light is lost, then green and yellow and finally blue. In very clear water, the blue light can penetrate to a maximum of 1000 m. Below this, all is dark.

The upper layers of the sea contain a large community of microscopic floating organisms called plankton, many of which are tiny plants known as phytoplankton. These act as a gigantic solar cell, which feeds all the animals of the sea and supplies both them and the atmosphere above with oxygen.

Nearer the shore, larger plants are found. Seaweeds grow on rocky shores, brown and green ones high on the shore, and red ones lower down, where they are covered with deep water when the tide is in. The colours of the seaweeds are due to their light-absorb-ing pigments, not all of which are chlorophyll.

(a) Why are no green plants found below the upper few hundred metres of the sea?
(b) Some living organisms are found in the permanently dark depths of the oceans. What might they feed on?
(c) What are phytoplankton?
(d) Explain as fully as you can the last sentence of paragraph 2, 'These act as .... with oxygen.'
(e) Chlorophyll is a green pigment. Which colours of light does it (i) absorb, and (ii) reflect?
(f) What colour light would you expect the pigment of red seaweeds to absorb?
(g) Why are red seaweeds normally found lower down the shore than green ones?

continued

6 An experiment was performed to find out how fast a plant photosynthesised as the concentration of CO_2 in the air around it was varied. The results were as follows.

CO_2 concentration % by volume in air	Rate of photosynthesis in arbitrary units	
	low light intensity	high light intensity
0	0	0
0.02	20	33
0.04	29	53
0.06	35	68
0.08	39	79
0.10	42	86
0.12	45	89
0.14	46	90
0.16	46	90
0.18	46	90
0.20	46	90

(a) Plot these results on a graph, drawing one line for low and one for high light intensity, both on the same pair of axes.

(b) What is the CO_2 concentration of normal air?

(c) What is the rate of photosynthesis at this CO_2 concentration in a high light intensity?

(d) Market gardeners often add carbon dioxide to the air in greenhouses. What is the advantage of doing this?

(e) Up to what values does CO_2 concentration act as a limiting factor at high light intensities?

6 Respiration

6.1 Respiration releases energy from food.

Every cell in every living organism needs energy. Cells get their energy from food. The energy is released from the food by a process called **respiration**.

6.2 Sugars release energy when oxidised.

A food which is often used for obtaining energy is sugar. Energy can be released from sugar, by combining it with oxygen. This is called **oxidation**. Fig 6.1 illustrates apparatus in which sugar and oxygen can be made to react together. Oxygen is fed into the space around the sugar. A small electric current is passed into the sugar. When it gets hot enough, the sugar suddenly begins to combine with the oxygen. As it does so, energy is released from it. The energy is heat energy. The sugar burns and the water around it heats up.

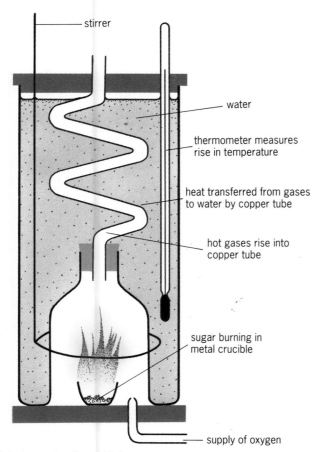

6.1 Apparatus for oxidising sugar

Practical 6.1 To show that peanuts release energy when they are oxidised

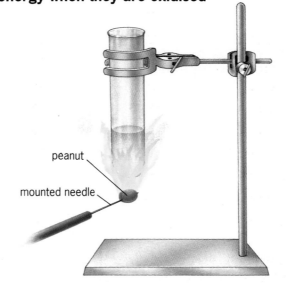

6.2 Burning a peanut

1 Set up your apparatus as shown in Fig 6.2. You will also need a thermometer.
2 Take the temperature of the water in the test tube, and record it.
3 Using the mounted needle, hold the peanut in the Bunsen flame. The heat from the flame will give the peanut enough energy for it to begin to combine with oxygen in the air, so it starts to burn. This reaction is called **oxidation**, or **combustion**.
4 Hold the burning peanut under the test tube of water until it stops burning.
5 Quickly take the temperature of the water again.

Questions

1 Where did the energy come from (a) to start off the reaction of the peanut with oxygen in the air and (b) to raise the temperature of the water?
2 Why is it important to keep the Bunsen burner well away from the test tube?
3 Has *all* the energy in your peanut been released during this experiment? Give a reason for your answer.
4 Do you think all the energy that was released from the peanut went into the water? Explain your answer.

6.3 Respiration oxidises sugars in stages.

Obviously, this does not happen in living cells. If sugar was oxidised like this, the cells would get so hot that they would be killed. In the apparatus in Fig 6.1, the sugar is oxidised quickly in one violent reaction. In a cell, during respiration, the sugar is oxidised very gradually in a series of small, controlled reactions. The reactions are controlled by enzymes. The result, though, is similar. Sugar is combined with oxygen, releasing energy. Carbon dioxide and water are formed.

6.4 The respiration equation.

The process of respiration can be summarised like this.

sugar + oxygen $\rightarrow$ carbon dioxide + water + energy

The sugar which is normally used is glucose, $C_6H_{12}O_6$. The balanced equation for respiration is this.

$$C_6H_{12}O_6 + 6O_2 \rightarrow 6CO_2 + 6H_2O + energy$$

The carbon dioxide and water are by-products. The reaction produces energy for the cell.

Practical 6.2 To show that carbon dioxide is produced in respiration

1 Set up the apparatus as in Fig 6.3.
2 Note the colour of the hydrogencarbonate indicator solution or lime water in each flask.
3 Turn on the pump, to draw air through the apparatus. Leave it running until one of the solutions has changed colour.

Hydrogencarbonate indicator solution changes from red to yellow when carbon dioxide is bubbled through it. Lime water changes from clear to milky white.

Questions

1 Potassium hydroxide solution absorbs carbon dioxide. Why was the air bubbled through this solution before it reached the mouse?
2 Why was the air bubbled through lime water or hydrogencarbonate indicator solution before reaching the mouse?
3 Which solution changed colour? What does this show?

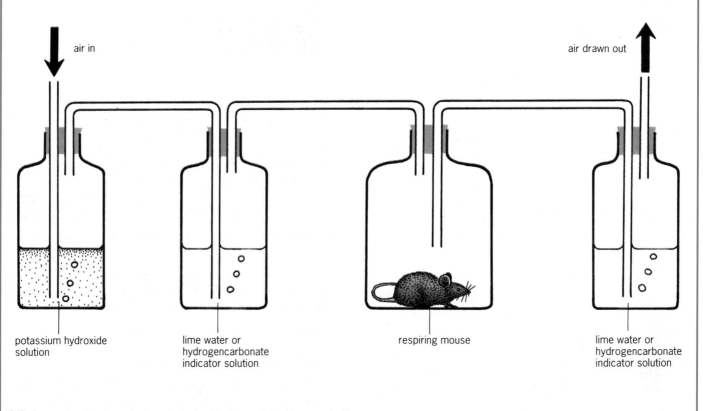

air in   air drawn out

potassium hydroxide   lime water or   respiring mouse   lime water or
solution   hydrogencarbonate   hydrogencarbonate
                             indicator solution   indicator solution

6.3 Apparatus to show that carbon dioxide is produced by respiration

Practical 6.3 To show the uptake of oxygen during respiration

1   Copy out the results table, ready to fill it in.
2   Set up both pieces of apparatus shown in Fig 6.4(a) and (b). Make sure that the connections between the capillary tube, bung and chamber are airtight. Vaseline will help to seal them.
3   Dip the end of the capillary tube of each apparatus into oil, so that a drop is introduced into it.
4   Watch the movement of the oil drop in apparatus (a). This should move quite quickly at first, as the soda lime absorbs any carbon dioxide already in the apparatus.
5   When the oil drop in apparatus (a) slows down or stops, set your stop clock to time 0, and record the position of the oil drop in *both* pieces of apparatus.
6   At suitable time intervals, note both time and distance

Results table

Time in minutes	0	1	2	3	4	etc.
Distance travelled by oil drop in (b) in cm						
Distance travelled by oil drop in (a) in cm						
Distance (b) − (a)						

travelled by both oil drops. Record these results in your results table.
7   Plot a graph of the distance in (b) minus distance in (a), against time. Put time on the bottom axis.

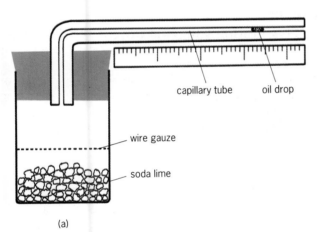

capillary tube   oil drop

wire gauze

soda lime

(a)

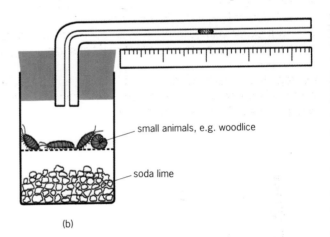

small animals, e.g. woodlice

soda lime

(b)

6.4 Apparatus to show the uptake of oxygen during respiration

Questions

1   What gas is absorbed by soda lime?
2   Why does the oil drop in apparatus (a) move quickly at first?
3   Why does the oil drop in (a) slow down or stop?
4   Why does the oil drop carry on moving in apparatus (b), when the oil drop stops in (a)?
5   Why does the CO_2 breathed out by the woodlice not cause the oil drop in (b) to move to the right?
6   What is the purpose of apparatus (a)?
7   What might cause the oil drop to move in apparatus (a) after its first rapid movement?
8   How could another similar apparatus be used to work out the amount of CO_2 breathed out by the woodlice?

6.5 ATP is the energy currency in cells.

Respiration is going on in all living cells all the time. What happens to the energy which is released?

In the cell are molecules of a substance called **ADP**. ADP stands for adenosine diphosphate. The energy which is released by respiration is used to join a phosphate group onto an ADP molecule. The molecule which is made is called ATP (adenosine triphosphate, Fig 6.5).

ADP + phosphate + energy → ATP

ADP has a low energy content, but ATP has a high energy content. When the cell needs energy, the ATP can be broken down again, releasing its energy.

ATP → ADP + phosphate + energy

6.6 Respiration produces heat.

The energy released by respiration is not all used to make ATP. Some of it does escape as heat. In fact, many animals use the heat from respiration to keep their bodies warm.

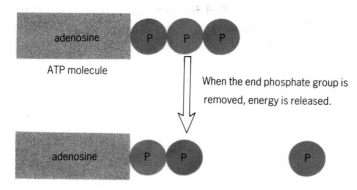

adenosine P P P

ATP molecule

When the end phosphate group is removed, energy is released.

adenosine P P   P

ADP molecule

This can be made into an ATP molecule by adding another phosphate group.

6.5 ATP and ADP

Questions

1 In respiration, sugar is oxidised. What does this mean?
2 What is special about the way that oxidation happens inside cells?
3 What is the purpose of respiration?
4 What is the energy released in respiration used for?
5 In which part of a cell does respiration take place?

6.7 ATP is made inside mitochondria.

Respiration happens inside every living cell, whether plant or animal. Inside these cells are **mitochondria** (Fig 1.5). Mitochondria are called the 'power-houses' of a cell, because it is there that most ATP is made. The more energy a cell needs, the more mitochondria it has. Muscle cells, for example, contain large numbers of mitochondria. So do the cells covering the villi in the small intestine, which use ATP for active transport of glucose.

6.8 Respiration sometimes occurs without oxygen.

The process described so far in this chapter releases energy from sugar by combining it with oxygen. It is called **aerobic respiration**, because it uses air (which contains oxygen).

Practical 6.4 To show that heat is produced in respiration

1 Soak some peas in water for a day, so that they begin to germinate.
2 Boil a second set of peas, to kill them.
3 Wash both sets of peas in dilute disinfectant, so that any bacteria and fungi on them are killed.
4 Put each set of peas into a vacuum flask as shown in Fig 6.6. Do not fill the flasks completely.
5 Note the temperature of each flask.
6 Support each flask upside down, and leave them for a few days.
7 Note the temperature of each flask at the end of your experiment.

Questions

1 Which flask showed the higher temperature at the end of the experiment? Explain your answer.
2 Why is it important to kill any bacteria and fungi on the peas?
3 Why should the flasks not be completely filled with peas?
4 Carbon dioxide is a heavy gas. Why were the flasks left upside down, with porous cotton wool plugs in them?
5 Not all of the energy produced by the respiring peas will be given off as heat. What happens to the rest of it?

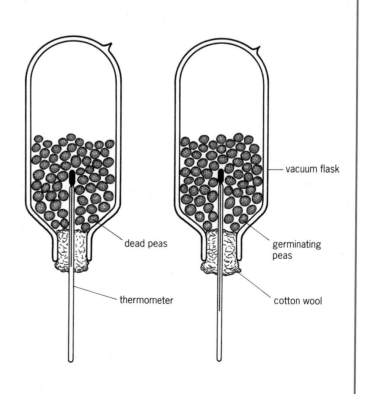

vacuum flask

dead peas

germinating peas

thermometer

cotton wool

6.6 Apparatus to show that heat is produced during respiration

Practical 6.5 To show that carbon dioxide is produced when yeast respires anaerobically

1 Boil some water, to drive off any dissolved air.
2 Dissolve a small amount of sugar in the boiled water, and allow it to cool.
3 When it is cool, add yeast and stir with a glass rod.
4 Set up the apparatus as in Fig 6.7. Add the liquid paraffin by trickling it gently down the side of the tube, using a pipette.
5 Set up an identical piece of apparatus, but use boiled yeast instead of living yeast.
6 Leave your apparatus in a warm place.
7 Observe what happens to the hydrogencarbonate indicator solution after half an hour.

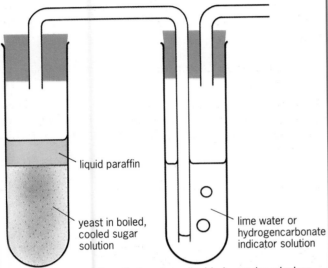

liquid paraffin

yeast in boiled, cooled sugar solution

lime water or hydrogencarbonate indicator solution

6.7 Apparatus to show that carbon dioxide is produced when yeast respires anaerobically

Questions

1 Why is it important to boil the water?
2 Why must the sugar solution be cooled before adding the yeast?
3 What is the liquid paraffin for?
4 What happened to the lime water or hydrogencarbonate indicator solution in each of your pieces of apparatus? What does this show?
5 What new substance would you expect to find in the sugar solution containing living yeast at the end of the experiment?

It is possible, though, to release energy from sugar without using oxygen. It is not such an efficient process and not much energy is released, but the process is used by some organisms. It is called **anaerobic respiration** ('an' means without).

Yeast, a single-celled fungus, can respire anaerobically. It breaks down sugar to alcohol.

$$sugar \rightarrow alcohol + carbon\ dioxide + energy$$
$$C_6H_{12}O_6 \rightarrow 2C_2H_5OH + 2CO_2 + energy$$

As in aerobic respiration, carbon dioxide is made and the energy is used to make ATP.

Some of the cells in your body, particularly muscle cells, can also respire anaerobically for a short time. They make lactic acid instead of alcohol. This is described in Section 6.23.

Table 6.1 A comparison of aerobic and anaerobic respiration

Similarities
1 Energy released by breakdown of sugar
2 ATP made
3 Some energy lost as heat

Differences	
aerobic respiration	*anaerobic respiration*
1 Uses oxygen gas	Does not use oxygen gas
2 No alcohol or lactic acid made	Alcohol or lactic acid made
3 Large amount of energy released	Small amount of energy released
4 CO_2 always made	CO_2 sometimes made

Gaseous exchange

6.9 Gaseous exchange occurs at respiratory surfaces.

If you look back at the respiration equation in Section 6.4, you will see that two substances are needed. They are glucose and oxygen. The way in which cells obtain glucose is described in Chapters 4 and 5. Animals get sugar from carbohydrates which they eat. Plants make theirs, by photosynthesis.

Oxygen is obtained in a different way. Animals and plants get their oxygen directly from their surroundings. The part of the organism through which oxygen enters the body is called the **respiratory surface**.

If you look again at the respiration equation you can see that carbon dioxide is made. This is a waste product and it must be removed from the organism. It leaves across the respiratory surface.

So, at a respiratory surface, oxygen comes in and carbon dioxide goes out. This is called **gaseous exchange**.

6.10 *Amoeba* exchanges gases through its membrane.

Amoeba is a single-celled organism which lives in water. Its respiratory surface is its **cell surface membrane** (Fig 6.8).

65

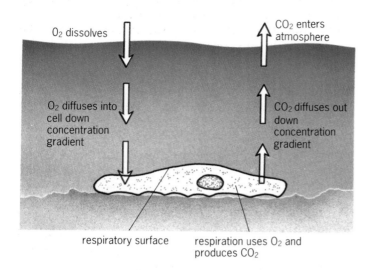

6.8 *Gaseous exchange in* Amoeba

Oxygen dissolves in water, so there are usually oxygen molecules in the water around *Amoeba*. Inside the cell, however, oxygen is being used up in respiration. Therefore, there is a higher concentration of oxygen molecules outside the cell, but a lower concentration inside. So oxygen diffuses into the cell, across the cell membrane, down a concentration gradient. Carbon dioxide diffuses in the opposite direction.

6.11 Large organisms need transport systems.

Amoeba is a very small organism made of only one cell. Oxygen can quickly diffuse into the centre of the cell because it does not have far to go.

This would not work, though, for a large organism like a human. It would take too long for oxygen to diffuse from the air to every cell in your body. Some sort of transport system is needed to get the oxygen all around the body as quickly as possible. In humans this is the blood system.

6.12 Surface area to volume ratio.

Large organisms have another problem with gaseous exchange. The larger their volume, the more oxygen they need. This oxygen has to get through their respiratory surface. The amount that can get into their body depends on the area of this surface.

So, the need for oxygen increases with an organism's **volume**, but the supply of oxygen increases with its **respiratory surface area**. This is a problem because, as an organism gets larger, its surface area and volume increase by different amounts.

Imagine a cube-shaped organism (Fig 6.9), where the outer surface is the respiratory surface. A good way to compare the surface area to the volume is to divide the surface area by the volume. This is called the surface

area to volume ratio. For the small cube, this is 6. For the medium sized cube it is 0.6, and for the large cube only 0.06. So, the larger an organism is, the smaller its surface area to volume ratio is.

A small organism, which has a large surface area compared to its volume, can use its body surface for gaseous exchange. But a large organism cannot use its ordinary body surface alone, because it is not large enough. Large organisms need special respiratory surfaces, which provide the large areas required for gaseous exchange. Specialised parts of their surface are highly divided or folded to provide this extra area for gaseous exchange (Fig 6.10). Sometimes, these surfaces are tucked inside the body for protection. This also helps to prevent too much water evaporating from organisms which live on land.

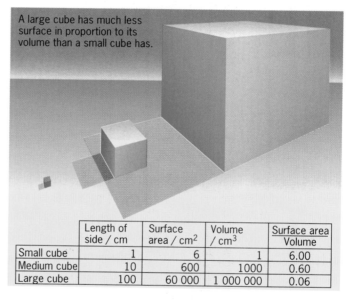

	Length of side / cm	Surface area / cm^2	Volume / cm^3	Surface area / Volume
Small cube	1	6	1	6.00
Medium cube	10	600	1000	0.60
Large cube	100	60 000	1 000 000	0.06

6.9 *Surface area to volume ratio*

6.13 Respiratory surfaces are thin and moist.

Respiratory surfaces are usually made of living cells. These cells must be kept moist, or they will die. If an organism is surrounded by water, this is no problem.

Table 6.2 Properties of respiratory surfaces of large organisms

1 They should be **thin** to allow gases to diffuse across them quickly.

2 They should be close to an efficient **transport system** to take gases to and from the cells which need them.

3 They should be kept **moist**, to stop the cells dying.

4 They should have a **large surface area** so that a lot of oxygen can diffuse across at the same time.

5 They should have a good **supply of oxygen**.

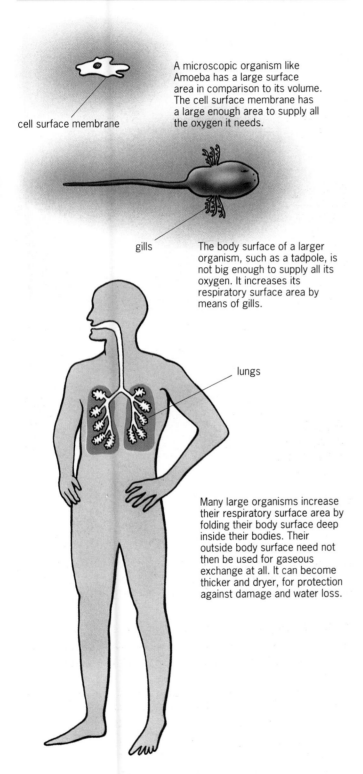

A microscopic organism like Amoeba has a large surface area in comparison to its volume. The cell surface membrane has a large enough area to supply all the oxygen it needs.

cell surface membrane

The body surface of a larger organism, such as a tadpole, is not big enough to supply all its oxygen. It increases its respiratory surface area by means of gills.

gills

lungs

Many large organisms increase their respiratory surface area by folding their body surface deep inside their bodies. Their outside body surface need not then be used for gaseous exchange at all. It can become thicker and dryer, for protection against damage and water loss.

6.10 Respiratory surfaces

A fish's gills, for example, are always surrounded by water in which the oxygen is dissolved.

On land, though, the respiratory surface must be kept moist by the organism itself. Your lungs, for example, contain cells which make a liquid to keep the respiratory surface wet (Fig 6.15).

A respiratory surface should also be as thin as possible. The thinner it is, the more quickly oxygen can diffuse across it. This means that respiratory surfaces are often very delicate.

6.14 Earthworms exchange gases through the skin.

An earthworm's respiratory surface is its skin. The skin is quite thin and has a good blood supply. The blood transports oxygen and carbon dioxide to and from all the cells of the earthworm's body. The blood contains **haemoglobin**, which helps to carry oxygen.

Humans are covered with quite a thick layer of dead cells, which help to stop us from drying out in the air. An earthworm's skin cannot be thick and dead, or it would be no good for allowing gases to diffuse through it quickly. Its skin is thin, and made of living cells which must be kept moist. This means that earthworms cannot live in dry places. They must live in moist soil, and can only come above ground to feed when it is cool or wet.

Questions

1 What is a respiratory surface?
2 What is the respiratory surface of *Amoeba*?
3 How does gaseous exchange take place across the respiratory surface of *Amoeba*?
4 Explain, as briefly as you can, why large organisms need special respiratory surfaces.
5 Why are the respiratory surfaces of most terrestrial (land living) animals inside their bodies?

Gaseous exchange in humans

6.15 The structure of the respiratory system.

Figure 6.11 shows the structures which are involved in gaseous exchange in a human. The most important are the two lungs. Each lung is filled with many tiny air spaces called air sacs or **alveoli**. It is here that oxygen diffuses into the blood. Because they are so full of spaces, lungs feel very light and spongy to touch. The lungs are supplied with air through the windpipe or **trachea**.

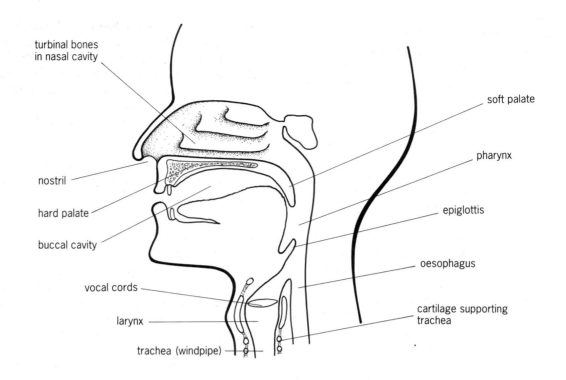

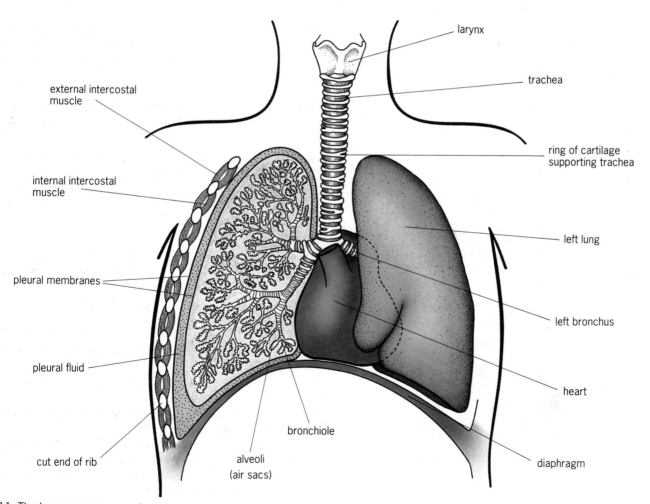

6.11 The human gaseous exchange system

6.16 The path taken by air to the lungs.

The nose and mouth Air can enter the body either through the nose or mouth. The nose and mouth are separated by the **palate** (Fig 6.11), so you can breathe through your nose even when you are eating.

It is better to breathe through your nose, because the structure of the nose allows the air to become warm, moist and filtered before it gets to the lungs. Inside the nose are some thin bones called **turbinal bones** which are covered with a thin layer of cells. Some of these cells make a liquid containing water and mucus which evaporates into the air in the nose and moistens it (Fig 6.12).

Other cells have very tiny hair-like projections called cilia. The cilia are always moving and bacteria or particles of dust get trapped in them and in the mucus. Cilia are found all along the trachea and bronchi, too. They waft the mucus, containing bacteria and dust, up to the back of the throat, so that it does not block up the lungs. Cilia in the nose also waft mucus into the oesophagus where it is swallowed.

The trachea The air then passes into the windpipe or **trachea**. At the top of the trachea is a piece of cartilage called the **epiglottis**. This closes the trachea and stops food going down the trachea when you swallow. This is a reflex action which happens automatically when a bolus of food touches the soft palate.

Just below the epiglottis is the voice box or **larynx**. This contains the vocal cords. The vocal cords can be tightened by muscles so that they make sounds when air passes over them. The trachea has rings of cartilage around it which keep it open.

The bronchi The trachea goes down through the neck and into the **thorax**. The thorax is the upper part of your body from the neck down to the bottom of the ribs and diaphragm. In the thorax the trachea divides into two. The two branches are called the right and left **bronchi**. One bronchus goes to each lung and then branches out into many smaller tubes called **bronchioles**.

The alveoli At the end of each bronchiole are many tiny air sacs or **alveoli** (Fig 6.13). This is where gaseous exchange takes place.

6.17 Alveolar walls form the respiratory surface.

The walls of the alveoli are the respiratory surface. Tiny blood vessels, called **capillaries**, are closely wrapped around the outside of the alveoli (Fig 6.13). Oxygen diffuses across the walls of the alveoli into the blood (Fig 6.15). Carbon dioxide diffuses the other way.

The walls of the alveoli have several features which make them an efficient respiratory surface.

They are very thin They are only one cell thick. The capillary walls are also only one cell thick. An oxygen molecule only has to diffuse across this small thickness to get into the blood.

They have an excellent transport system Blood is constantly pumped to the lungs along the pulmonary

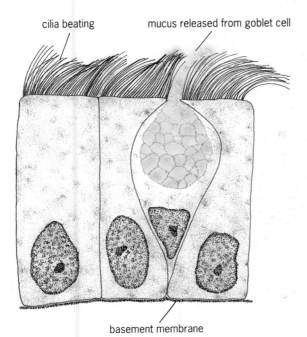

cilia beating   mucus released from goblet cell

basement membrane

6.12 Part of the lining of the respiratory passages

Practical 6.6 Examining lungs
1 Examine some sheep lungs obtained from a butcher's shop or abattoir.

Questions

1   What colour are the lungs? Why are they this colour?
2   Push them gently with your finger. What do they feel like? Why do they feel like this?
3   What is covering the surface of the lungs? What is its name, and why is it there?
4   Find the two tubes leading down to the lungs. Which one is the oesophagus? Follow it along, and notice that it goes right past the lungs. Where is it going to?
5   The other tube is the trachea. What does it feel like? Why does it feel like this?
6   What is the name of the wide part at the top of the trachea? What is its function?
7   If the lungs have not been badly cut, take a long glass tube (such as a burette tube) and push it down through the trachea. Hold the trachea tightly against it, and blow down it. What happens?

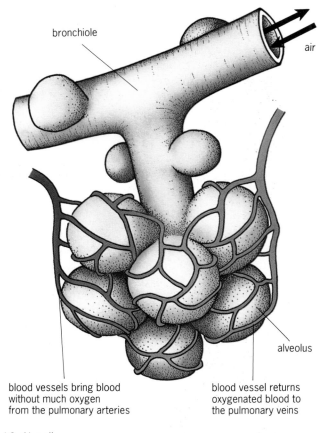

6.13 Alveoli

bronchiole

air

blood vessels bring blood without much oxygen from the pulmonary arteries

alveolus

blood vessel returns oxygenated blood to the pulmonary veins

artery. This branches into thousands of capillaries which take blood to all parts of the lungs. Carbon dioxide in the blood can diffuse out into the air spaces in the alveoli and oxygen can diffuse into the blood. The blood is then taken back to the heart in the pulmonary vein, ready to be pumped to the rest of the body.

The way in which the blood carries oxygen and carbon dioxide is explained in Section 7.19.

They have a large surface area In fact, the surface area is enormous! The total surface area of all the alveoli in your lungs is over 100 m^2.

They have a good supply of oxygen Your breathing movements keep your lungs well supplied with oxygen.

Questions

1 Why is it better to breathe through your nose than through your mouth?
2 What is the function of the cilia in the respiratory passages?
3 What is the larynx?
4 What is the respiratory surface of a human?
5 How many cells does an oxygen molecule have to pass through, to get from an alveolus into the blood?

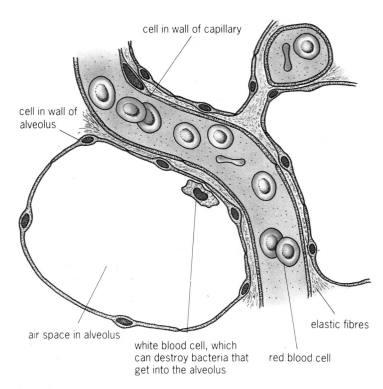

cell in wall of capillary

cell in wall of alveolus

air space in alveolus

white blood cell, which can destroy bacteria that get into the alveolus

red blood cell

elastic fibres

6.14 *Section through part of a lung, magnified*

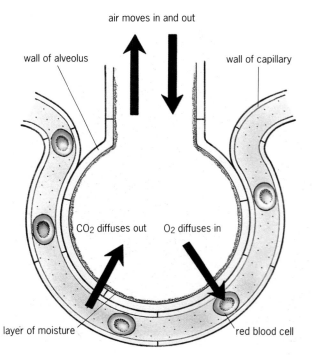

air moves in and out

wall of alveolus

wall of capillary

CO_2 diffuses out O_2 diffuses in

layer of moisture

red blood cell

6.15 *Gaseous exchange in an alveolus*

6.18 Ribs and diaphragm move during breathing.

To make air move in and out of the lungs, you must keep changing the volume of your thorax. First, you make it large so that air is sucked in. Then you make it smaller again so that air is squeezed out. This is called breathing.

There are two sets of muscles which help you to breathe. One set is in between the ribs. This set is called the **intercostal muscles** (Fig 6.16). The other set is in the **diaphragm**. The diaphragm is a large sheet of muscle and elastic tissue which stretches across your body, underneath the lungs and heart.

6.19 Breathing in is called inspiration.

When breathing in, the muscles of the diaphragm contract. This pulls the diaphragm downwards, which increases the volume in the thorax (Fig 6.17a). At the same time, the external intercostal muscles contract. This pulls the rib cage upwards and outwards (Fig 6.18). Together, these movements increase the volume of the thorax.

As the volume of the thorax increases, the pressure inside it falls below atmospheric pressure. Extra space has been made and something must come in to fill it up. Air therefore rushes in along the trachea and bronchi into the lungs.

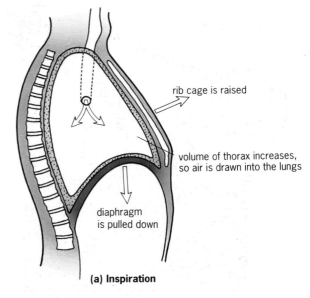

rib cage is raised

volume of thorax increases, so air is drawn into the lungs

diaphragm is pulled down

(a) Inspiration

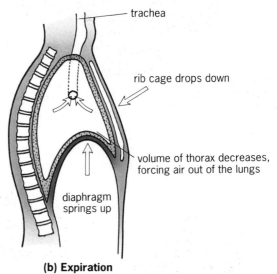

trachea

rib cage drops down

volume of thorax decreases, forcing air out of the lungs

diaphragm springs up

(b) Expiration

6.17 How the thorax changes shape during breathing

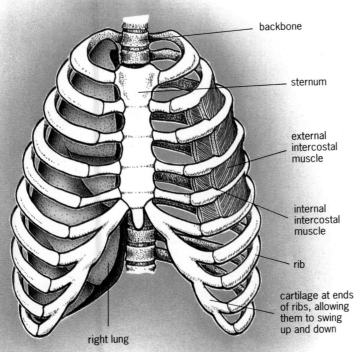

backbone

sternum

external intercostal muscle

internal intercostal muscle

rib

cartilage at ends of ribs, allowing them to swing up and down

right lung

6.16 The rib cage

6.20 Breathing out is called expiration.

When breathing out the muscles of the diaphragm relax. The diaphragm springs back up into its domed shape because it is made of elastic tissue. This decreases the volume in the thorax. The external intercostal muscles also relax. The rib cage drops down again into its normal position. This also decreases the volume of the thorax (Fig 6.17b).

As the volume of the thorax decreases, the pressure inside it increases. Air is squeezed out through the trachea into the nose and mouth, and on out of the body.

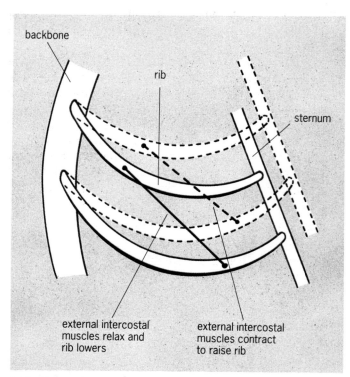

6.18 *The external intercostal muscles raise and lower the ribs*

Practical 6.7 Using a model to show the action of the diaphragm

1 Use the apparatus in Fig 6.19. Begin with the plunger in as far as it will go. Put your thumb tightly over the hole, and pull the plunger outwards.
2 Repeat this, but this time do not cover the hole with your thumb.

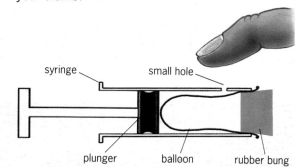

6.19 *A model to show the action of the diaphragm*

Questions

1 What does the balloon represent?
2 What does the plunger represent?
3 What happens to the balloon when you cover the hole and pull the plunger? Explain why.
4 What happens to the balloon when you pull the plunger without covering the hole? Explain why.
5 In what ways is this a misleading demonstration of the mechanism of breathing?

6.21 Internal intercostal muscles can force air out.

Usually, you breathe out by relaxing the external intercostal muscles and the muscles of the diaphragm, as explained in Section 6.20. Sometimes, though, you breathe out more forcefully – when coughing, for example. Then the internal intercostal muscles contract strongly, making the rib cage drop down even further. The muscles of the abdomen wall also contract, helping to squeeze extra air out of the thorax.

Practical 6.8 Comparing the carbon dioxide content of inspired and expired air

You can use either lime water or hydrogencarbonate indicator solution for this experiment. Lime water changes from clear to cloudy when carbon dioxide dissolves in it. Hydrogencarbonate indicator solution changes from red to yellow when carbon dioxide dissolves in it.
1 Set up the apparatus as in Fig 6.20.
2 Breathe in and out gently through the rubber tubing. Do not breathe too hard. Keep doing this until the liquid in one of the flasks changes colour.

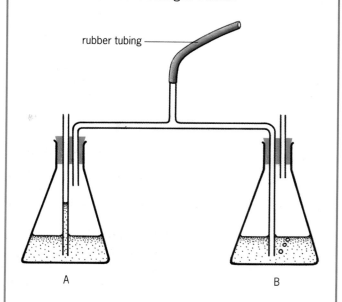

6.20 *Comparing the carbon dioxide content of inspired and expired air*

Questions

1 In which flask did bubbles appear when you breathed out? Explain why.
2 In which flask did bubbles appear when you breathed in? Explain why.
3 What happened to the liquid in flask A?
4 What happened to the liquid in flask B?
5 What do your results tell you about the amount of carbon dioxide in inspired air and expired air?

Table 6.3 Comparison of inspired and expired air.
Inspired air is the air you breathe in. Expired air is the air you breathe out.

	Inspired air	Expired air	Reason for difference
Oxygen	21%	16%	Oxygen is absorbed across respiratory surface, then used by cells in respiration
Carbon dioxide	0.03%	4%	Carbon dioxide is made by cells as a waste product of respiration, and is released across the respiratory surface
Argon and other noble gases	1%	1%	
Nitrogen	78%	78%	Nitrogen gas is not used by cells
Water content (humidity)	Variable	Always high	Respiratory surface must be kept moist. Some of this moisture evaporates and is lost as air is breathed out
Temperature	Variable	Always high	Air is warmed as it passes through the respiratory passages

6.22 Pleural membranes help with breathing.

Each lung is covered with a thin, smooth membrane. Another similar membrane lines the inside of the rib cage. These are called the **pleural membranes** (Fig 6.11).

The pleural membranes make a liquid called pleural fluid. This fills the space between the two membranes. As the lungs inflate and deflate, the pleural fluid helps to lubricate them so that they do not rub against the

Table 6.4 The differences between respiration, gaseous exchange and breathing

Respiration is chemical reactions which happen in all living cells, in which food is broken down to release energy, usually by combining it with oxygen.

Gaseous exchange is the exchange of gases across a respiratory surface. For example, oxygen is taken into the body, and carbon dioxide is removed from it. Gaseous exchange also takes place during photosynthesis and respiration in plants.

Breathing is muscular movements which keep the respiratory surface supplied with oxygen.

rib cage too much. Also, as the rib cage expands, the pleural fluid ensures that the lungs adhere closely to the moving ribs.

Sometimes, in a car accident for example, the thorax becomes punctured so that air gets in between the pleural membranes. If this happens, then the lungs will not work and they collapse.

The pleural membranes also help to keep the two lungs separate from one another. If one lung is punctured in an accident so that it collapses, the other pleural cavity will still be airtight, so the other lung can work normally.

Questions
1. What is breathing?
2. Which muscles help in breathing?
3. Where are the pleural membranes?
4. Give two functions of pleural fluid.

6.23 Exercise can create an oxygen debt.

All the cells in your body need oxygen for respiration and all of this oxygen is supplied by the lungs. The oxygen is carried by the blood to every part of the body.

Sometimes, cells may need a lot of oxygen very quickly. Imagine you are running in a race. The muscles in your legs are using up a lot of energy. To produce this energy, the mitochondria in the muscles will be combining oxygen with glucose as fast as they can, to make ATP which will provide the energy for the muscles.

A lot of oxygen is needed to work as hard as this. You breathe deeper and faster to get more oxygen into your blood. Your heart beats faster to get the oxygen to the leg muscles as quickly as possible. Eventually a limit is reached. The heart and lungs cannot supply oxygen to the muscles any faster. But more energy is

6.21 *An athlete pays back his oxygen debt at the end of a race*

73

still needed for the race. How can that extra energy be found?

Extra energy can be produced by anaerobic respiration. Some glucose is broken down without combining it with oxygen.

glucose → lactic acid + energy

As explained in Section 6.8, this does not release very much energy, but a little extra might make all the difference.

When you stop running, you will have quite a lot of lactic acid in your muscles and your blood. This lactic acid must be broken down by combining it with oxygen. So, even though you do not need the energy any more, you go on breathing hard. You are taking in extra oxygen to break down the lactic acid.

While you were running, you built up an **oxygen debt**. You 'borrowed' some extra energy, without 'paying' for it with oxygen. Now, as the lactic acid is combined with oxygen, you are paying off the debt. Not until all the lactic acid has been used up, does your breathing rate and rate of heart beat return to normal.

Practical 6.9 Investigating how breathing rate changes with exercise

1 Copy the table, ready to fill in your results.
2 Sit quietly for two minutes, to make sure you are completely relaxed.
3 Count how many breaths you take in one minute. Record it in your table.
4 Wait one minute, then count breaths again, and record.
5 Now do some vigorous exercise, such as stepping up and down onto a chair, for exactly two minutes. At the end of this time, sit down. Immediately count your breaths in the next minute, and record.
6 Continue to record your breaths per minute every other minute, until they have returned to near the level before you started to exercise.
7 Draw a graph of your results, putting time on the bottom (x) axis.

Results table

Time	Number of breaths per minute
1st minute	
3rd minute	
6th minute	
8th minute	
10th minute	

Questions

1 Why does your breathing rate rise so quickly during exercise?
2 Why did your breathing rate not go back to normal as soon as you finished exercising?
3 Work out how many minutes it took your breathing rate to return to normal after exercise. Collect everyone's results for this, and work out the class average.
   Now compare individual results with the average one. Do fit people who regularly play a lot of sport come above or below this average result? Try to explain this.

Smoking

6.24 Cigarette smoking damages lungs and heart.

Cigarette smoke is very harmful to a person's lungs. Everyone who smokes does some damage to their lungs. Heavy smoking can also damage the heart and blood vessels.

Even people who do not smoke may be harmed by other people's cigarettes. If a baby's parents each smoke 20 cigarettes a day, the child will have indirectly smoked 80 cigarettes by the time it is one year old. Non-smokers are more likely to get coughs and bronchitis if they spend much time in a room with people who are smoking.

Cigarette smoke contains three main ingredients. These are nicotine, tar and carbon monoxide. Each of these has its own effects on the body.

6.25 Nicotine is addictive.

Nicotine affects the brain. It is a stimulant, which means that it makes you feel more alert and active. It makes heart rate and blood pressure increase. People who smoke are more likely to suffer from heart disease than people who do not.

Nicotine is a very poisonous substance. It is used in some insecticides. A smoker takes in about 2 mg of nicotine for each cigarette that he smokes. The nicotine is absorbed into the blood. But fifteen minutes after smoking the cigarette, half of this nicotine has been broken down, so only 1 mg remains in the blood.

Nicotine is **addictive**. This means that once your body has got used to it, it is very hard to do without it. This is why many smokers find it difficult to give up smoking.

6.26 Tar increases the chances of getting lung cancer.

The tar in cigarette smoke is absorbed by some of the cells in the lungs, especially the ones lining the bronchi and bronchioles. Normally, these cells form a thin,

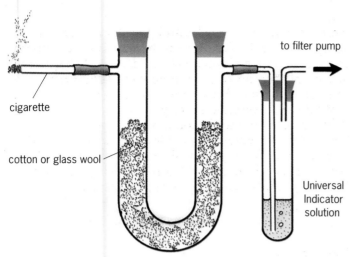

cigarette

cotton or glass wool

to filter pump

Universal
Indicator
solution

Smoke particles and tar are trapped in the cotton wool. The Universal Indicator solution changes from green (neutral) to yellow (acidic) because substances in the smoke form an acidic solution.

6.22 Apparatus to show what is contained in cigarette smoke

protective layer (Fig 6.12). But the tar makes them divide, and build up into a thicker layer. Some of these groups of dividing cells may go on and on dividing, developing into **cancer**.

Non-smokers do occasionally get lung cancer, but this is very rare. Most deaths from lung cancer are of people who smoked.

Tar is an irritant. It makes the linings of the respiratory passages inflamed, causing chronic bronchitis. It also damages the cilia lining these passages, and causes extra mucus to be made by the goblet cells. This mucus trickles down into the lungs – the cilia are no longer able to beat and sweep it upwards.

Bacteria breed in the mucus, causing infections. The person coughs, to try to move the mucus upwards. The constant coughing can damage the delicate alveoli in the lungs. This makes it much more difficult for the person to get enough oxygen into their blood. This person has an illness called emphysema.

6.27 Carbon monoxide cuts down oxygen supply.

Carbon monoxide is absorbed into the blood. Here it combines rapidly with haemoglobin inside the red cells (Section 7.19). This means that there is less haemoglobin available to carry oxygen. In a heavy smoker who inhales, up to one fifth of his haemoglobin is combined with carbon monoxide instead of oxygen.

As well as cutting down the amount of oxygen *in* the blood, carbon monoxide also makes body cells less able to absorb oxygen *from* the blood. Brain cells are especially sensitive to this.

Babies born to mothers who smoke tend to be smaller than babies of non-smokers, and this is probably because of the effects of carbon monoxide on the baby in the womb.

Solvent abuse

6.28 Glue-sniffing can kill.

Some glues and other substances contain organic solvents. When a substance containing the solvent is sniffed, the solvent goes into the nose and gaseous exchange system. It can then be absorbed into the blood.

Many of these organic solvents are dangerous. They cause dizziness, loss of coordination, and sometimes unconsciousness. Many young people have died from sniffing solvents. This is sometimes because of the toxic effects of the solvent on the brain. Sometimes the solvent makes the person vomit while they are unconscious, and they choke on their vomit. Sometimes the person loses control of their actions while under the influence of the solvent, and has a fatal accident.

Gaseous exchange in fish

6.29 Fish absorb oxygen through gills.

Fish use oxygen which is dissolved in water, just as *Amoeba* do. Their respiratory surface is the surface of their **gills**.

Figure 6.23 shows the structure of a fish's gills. A fish has several gills. These have spaces in between them called **gill pouches**. The gill pouches open to the outside. In bony fish, the opening is covered by a piece of skin and bone called the **operculum**.

Each gill is supported by a piece of bone called a **gill bar**. On the outer surface of the gill bar are many thin, soft flaps of tissue. These are the **gill lamellae** and it is here where gaseous exchange takes place. Because they are so finely divided, they have a very large surface area. They are thin and have a good blood supply.

On the other side of each gill bar are the **gill rakers**. These trap particles of dirt and stop them from clogging up the lamellae. Some fish, such as the herring, use their gill rakers for filter feeding.

6.30 Some fish make breathing movements.

Oxygen is brought to the gills as water flows over them. Water flows in through the mouth, over the gills and out through the gill slits.

Some fish, such as the herring, swim fast with their mouths open. This makes water pass over their gills. Others, such as trout, lie in fast running water, facing upstream. Fish which cannot swim fast, or which live in still water, have to make breathing movements. These are explained in Fig 6.24.

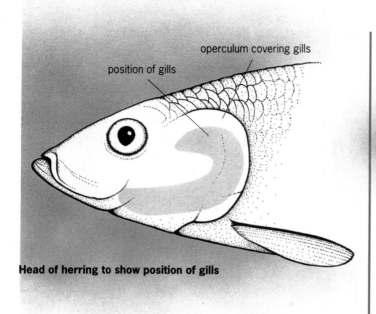

Head of herring to show position of gills

position of gills

operculum covering gills

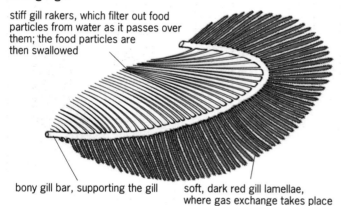

A single gill

stiff gill rakers, which filter out food particles from water as it passes over them; the food particles are then swallowed

bony gill bar, supporting the gill

soft, dark red gill lamellae, where gas exchange takes place

6.23 A herring's gills

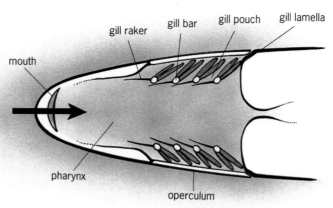

gill raker gill bar gill pouch gill lamella

mouth

pharynx

operculum

Inspiration In inspiration the mouth opens. The floor of the pharynx is pulled down, increasing the space inside it. Water therefore flows into the mouth and pharynx.

Expiration

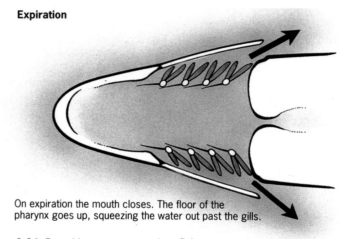

On expiration the mouth closes. The floor of the pharynx goes up, squeezing the water out past the gills.

6.24 Breathing movements in a fish

Practical 6.10 Investigating the structure of gills

1 Examine a dead fish. Find the operculum. Using a seeker, lift it up gently. Notice the gills lying underneath. What colour are they? Why are they this colour?

2 Gently push a seeker into the fish's mouth, and out under the operculum. What normally travels along this path?

3 Using scissors, cut the operculum neatly where it joins the body. Using forceps and scissors, cut out *one* gill, as close to its ends as possible.

4 Put the gill into a small dish containing water. Make a drawing of it. Label gill bar, gill lamellae and gill rakers. What is the function of each of these?

5 Take the gill out of the water, and lay it on a dry tile. What difference is there between the position of the gill lamellae now, and when they were floating in the water? Can you think of one reason why a fish cannot breathe out of the water?

Gaseous exchange in flowering plants

6.31 Plants respire and photosynthesise.

Green plants photosynthesise. They make glucose by combining water and carbon dioxide.

$$\text{carbon dioxide} + \text{water} \xrightarrow[\text{chlorophyll}]{\text{sunlight}} \text{glucose} + \text{oxygen}$$

$$6CO_2 + 6H_2O \xrightarrow[\text{chlorophyll}]{\text{sunlight}} C_6H_{12}O_6 + 6O_2$$

This needs energy which comes from sunlight. The energy is trapped by chlorophyll. The glucose which is made contains some of this energy.

When the plant needs energy, it releases it from the glucose in the same way that an animal does – that is, by respiration.

glucose + oxygen → carbon dioxide + water + energy

$$C_6H_{12}O_6 + 6O_2 \longrightarrow 6CO_2 + 6H_2O + energy$$

At first sight, this reaction looks like photosynthesis going 'backwards'. In some ways it is. The photosynthesis reaction makes glucose and the respiration reaction breaks it down. However, the reactions are really very different. In photosynthesis, the energy which goes into the reaction is light energy which is trapped by the chloroplast. In respiration, the energy which comes out is chemical energy. This process occurs in the mitochondrion.

As in animals, the energy which is released during respiration is used to make ATP. The ATP can then be used whenever the plant needs energy.

6.32 Plants, like animals, need energy.

Plants do not need as much energy as animals. They are not so active, partly because they do not have to move to find their food. However, all living cells need some energy. Plant cells need energy for growth, reproduction and for transporting food material between

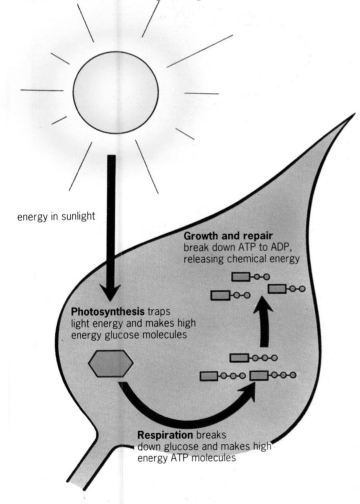

energy in sunlight

Growth and repair break down ATP to ADP, releasing chemical energy

Photosynthesis traps light energy and makes high energy glucose molecules

Respiration breaks down glucose and makes high energy ATP molecules

6.25 How the energy in sunlight is changed to useful energy by a green plant

cells and inside cells. They need it for building up large molecules from small ones, for example starch and cellulose from sugars, and proteins from amino acids. So all living plant cells, like animal cells, are always respiring.

Practical 6.11 To investigate the effect that plants and animals have on the carbon dioxide concentration of water

1 Copy the results chart, ready to fill it in.
2 Take four clean tubes, and put an equal quantity of hydrogencarbonate indicator solution into each. Note the colour of the solution, and fill it in on your results chart.
3 Put watersnails and water plants into each tube as shown in Fig 6.26.

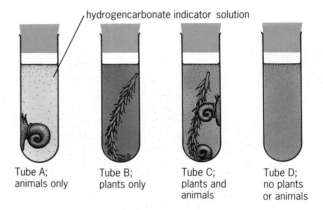

hydrogencarbonate indicator solution

Tube A; animals only

Tube B; plants only

Tube C; plants and animals

Tube D; no plants or animals

6.26 To investigate the effect that plants and animals have on the carbon dioxide concentration of water

4 Stopper each tube firmly with a rubber bung.
5 Leave all four tubes in a light place for 30 – 45 minutes.

Results table	A	B	C	D
Contents of tube				
Colour of indicator solution at beginning				
Colour of indicator solution at end				

Questions

1 Remembering that animals and plants respire, and that plants also photosynthesise in the light, explain the differences in the colour of the hydrogencarbonate indicator solution in each tube.
2 What would you expect to happen to the animals and/or the plants in each tube if you left them for a long time?
3 What would happen to the colour of the solution in each of your four tubes if you left them in the dark?

6.33 The balance between photosynthesis and respiration.

Some plant cells, however, also photosynthesise. The cells in a leaf have chloroplasts and they use carbon dioxide and release oxygen during the daytime. At the same time, respiration is happening inside the mitochondria (Fig 6.27).

In the daytime, photosynthesis is going on much faster than respiration. All of the carbon dioxide that the plant makes by respiration is used up by the chloroplasts in photosynthesis. Even this is not enough, and the plant takes in extra carbon dioxide from the air.

Some of the oxygen which is made by photosynthesis is used up for respiration. There is a lot left over, however, and this diffuses out of the cell.

At night, the chloroplasts stop photosynthesising. The mitochondria, however, continue to respire. Oxygen is used up, and carbon dioxide is released.

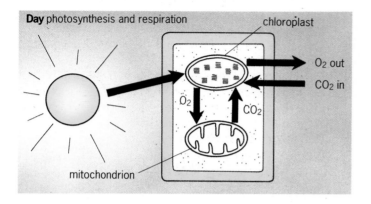 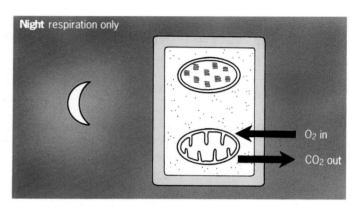

6.27 *The balance between photosynthesis and respiration in a green plant*

Table 6.5 Comparison of gaseous exchange in living organisms

Organism	Respiratory surface (RS)	How is the RS kept moist?	How is the RS provided with oxygen?	Transport system in the organism	How is the surface area of the RS increased?
Amoeba	Cell surface membrane	Surrounded by water	Water currents, diffusion	Diffusion only	Not necessary, as organism is small
Earthworm	Skin	Moisture in soil and on damp vegetation; coelomic fluid leaks through pores	Diffusion	Blood containing haemoglobin	Not necessary, as organism is small and not very active
Mammal	Alveoli in lungs	Cells in alveoli secrete fluid	Breathing movements; muscles of diaphragm and intercostal muscles vary volume of thorax, so that air moves up and down trachea	Blood containing haemoglobin	Many alveoli create very large surface area inside lungs
Fish	Lamellae of gills	Surrounded by water	Water currents and breathing movements; continuous movement of water into mouth and out under operculum	Blood containing haemoglobin	Each gill divided into many thin lamellae and each lamella also subdivided
Flowering plant	Surface of cells inside leaf, stem and roots	Cells in leaf surrounded by thin film of water brought by xylem vessels	By diffusion through stomata into leaf and stem; from photosynthesising cells; through lenticels in woody stem, by diffusion; from air spaces in soil through epidermis of root, by diffusion	By diffusion	Leaf is very thin, so has large surface area compared with volume

6.34 Plants get oxygen by diffusion.

Plants have a branching shape, so they have quite a large surface area in comparison to their volume. Therefore, diffusion alone can supply all their cells with as much oxygen as they need for respiration. Diffusion occurs in the leaves, stems and roots of plants.

Leaves In the daytime, leaves are photosynthesising. This supplies plenty of oxygen for respiration. At night, oxygen diffuses into the leaves through the stomata. It dissolves in the thin layer of moisture around the cells and diffuses in across their cell walls and membranes.

Stems The stems of herbaceous plants have stomata. Woody stems are covered with a layer of **cork cells** which make up the bark. These cells will not let air through, so the cork cells are packed loosely in places, to let oxygen diffuse in to the cells underneath. These places are called **lenticels** (Fig 6.28).

Roots Roots get their oxygen from the air spaces in the soil. If the soil is waterlogged for very long, the roots become short of oxygen. Under these conditions the roots will respire anaerobically, producing alcohol. This may kill the plant.

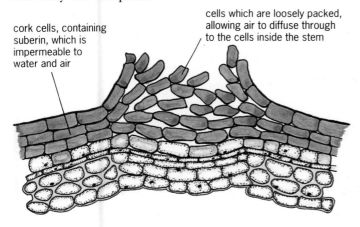

cork cells, containing suberin, which is impermeable to water and air

cells which are loosely packed, allowing air to diffuse through to the cells inside the stem

6.28 *Section through a lenticel on a woody stem*

Questions

1 Why is respiration not really like 'photosynthesis backwards'?
2 Why do plants need energy?
3 In which parts of a plant cell does (a) respiration, and (b) photosynthesis happen?
4 At what times of day do plant cells respire?
5 At what times of day do plant cells photosynthesise?
6 Why do plants not need a transport system to carry oxygen around their bodies?

Chapter revision questions

1 Match each of these words with its definition listed below: operculum, stoma, alveolus, lenticel, lamellae, fermentation, mitochondrion, cilia.
(a) A type of anaerobic respiration which makes alcohol and carbon dioxide
(b) Finely divided parts of a fish's gills
(c) A bony covering over a fish's gills
(d) An air sac inside a mammal's lungs
(e) Small hair-like projections from a cell
(f) Part of a woody stem through which gaseous exchange takes place
(g) A small hole on the surface of a leaf, through which gases diffuse
(h) The part of a cell where sugar is oxidised
2 Which of these descriptions applies to aerobic respiration, which to anaerobic respiration, and which to both?
(a) lactic acid or alcohol made
(b) carbon dioxide made
(c) energy released from glucose
(d) heat produced
(e) ATP made
(f) glucose oxidised
3 (a) What is meant by a respiratory surface?
(b) Describe, with the aid of diagrams, how the respiratory surfaces of (i) a fish, and (ii) a human are kept supplied with oxygen.
(c) List three properties which these two types of respiratory surface have in common.
4 Describe an experiment you could do to see if germinating seeds give off carbon dioxide. Include a labelled diagram of your apparatus, a control, and explain what you think your results would be.
5 Construct a table to compare the processes of respiration and photosynthesis in a green plant.
6 The chart below shows the results of an investigation into the effects of smoking during pregnancy.
(a) Plot graphs to show these results.
(b) What effect does smoking during pregnancy have on the growth of the embryo and child?
(c) Describe three other harmful effects of smoking, explaining the cause of each one.

Number of cigarettes smoked per day by mother during pregnancy	Average birth weight of baby in grams	Average height of child at 14 years, in centimetres
0	3600	161.5
1–9	3500	161.0
10 or more	3200	160.4

7 Transport

7.1 Large organisms need transport systems.

Large organisms need transport systems to supply all their cells with food, oxygen and other materials. This chapter describes the transport systems of mammals and flowering plants, and describes the parts which make up these systems.

Layout of a mammal transport system

7.2 Mammals have double circulatory systems.

The main transport system of a mammal is its blood system. This is sometimes called the vascular system. It is a network of tubes, called **blood vessels**. A pump, the **heart**, keeps blood flowing through the vessels.

Figure 7.1 illustrates the general layout of the blood system. The arrows show the direction of blood flow.

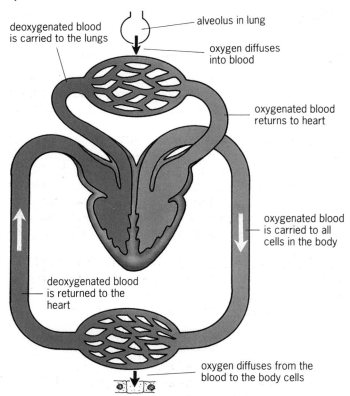

deoxygenated blood is carried to the lungs

alveolus in lung

oxygen diffuses into blood

oxygenated blood returns to heart

oxygenated blood is carried to all cells in the body

deoxygenated blood is returned to the heart

oxygen diffuses from the blood to the body cells

7.1 *The general layout of the circulatory system of a human, as seen from the front*

If you follow the arrows, beginning at the lungs, you can see that blood flows into the left-hand side of the heart, and then out to the rest of the body. It is brought back to the right-hand side of the heart, before going back to the lungs again.

This is called a **double circulatory system**, because the blood travels through the heart twice on one complete journey around the body.

7.3 Oxygenated and deoxygenated blood.

The blood in the left-hand side of the heart has come from the lungs. It contains oxygen, which was picked up by the capillaries surrounding the alveoli. It is called **oxygenated blood**.

This oxygenated blood is then sent around the body. Some of the oxygen in it is taken up by the body cells, which need oxygen for respiration. When this happens the blood becomes **deoxygenated**. The deoxygenated blood is brought back to the right-hand side of the heart. It then goes to the lungs, where it becomes oxygenated once more.

Questions

1 Why do large organisms need transport systems?
2 What is a double circulatory system?
3 What is oxygenated blood?
4 Where does blood become oxygenated?
5 Which side of the heart contains oxygenated blood?

The heart

7.4 The structure of the heart.

The function of the heart is to pump blood around the body. It is made of a special type of muscle called **cardiac muscle**. This muscle contracts and relaxes regularly, throughout life.

Figure 7.2 illustrates a section through a heart. It is divided into four chambers. The two upper chambers are called **atria**. The two lower chambers are **ventricles**. The chambers on the left-hand side are completely separated from the ones on the right-hand side by a **septum**.

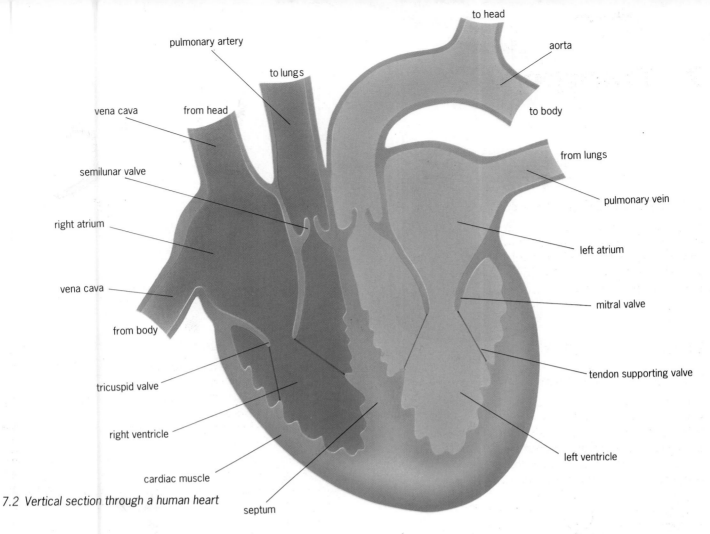

pulmonary artery

to head

aorta

to lungs

vena cava

from head

to body

semilunar valve

from lungs

pulmonary vein

right atrium

left atrium

vena cava

mitral valve

from body

tendon supporting valve

tricuspid valve

right ventricle

left ventricle

cardiac muscle

7.2 Vertical section through a human heart

septum

If you look at Fig 7.1, you will see that blood flows into the heart at the top, into the atria. Both of the atria receive blood. The left atrium receives blood from the **pulmonary veins**, which come from the lungs. The right atrium receives blood from the rest of the body, arriving through the **venae cavae**.

From the atria, the blood flows into the ventricles. The ventricles then pump it out of the heart. The blood in the left ventricle is pumped into the **aorta**, which takes the blood around the body. The right ventricle pumps blood into the **pulmonary artery**, which takes it to the lungs.

The job of the ventricles is quite different from the job of the atria. The atria simply receive blood, either from the lungs or the body and supply it to the ventricles. The ventricles pump blood out of the heart and all round the body. To help them to do this, the ventricles have much thicker, more muscular walls than the atria.

There is also a difference in the thickness of the walls of the right and left ventricles. The right ventricle pumps blood to the lungs, which are very close to the heart. The left ventricle, however, pumps blood all around the body. The left ventricle has an especially thick wall of muscle to enable it to do this.

7.5 Coronary arteries supply heart muscle.

In Fig 7.3, you can see that there are blood vessels on the outside of the heart. They are called the **coronary arteries**. These vessels supply blood to the heart muscles.

It may seem odd that this is necessary, when the heart is full of blood. However, the muscles of the heart are so thick that the food and oxygen in the blood inside the heart would not be able to diffuse to all the muscles quickly enough. The heart muscle needs a constant supply of food and oxygen, so that it can keep contracting and relaxing. The coronary artery supplies this.

If the coronary artery gets blocked, for example by a blood clot, the cardiac muscles run short of oxygen. They cannot contract, so the heart stops beating. This is called a heart attack or **cardiac arrest**.

Fact!

The longest heart stoppage was 4 hours. A Norwegian fell into the sea in December 1987. Survival was due to the low temperature of his body in the sea.

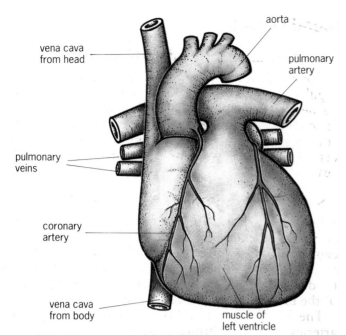

7.3 External appearance of a human heart

Labels on figure 7.3:
- aorta
- vena cava from head
- pulmonary artery
- pulmonary veins
- coronary artery
- vena cava from body
- muscle of left ventricle

Questions

1 What kind of muscle is found in the heart?
2 Which parts of the heart receive blood from (a) the lungs, and (b) the body?
3 Which parts of the heart pump blood into (a) the pulmonary artery, and (b) the aorta?
4 Why do the ventricles have thicker walls than the atria?
5 Why does the left ventricle have a thicker wall than the right ventricle?
6 What is the function of the coronary artery?

7.6 Heart beat.

The heart beats as the cardiac muscles in its walls contract and relax. When they contract, the heart becomes smaller, squeezing blood out. This is called **systole**. When they relax, the heart becomes larger, allowing blood to flow into the atria and ventricles. This is called **diastole**. Fig 7.4 illustrates this.

The rate at which the heart beats is controlled by a patch of muscle in the right atrium called the **pacemaker**. The pacemaker sends electrical signals through the walls of the heart at regular intervals, which make the muscle contract. The pacemaker's rate, and therefore the rate of heart beat, changes according to the needs of the body. For example, during exercise, when extra oxygen is needed by the muscles, the brain sends messages along nerves to the pacemaker, to make the heart beat faster.

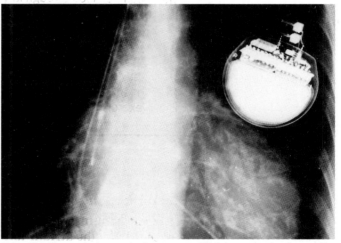

7.5 The X-ray photograph shows an artificial pacemaker in position next to someone's heart

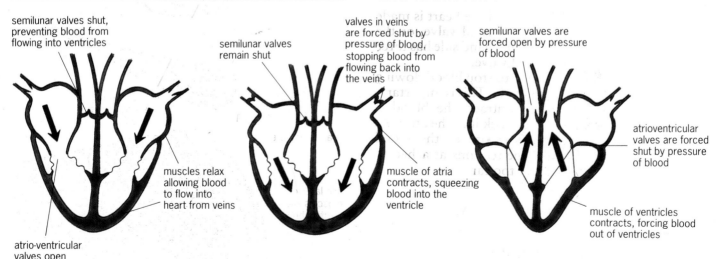

Diastole All muscles relaxed. Blood flows into heart.

Labels (left diagram):
- semilunar valves shut, preventing blood from flowing into ventricles
- muscles relax allowing blood to flow into heart from veins
- atrio-ventricular valves open

Atrial systole Muscles of atria contract. Muscles of ventricles remain relaxed. Blood forced from atria into ventricles.

Labels (middle diagram):
- semilunar valves remain shut
- valves in veins are forced shut by pressure of blood, stopping blood from flowing back into the veins
- muscle of atria contracts, squeezing blood into the ventricle

Ventricular systole Muscles of atria relax. Muscles of ventricles contract. Blood forced out of ventricles into arteries.

Labels (right diagram):
- semilunar valves are forced open by pressure of blood
- atrioventricular valves are forced shut by pressure of blood
- muscle of ventricles contracts, forcing blood out of ventricles

7.4 How the heart pumps blood

Sometimes, the pacemaker stops working properly. An **artificial pacemaker** can then be placed in the person's heart. Fig 7.5 shows one kind of artificial pacemaker. It produces an electrical impulse at a regular rate of about one impulse per second. Artificial pacemakers last for up to ten years before they have to be replaced.

Practical 7.1 To find the effect of exercise on the rate of heart beat

The best way to measure the rate of your heart beat is to take your pulse. Use the first two fingers of your right hand and lie them on the inside of your left wrist. Feel for the tendon near the outside of your wrist. If you rest your fingers lightly just over this tendon, you can feel the artery in your wrist pulsing as your heart pumps blood through it.

Perform the experiment as explained in Practical 6.9.

Questions

1 Why does your heart beat faster during exercise?
2 Why does the heart not return to its normal rate of beating as soon as you finish exercising?

7.7 Blood flows one way through heart valves.

There is a valve between the left atrium and the left ventricle, and another between the right atrium and ventricle. These are called **atrio-ventricular valves** (Fig 7.4).

The valve on the left-hand side of the heart is made of two parts and is called the **bicuspid valve**, or the **mitral valve**. The valve on the right-hand side has three parts, and is called the **tricuspid valve**.

The function of these valves is to stop blood flowing from the ventricles back to the atria. This is important, so that when the ventricles contract, the blood is pushed up into the arteries, not back into the atria. As the ventricles contract, the pressure of the blood pushes the valves upwards. The tendons attached to them stop them from going up too far.

Questions

1 What is (a) systole, and (b) diastole?
2 Where are the atrio-ventricular valves?
3 What is their function?
4 Why are these valves supported by tendons?

Blood vessels

7.8 There are three kinds of blood vessels.

There are three main kinds of blood vessels: arteries, capillaries and veins. **Arteries** carry blood away from the heart. They divide again and again, and eventually form very tiny vessels called **capillaries**. The capillaries gradually join up with one another to form large vessels called **veins**. Veins carry blood towards the heart.

7.9 Arteries have thick elastic walls.

When blood flows out of the heart, it enters the arteries. The blood is then at very high pressure, because it has been forced out of the heart by the contraction of the muscular ventricles. Arteries therefore need very strong walls to withstand the high pressure of the blood flowing through them.

The blood does not flow smoothly through the arteries. It pulses through, as the ventricles contract and relax. The arteries have elastic tissue in their walls which can stretch and recoil with the force of the

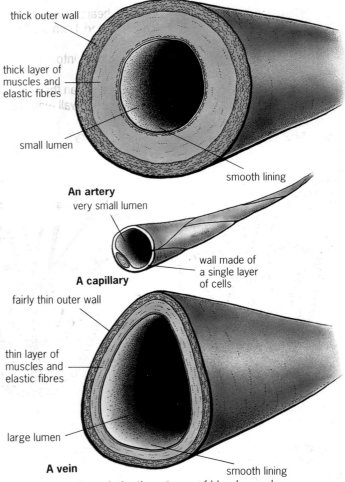

thick outer wall

thick layer of muscles and elastic fibres

small lumen

smooth lining

An artery

very small lumen

A capillary

wall made of a single layer of cells

fairly thin outer wall

thin layer of muscles and elastic fibres

large lumen

A vein

smooth lining

7.6 Sections through the three types of blood vessels

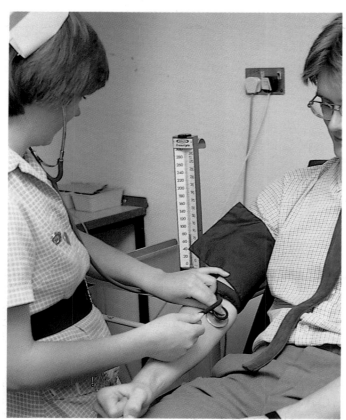

7.7 A sphygmomanometer being used to measure blood pressure

blood. This helps to make the flow of blood smoother. You can feel your arteries stretch and recoil when you feel your pulse in your wrist.

The blood pressure in the arteries of your arm can be measured using a **sphygmomanometer** (Fig 7.7).

7.10 Capillaries are very narrow, with thin walls.

The arteries gradually divide to form smaller and smaller vessels (Fig 7.8). These are the capillaries. The capillaries are very small and penetrate to every part

of the body. No cell is very far away from a capillary.

The function of the capillaries is to take food, oxygen and other materials to all the cells in the body, and to take away their waste materials. To do this, their walls must be very thin so that substances can get in and out of them easily. The walls of the smallest capillaries are only one cell thick (Fig 7.6).

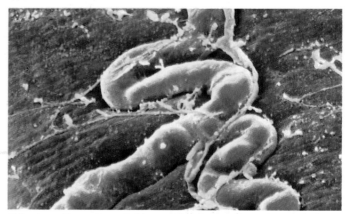

7.9 A capillary, shown in blue, snakes its way through muscle tissue. This is magnified about 600 times.

7.11 Veins have one-way valves.

The capillaries gradually join up again to form veins. By the time the blood gets to the veins, it is at a much lower pressure than it was in the arteries. The blood flows more slowly and smoothly now. There is no need for veins to have such thick, strong, elastic walls.

If the veins were narrow, this would slow down the blood even more. To help to keep the blood moving easily through them, the space inside the veins, called the **lumen**, is much wider than the lumen of the arteries.

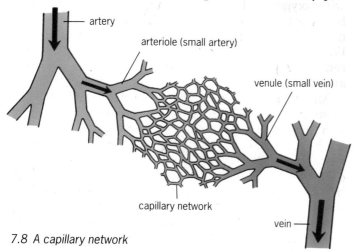

7.8 A capillary network

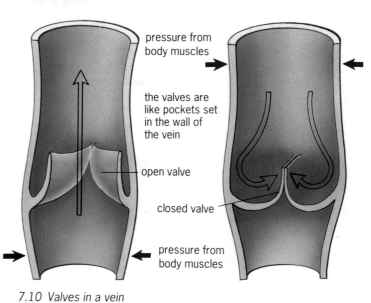

7.10 Valves in a vein

Table 7.1 Arteries, veins, and capillaries

	Function	Structure of wall	Width of lumen	Reasons for structure
Arteries	carry blood away from the heart	thick, strong, containing muscles and elastic fibres	varies, as elastic fibres stretch and recoil	strength and elasticity needed to resist pulsing of blood as it is pumped by the heart
Capillaries	supply all cells with their requirements, and take away waste products	very thin, often only one cell thick	very narrow, just wide enough for a red blood cell to squeeze through	no need for strong walls, as most of force of blood has been lost; thin walls and narrow lumen bring blood into close contact with tissues
Veins	return blood to heart	quite thin, containing far fewer muscles and elastic fibres than arteries	wide, contain valves	no need for strong walls, as most of force of blood has been lost; wide lumen offers less resistance to blood flow; valves prevent backflow

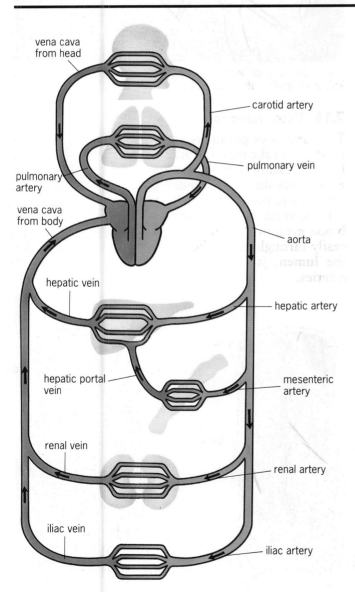

7.11 *Plan of the main blood vessels in the human body*

Veins have valves in them to stop the blood flowing backwards (Fig 7.10). Valves are not needed in the arteries, because the force of the heart beat keeps blood moving forwards through them.

Blood is also kept moving in the veins by the contraction of muscles around them. The large veins in your legs are squeezed by your leg muscles when you walk. This helps to push the blood back up to your heart. If a person is confined to bed for a long time, then there is a danger that the blood in these veins will not be kept moving. A clot may form in them, called a **thrombosis**. If the clot is carried to the lungs, it could get stuck in the arterioles of the lung. This is called a **pulmonary embolism**, and it may prevent the circulation reaching part of the lungs. In serious cases this can cause death.

7.12 Each organ has its own blood supply.

Figures 7.11 and 7.12 illustrate the positions of the main arteries and veins in the body.

Each organ of the body, except the lungs, is supplied with oxygenated blood from an artery. Deoxygenated blood is taken away by a vein. The artery and vein are named according to the organ they are connected with. For example, the blood vessels of the kidneys are the renal artery and vein. The liver has the hepatic artery and vein.

All arteries, other than the pulmonary artery, branch from the aorta. All veins, except the pulmonary veins, join up to one of the two venae cavae.

The liver has two blood vessels supplying it with blood. The first is the **hepatic artery**, which supplies oxygen. The second is the **hepatic portal vein**. This vein brings blood from the digestive system (Fig 4.26), so that the liver can process the food which has been absorbed, before it travels to other parts of the body. All the blood leaves the liver in the **hepatic vein**.

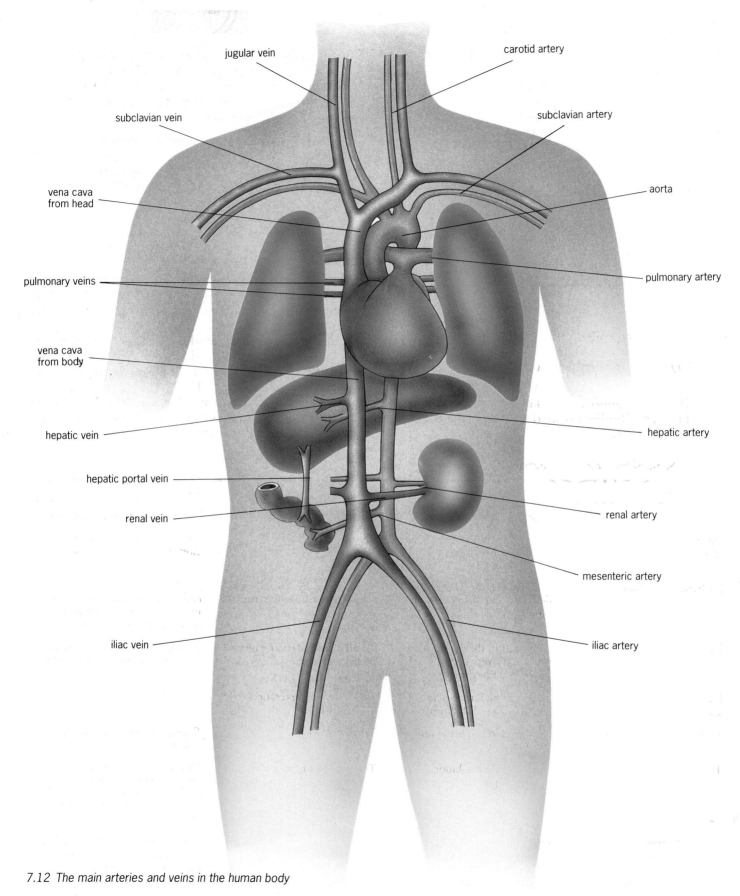

jugular vein

carotid artery

subclavian vein

subclavian artery

vena cava
from head

aorta

pulmonary veins

pulmonary artery

vena cava
from body

hepatic vein

hepatic artery

hepatic portal vein

renal vein

renal artery

mesenteric artery

iliac vein

iliac artery

7.12 The main arteries and veins in the human body

1 Which blood vessels carry blood (a) away from, and (b) towards the heart?
2 Why do arteries need strong walls?
3 Why do arteries have elastic walls?
4 What is the function of capillaries?
5 Why do veins have a large lumen?
6 How is blood kept moving in the large veins of the legs?
7 What is unusual about the blood supply to the liver?

Fact!

The body adjusts to changes in blood volume so quickly that there is no detectable change in blood volume when the standard 450 cm^3 – about one tenth of the total blood volume – is taken in a blood donation clinic.

Large quantities of blood are sometimes needed during operations. A 50-year-old haemophiliac, who underwent open heart surgery in Chicago in 1970 needed 1080 litres of blood.

Blood

7.13 Blood consists of cells floating in plasma.

The liquid part of blood is called **plasma**. Floating in the plasma are cells. Most of these are **red blood cells**. A much smaller number are **white blood cells**. There are also small fragments formed from special cells in the bone marrow, called **platelets** (Fig 7.13).

7.14 Plasma is a complex solution.

Plasma is mostly water. Many substances are dissolved in it. Glucose, amino acids, salts, hormones, blood proteins and antibodies are all dissolved in the plasma. Look at Table 7.2.

7.15 Red blood cells carry oxygen.

Red blood cells are made in the bone marrow of some bones, including the ribs, vertebrae and some limb bones. They are produced at a very fast rate – about 9000 million per hour!

Red cells have to be made so quickly because they do not live for very long. Each red cell only lives for about four months. One reason for this is that they do not have a nucleus (Fig 7.13).

Red cells are red because they contain the pigment **haemoglobin**. This carries oxygen. Haemoglobin is a protein, and contains iron.

Table 7.2 Some of the main components of blood plasma

Substance	Source	Destination	Notes
Water	Absorbed in colon.	All cells.	Excess is removed by kidneys.
Plasma proteins e.g. fibrinogen, antibodies	Fibrinogen made in the liver. Antibodies made by lymphocytes.	Remain in the blood.	Fibrinogen helps in blood clotting. Antibodies kill bacteria.
Cholesterol and fats	Absorbed in the ileum. Also derived from fat reserves in the body.	To the liver, for breakdown. To adipose tissue, for storage.	Breakdown of fats yields energy. High cholesterol levels in the blood may increase the chances of heart disease.
Glucose	Absorbed in the ileum. Also produced by glycogen breakdown in the liver.	To all cells, for energy release by respiration.	Excess glucose is converted to glycogen and stored in liver and muscles.
Excretory substances e.g. urea	Produced by amino acid deamination in the liver.	To kidneys for excretion.	
Mineral ions e.g. Na$^+$, Cl$^-$	Absorbed in the ileum and colon.	To all cells.	Excess ions are excreted by the kidneys.
Hormones	Secreted into the blood by endocrine glands.	To all parts of the body.	Hormones only affect their own target organs. Hormones are broken down in the liver, and they are also excreted by the kidneys.
Dissolved gases e.g. carbon dioxide	Carbon dioxide is released from all cells as a waste product of respiration.	To the lungs for excretion.	Most carbon dioxide is carried as hydrogencarbonate ions HCO_3^- in the plasma.

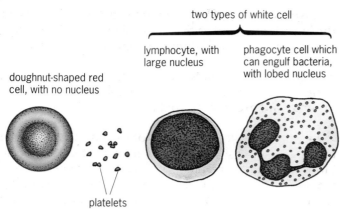

two types of white cell

doughnut-shaped red cell, with no nucleus

lymphocyte, with large nucleus

phagocyte cell which can engulf bacteria, with lobed nucleus

platelets

7.13 Blood cells

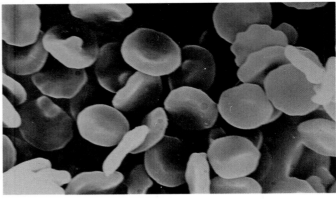

7.14 Scanning electronmicrograph of red blood cells

Old red blood cells are broken down in the liver, spleen and bone marrow. Some of the iron from the haemoglobin is stored, and used for making new haemoglobin. Some of it is turned into bile pigment and excreted.

7.16 White blood cells fight infection.

White cells are made in the bone marrow and in the **lymph nodes** (Section 7.25). White cells do have a nucleus, which is often quite large and lobed (Fig 7.13). They can move around, like *Amoeba*, and can squeeze out through the walls of blood capillaries into almost all parts of the body. Their function is to fight infection, and to clear up any dead body cells.

7.17 Platelets help blood to clot.

Platelets are small fragments of cells, with no nucleus. They are made in the bone marrow, and they are involved in blood clotting (Fig 18.13).

7.18 Blood has many functions.

Blood has three main functions. These are transport, defence against disease, and regulation of body temperature.

Questions

1 List five components of plasma.
2 Where are red blood cells made?
3 What is unusual about red blood cells?
4 What is haemoglobin?
5 Where are white blood cells made?
6 What are platelets?

7.19 Many substances are transported by blood.

Transport of oxygen In the lungs, oxygen diffuses from the alveoli into the blood. The oxygen diffuses into the red blood cells, where it combines with the haemoglobin (Hb) to form oxyhaemoglobin (oxyHb).

The blood is then taken to the heart in the pulmonary veins and pumped out of the heart in the aorta. Arteries branch from the aorta to supply all parts of the body with oxygenated blood. When it reaches a tissue which needs oxygen, the oxyHb gives up its oxygen, to become Hb again.

Because capillaries are so narrow, the oxyHb in the

Table 7.3 Components of blood

Component	Structure	Functions
Plasma	Water, containing many substances in solution	1 Liquid medium in which cells and platelets can float 2 Transports CO_2 in solution 3 Transports food materials in solution 4 Transports urea in solution 5 Transports hormones in solution 6 Transports heat 7 Transports substances needed for blood clotting 8 Transports antibodies
Red cells	Biconcave discs, with no nucleus, containing haemoglobin	1 Transport oxygen 2 Transport small amount of CO_2
White cells	Variable shape, with nucleus	1 Engulf and destroy bacteria (phagocytosis) 2 Make antibodies
Platelets	Small particles, with no nucleus	1 Help in blood clotting

red blood cells is taken very close to the tissues which need the oxygen. The oxygen only has a very short distance to diffuse.

OxyHb is bright red, whereas Hb is purplish-red. The blood in arteries is therefore a brighter red colour than the blood in veins.

Transport of carbon dioxide Carbon dioxide is made by all the cells in the body as they respire. The carbon dioxide diffuses through the walls of the capillaries, into the blood.

Most of the carbon dioxide is carried by the blood plasma in the form of hydrogencarbonate ions, HCO_3^-. A small amount is carried by Hb in the red cells.

Blood containing carbon dioxide is returned to the heart in the veins, and then to the lungs in the pulmonary arteries. The carbon dioxide diffuses out of the blood and is passed out of the body on expiration.

Transport of food materials Digested food is absorbed in the ileum. It includes amino acids, fatty acids and glycerol, monosaccharides (such as glucose), water, vitamins and minerals. These all dissolve in the plasma in the blood capillaries in the villi.

These capillaries join up to form the hepatic portal vein. This takes the dissolved food to the liver. The liver processes the food and returns some of it to the blood.

The food is then carried, dissolved in the blood plasma, to all parts of the body.

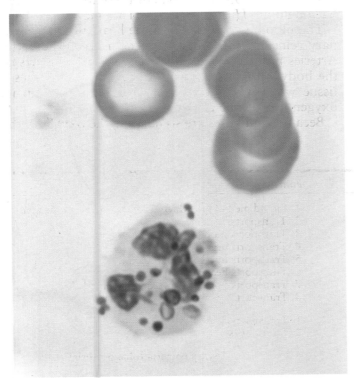

7.15 *A light micrograph of human blood. You can see several red cells, and also a white cell which is taking in and digesting bacteria.*

Transport of urea Urea, a waste substance, is made in the liver. It dissolves in the blood plasma, and is carried to the kidneys. The kidneys excrete it in the urine.

Transport of hormones Hormones are made in endocrine glands. The hormones dissolve in the blood plasma, and are transported all over the body.

Transport of heat Some parts of the body, such as the liver, muscles and brown fat, make a lot of heat. The blood transports the heat to all parts of the body. This prevents the liver, muscles and brown fat becoming too hot, and helps to keep the rest of the body warm.

7.20 Blood defends the body.

The ways in which the blood defends the body are described in Chapter 18. They include blood clotting, phagocytosis, and the production of antibodies.

7.21 Blood helps to regulate temperature.

The capillaries in the skin help to keep your body temperature constant at about 36.8 °C. This is described in Chapter 10.

Questions

1 Why is blood in arteries a brighter red than the blood in veins?
2 Which vessel transports digested food to the liver?
3 How is urea transported?
4 Name two functions of blood other than transport.

Lymph and tissue fluid

7.22 Tissue fluid is leaked plasma.

Capillaries leak! The cells in their walls do not fit together exactly, so there are small gaps between them. Plasma can therefore leak out from the blood.

White blood cells can also get through these gaps. They are able to move, like *Amoeba*, and can squeeze through, out of the capillaries. Red blood cells cannot get out. They cannot change their shape very much in contrast to white blood cells.

So plasma and white cells are continually leaking out

Fact!

A human being contains about 70ml of blood per kilogram of body weight. For an adult, this is about 4 or 5 litres.

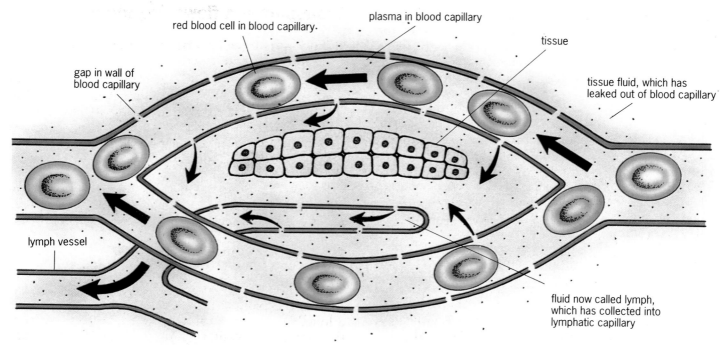

7.16 *Part of a capillary network, to show how tissue fluid and lymph are formed*

of the blood capillaries. The fluid formed in this way is called **tissue fluid**. It surrounds all the cells in the body (Fig 7.16).

7.23 The functions of tissue fluid.

Tissue fluid is very important. It supplies cells with all their requirements. These requirements, such as oxygen and food materials, diffuse from the blood, through the tissue fluid, to the cells. Waste products, such as carbon dioxide, diffuse in the opposite direction.

The tissue fluid is the immediate environment of every cell in your body. It is easier for a cell to carry out its functions properly if its environment stays constant. For example this means it should stay at the same temperature, and at the same osmotic concentration.

Several organs in the body work to keep the composition and temperature of the blood constant, and therefore the tissue fluid as well. This process is called **homeostasis**, and is described in Chapter 10.

7.24 Lymph is drained tissue fluid.

The plasma and white cells which leak out of the blood capillaries must eventually be returned to the blood. In the tissues, as well as blood capillaries, are other small vessels. They are **lymphatic capillaries** (Fig 7.16). The tissue fluid slowly drains into them. The fluid is now called **lymph**.

The lymphatic capillaries gradually join up to form larger **lymphatic vessels**. These carry the lymph to the subclavian veins which bring blood back from the

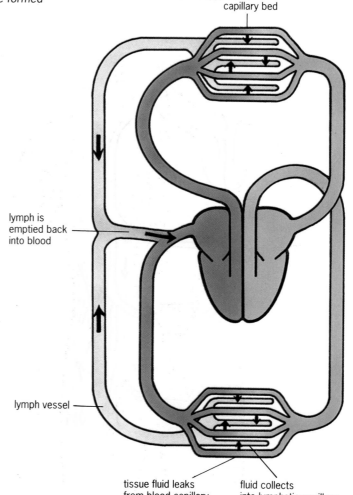

7.17 *Relationship between blood circulation and lymphatic circulation*

arms (Fig 7.18). Here the lymph enters the blood again.

The lymphatic system has no pump to make the lymph flow. Lymph vessels do have valves in them, however, to make sure that movement is only in one direction. Lymph flows much more slowly than blood.

7.25 Lymph nodes contain white blood cells.

On its way from the tissues to the subclavian vein, lymph flows through several **lymph nodes**. Some of these are shown in Fig 7.18.

Lymph nodes contain large numbers of white cells. Most bacteria or toxins (Section 18.13) in the lymph can be destroyed by these cells.

Questions

1 What is tissue fluid?
2 Give two functions of tissue fluid.
3 What is lymph?
4 Why do lymphatic capillaries have valves in them?
5 Name two places where lymph nodes are found.
6 What happens inside lymph nodes?

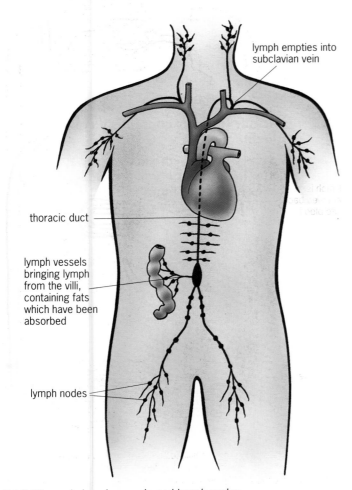

lymph empties into subclavian vein

thoracic duct

lymph vessels bringing lymph from the villi, containing fats which have been absorbed

lymph nodes

7.18 The main lymph vessels and lymph nodes

Transport in a flowering plant

7.26 Plants have two transport systems – phloem and xylem.

Transport systems in plants are less elaborate than in mammals. Plants are less active than mammals, and so their cells do not need to be supplied with materials so quickly. Also, the branching shape of a plant means that all the cells can get their oxygen for respiration, and carbon dioxide for photosynthesis, directly from the air, by diffusion.

Plants have two transport systems. The **xylem vessels** carry water and minerals, while the **phloem tubes** carry food materials which the plant has made.

7.27 Xylem helps to support plants.

A xylem vessel is like a long drainpipe (Figs 7.19 and 7.20). It is made of many hollow, dead cells, joined end to end. The end walls of the cells have disappeared, so a long, open tube is formed. Xylem vessels run from the roots of the plant, right up through the stem. They branch out into every leaf.

Xylem vessels contain no cytoplasm or nuclei. Their walls are made of cellulose and **lignin**. Lignin is very strong, so xylem vessels help to keep plants upright. Wood is made almost entirely of lignified xylem vessels.

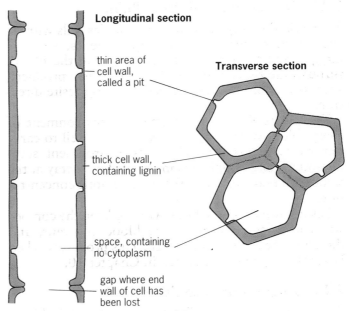

Longitudinal section

thin area of cell wall, called a pit

Transverse section

thick cell wall, containing lignin

space, containing no cytoplasm

gap where end wall of cell has been lost

7.19 Xylem vessels

7.28 Phloem contains sieve-tube elements.

Like xylem vessels, phloem tubes are made of many cells joined end to end. However, their end walls have not completely broken down. Instead, they form **sieve plates** (Figs 7.21 and 7.22), which have small holes in them. The cells are called **sieve tube elements**. Sieve

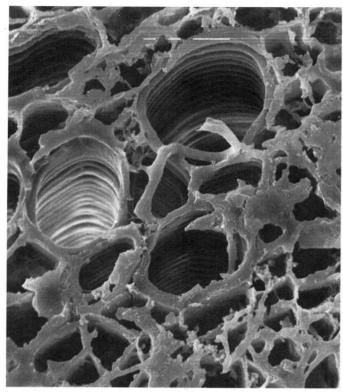

7.20 *A scanning electronmicrograph of xylem tissue in a plant stem. The walls are made of lignin, arranged in a spiral pattern.*

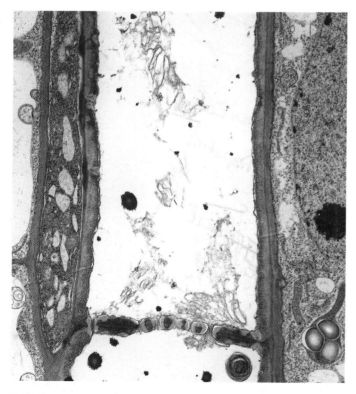

7.21 *Electronmicrograph of a phloem tube, which carries food such as sugars; a companion cell lies alongside the tube on the left, and a sieve plate can be seen at the bottom. The holes in the plate allow food to pass along the tube.*

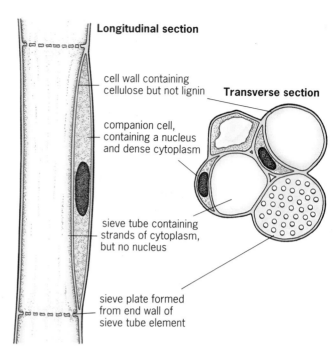

Longitudinal section

cell wall containing cellulose but not lignin

Transverse section

companion cell, containing a nucleus and dense cytoplasm

sieve tube containing strands of cytoplasm, but no nucleus

sieve plate formed from end wall of sieve tube element

7.22 *Phloem tubes*

tube elements contain cytoplasm, but no nucleus. They do not have lignin in their cell walls.

Each sieve tube element has a **companion cell** next to it. The companion cell does have a nucleus, and also contains many other organelles. Companion cells probably supply sieve tube elements with some of their requirements.

7.29 Vascular bundles contain xylem and phloem.

Xylem vessels and phloem tubes are usually found close together. A group of xylem vessels and phloem tubes is called a **vascular bundle**.

The positions of vascular bundles in roots and shoots is shown in Figs 7.23 and 7.24. In a root,

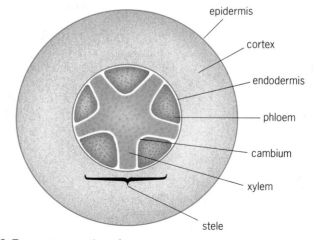

epidermis

cortex

endodermis

phloem

cambium

xylem

stele

7.23 *Transverse section of a root*

vascular tissue is found at the centre, whereas in a shoot vascular bundles are arranged in a ring near the outside edge. They help to support the plant.

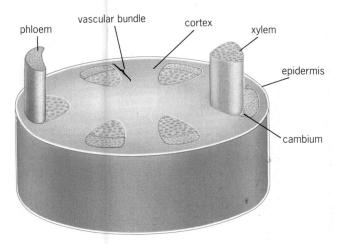

7.24 Transverse section of a stem

Questions

1 Why do plants not need such elaborate transport systems as mammals?
2 What do xylem vessels carry?
3 What do phloem tubes carry?
4 What substance makes up the cell walls of xylem vessels?
5 Give three ways in which phloem tubes differ from xylem vessels.
6 What is a vascular bundle?

The transport of water

7.30 The structure of a root.

Plants take in water from the soil, through their **root hairs**. The water is carried in the xylem vessels to all parts of the plant.

Figure 7.25 shows the structure of a root. At the very tip is the **root cap**. This is a layer of cells which protects the root as it grows through the soil. The rest of the root is covered by a layer of cells called the **epidermis**.

The **root hairs** are a little way up from the root tip. Each root hair is a long epidermal cell (Fig 7.26). Root hairs do not live for very long. As the root grows, they are replaced by new ones.

7.31 Root hairs absorb water by osmosis.

The function of a root hair is to absorb water and minerals from the soil. Water gets into a root hair by osmosis. The cytoplasm and cell sap inside it are quite concentrated solutions. The water in the soil is normally a dilute solution. Water therefore diffuses into the root hair, down its concentration gradient, through the partially permeable cell membrane.

7.32 Absorbed water enters the xylem.

The root hairs are on the edge of the root. The xylem vessels are in the centre. Before the water can be taken to the rest of the plant, it must travel to these xylem vessels.

The path it takes is shown in Fig 7.26. It travels by osmosis through the cortex, from cell to cell. Some of it also travels through the spaces between the cells.

7.33 Water is sucked up the xylem.

Water moves up xylem vessels in the same way that a drink moves up a straw when you suck it. When you suck a straw, you are reducing the pressure at the top of the straw. The liquid at the bottom of the straw is at a higher pressure, so it flows up the straw into your mouth.

The same thing happens with the water in xylem vessels. The pressure at the top of the vessels is lowered, while the pressure at the bottom stays high. Water therefore flows up the xylem vessels.

How is the pressure at the top of the xylem vessels reduced? It happens because of transpiration.

7.25 A root tip, showing the root cap and root hairs

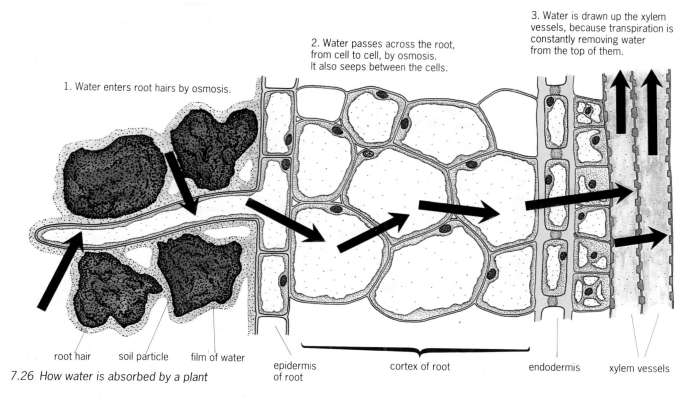

1. Water enters root hairs by osmosis.

2. Water passes across the root, from cell to cell, by osmosis. It also seeps between the cells.

3. Water is drawn up the xylem vessels, because transpiration is constantly removing water from the top of them.

| root hair | soil particle | film of water | epidermis of root | cortex of root | endodermis | xylem vessels |

7.26 How water is absorbed by a plant

7.34 Transpiration is evaporation from leaves.

Transpiration is the evaporation of water from a plant. Most of this evaporation takes place from the leaves.

If you look back at Fig 5.4, you will see that there are openings on the underside of the leaf called **stomata**. The cells inside the leaf are each covered with a thin film of moisture.

Some of this film of moisture evaporates from the cells, and diffuses out of the leaf through the stomata. Water from the xylem vessels in the leaf will travel to the cells by osmosis to replace it.

Water is constantly being taken from the top of the xylem vessels, to supply the cells in the leaves. This reduces the effective pressure at the top of the xylem vessels, so that water flows up them. This process is known as the **transpiration stream** (Fig 7.27).

7.35 A potometer compares transpiration rates.

It is not easy to measure how much water is lost from the leaves of a plant. It is much easier to measure how fast the plant *takes up* water. The rate at which a plant takes up water depends on the rate of transpiration – the faster a plant transpires, the faster it takes up water.

Figure 7.29 illustrates apparatus which can be used to compare the rate of transpiration in different conditions. It is called a **potometer**. By recording how fast the air/water meniscus moves along the capillary tube, you can compare how fast the plant takes up water in different conditions.

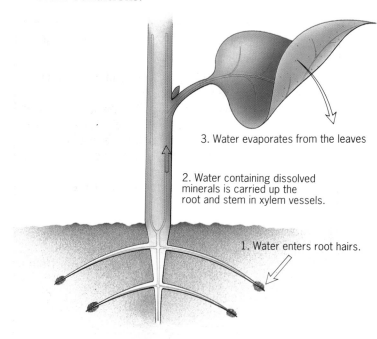

3. Water evaporates from the leaves

2. Water containing dissolved minerals is carried up the root and stem in xylem vessels.

1. Water enters root hairs.

7.27 The transpiration stream

Fact!

An oak tree 16 m high and with a trunk about 1 m in diameter would transpire about 150 litres of water on a warm, sunny day.

Practical 7.2 To see which part of a stem transports water and solutes

1 Take a plant, such as groundsel, with a root system intact. Wash the roots thoroughly.
2 Put the roots of the plant into eosin solution. Leave overnight.
3 Set up a microscope.
4 Remove the plant from the eosin solution, and wash the roots thoroughly.
5 Use a razor blade to cut across the stem of the plant about half way up. Take great care when using a razor blade and do not touch its edges.
6 Now cut very thin sections across the stem. Try to get them so thin that you can see through them. It does not matter if your section is not a complete circle.
7 Choose your thinnest section, and mount it in a drop of water on a microscope slide. Cover with a coverslip.
8 Observe the section under a microscope. Compare what you can see with Fig 7.24. Make a labelled drawing of your section.

Questions

1 Which part of the stem contained the dye? What does this tell you about the transport of water and solutes (substances dissolved in water) up a stem?
2 Why was it important to wash the roots of the plant:
(a) before putting it into the eosin solution, and
(b) before cutting sections?
3 Design an experiment to find out how quickly the dye is transported up the stem.

Practical 7.3 To see which surface of a leaf loses most water

Cobalt chloride paper is blue when dry and pink when wet. Use forceps to handle it.
1 Use a healthy, well-watered potted plant, with leaves which are not too hairy. Fix a small square of blue cobalt chloride paper onto each surface of one leaf, using clear sticky tape. Make sure there are no air spaces around the paper.
2 Leave the paper on the leaf for a few minutes.

Questions

1 Which piece of cobalt chloride paper turned pink first? What does this tell you about the loss of water from a leaf?
2 Why does this surface lose water faster than the other?
3 Why is it important to use forceps, not fingers, for handling cobalt chloride paper?

Practical 7.4 To measure the rate of transpiration of a potted plant

1 Use two similar well-watered potted plants. Enclose one plant entirely in a polythene bag, including its pot. This is the control.
2 Enclose only the pot of the second plant in a polythene bag. Fix the bag firmly around the stem of the plant, and seal with Vaseline (Fig 7.28).
3 Place both plants on balances, and record their masses.
4 Record the mass of each plant every day, at the same time, for at least a week.
5 Draw a graph of your results.

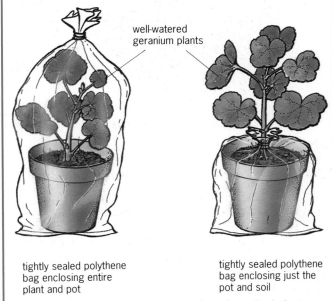

well-watered geranium plants

tightly sealed polythene bag enclosing entire plant and pot

tightly sealed polythene bag enclosing just the pot and soil

7.28 Measuring the rate of transpiration of a potted plant

Questions

1 Which plant lost weight? Why?
2 Do you think this is an accurate method of measuring transpiration rate? How could it be improved?

7.36 Conditions which affect transpiration rate.

Temperature On a hot day, water will evaporate quickly from the leaves of a plant. Transpiration increases as temperature increases.

Humidity Humidity means the moisture content of the air. The higher the humidity, the less water will evaporate from the leaves. Transpiration decreases as humidity increases.

Wind speed On a windy day, water evaporates more quickly than on a still day. Transpiration increases as wind speed increases.

Practical 7.5 Using a potometer to compare rates of transpiration under different conditions

1. Set up the potometer as in Fig 7.29. The stem of the plant must fit exactly into the rubber tubing, with no air gaps. Vaseline will help to make an airtight seal.
2. Fill the apparatus with water, by opening the screw clip.
3. Close the clip again, and leave the apparatus in a light, airy place. As the plant transpires, the water it loses is replaced by water taken up the stem. Air will be drawn in at the end of the capillary tube.
4. When the air/water meniscus reaches the scale, begin to record the position of the meniscus every two minutes.
5. When the meniscus reaches the end of the scale, refill the apparatus with water from the reservoir as before.
6. Now repeat the experiment, but with the apparatus in a different situation. You could try each of these.
   (a) blowing it with a fan
   (b) putting it in a cupboard
   (c) putting it in a refrigerator
7. Draw a graph of your results.

Questions

1. Under which conditions did the plant transpire (a) most quickly, and (b) most slowly?
2. You have been using the potometer to compare the rate of uptake of water under different conditions. Does this really give you a good measurement of the rate of transpiration? Explain your answer.

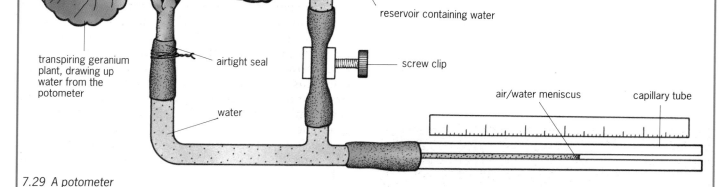

transpiring geranium plant, drawing up water from the potometer

airtight seal

water

reservoir containing water

screw clip

air/water meniscus

capillary tube

7.29 A potometer

Light intensity In bright sunlight, a plant may open its stomata to supply plenty of carbon dioxide for photosynthesis. More water can therefore evaporate from the leaves.

Water supply If water is in short supply, then the plant will close its stomata. This will cut down the rate of transpiration. Transpiration decreases when water supply decreases below a certain level.

7.37 Many plants can cut down water loss.

Transpiration is useful to plants, because it keeps water moving up the xylem vessels. But if the leaves lose too much water, the roots may not be able to take up enough to replace it. If this happens, the plant **wilts**. To stop this happening, many plants have ways of cutting down the rate of transpiration.

Closing stomata Plants lose most water through their stomata. If they close their stomata, then transpiration will slow right down. Fig 7.30 shows how they do this.

However, if its stomata are closed, then the plant cannot photosynthesise, because carbon dioxide cannot diffuse into the leaf. Plants only close their stomata when they really need to, such as when it is very hot and dry, or when they could not photosynthesise anyway, such as at night.

Waxy cuticle Many leaves, such as holly leaves, are covered with a waxy cuticle, made by the cells in the epidermis. The wax waterproofs the leaf.

Hairy leaves Some plants have hairs on their leaves (Fig 7.31). These hairs trap a layer of moist air next to the leaf.

Stomata on underside of leaf In most leaves, there are more stomata on the lower surface than on the upper surface. The lower surface is usually cooler than the upper one, so less water will evaporate.

Cutting down the surface area The smaller the surface area of the leaf, the less water will evaporate from it. Plants like cacti (Fig 7.32) have leaves (the spines) with a small surface area, to help them to conserve water. However, this slows down photosynthesis, because it means less light and carbon dioxide can be absorbed.

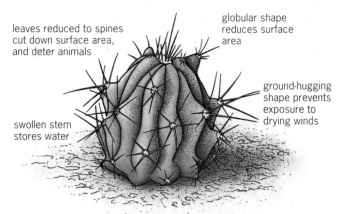

7.32 *Ferocactus – a plant adapted to live in deserts*

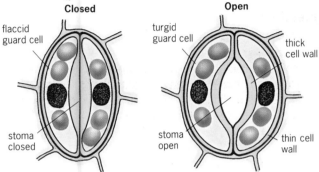

When a plant is short of water, the guard cells become flaccid closing the stoma.

When a plant has plenty of water, the guard cells become turgid. The cell wall on the inner surface is very thick, so it cannot stretch as much as the outer surface. So as the guard cells swell up, they curve away from each other, opening the stoma.

7.30 *How stomata open and close*

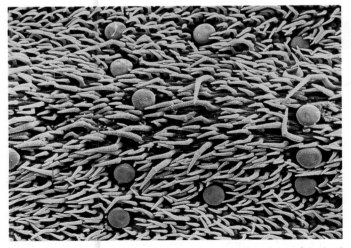

7.31 *A scanning electronmicrograph of the leaf surface of the herb thyme. Thyme is adapted for growing in hot, dry conditions. The tiny hairs trap a layer of moist air next to the leaf, stopping too much water being lost from its surface. The red spheres are glands which make the oil which gives thyme its flavour.*

Uptake of mineral salts

7.38 Root hairs absorb minerals by active transport.

As well as absorbing water by osmosis, root hairs absorb mineral salts. These are in the form of ions dissolved in the water in the soil. They travel to the xylem vessels along with the water which is absorbed, and are transported to all parts of the plant.

These minerals are usually present in the soil in quite low concentrations. The concentration inside the root hairs is higher. In this situation, the mineral ions would normally diffuse out of the root hair into the soil. Root hairs can, however, take up mineral salts against their concentration gradient. It is the cell membrane which does this. Special carrier molecules in the cell membrane of the root hair carry the mineral ions across the cell membrane into the cell, against their concentration gradient.

This is called **active transport**. It uses a lot of energy. The energy is supplied by mitochondria in the root hair cells.

Transport of manufactured food

7.39 Phloem translocates organic foods.

Leaves make carbohydrates by photosynthesis. They also use some of these carbohydrates to make amino acids, proteins, oils and other organic substances.

Some of the organic food material, especially sugar, that the plant makes is transported in the phloem tubes. It is carried from the leaves to whichever part of the plant needs it. This is called **translocation**. The sap inside phloem tubes therefore contains a lot of sugar, particularly sucrose. Energy is needed to make sap move through phloem tubes. It is an active process.

97

Chapter revision questions

1 Using Fig 7.11 to help you, list in order the blood vessels and parts of the heart which:
(a) a glucose molecule would travel through on its way from your digestive system to a muscle in your leg
(b) a carbon dioxide molecule would travel through on its way from the leg muscle to your lungs.

2 Explain the difference between each of the following pairs.
(a) blood, lymph
(b) diastole, systole
(c) artery, vein
(d) deoxygenated blood, oxygenated blood
(e) atrium, ventricle
(f) hepatic vein, hepatic portal vein
(g) red blood cell, white blood cell
(h) xylem, phloem
(i) diffusion, active transport

3 Arteries, veins, capillaries, xylem vessels and phloem tubes are all tubes used for transporting substances in mammals and flowering plants. Describe how each of these tubes is adapted for its particular function.

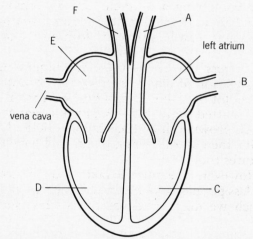

7.33

4 (a) What is meant by a double circulatory system?
(b) Copy the diagram in Fig 7.33 of a section through a heart. Fill in the labels A to F, and draw in arrows to show the direction of blood flow through it.
(c) In an unborn child, the lungs do not work. The baby gets its oxygen from the mother, to which it is connected by the umbilical cord. This cord contains a vein, which carries the oxygenated blood to the baby's vena cava.
(i) Which chamber of the heart does oxygenated blood enter in an adult person?
(ii) Which chamber of the heart does oxygenated blood enter in an unborn baby?
(iii) In an unborn child, there is a hole in the septum between the left and right atria. What purpose do you think this has?

(iv) As soon as the baby takes its first breath, this hole closes up. Why is this important?

5 An experiment was performed where a solution of human haemoglobin was exposed to samples of air containing different amounts of oxygen (measured in kilopascals, kPa). At each oxygen concentration, the haemoglobin sample was tested to see how much oxygen it had absorbed. If it had absorbed as much oxygen as it could possibly carry, it was said to be 100% saturated. If it only carried half this amount, it was 50% saturated, and so on. The graph shows the results obtained.

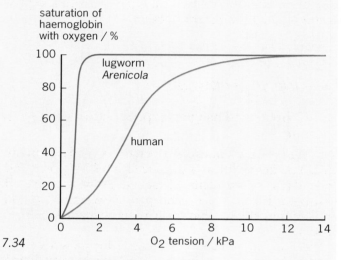

7.34

(a) What is the approximate percentage saturation of human haemoglobin with oxygen, at an oxygen tension of (i) 2 kPa and (ii) 6 kPa?
(b) If haemoglobin which had been exposed to an oxygen tension of 6 kPa was then exposed to an oxygen tension of 2 kPa, would it absorb or give up oxygen?
(c) In the lungs, the oxygen tension is usually about 13 kPa. In the muscles, it is around 4 kPa. Explain why.
(d) Using the information in part (c), and your answer to part (b), explain how haemoglobin transports oxygen from the lungs to a muscle.
(e) What would be the disadvantage of having haemoglobin which absorbed a lot of oxygen at low oxygen tensions?
(f) The lugworm, *Arenicola*, lives in burrows on muddy beaches. There is often only very little oxygen available. *Arenicola* is not a very active animal. The blood of *Arenicola* contains haemoglobin, which behaves rather differently from human haemoglobin (see graph). Can you explain why this type of haemoglobin suits *Arenicola*'s way of life better than human haemoglobin would?

8 Reproduction

8.1 Reproduction may be sexual or asexual.

Living organisms may be killed by other organisms, or die of old age. New organisms have to be produced to replace those that die. This is reproduction.

Each species reproduces in a different way. However, there are only two basic types – **asexual reproduction**, and **sexual reproduction**.

Asexual reproduction

8.2 Growth and asexual reproduction involve mitosis.

A living organism such as a person is made of many cells. You began life as a single cell. This cell grew, and divided to form two cells. These cells grew, and divided again to form four cells. This process went on and on until all the cells of which you are now made had been produced.

The way in which cells divide during growth is shown in Fig 8.2. It is called **mitosis**. Many living organisms also use mitosis to make complete new organisms – they just grow a new one out of themselves. This is called **asexual reproduction**.

8.3 Mitosis makes new cells with the same genes as the old one.

The nucleus of a cell contains threads of **DNA**, called **chromosomes** (Fig 8.1). Different species of organisms have different numbers of chromosomes. Human cells, for example, have 46 chromosomes. The DNA is a coded recipe for making proteins. Each chromosome contains many recipes, or **genes**. You can find out more about DNA, genes and chromosomes in Chapter 15.

Mitosis is a method of cell division which makes two new cells with exactly the same number of chromosomes, carrying exactly the same genes, as the old cell. Figs 8.2 and 8.3 show how mitosis takes place.

8.4 Asexual reproduction produces genetically identical offspring.

As asexual reproduction takes place by means of mitosis, the new organisms produced are genetically identical to their parent, and to each other. A group of genetically identical organisms is called a **clone**.

Figures 8.4, 8.5, 8.6 and 8.7 illustrate four ways in which clones of plants can be produced. The first two – runners and bulbs – are natural methods, which many different kinds of plants use. The second two – cuttings and grafts – are artificial methods, which horticulturalists use to produce new plants.

Another way of producing large numbers of genetically identical plants is **tissue culture**. A small number of cells are taken from a plant, and put onto a sterile jelly. The cells divide to form a shapeless lump called a **callus**. The callus is then moved to a different jelly, containing hormones which stimulate the callus to develop roots. It may then be moved to yet another jelly containing a different set of hormones, which stimulate the development of shoots. Eventually, many tiny plants can be produced from just a few original cells.

Growers use all of these techniques of artificial propagation of plants, because they can quickly produce a lot of plants all genetically identical to the one they started with. If the plant is a popular variety, which grows well and has a good yield of flowers or fruits, then all the young plants will have these good features too.

However, care must be taken that we keep some of the less popular varieties, too. They may contain genes which we might find useful one day, such as ones

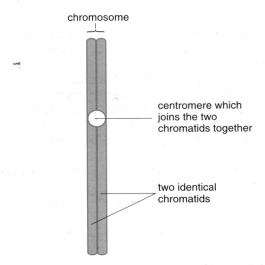

8.1 A chromosome just before division

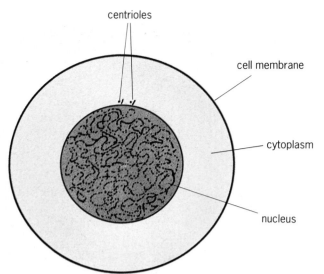

centrioles

cell membrane

cytoplasm

nucleus

1 **Interphase** When a cell is not dividing, no chromosomes can be seen clearly in the nucleus. They are there, but are so long and thin that they are invisible.

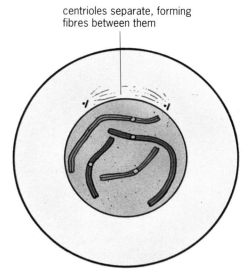

centrioles separate, forming fibres between them

2 **Prophase** The chromosomes get short and fat, so they can now be seen with a light microscope. Each chromosome contains two chromatids (see Fig 8.1).

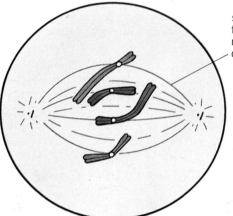

spindle, formed from the fibres made by the centrioles

3 **Metaphase** The nuclear membrane vanishes. The chromosomes line up on the equator of the spindle.

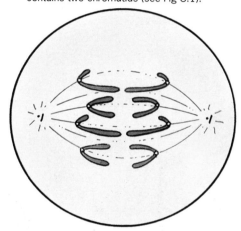

4 **Anaphase** The centromere of each chromosome splits, so the two chromatids separate. The chromatids move away from each other, along the spindle fibres.

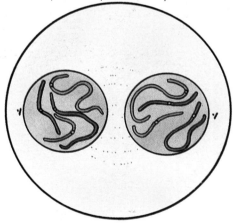

5 **Telophase** The chromatids arrive at opposite ends of the cell, and form into groups. A nuclear membrane appears round each group. The spindle fibres fade away.

8.2 Mitosis in an animal cell with four chromosomes

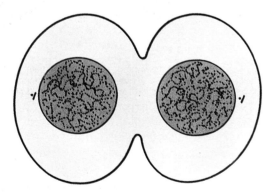

6 **Late telophase** The chromosomes become long and thin again, so that they are invisible. The cytoplasm divides, forming two daughter cells. Each cell now goes into interphase again.

100

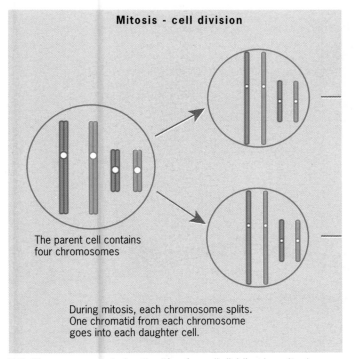

Mitosis - cell division

The parent cell contains four chromosomes

During mitosis, each chromosome splits. One chromatid from each chromosome goes into each daughter cell.

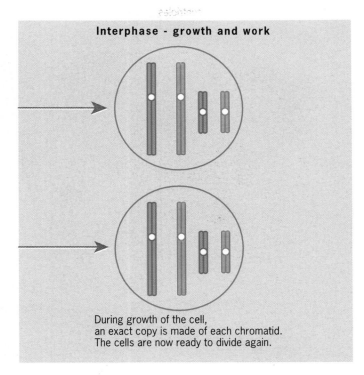

Interphase - growth and work

During growth of the cell, an exact copy is made of each chromatid. The cells are now ready to divide again.

8.3 Chromosomes during the life of a cell dividing by mitosis

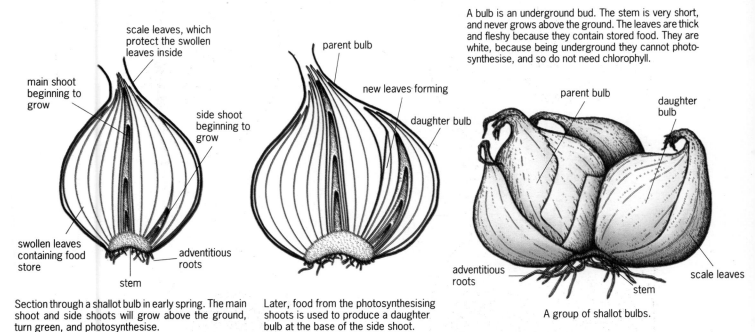

scale leaves, which protect the swollen leaves inside

main shoot beginning to grow

side shoot beginning to grow

swollen leaves containing food store

adventitious roots

stem

Section through a shallot bulb in early spring. The main shoot and side shoots will grow above the ground, turn green, and photosynthesise.

parent bulb

new leaves forming

daughter bulb

Later, food from the photosynthesising shoots is used to produce a daughter bulb at the base of the side shoot.

A bulb is an underground bud. The stem is very short, and never grows above the ground. The leaves are thick and fleshy because they contain stored food. They are white, because being underground they cannot photosynthesise, and so do not need chlorophyll.

parent bulb

daughter bulb

adventitious roots

stem

scale leaves

A group of shallot bulbs.

8.4 Asexual reproduction of a shallot bulb

which help them to resist a particular kind of disease. We may not want these genes now, but we might need them later! 'Gene banks' are now being kept for most kinds of plants, where seeds of all the different varieties are kept, in case breeders may want to use them in years to come.

Some animals can also reproduce asexually and form clones. One example is a tiny freshwater organism called *Hydra*, which is shown in Fig 8.8. Animal breeders can also artificially produce clones of larger animals, such as sheep or cattle. A fertilised cow's egg, for example, can be split into two to make two eggs,

101

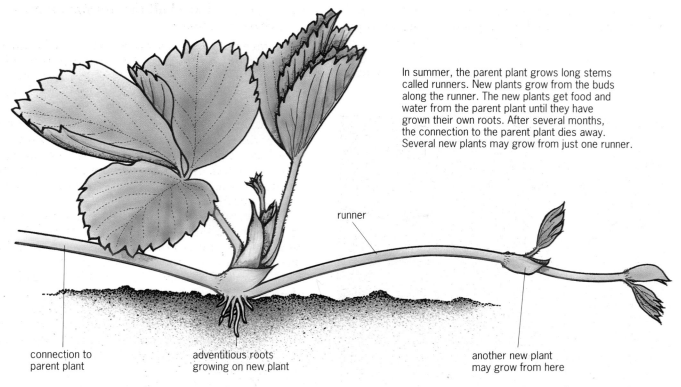

In summer, the parent plant grows long stems called runners. New plants grow from the buds along the runner. The new plants get food and water from the parent plant until they have grown their own roots. After several months, the connection to the parent plant dies away. Several new plants may grow from just one runner.

runner

connection to
parent plant

adventitious roots
growing on new plant

another new plant
may grow from here

8.5 Asexual reproduction of a strawberry plant

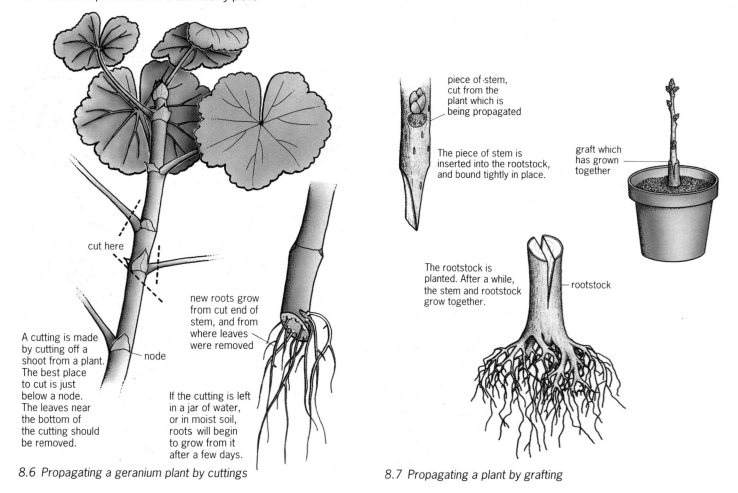

cut here

A cutting is made
by cutting off a
shoot from a plant.
The best place
to cut is just
below a node.
The leaves near
the bottom of
the cutting should
be removed.

node

new roots grow
from cut end of
stem, and from
where leaves
were removed

If the cutting is left
in a jar of water,
or in moist soil,
roots will begin
to grow from it
after a few days.

8.6 Propagating a geranium plant by cuttings

piece of stem,
cut from the
plant which is
being propagated

The piece of stem is
inserted into the rootstock,
and bound tightly in place.

The rootstock is
planted. After a while,
the stem and rootstock
grow together.

rootstock

graft which
has grown
together

8.7 Propagating a plant by grafting

each of which will grow into an embryo. (This is the same as the process which happens naturally to produce identical twins, which is described in Section 8.23.) The two eggs can be put into the cow's uterus to grow into calves, which will be genetically identical to each other.

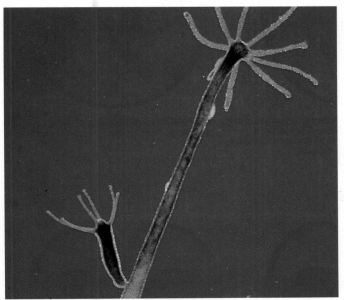

8.8 *The tiny freshwater cnidarian,* Hydra viridis, *reproduces asexually by growing young ones from its body. This is called budding.*

Questions

1 What kind of cell division is involved in asexual reproduction?
2 Explain why gardeners and other plant growers often use cuttings or tissue culture to produce new plants.
3 What problems might occur if we just keep producing plants of a few favourite varieties, rather than some of the less popular ones as well?

Sexual reproduction

8.5 Sexual reproduction involves fertilisation.

In sexual reproduction, the parent organism produces sex cells or **gametes**. Eggs and sperm are examples of gametes. Two of these gametes then join together. This is called **fertilisation**. The new cell which is formed by fertilisation is called a **zygote**. The zygote divides again and again, and eventually grows into a new organism.

The new organisms produced by sexual reproduction are not identical to each other or to their parents. They contain different combinations of genes. You will see why this is so in Section 8.7.

8.6 Gametes have half the normal number of chromosomes.

Gametes are different from ordinary cells, because they contain only half as many chromosomes as usual. This is so that when two of them fuse together, the zygote they form will have the correct number of chromosomes.

Humans, for example, have 46 chromosomes in each of their body cells. But human egg and sperm cells only have 23 chromosomes each. When an egg and sperm fuse together at fertilisation, the zygote which is formed will therefore have 46 chromosomes, the normal number (Fig 8.9).

The 46 chromosomes in an ordinary human cell are of 23 different kinds. There are two of each kind. The two chromosomes of one kind are called **homologous chromosomes**. A cell which has the full number of chromosomes, with two of each kind, is called a **diploid cell**.

An egg or sperm, though, only has 23 chromosomes, one of each kind. It is called a **haploid cell**. Gametes are always haploid. When two gametes fuse together, they form a **diploid zygote**.

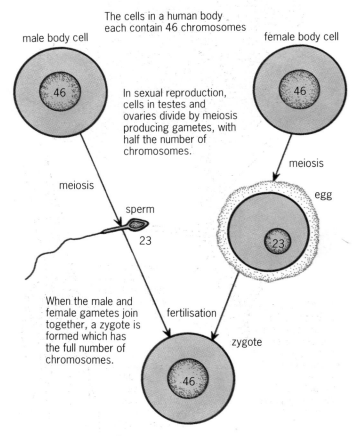

The cells in a human body each contain 46 chromosomes

male body cell

female body cell

In sexual reproduction, cells in testes and ovaries divide by meiosis producing gametes, with half the number of chromosomes.

meiosis

meiosis

egg

sperm

When the male and female gametes join together, a zygote is formed which has the full number of chromosomes.

fertilisation

zygote

8.9 *Sexual reproduction*

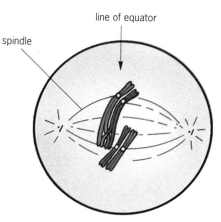

centrioles separate,
forming fibres between them

spindle   line of equator

1 Early Prophase I The chromosomes get short and fat, so they can be seen with a light microscope. Each chromosome contains two chromatids, just as in mitosis.

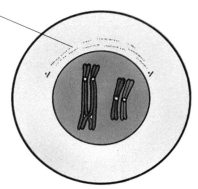

2 Late Prophase I Homologous chromosomes come together, forming two bivalents. Chromatids of homologous chromosomes may break and rejoin with each other, forming crossover points.

3 Metaphase I The bivalents line up on the equator of the spindle.

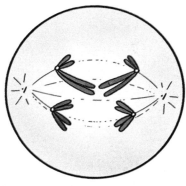

4 Anaphase I The bivalents separate, and the homologous chromosomes move away from one another along the spindle fibres. Notice that the centromeres do not split, so the two chromatids of each chromosome are still joined together.

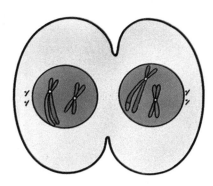

5 Telophase I The chromosomes arrive at opposite ends of the cell. A nuclear membrane forms round each group. The spindle fibres fade away. The centrioles divide, and so does the cytoplasm.

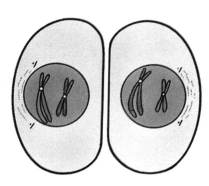

6 Prophase II The centrioles begin to form new spindles at right angles to the first one.

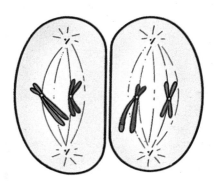

7 Metaphase II The chromosomes line up on the equators of the spindles.

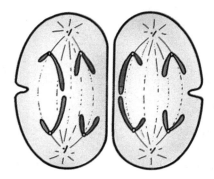

8 Anaphase II The centromeres of each chromosome split, so the two chromatids separate. The chromatids move away from each other, along the spindle fibres.

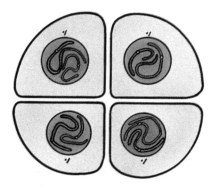

9 Telophase II The chromatids arrive at opposite ends of the cell, and nuclear membranes form around them. The cytoplasm divides.
  Four daughter cells have been formed, each with half the number of chromosomes of the parent cell. Each of these cells is called a gamete.

8.10 Meiosis in an animal cell with four chromosomes. In meiosis, the cell divides twice. In the first division, homologous chromosomes separate from one another. In the second division, chromatids separate, as in mitosis.

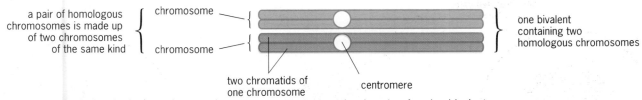

a pair of homologous chromosomes is made up of two chromosomes of the same kind

chromosome

chromosome

two chromatids of one chromosome

centromere

one bivalent containing two homologous chromosomes

8.11 A bivalent. During meiosis, homologous chromosomes come together in pairs, forming bivalents.

8.7 Gametes are made by meiosis.

Gametes are made by ordinary body cells dividing. For example, human sperm are made when cells in a testis divide.

Because gametes need to have only half as many chromosomes as their parent cell, division by mitosis will not do. When gametes are being made, cells divide in a different way, called **meiosis**. This process is shown in Fig 8.10 and 8.12.

In flowering plants and animals, meiosis only happens when gametes are being made. Meiosis produces new cells with only half as many chromosomes as the parent cell.

If you look carefully at Figs 8.10 and 8.12, you will see that the pairs of chromosomes have swapped some pieces between themselves. These pieces may carry different versions of genes. This means that the gametes which are produced carry different combinations of genes – they do not have the same combination as the cell which made them, nor the same as each other. You can find out more about how this can produce variation amongst the offspring produced by sexual reproduction in Chapter 15.

8.8 Male gametes move – female ones stay still.

In many organisms, there are two different kinds of gamete. One kind is quite large, and does not move much. This is called the female gamete. In humans, the female gamete is the egg.

The other sort of gamete is smaller, and moves actively in search of the female gamete. This is called the male gamete. In humans, the male gamete is the sperm.

Often, one organism can only produce one kind of gamete. Its sex is either male or female, depending on what kind of gamete it makes. All mammals, for example, are either male or female.

Sometimes, though, an organism can produce both sorts of gamete. Earthworms, for example, can produce both eggs and sperm. An organism which produces both male and female gametes is a **hermaphrodite**. Many flowering plants are also hermaphrodite.

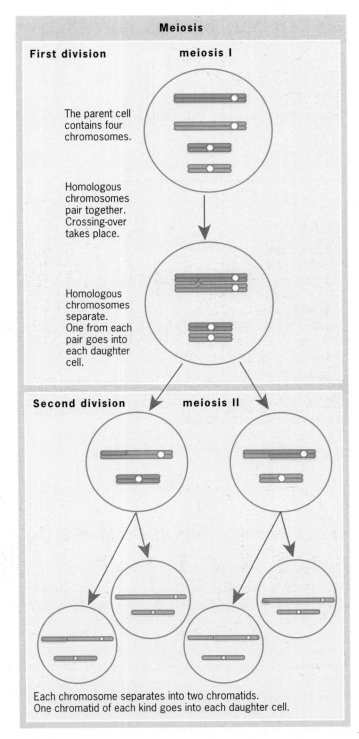

Meiosis

First division   **meiosis I**

The parent cell contains four chromosomes.

Homologous chromosomes pair together. Crossing-over takes place.

Homologous chromosomes separate. One from each pair goes into each daughter cell.

Second division   **meiosis II**

Each chromosome separates into two chromatids. One chromatid of each kind goes into each daughter cell.

8.12 Summary of chromosome behaviour during meiosis

Table 8.1 A comparison of chromosome behaviour during mitosis and meiosis

Mitosis	Meiosis
Prophase Chromosomes appear. They do not associate with one another.	*Prophase I* Chromosomes appear. Homologous chromosomes pair up and form bivalents.
Metaphase Chromosomes line up individually on equator of spindle.	*Metaphase I* Bivalents line up on equator of spindle.
Anaphase Centromeres split. *Chromatids* separate and travel to opposite ends of the cell.	*Anaphase I* Centromeres do not split. Homologous *chromosomes* separate and travel to opposite ends of the cell.
Telophase Two groups of chromatids come together at opposite ends of the cell, and begin to uncoil.	*Telophase I* Two groups of chromosomes come together at opposite ends of the cell, but do not uncoil.
There is no second division of the nucleus. Division has now been completed.	*Second division* The cell goes into another division, at right angles to the first one. The chromatids separate as in mitosis.
Interphase Chromatids are completely uncoiled, and are not visible.	*Interphase* Chromatids are completely uncoiled, and are not visible.
Result Two new cells are formed with exactly the same number and kind of chromosomes as their parent cell.	*Result* Four new cells are formed, each with only half the number of chromosomes of their parent cell.

Questions

1 What is a gamete?
2 What is a zygote?
3 Why do gametes contain only half the normal number of chromosomes?
4 What is meant by a diploid cell?
5 Name one part of your body where you have diploid cells.
6 What is meant by a haploid cell?
7 Give one example of a haploid cell.
8 When do cells divide by meiosis?
9 What is the purpose of meiosis?
10 What does hermaphrodite mean?
11 Give one example of a hermaphrodite organism.

Sexual reproduction in a mammal

8.9 The female reproductive organs.

Figure 8.13 shows the reproductive organs of a woman. The female gametes, called eggs or **ova**, are made in the two **ovaries**. Leading away from the ovaries are the **oviducts**, sometimes called Fallopian tubes. They do not connect directly to the ovaries, but have a funnel shaped opening just a short distance away.

The two oviducts lead to the womb or **uterus**. This has very thick walls, made of muscle. It is quite small – only about the size of a clenched fist – but it can stretch a great deal when a woman is pregnant.

At the base of the uterus is a narrow opening, guarded by muscles. This is the neck of the womb, or **cervix**. It leads to the **vagina**, which opens to the outside.

The opening from the bladder, called the **urethra**, runs in front of the vagina, while the **rectum** is just behind it. The three tubes open quite separately to the outside.

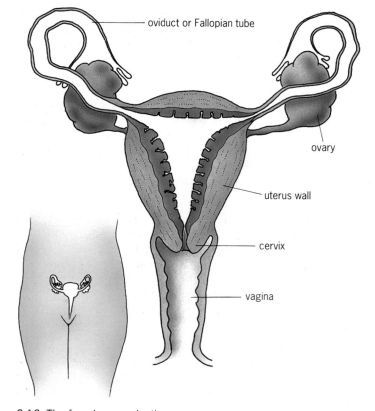

8.13 The female reproductive organs

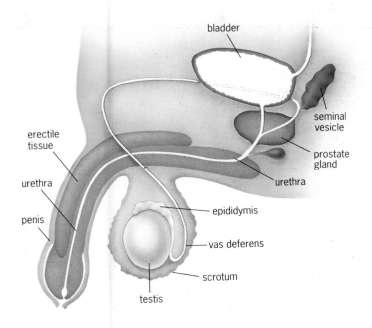

8.14 *The male reproductive organs*

8.10 The male reproductive organs.

Figure 8.14 shows the reproductive organs of a man. The male gametes, called **spermatozoa** or sperm, are made in two **testes**. These are outside the body, in two sacs of skin called the **scrotum**.

The sperm are carried away from each testis in a tube called the **vas deferens**. The vasa deferentia from the testes join up with the **urethra** just below the bladder. The urethra continues downwards, and opens at the tip of the **penis**. The urethra can carry both urine and sperm at different times.

Where the vasa deferentia join the urethra, there is a gland called the **prostate gland**. This makes a fluid which the sperm swim in. Just behind the prostate gland are the **seminal vesicles**, which also secrete fluid.

8.11 Ovaries make eggs.

Figure 8.15 shows a section through a human ovary. The eggs are made from cells in the outside layer, or **epithelium**, of the ovary. Some of these cells move towards the centre of the ovary. A small space, filled with liquid, forms around each one. The space and the cell inside it is called a **follicle**.

This has happened inside a girl's ovaries before she is born. At birth, she will already have many thousands of follicles inside her ovaries.

When she reaches puberty, some of these follicles will begin to develop. Usually, only one develops at a time. The cell inside the follicle grows bigger, and so does the fluid-filled space around it. The follicle moves to the edge of the ovary.

It is now called a **Graafian follicle**. It is little more than 1 cm across, and bulges from the outside of the ovary.

Throughout this process the developing egg has been undergoing meiosis. Only one of the cells which are made becomes an egg. The follicle bursts, and the egg shoots out of the ovary. This is called **ovulation**. In humans, it happens about once a month.

8.12 Testes make sperm.

Figure 8.17 shows a section through a testis. It contains thousands of very narrow, coiled tubes or **tubules**. These are where the sperm are made. They develop from cells in the walls of the tubules, which divide by meiosis. Sperm are made continually from puberty onwards.

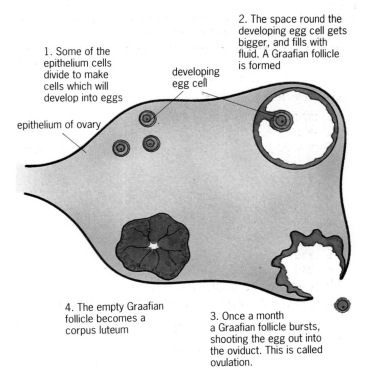

1. Some of the epithelium cells divide to make cells which will develop into eggs

epithelium of ovary

developing egg cell

2. The space round the developing egg cell gets bigger, and fills with fluid. A Graafian follicle is formed

4. The empty Graafian follicle becomes a corpus luteum

3. Once a month a Graafian follicle bursts, shooting the egg out into the oviduct. This is called ovulation.

8.15 *How eggs are made*

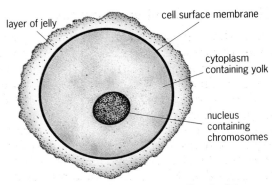

layer of jelly

cell surface membrane

cytoplasm containing yolk

nucleus containing chromosomes

diameter 0.1 mm

8.16 *An egg or ovum*

Sperm production is very sensitive to heat. If they get too hot, the cells in the tubules will not develop into sperm. This is why the testes are outside the body, where they are cooler than they would be inside.

8.13 Mating introduces sperm into the vagina.

After ovulation, the egg is caught in the funnel of the oviduct. The funnel is lined with cilia which beat rhythmically, wafting the egg into the entrance of the oviduct.

Very slowly, the egg travels towards the uterus. Cilia lining the oviduct help to sweep it along. Muscles in the wall of the oviduct also help to move it, by peristalsis (Section 4.33).

If the egg is not fertilised by a sperm within 8–24 hours after ovulation, it will die. By this time, it has only travelled a short way along the oviduct. So a sperm must reach an egg while it is quite near the top of the oviduct if fertilisation is to be successful.

When the man is sexually excited, blood is pumped into spaces inside the penis, so that it becomes erect. To bring the sperm as close as possible to the egg, the man's penis is placed inside the vagina of the woman.

Sperm are pushed out of the penis into the vagina. This happens when muscles in the walls of the tubes containing the sperm contract rhythmically. The wave of contraction begins in the testes, travels along the vasa deferentia, and into the penis. The sperm are squeezed along, and out of the man's urethra into the woman's vagina. This is called **ejaculation**.

Section through a testis

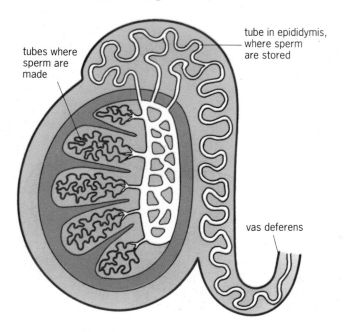

tubes where sperm are made

tube in epididymis, where sperm are stored

vas deferens

Section through one of the tubes where sperm are made

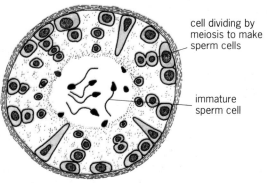

cell dividing by meiosis to make sperm cells

immature sperm cell

8.17 How sperm are made

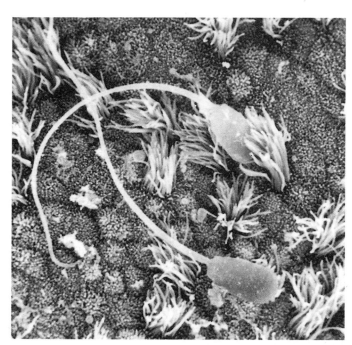

8.19 Scanning electron micrograph of sperm cells swimming over the ciliated cells of the oviduct

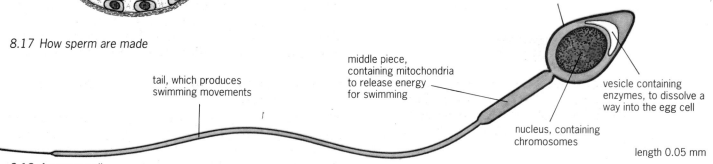

head

middle piece, containing mitochondria to release energy for swimming

tail, which produces swimming movements

vesicle containing enzymes, to dissolve a way into the egg cell

nucleus, containing chromosomes

length 0.05 mm

8.18 A sperm cell

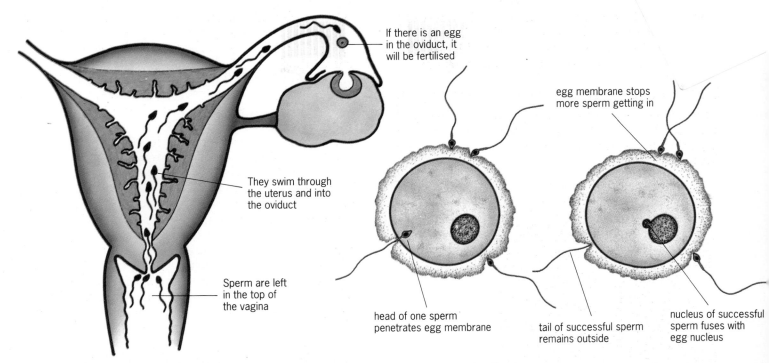

8.20 How sperm get to the egg (sperm and egg drawn to different scales)

Labels in figure 8.20:
- If there is an egg in the oviduct, it will be fertilised
- They swim through the uterus and into the oviduct
- Sperm are left in the top of the vagina

8.21 Fertilisation

Labels in figure 8.21:
- egg membrane stops more sperm getting in
- head of one sperm penetrates egg membrane
- tail of successful sperm remains outside
- nucleus of successful sperm fuses with egg nucleus

The fluid containing the sperm is called **semen**. Ejaculation deposits the semen at the top of the vagina, near the cervix.

8.14 Fertilisation happens in the oviduct.

The sperm are still quite a long way from the egg. They swim, using their tails, up through the cervix, through the uterus, and into the oviduct (Fig 8.20).

Sperm can only swim at a rate of about 4 mm per minute, so it takes quite a while for them to get as far as the oviducts. Many will never get there at all. But one ejaculation deposits about a million sperm in the vagina, so there is a good chance that some of them will reach the egg.

One sperm enters the egg. Only the head of the sperm goes in; the tail is left outside. The nucleus of the sperm fuses with the nucleus of the egg. This is **fertilisation** (Fig 8.21).

As soon as the successful sperm enters the egg, the egg membrane becomes impenetrable, so that no other sperm can get in. The unsuccessful sperm will all die.

Fact!

The most children one woman has ever had is 69. A Russian woman who lived between 1707 and 1782 had sixteen pairs of twins, seven sets of triplets and four sets of quadruplets, all born between 1725 and 1765.

Questions

1 What is the name for the narrow opening between the uterus and the vagina?
2 Where is the prostate gland, and what is its function?
3 What is a Graafian follicle?
4 Explain how ovulation happens.
5 Where are sperm made?
6 How does an egg travel along the oviduct?
7 What is semen?
8 Where does fertilisation take place?

8.15 The zygote implants in the uterus wall.

When the sperm nucleus and the egg nucleus have fused together, they form a zygote. The zygote continues to move slowly down the oviduct. As it goes, it divides by mitosis. After several hours, it has formed a ball of cells. This is called an **embryo**. The embryo obtains food from the yolk of the egg.

It takes several hours for the embryo to reach the uterus, and by this time it is a ball of 16 or 32 cells. The uterus has a thick, spongy lining, and the embryo sinks into it. This is called **implantation** (Fig 8.22).

8.16 The embryo's life-support system is its placenta.

The cells in the embryo, now buried in the soft wall of the uterus, continue to divide. As the embryo grows, a **placenta** also grows, which connects it to the wall of the uterus (Figs 8.23 and 8.24). The placenta is soft

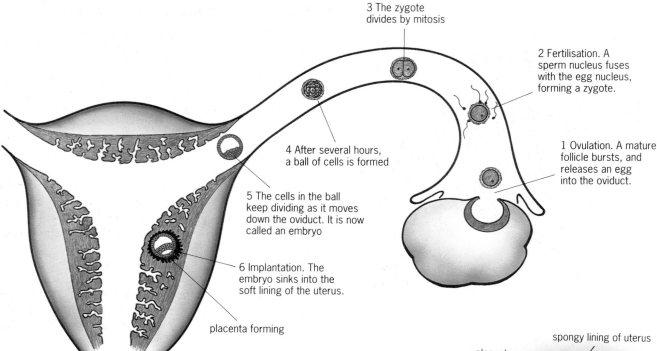

3 The zygote divides by mitosis

2 Fertilisation. A sperm nucleus fuses with the egg nucleus, forming a zygote.

1 Ovulation. A mature follicle bursts, and releases an egg into the oviduct.

4 After several hours, a ball of cells is formed

5 The cells in the ball keep dividing as it moves down the oviduct. It is now called an embryo

6 Implantation. The embryo sinks into the soft lining of the uterus.

placenta forming

8.22 Stages leading to implantation

and dark red, and has finger-like projections called **villi**. The villi fit closely into the uterus wall.

The placenta is joined to the embryo by the **umbilical cord**. Inside the cord is an artery and a vein. The artery takes blood from the embryo into the placenta, and the vein returns the blood to the embryo.

In the placenta are capillaries filled with the embryo's blood. In the wall of the uterus are large spaces filled with the mother's blood. The embryo's and mother's blood do not mix. They are separated by the wall of the placenta. But they are brought very close together, because the wall of the placenta is very thin.

Oxygen and food materials in the mother's blood diffuse across the placenta into the embryo's blood, and are then carried along the umbilical cord to the embryo. Carbon dioxide and waste materials diffuse the other way, and are carried away in the mother's blood.

As the embryo grows, the placenta grows too. By the time the embryo is born, the placenta will be a flat disc, about 12 cm in diameter, and 3 cm thick.

8.17 An amnion protects the embryo.

The embryo is surrounded by a strong membrane, called the **amnion**. The amnion makes a liquid called **amniotic fluid**. This fluid helps to support the embryo, and to protect it.

8.18 A baby develops during gestation.

No-one fully understands how the cells in the ball

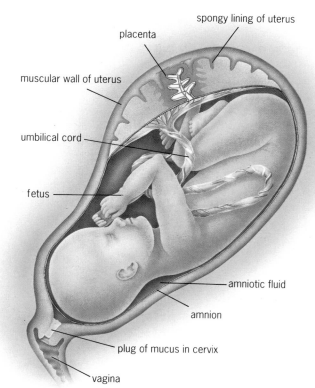

spongy lining of uterus

placenta

muscular wall of uterus

umbilical cord

fetus

amniotic fluid

amnion

plug of mucus in cervix

vagina

8.23 Side view of developing fetus inside uterus

Fact!

The mammal with the longest gestation period is the Asiatic elephant – it is 609 days on average, but may last as long as 760 days.

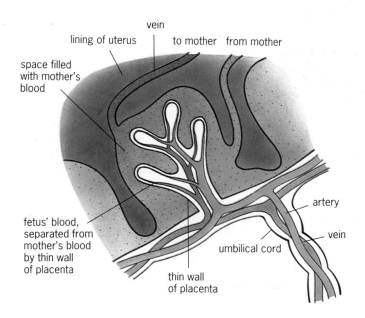

space filled with mother's blood

lining of uterus

vein

to mother   from mother

fetus' blood, separated from mother's blood by thin wall of placenta

artery

vein

umbilical cord

thin wall of placenta

8.24 Part of the placenta

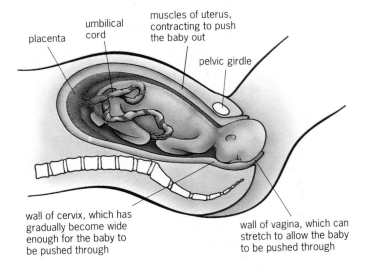

placenta

umbilical cord

muscles of uterus, contracting to push the baby out

pelvic girdle

wall of cervix, which has gradually become wide enough for the baby to be pushed through

wall of vagina, which can stretch to allow the baby to be pushed through

8.25 Birth

which embedded itself in the wall of the uterus become arranged to form a baby. The cells gradually divide and grow. By eleven weeks after fertilisation they have become organised into all the different organs. By this stage the embryo is called a fetus.

After this, the fetus just grows. It takes nine months before it is ready to be born. This length of time between fertilisation and birth is called the **gestation period**.

8.19 Muscular contractions cause birth.

A few weeks before birth, the fetus usually turns over in the uterus, so that it is lying head downwards. Its head lies just over the opening of the cervix.

Birth begins when the strong muscles in the wall of the uterus start to contract. This is called **labour**. To begin with, the contractions are quite gentle, and only happen about once an hour. Gradually, they become stronger and more frequent. The contractions of the muscles slowly stretch the opening of the cervix (Fig 8.25).

After several hours, the cervix is wide enough for the head of the baby to pass through. Now, the muscles start to push the baby down through the cervix and the vagina. This part of the birth happens quite quickly.

The baby is still attached to the uterus by the umbilical cord and the placenta. Now that it is in the open air, it can breathe for itself, so the placenta is no longer needed. The placenta falls away from the wall of the uterus, and passes out through the vagina. It is called the **afterbirth**.

The umbilical cord is cut, and clamped just above the point where it joins the baby. This is completely painless, because there are no nerves in the cord. The stump of the cord forms the baby's navel.

The contractions of the muscles of the uterus are sometimes painful. They feel rather like cramp. However, there is now no need for any mother to suffer really bad pain. She can help herself a lot by preparing her body with exercises before labour begins and by breathing in a special way during labour, and she can also be given pain killing drugs if she needs them.

8.20 Mammals care for their young.

Although it has been developing for nine months, a human baby is very helpless when it is born. Usually, both parents help to care for it.

During pregnancy, the glands in the mother's breasts will have become larger. Soon after the birth of the baby, they begin to make milk. This is called **lactation**. Lactation happens in all mammals, but not in other animals (Fig 8.26).

Milk contains all the nutrients that the baby needs. It also contains **antibodies** (Section 18.14) which will help the baby to resist infection.

As well as being fed, the baby needs to be kept warm. Because it is so small, a baby has a large surface area

Fact!

The most children surviving at a single birth is six. This has happened three times – once in South Africa in 1974, once in 1980, in Italy, and once in England in 1983.

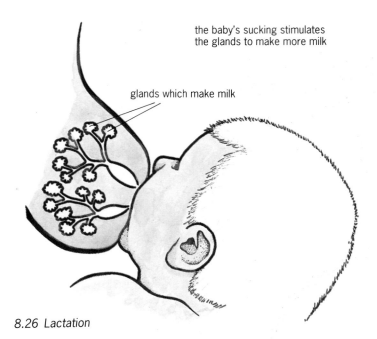

the baby's sucking stimulates the glands to make more milk

glands which make milk

8.26 Lactation

in relation to its volume, so it loses heat very quickly.

It is extremely important that a young baby is cared for emotionally, as well as physically. Babies need a lot of close contact with their parents.

Most mammals care for their young by feeding them and keeping them warm. In humans, parental care also involves teaching the baby and young child how to look after itself, and how to live in society. This continues into its 'teens – a much longer time than for any other animal.

Questions

1. What is formed when an egg and sperm fuse together?
2. What kind of cell division takes place in the growth of an embryo?
3. From where does the very young embryo obtain its food?
4. What is implantation?
5. What is a fetus?
6. How is the fetus connected to the placenta?
7. Describe two ways in which the structure of the placenta helps diffusion between the mother's and the fetus's blood to take place quickly.
8. List two substances which pass from the mother's blood into the fetus's blood.
9. What is the function of the amnion?
10. How long is the gestation period in humans?
11. Describe what happens to each of the following during the birth of a baby.
    (a) muscles in the uterus wall
    (b) the cervix
    (c) the placenta
12. Why must babies be kept warm?

8.21 The menstrual cycle.

Usually, one egg is released into the oviduct every month in an adult woman. Before the egg is released, the lining of the uterus becomes thick and spongy, to prepare itself for the fertilised egg. It is full of tiny blood vessels, ready to supply the embryo with food and oxygen if it should arrive.

If the egg is not fertilised, it is dead by the time it reaches the uterus. It does not sink into the spongy wall, but continues onwards, down through the vagina. As the spongy lining is not needed now, it gradually disintegrates. It, too, is slowly lost through the vagina. This is called **menstruation**, or a period. It usually lasts for about five days.

After menstruation, the lining of the uterus builds up again, so that it will be ready to receive the next egg, if it is fertilised.

The menstrual cycle is controlled by hormones. This is described in Section 9.27.

8.22 Sexual maturity is reached at puberty.

The time when a person approaches sexual maturity is called **adolescence**. Sperm production begins in a boy, and ovulation in a girl.

During adolescence, the secondary sexual characteristics develop. In boys, these include growth of facial and pubic hair, breaking of the voice, and muscular development. In girls, pubic hair begins to grow, the breasts develop, and the pelvic girdle becomes broader.

These changes are brought about by hormones. The male hormones are called **androgens** of which the most important is **testosterone**. The female hormones are called **oestrogens**.

The point at which sexual maturity is reached is called **puberty**. This is often several years earlier for girls than for boys. At puberty, a person is still not completely adult, because emotional development is not complete.

8.23 Twins can be identical or non-identical.

Most mammals have several young at a time. Humans are unusual in only having single babies. But sometimes, a mother may have twins, triplets or even more children at a time. Having twins tends to run in families.

There are two types of twins – identical and non-identical.

Identical twins result when the ball of cells formed from the zygote divides completely into two soon after fertilisation. Each ball of cells then grows into a separate embryo, although they often share the same placenta. The two embryos have each developed from the same egg and sperm, so they have exactly the same genes. They are the same sex, and often very difficult to tell apart.

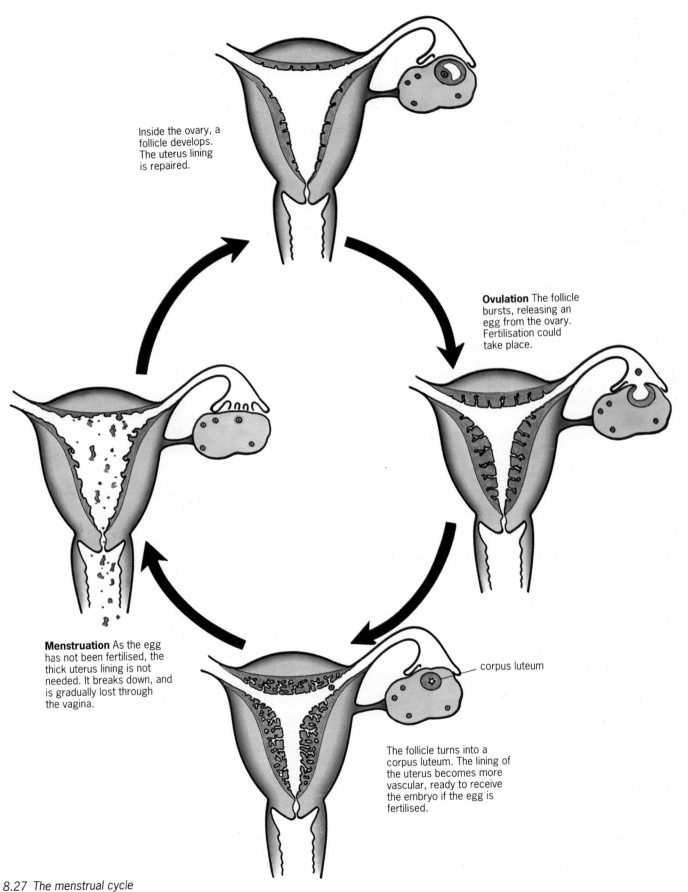

Inside the ovary, a follicle develops. The uterus lining is repaired.

Ovulation The follicle bursts, releasing an egg from the ovary. Fertilisation could take place.

corpus luteum

The follicle turns into a corpus luteum. The lining of the uterus becomes more vascular, ready to receive the embryo if the egg is fertilised.

Menstruation As the egg has not been fertilised, the thick uterus lining is not needed. It breaks down, and is gradually lost through the vagina.

8.27 The menstrual cycle

Non-identical twins are formed when two separate eggs are fertilised by two separate sperm. This can only happen when more than one egg is released from the

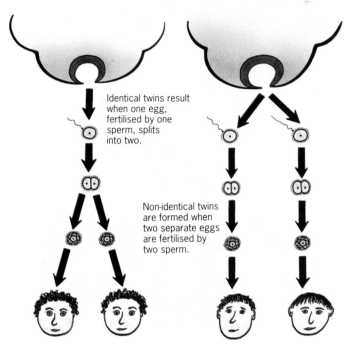

Identical twins result when one egg, fertilised by one sperm, splits into two.

Non-identical twins are formed when two separate eggs are fertilised by two sperm.

8.28 How twins are formed

ovaries at the same time. Each embryo has its own placenta. The two embryos are no more alike than normal brothers and sisters, because each has developed from a separate egg and sperm. Non-identical twins can be both girls, both boys, or a boy and a girl.

Very rarely, several eggs are released from the ovaries at the same time, resulting in a **multiple birth**. Most multiple births have occurred when a woman has been given hormone treatment to help her to produce and release eggs.

8.24 Contraception prevents fertilisation.

Contraception is the prevention of fertilisation when sexual intercourse takes place. Contraception is important in keeping family sizes small, and in limiting the increase in the human population. Careful and responsible use of contraceptive methods means no unwanted children need ever be born.

Contraceptive methods all work by preventing sperm from coming into contact with an egg.

Barrier methods work by putting a barrier between the eggs and sperm. Two examples are the condom and the cap.

The pill stops eggs being produced. It contains hormones like those that a woman's body makes when she is pregnant. These are progesterone and oestrogen. One of the effects of these hormones is to stop eggs

Table 8.2 Some methods of contraception

Method	How it works	Advantages and disadvantages
Condom	The condom is placed over the erect penis. It traps semen as it is released, stopping it from entering the vagina.	This is a very safe method of contraception if used correctly, but care must be taken that no semen is allowed to escape before it is put on or after it is removed. It can also help to prevent the transfer of infection, such as gonorrhoea and HIV, from one partner to the other.
Cap	The cap is a circular sheet of rubber which is placed over the cervix, at the top of the vagina. Spermicidal (sperm-killing) cream is first applied round its edges. Sperm deposited in the vagina cannot get past the cap into the uterus.	This is an effective method, if used and fitted correctly. Fitting must be done by a doctor, but after that a woman can put her own cap in and take it out as needed.
The pill or oral contraceptive	The pill contains female sex hormones. One pill is taken every day. The hormones are like those that are made when a woman is pregnant, and stop egg production.	This is a very effective method, so long as the pills are taken at the right time. However, some women do experience unpleasant side effects, and it is important that women on the pill have regular check-ups with their doctor.
Sterilisation	In a man, the vasa deferentia are cut or tied, stopping sperm from travelling from the testes to the penis. In a woman, the oviducts are cut or tied, stopping eggs from travelling down the oviducts.	An extremely sure method of contraception, with no side effects. However, the tubes often cannot be re-opened if the person later decides they do want to have children, so it is not a method for young people.
Rhythm	The woman keeps a careful record of her menstrual cycle over several months, so that she can predict roughly when an egg is likely to be present in her oviducts. She must avoid sexual intercourse for several days around this time.	This is a very unsafe method, because it is never possible to be 100% certain when ovulation is going to happen. Nevertheless, it is used by many people who do not want to use one of the other contraceptive methods.

from being released until the pregnancy is over. A woman on the pill has no eggs present to be fertilised.

Sterilisation is a common method of contraception for couples who already have as many children as they want. The operation for a man is called a vasectomy. It is a quick and simple operation, usually done under local anaesthetic. The operation for a woman usually involves a short stay in hospital, and a general anaesthetic.

The rhythm method involves the woman in trying to work out when she is likely to have eggs in her oviduct, and to avoid sexual intercourse at that time. It is a risky method, and only works for women who have very regular and predictable menstrual cycles. However, it is useful for couples who do not wish to use other contraceptive methods for religious or other reasons.

Questions

1 Why does the uterus wall become thick and spongy before ovulation?
2 What happens if the egg is not fertilised?
3 What is meant by (a) adolescence, and (b) puberty?
4 What are androgens?
5 List two effects of androgens.

Sexual reproduction in a fish

8.25 Fish use external fertilisation.

The herring is a marine fish, which lives in the northern parts of the Atlantic Ocean. Between spring and summer, large numbers of adult herring collect at their spawning grounds. The females have enormous numbers of eggs in their ovaries, while the males have sperm in their testes.

The female lays her eggs in water, and the male releases sperm onto them. This is called **spawning**. The sperm swim to the eggs, and fertilise them. This is called **external fertilisation**, because it happens outside the female's body.

8.26 Few eggs survive to grow into fish.

The eggs sink to the bottom of the sea. There are so many of them that they attract other fish, such as haddock, which eat them. The parent fish do not look after the eggs.

The eggs contain **yolk**, which supplies the developing embryo with food. They are surrounded by a layer of jelly-like **albumen**, which helps to protect the developing fish. Albumen is a protein. The embryo obtains its oxygen by diffusion, from the water.

After a few days, the young fish hatches from the

Fact!

The fish which lays the largest number of eggs is the Ocean Sunfish – it may lay up to 30 000 000 at one time.

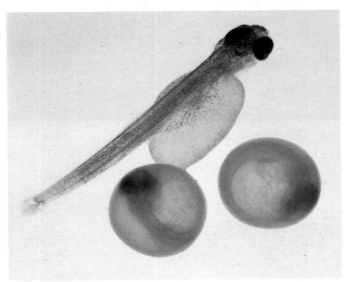

8.29 This small trout has just hatched from an egg, and still has its yolk sac attached. You can also see the yolk in the two unhatched eggs.

egg. It is now called a **larva**. The remains of the yolk are still attached to it, and it uses this for food for the next day or so.

The young larvae feed on microscopic plants floating in the water, called **phytoplankton**. Many of them are eaten by predators. Of the thousands of eggs laid by the female fish, only a very few will survive to become adult herrings.

Sexual reproduction in an amphibian

8.27 Frogs return to water to fertilise eggs.

The common frog is an amphibian which lives near ponds and slow-moving streams. Like fish, frogs use external fertilisation. In spring, male and female frogs collect together in ponds. The male frogs, which are usually slightly smaller than the females, climb onto the females' backs. The male clings firmly to the female using his front legs. He has a horny pad on each thumb, which helps him to grip.

The female lays her eggs in the water. The male releases sperm onto them immediately. He must do this very quickly, because the eggs swell as soon as they get into the water. Once they are swollen, the sperm cannot get in.

115

8.30 *Mating frogs*

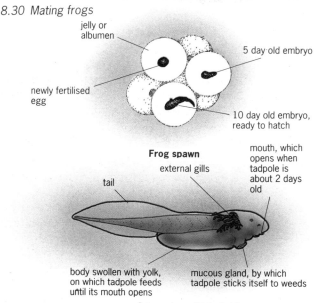

jelly or albumen

newly fertilised egg

5 day old embryo

10 day old embryo, ready to hatch

Frog spawn

tail

external gills

mouth, which opens when tadpole is about 2 days old

body swollen with yolk, on which tadpole feeds until its mouth opens

mucous gland, by which tadpole sticks itself to weeds

A two day old tadpole

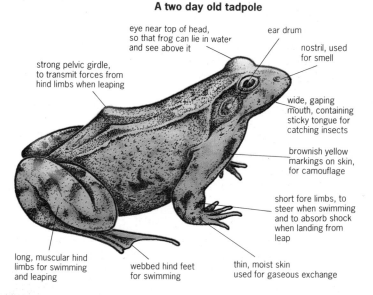

eye near top of head, so that frog can lie in water and see above it

ear drum

nostril, used for smell

strong pelvic girdle, to transmit forces from hind limbs when leaping

wide, gaping mouth, containing sticky tongue for catching insects

brownish yellow markings on skin, for camouflage

short fore limbs, to steer when swimming and to absorb shock when landing from leap

long, muscular hind limbs for swimming and leaping

webbed hind feet for swimming

thin, moist skin used for gaseous exchange

An adult frog

8.31 *Development of a frog*

8.28 Tadpoles are adapted to life in water.

Like a fish's egg, a frog's egg contains an embryo, yolk and albumen (Fig 8.31). The albumen helps to stick the eggs together in a large group.

The embryo is ready to hatch after about ten days. It is now called a larva or tadpole.

Tadpoles are well adapted for life in water. They respire using gills, first external ones and later internal ones. Their mouths and digestive systems are designed to eat first water plants, and then small aquatic (water living) animals. They have muscular tails to help them to swim.

8.29 Frogs are adapted to spend some time on land.

In late spring and early summer, the tadpoles change into frogs. This change is called **metamorphosis**. Metamorphosis changes the aquatic tadpole into a terrestrial (land living) frog.

The tadpole's tail is digested by special cells which secrete enzymes into it, and it is absorbed into the tadpole's body. It would be a hindrance when the frog is living on land.

The gills are also reabsorbed, and are replaced by lungs, adapted for breathing in the air. The adult frog also breathes through its thin, moist skin.

The mouth becomes wider, and a sticky tongue develops, fixed to the front of the mouth. The tongue can be flicked out to catch insects. The eyes move to the top of the head, so that the frog can see above the surface of the water.

The hind limbs develop strong muscles, which enable the frog to leap. Webs grow between the toes, to provide a large surface to push against the water when swimming. The front limbs are smaller. They are used for balance on land, and for steering when the frog is swimming.

After metamorphosis, the young frog is still very small, and does not become sexually mature for about four years.

Questions

1 What type of fertilisation do herrings use?
2 Explain how an embryo herring is (a) supplied with food, and (b) protected.
3 Why do female herrings lay so many eggs?
4 What type of fertilisation do frogs use?
5 How do tadpoles breathe when they are (a) two days old, and (b) four weeks old?
6 What is metamorphosis?
7 List four changes that occur at metamorphosis, which are associated with the change from an aquatic to a terrestrial life.

Sexual reproduction in birds

8.30 Robins establish breeding territories.

Robins (Fig 8.32) live in woods and gardens throughout Great Britain and much of Europe. They breed in April and May. The male robin begins to claim a territory in August of the previous year. He does this by singing. His song warns off rival males, and advertises his presence to females. He sings all through autumn, winter and spring.

During the winter, a female bird will pair up with a male. The two birds then share the territory, although they usually take very little notice of one another at this time. Only males which have a territory will obtain mates. This ensures that the parents will be able to find enough food to support their young in the spring.

In April, the two birds build a nest. It is usually built in a hollow, and made of dead leaves and moss.

8.31 Birds use internal fertilisation.

During the nest building period, eggs are developing in the female robin's ovary. Each egg has a very large amount of yolk.

Robins, like all birds, use **internal fertilisation**. The male robin balances on the female's back, and passes sperm into her oviduct. The sperm swim up the oviduct, where fertilisation takes place.

The fertilised egg then travels down the oviduct. As it goes, the walls of the oviduct secrete a layer of

> ### Fact!
>
> The largest bird's egg is that of the ostrich, which is about 15–20 cm long. It weighs around 1.7 kg, and takes 40 minutes to boil.

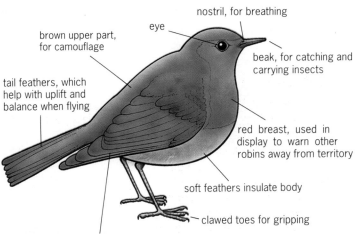

8.32 A robin

- nostril, for breathing
- eye
- brown upper part, for camouflage
- beak, for catching and carrying insects
- tail feathers, which help with uplift and balance when flying
- red breast, used in display to warn other robins away from territory
- soft feathers insulate body
- clawed toes for gripping
- flight feathers, to give large surface area to increase uplift when flying

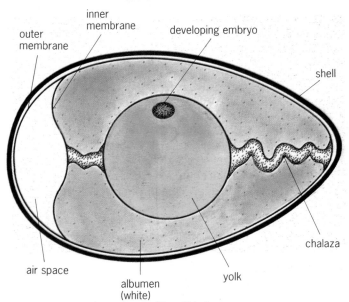

8.33 A section through a fertilised bird's egg

- outer membrane
- inner membrane
- developing embryo
- shell
- chalaza
- air space
- albumen (white)
- yolk

albumen, which surrounds the yolk. Just before it is laid, the oviduct walls secrete a calcium rich substance over it, which hardens into the shell (Fig 8.33).

8.32 Bird embryos develop inside shelled eggs.

The female robin lays about five eggs. The shells are white, with reddish brown markings. This helps to camouflage the eggs from predators.

As soon as she has laid all her eggs, the female robin begins to incubate them. Her body heat keeps them warm, and the embryo in each egg begins to develop.

The embryo grows on top of the yolk (Fig 8.33). It grows blood vessels over the surface of the yolk, which absorb food from it.

The albumen helps to protect the embryo from damage. It also insulates it from extreme temperatures, and stops it from drying out.

The chalaza supports the embryo in the centre of the egg. When the egg is turned, the yolk always swings round so that the embryo lies on top. The robin turns her eggs frequently.

The embryo obtains its oxygen by diffusion through the shell and membranes.

The embryo's nitrogenous waste (Section 10.18) is excreted in the form of **uric acid**. This is a white paste, which collects in one part of the egg, where it will not interfere with the embryo's growth.

8.33 Birds care for their young.

Robins, like most birds, take great care of their eggs and young. The young robins hatch after thirteen or fourteen days. They break the shell of the egg using a hard growth on the top of their beak, called an **egg tooth**. The parent birds remove the egg shells from the nest, as these might attract predators.

Practical 8.1 Examining the structure of a hen's egg

You will need a hard-boiled egg, and a fresh egg.

1 Firstly, examine the hard-boiled egg. Very carefully remove the shell. Look at a piece of the shell under a binocular microscope, and notice the pores in the shell. What do you think goes in and out of the egg through these pores? What other functions does the shell have?

2 What is lying between the shell and the white of the egg? What is its function?

3 The white of the egg is made of protein. What is the name of this protein?

4 Put the shelled egg onto a tile. Cut it through lengthways. Make a labelled drawing of the surface of one half. Label membranes, white and yolk.

5 Now examine a fresh, unfertilised egg. Put it into a petri dish, on a paper towel to hold it steady. Using the blunt end of your forceps, make a small crack in the shell. Carefully pick off pieces of shell with forceps. Can you see anything lying on top of the yolk?

6 Gently tip the contents of the shell into a dish containing a little water. Examine the white, and look for the twisted parts called the chalaza. What is their function?

7 Look at a fertilised egg, in which a window has been made. Look for a small spot or circle near the top of the yolk. What is it? Why could you not see this on the yolk of the other egg?

The female continues to sit on the young birds just as she did on the eggs, until they are about a week old. By this time, they have brown feathers, which camouflage them.

Both the male and female robins bring food to their young. The young robins leave the nest after about a fortnight. Within five weeks of hatching they are completely independent of their parents.

Questions

1 How do male robins claim a territory?
2 What is the advantage of claiming a territory?
3 What type of fertilisation do robins use?
4 How is an embryo robin (a) supplied with food, (b) protected, and (c) supplied with oxygen?
5 List three ways in which the parent birds care for their young after they have hatched.

Fact!

The smallest bird's egg belongs to the Vervain humming bird. It is less than 10mm long and weighs 0.37 g.

Sexual reproduction in insects

8.34 Insects undergo metamorphosis.

Figure 8.34 shows the life cycle of a locust. Locusts live in quite hot places, which are often dry. The females lay their eggs in sand or dusty soil, protected from drying out by a waterproof covering. The young locusts which hatch are very small, and do not have wings. They are called nymphs or hoppers.

Insects have to moult as they grow. This is because they have a hard covering, or **exoskeleton**, on the outside of their bodies. The exoskeleton cannot grow. As the insect – inside its exoskeleton – gets bigger, it has to shed its exoskeleton every now and then, and produce a new one. This is called moulting, or **ecdysis**.

8.35 New exoskeletons can stretch.

As the young locust feeds, it increases in weight inside its exoskeleton. When it has filled up all the space inside the exoskeleton, it stops feeding. It climbs onto a branch, and hangs upside down.

Underneath the exoskeleton, a liquid called **moulting fluid** is made. It dissolves the inner layer of the exoskeleton, so that it is loosened from the insect's body. In the space that the moulting fluid has made, a new, soft exoskeleton forms.

The locust now pumps blood into its thorax, so that it expands. The new exoskeleton stretches, and the old one splits. The locust wriggles out of its old exoskeleton. Underneath is the new, soft one. This expands, so the locust is suddenly a lot bigger. It takes a few hours for the new exoskeleton to harden. The young locust begins to feed, and will need to moult again in a few weeks' time.

8.36 Insects grow in stages.

Figure 8.35a shows the length changes during the growth of a locust. Between moults, it stays the same size, because the exoskeleton cannot grow. At ecdysis, the new exoskeleton expands quickly, so there is a sudden increase in length.

Figure 8.35b shows the weight changes. The locust gradually increases in weight underneath its exoskeleton. When it moults, its old exoskeleton is shed, so it loses a little weight. As soon as it begins feeding again, its weight goes up.

8.37 Metamorphosis is a change from young to adult.

When a locust hatches from an egg, it is not a miniature version of an adult locust. It is called a **nymph**. Quite a lot of changes will have to take place before it becomes an adult locust. The changes are called **metamorphosis**.

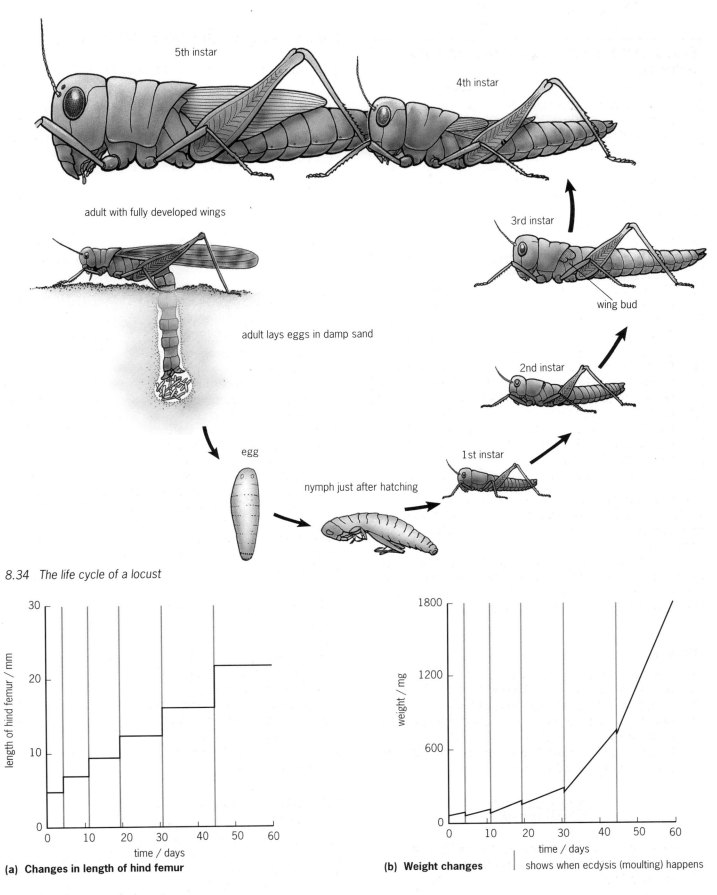

5th instar

4th instar

adult with fully developed wings

3rd instar

wing bud

adult lays eggs in damp sand

2nd instar

1st instar

egg

nymph just after hatching

8.34 The life cycle of a locust

(a) Changes in length of hind femur

length of hind femur / mm

time / days

(b) Weight changes

weight / mg

time / days

shows when ecdysis (moulting) happens

8.35 Growth curves of a locust

8.38 Locusts show incomplete metamorphosis.

A locust moults five times before it is adult. Each stage in between moults is called an **instar**.

The five instars of a locust are shown in Fig 8.34. At each moult, the instars become more like the adult. This gradual change from a nymph to an adult insect is called **incomplete metamorphosis**.

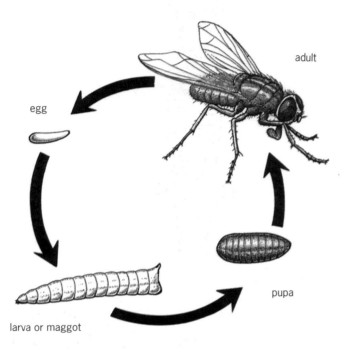

8.36 The life cycle of a blowfly – an example of complete metamorphosis

8.39 Houseflies show complete metamorphosis.

Many insects, such as houseflies, undergo more dramatic changes when they moult. The **larva** or maggot which hatches from a blowfly's egg is very different from the adult. When fully grown the larva changes into a pupa. After some time the adult blowfly emerges from inside the pupa's skin. These changes from a larva to an adult are called **complete metamorphosis** (Fig 8.36).

8.40 Metamorphosis reduces competition.

Why do insects undergo metamorphosis? Would it not be simpler if they hatched as miniature adults, and then just grew?

One reason is that, if the young and adults are different from one another, then they do not **compete** with each other. Blowfly maggots, for example, feed on rotting meat. The female chooses the spot in which she lays her eggs carefully, to ensure that the larvae will find themselves on a good food supply. The adult blowflies, however, feed on carbohydrate-rich foods,

such as sugary things. Therefore, as the larva and the adult eat different kinds of foods, rather than competing for the same food, there will be more for each of them.

Another reason is that the young and the adult have different functions. The larva has to **grow**, and it is adapted for eating and growing as fast as possible. The adult has to **reproduce**. It needs wings to find a mate, and to find a suitable place to lay its eggs. It would be a waste of energy for the larva to fly around, as it has all the food it needs where it is.

Questions

1 Why is the growth curve for an insect not a smooth one?
2 What is a nymph?
3 Explain the difference between incomplete and complete metamorphosis.
4 Give two reasons why some animals undergo metamorphosis.

Sexual reproduction in flowering plants

8.41 Flowers are for sexual reproduction.

Many flowering plants can reproduce in more than one way. Often, they can reproduce asexually, by vegetative propagation and also sexually, by means of flowers.

The function of a flower is to make gametes, and to ensure that fertilisation will take place. Fig 8.38 illustrates the structure of a wallflower. On the outside of the flower are four **sepals**. The sepals protect the flower while it is a bud. In wallflowers, the colour of the sepals

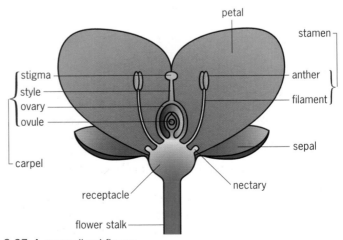

8.37 A generalised flower

120

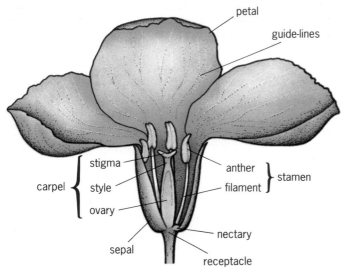

8.38 *A wallflower with one petal removed*

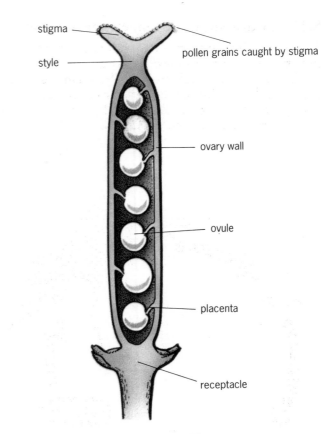

8.39 *Section through the carpel of a wallflower*

depends on the colour of the petals. In other flowers, the sepals are often green.

Just inside the sepals are four **petals**. These are brightly coloured, and have lines on them running from top to bottom. The petals attract insects to the flower. The lines are called **guide-lines**, because they guide the insect to the base of the petal. Here, there is a gland called a **nectary**. The nectary makes a sugary liquid called nectar, which insects feed on.

Inside the petals are six **stamens**. These are the male parts of the flower. Each stamen is made up of a long **filament**, with an **anther** at the top. The anthers contain **pollen grains**, which contain the male gametes.

The female part of the flower is in the centre. It is called a **carpel**. Most of it consists of an **ovary**. Inside the ovary are many **ovules**, which contain the female gametes. At the top of the ovary is a short **style**, with a forked **stigma** at the tip. The function of the stigma is to catch pollen grains.

The wallflower makes both male and female gametes, so it is a hermaphrodite flower. Most, but not all, flowers are hermaphrodite.

8.42 Pollen grains contain male gametes.

The male gametes are inside the pollen grains, which are made in the anthers.

Figure 8.40a illustrates a young anther, as it looks before the flower bud opens. The anther has four spaces or **pollen sacs** inside it. Some of the cells around the edge of the pollen sacs divide by meiosis to make pollen grains. When the flower bud opens, the anthers split open (Fig 8.40c). Now the pollen is on the outside of the anther.

Pollen looks like a fine, yellow powder. Under the microscope, you can see the shape of individual grains. Pollen grains from other kinds of flowers have different shapes.

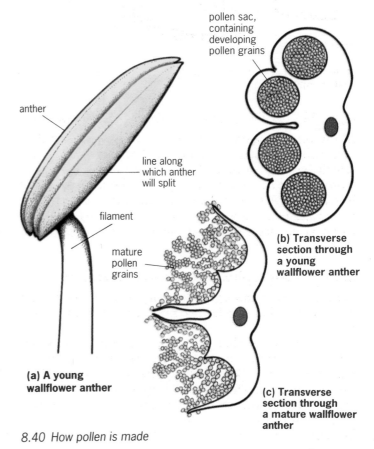

8.40 *How pollen is made*

121

8.41 *Scanning electronmicrograph of wallflower pollen on a petal*

Practical 8.2 Investigating the structure of a wallflower

1 Take an open, fresh looking flower. Can you suggest two ways in which the flower advertises itself to insects?

2 Gently remove the four sepals from the outside of the flower. Look at the sepals on a flower bud, near the top of the stem. What is the function of the sepals?

3 Now remove the four petals from your flower. Make a labelled drawing of one of them, to show the markings. What is the function of these markings?

4 Find the six stamens. If you have a young flower there will be pollen on the anthers at the top of the stamens. Dust some onto a microscope slide, and look at it under a microscope. Draw a few pollen grains.

5 Now remove the six stamens. What do you think is the function of the filaments?

6 Using a hand lens, try to find the nectaries at the bottom of the flower. What is their function?

7 The carpel is now all that is left of the flower. Find the ovary, style and stigma. Look at the stigma under a binocular microscope. What is its function, and how is it adapted to perform it?

8 Using a sharp razor blade, make a clean cut lengthways through the ovary, style and stigma. You have made a longitudinal section. Find the ovules inside the ovary. How big are they? What colour are they? About how many are there?

Each grain is surrounded by a hard coat, so that it can survive in difficult conditions if necessary. Wallflower pollen has a smooth, sticky coat, so that it will stick to insects' bodies.

8.43 Each ovule contains a female gamete.

The female gametes are inside the ovules, in the ovary. They have been made by meiosis. Each ovule contains just one gamete.

8.44 Pollen must be carried from anther to stigma.

For fertilisation to take place, the male gametes must travel to the female gametes. The first stage of this journey is for pollen to be taken from the anther where it was made, to a stigma. This is called **pollination**.

In wallflowers, pollination is carried out by insects. Small insects, such as beetles and honey bees, come to the flowers, attracted by their colour and strong, sweet scent. The bee follows the guide-lines to the nectaries, brushing past the anthers as it goes. Some of the pollen will stick to its body.

The bee will probably then go to another wallflower, looking for more nectar. Some of the pollen it picked up at the first flower will stick onto the stigma of the second flower when the bee brushes past it. The stigma is sticky, and many pollen grains get stuck on it (Fig 8.42).

8.45 Flowers can be self- or cross-pollinated.

Sometimes, pollen is carried to the stigma of the same flower, or to another flower on the same plant. This is called **self-pollination**.

8.42 *Pollen grains on the sticky surface of a wallflower stigma*

If pollen is taken to a flower on a different plant of the same species, this is called **cross-pollination**. If pollen lands on the stigma of a different species of plant, it usually dies.

8.46 Some flowers are wind-pollinated.

In the wallflower, pollen is carried from an anther to a stigma by insects. In some flowers, it is the wind which does this.

Figure 8.43 illustrates an oat flower which is an example of a wind-pollinated flower. Table 8.3 compares insect-pollinated and wind-pollinated flowers.

8.47 Pollen tubes take male gametes to ovules.

After pollination, the male gamete inside the pollen grain on the stigma still has not reached the female gamete. The female gamete is inside the ovule, and the ovule is inside the ovary.

If it has landed on the right kind of stigma, the pollen grain begins to grow a tube. You can try growing some pollen tubes, in Practical 8.3. The pollen tube grows down through the style and the ovary, towards the ovule (Fig 8.44). It secretes enzymes to digest a pathway through the style.

The ovule is surrounded by a double layer of cells called the **integuments**. At one end, there is a small hole

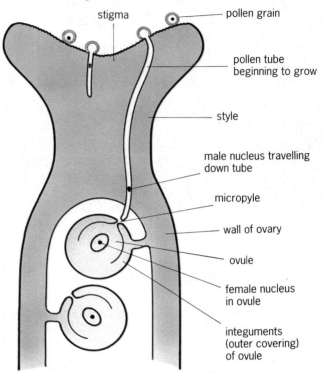

8.44 Fertilisation in a wallflower

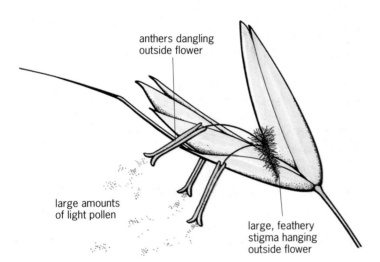

8.43 An example of a wind-pollinated flower – an oat flower

Table 8.3 A comparison between wind-pollinated and insect-pollinated flowers

Insect-pollinated, e.g. wallflower	Wind-pollinated, e.g. grass
Large, conspicuous petals, often with guide-lines	Small, inconspicuous petals, or no petals at all
Often strongly scented	No scent
Often have nectaries at base of flower	No nectaries
Anthers inside flower, where insect has to brush past them to get to nectar	Anthers dangling outside flower, where they catch the wind
Stigma inside flower, where insect has to brush past it to get to nectar	Stigma large and feathery, dangling outside flower, where pollen in the air may land on it
Sticky or spiky pollen grains, which will stick to insects	Smooth, light pollen, which can be blown in the wind
Quite large quantities of pollen made, because some will be eaten, or carried to the wrong sort of flower	Very large quantities of pollen made, because most will be blown away and lost
Flowers usually appear at warm times of year, when there are plenty of active insects	Flowers sometimes appear at colder times of year

in the integuments, called the **micropyle**. The pollen tube grows through the micropyle, into the ovule.

The male gamete travels along the pollen tube, and into the ovule. It fuses with the female gamete. Fertilisation has now taken place.

Practical 8.3 Growing pollen tubes

When a stigma is ripe, it secretes a fluid which stimulates pollen grains on it to grow tubes. The fluid contains sugar. In this experiment, you can try germinating different kinds of pollen grains in different concentrations of sugar solution.

It is best if the class is divided into groups. Each group should use sugar solution of just one concentration.

1   Collect four cavity slides. Using your finger, make a neat ring of Vaseline around the outer edge of each cavity.
2   Stick a label on each slide. Write your initials on it, and the concentration of sugar solution your group is using.
3   Fill the cavity in each slide with sugar solution.
4   Choose one flower of each kind which has pollen on its anthers. Dust pollen from one flower onto the solution on one of your slides. Gently lower a coverslip over it, without squashing the Vaseline ring. Write the name of the flower on the label.
5   Repeat step 4 with the other three flowers.
6   Place each slide in a warm incubator, and leave for at least an hour.
7   Set up a microscope. Examine each of your slides under the microscope. Look carefully for pollen tubes. Record your results in the table, and collect results from groups using other concentrations of sugar solution.

Results table

Concentration of sugar solution	distilled water	0.1 mol dm⁻³ solution	0.5 mol dm⁻³ solution	1 mol dm⁻³ solution	etc
Flower A					
Flower B					
Flower C					
Flower D					

Questions

1   Why was a ring of Vaseline put around the cavity in each slide?
2   In which solution did each of the four types of pollen germinate best?
3   Can you suggest why pollen dies if it lands on an unripe stigma, or a stigma of the wrong sort of flower?
4   Why do pollen grains grow tubes?

One pollen grain can only fertilise one ovule. If there are many ovules in the ovary, then many pollen grains will be needed to fertilise them all.

8.48 Fertilised ovules become seeds.

Once the ovules have been fertilised, many of the parts of the flower are not needed any more. The sepals, petals and stamens have all done their job. They wither, and fall off.

Inside the ovary, the ovules start to grow. Each ovule now contains a zygote, which was formed at fertilisation. The zygote divides by mitosis to form an embryo plant. The structure of the embryo is shown in Fig 8.47.

The ovule is now called a **seed**. The integuments of the ovule become hard and dry, to form the testa of the seed. Water is withdrawn from the seed, so that it becomes dormant (Section 8.52).

The ovary also grows. It is now called a **fruit**. The wall of the fruit is called the **pericarp**.

Questions

1   What is the function of a flower?
2   In which part of a flower are male gametes made?
3   In which part of a flower are female gametes made?
4   What is pollination?
5   Why do wind-pollinated flowers usually produce more pollen than insect-pollinated ones?
6   After pollination, how does the male gamete reach the ovule?
7   What is a micropyle?
8   What happens to each of the following once a flower's female gametes have been fertilised?
    (a) petals
    (b) stamens
    (c) zygote
    (d) ovule
    (e) integuments of the ovules
    (f) ovary

8.49 Fruits protect and disperse seeds.

The function of the fruit is to protect the seeds inside it until they are ripe, and then to help disperse the seeds. In the wallflower, the fruit is hard and dry. When the seeds are ripe, the fruit splits open. The seeds are very small and light, and can be carried a short distance on the wind (Fig 8.45).

Dispersal of seeds is important, because it prevents too many plants growing close together. If this happens, they compete for light, water and nutrients, so that none of them can grow properly. Dispersal also allows the plant to colonise new areas.

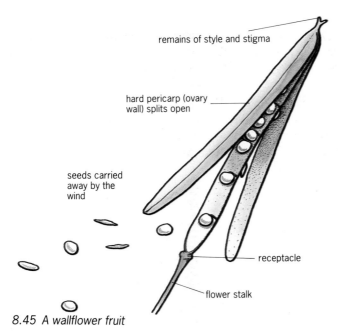

remains of style and stigma

hard pericarp (ovary wall) splits open

seeds carried away by the wind

receptacle

flower stalk

8.45 A wallflower fruit

8.50 Fruits are ovaries after fertilisation.

Plants have an enormous variety of fruits, all adapted to disperse their seeds as effectively as possible.

It is important to remember that, in biology, the word 'fruit' has a very particular meaning. Most people use the word to mean any sweet part of a plant which you can eat. Some of these are not real fruits at all. Rhubarb, for example, is really a leaf stalk, or petiole.

The biological definition of a fruit is an ovary after fertilisation, containing seeds. Blackberries, plums and oranges are true fruits, but so also are tomatoes, cucumbers and pea pods! You can tell a fruit because (a) it contains one or more seeds, and (b) it has two scars – one where it was attached to the plant, and one where the style and stigma were attached to it.

Sometimes, it is not easy to tell a fruit from a seed. A seed, though, only has one scar, called the **hilum**, where it was joined onto the fruit.

Animal dispersal – tomato

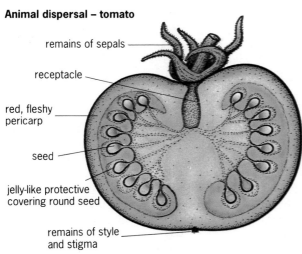

remains of sepals

receptacle

red, fleshy pericarp

seed

jelly-like protective covering round seed

remains of style and stigma

the tough testas and coat of jelly around the seeds allow them to pass unharmed through an animal's digestive system

Animal dispersal – goosegrass

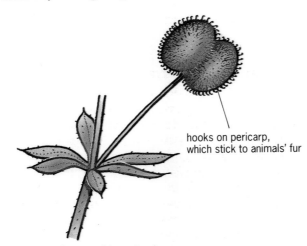

hooks on pericarp, which stick to animals' fur

8.46a Fruits dispersed by animals

Self dispersal – broom

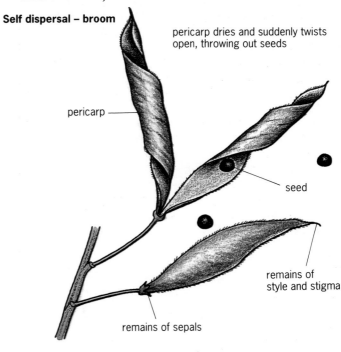

pericarp dries and suddenly twists open, throwing out seeds

pericarp

seed

remains of style and stigma

remains of sepals

Wind dispersal – sycamore

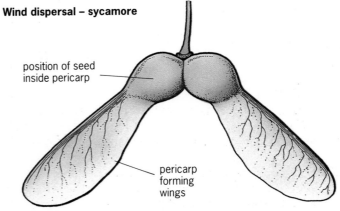

position of seed inside pericarp

pericarp forming wings

8.46b Fruits dispersed through the air

125

1 Give two functions of a fruit.
2 List three different ways in which seeds may be dispersed, giving one example for each.
3 Give two differences between fruits and seeds.
4 Which of the following are fruits, and which are not?
(a) blackberry (b) tomato (c) potato (d) cabbage
(e) pear (f) bean pod (g) rhubarb (h) cucumber

8.51 The structure of a seed.

Figure 8.47 shows the structure of a French bean seed. The seed has developed from a fertilised ovule.

A seed contains an embryo plant. The embryo consists of a **radicle**, which will grow into a root, and a **plumule**, which will grow into a shoot.

There is also food for the embryo. In a French bean seed, the food is stored in two cream-coloured cotyle-

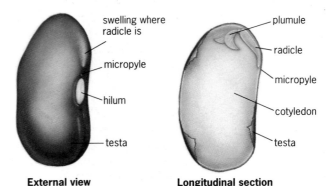

External view   **Longitudinal section**

8.47 *Structure of a French bean seed*

Practical 8.4 To find the conditions necessary for the germination of mustard seeds

1 Set up five tubes as shown in Fig 8.48.
2 Put tubes A, D and E in a warm place in the laboratory, in the light.

3 Put tube B in a refrigerator.
4 Put tube C in a warm, dark cupboard.
5 Fill in the results table to show what conditions the seeds in each tube have. The first line has been done for you.
6 Leave all the tubes for several days, then examine them to see if the seeds have germinated or not.

Results   Tube

	A	B	C	D	E
Water					
Warmth					
Oxygen					
Light					
Did seeds germinate?					

Questions

1 What three conditions do mustard seeds need for germination?
2 Read Sections 8.52 and 8.53, and then explain why each of these conditions is needed for successful germination.

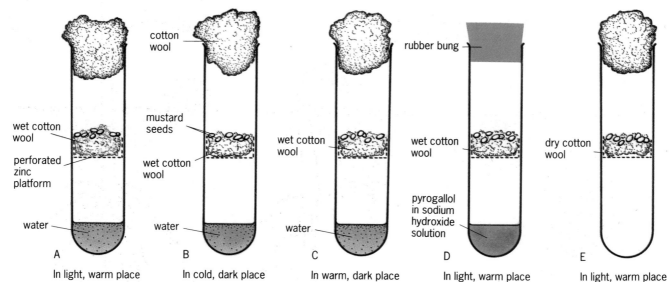

A	B	C	D	E
In light, warm place	In cold, dark place	In warm, dark place	In light, warm place	In light, warm place

8.48 *Experiment to find the conditions necessary for the germination of mustard seeds*

dons. These contain starch and protein. The cotyledons also contain enzymes.

Surrounding the cotyledons is a tough, protective covering called the **testa.** The testa stops the embryo from being damaged and it prevents bacteria and fungi from entering the seed.

The testa has a tiny hole in it called the **micropyle.** Near the micropyle is a scar, the **hilum**, where the seed was joined onto the pod.

8.52 Uptake of water begins seed germination.

A seed contains hardly any water. When it was formed on the plant, the water in it was drawn out, so that it became dehydrated. Without water, almost no metabolic reactions can go on inside it. The seed is inactive or **dormant.** This is very useful, because it means that the seed can survive harsh conditions, such as cold or drought, which would kill a growing plant.

A seed must have certain conditions before it will begin to germinate. You can find out what they are if you do Practical 8.4.

When a seed germinates, it first takes up water through the micropyle. As the water goes into the cotyledons, they swell. Eventually, they burst the testa (Fig 8.49).

Once there is sufficient water, the enzymes in the cotyledons become active. Amylase begins to break down the stored starch molecules to maltose. Proteases break down the protein molecules to amino acids.

Maltose and amino acids are soluble, so they dissolve in the water. They diffuse to the embryo plant, which uses these foods for growth. The way in which the embryo plant grows is shown in Fig 8.49.

8.53 During germination, enzymes digest food stores.

When a seed first begins to germinate, it increases in weight. This is because it absorbs water from the soil.

As soon as it begins to grow, it starts to use its food stores. The stored protein is broken down to amino acids, which are used to make new protein molecules for cell membranes and cytoplasm. The stored starch is broken down to maltose and then to glucose. Some of the glucose will be made into cellulose, to make cell walls for the new cells.

All this requires energy. The seed, like all living organisms, gets its energy by breaking down glucose, in respiration. Quite a lot of the glucose from the stored starch will be used up in respiration, so the seed loses weight.

After a few days, the plumule of the seed grows above the surface of the ground. The first leaves open out and begin to photosynthesise. The plant can now make its own food faster than it is using it up. It begins to increase in weight.

Figure 8.50 summarises the changes in weight of an annual plant, such as a French bean, from germination until death. An annual plant is one which lives for less than one year.

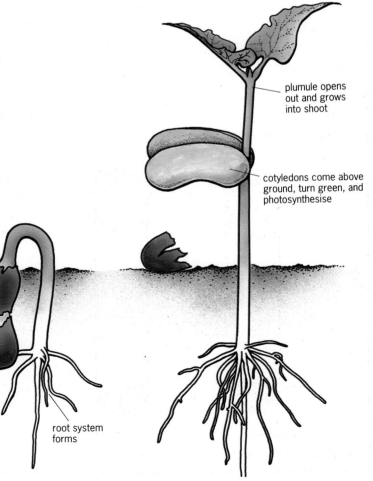

plumule opens out and grows into shoot

cotyledons come above ground, turn green, and photosynthesise

radicle emerges from testa

lateral roots begin to grow

testa falls off

root system forms

8.49 Stages in germination of a French bean seed

127

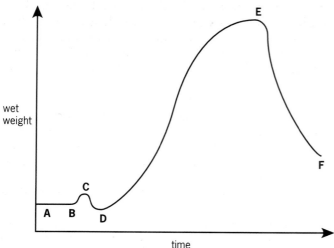

A to B: seed is dormant
B to C: germination begins, and seed increases in weight as it absorbs water
C to D: seed loses weight, as it uses up food stores to provide energy for growth
D to E: plant is photosynthesising, building up new cells
E to F: plant loses weight quickly, as it flowers and produces seeds and fruits, which are dispersed; plant gradually dies

8.50 Growth curve for an annual plant

Questions
1 What do the cotyledons of a French bean seed contain?
2 What does dormant mean?
3 What is the advantage of dormancy?
4 What activates the enzymes in the cotyledons?
5 What do the enzymes do?

A comparison of various methods of sexual reproduction

This chapter has described sexual reproduction in an insect, a fish, an amphibian, a bird, a mammal and a flowering plant. Basically, their methods of reproduction are the same. First, gametes are made by meiosis, then fertilisation takes place. A zygote is formed, which grows into a new organism.

There are, however, some important differences in the details of reproduction in these organisms. What are they, and what are the reasons for them?

8.54 Terrestrial organisms use internal fertilisation.

Male gametes need water to swim through to get to the female gametes. If an organism lives in water, then it can use **external fertilisation**, releasing male gametes into the water near the female. Most fish and amphibians do this.

A terrestrial organism, though, cannot use external fertilisation. The male gametes must be provided with a liquid to swim in, and not allowed to dry out. This is why insects, birds and mammals use **internal fertilisation**. Liquid is provided by the male, with the gametes, and also by the female, inside her body.

Flowering plants have a different solution to this problem. They cannot move around, so the animal type of internal fertilisation is not possible. Instead, the male gamete is enclosed in a tough, waterproof case, forming a pollen grain. Insects or the wind carry the pollen grain to a stigma, where the male gamete can travel along a pollen tube which grows towards the ovule.

8.55 Many gametes are lost in external fertilisation.

All organisms produce more male gametes than female ones. Female gametes are larger and more 'expensive' to make, so fewer are made. Many more male gametes are needed, because many will be lost on their way to the female gametes.

Animals with external fertilisation waste more gametes than animals with internal fertilisation. Fish and frogs therefore produce more gametes than birds or mammals.

Even after fertilisation, not all the embryos will survive. Organisms which do not look after their offspring, such as herrings and frogs, must produce a large number of eggs to make up for ones which are eaten by predators. Birds and mammals care for their eggs and young, so fewer eggs need be produced. The embryo of a flowering plant is protected inside the seed and fruit. Extra seeds, though, are needed, to allow for ones which will land in places unsuitable for growth, or which are eaten by animals.

8.56 Birds' eggs are large to store food.

Female gametes are larger than male ones, because they contain food stores for the embryo. In animal eggs, this is the yolk. Fish and frog eggs have a fairly large yolk, to supply the embryo for several days. Birds' eggs have a very large yolk, to supply the embryo for several weeks before it hatches. Human eggs only have a tiny amount. This is used to feed the embryo only until it arrives at the uterus wall and implants.

The ovules of a flowering plant contain very little stored food, because the ovule is still attached to the parent plant and can get its food from it. Once the ovule is fertilised, it is supplied with food from the parent, to build up food stores.

Sexual and asexual reproduction

8.57 Sexual reproduction produces variation.

This chapter has described several methods of asexual reproduction, and of sexual reproduction. There are some very important differences between them.

In asexual reproduction, some of the parent's cells divide by mitosis. This makes new cells with the same number and kind of chromosomes as the parent's cells. The new organisms are just like their parents. **Asexual reproduction does not produce variation.**

But in sexual reproduction some of the parent's cells divide by meiosis. The cells which are made are called gametes, and they have only half as many chromosomes as the parent cell. When two sets of chromosomes in two gametes combine during fertilisation, a new combination of genes is produced. The new organism will be different from either of its parents. **Sexual reproduction produces variation.**

8.58 Sexual and asexual reproduction each have advantages.

Is it useful or not to have variation amongst offspring? Sometimes, it is a good thing not to have variation. If a plant, for example, is growing well in a particular place, and if there is plenty of room for it, then it is advantageous if it produces a lot more plants just like itself. The plant is well adapted to living in these conditions, and if its offspring are identical to it, then they will be well adapted, too. Also, asexual reproduction is likely to be a quicker method than sexual reproduction, because there is no need to find a mating partner.

However, if the plant is having difficulty in surviving, or if space is very limited, then sexual reproduction might be more advantageous. The seeds produced could be scattered over a wide area. The new plants which grow from them will all be slightly different from one another, and there is a good chance that some of them will be well adapted to the new conditions they find themselves in.

In general, asexual reproduction is beneficial in an unchanging environment, or when spreading out in a new area where the parent organism is well adapted to survive. Sexual reproduction is most useful in an unstable environment, where variation in the offspring might produce organisms able to survive in a variety of conditions. This helps organisms to begin to colonise new areas.

You will find more about variation, and its importance in evolution, in Chapter 16.

Table 8.4 A comparison of sexual reproduction in fish, amphibians, birds, mammals and flowering plants

	Fish (e.g. herring)	Amphibian (e.g. frog)	Bird (e.g. robin)	Mammal (e.g. human)	Flowering plant (e.g. wallflower)
Number of eggs	Large	Quite large	Small	Small	Small
Size of eggs	Quite large	Quite large	Large	Small	Quite small
Fertilisation	External	External	Internal	Internal	Internal
How embryo feeds	Yolk in egg	Yolk in egg	Yolk in egg	Yolk in egg, then by diffusion from mother's blood through placenta	From parent plant, then from cotyledons of seed
How embryo obtains water	By osmosis from sea water	By osmosis from pond water	From albumen	By osmosis from mother's blood through placenta	By osmosis from parent until seed is fully developed, but then dries. At germination, water is absorbed from soil by osmosis
How embryo obtains oxygen	By diffusion from sea water	By diffusion from pond water	By diffusion from air	By diffusion from mother's blood through placenta	By diffusion from air
Protection of embryo	By albumen	By albumen	By albumen, shell, nest and parents	By amniotic fluid and mother's body wall	By testa of seed and pericarp of fruit
Protection of young organism	None	None	By nest and parents	By parents	None

Chapter revision questions

1 Match each of these words with its definition.
Zygote, mitosis, meiosis, gamete, albumen, pollination, fertilisation, pericarp, fruit, seed
(a) a sex cell, containing only half the normal number of chromosomes
(b) an ovary after fertilisation
(c) a diploid cell, formed by the fusion of two gametes
(d) a jelly-like protein which protects the embryos of fish, amphibians and birds
(e) a type of cell division which produces daughter cells just like the parent cell
(f) a type of cell division which produces daughter cells with only half the number of chromosomes as the parent cell
(g) an ovary wall after fertilisation
(h) the transfer of pollen from an anther to a stigma
(i) an ovule after fertilisation
(j) the fusion of two gametes

2 (a) Which type of cell division is involved in (i) the production of a new organism by asexual reproduction, (ii) the production of gametes, and (iii) the growth of a zygote?
(b) With the aid of diagrams, describe one way in which a named plant naturally reproduces asexually.
(c) What advantages are there to the plant in reproducing in this way?
(d) Many plants also reproduce sexually. What are the advantages to a plant in reproducing in this way?

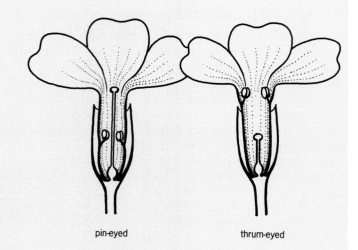

pin-eyed   thrum-eyed

3 The diagram shows two types of primrose flower. These types of flower are often found growing close together. Any one primrose plant, however, only has one type of flower.
(a) Describe the difference in the arrangement of the anthers and stigmas in the pin-eyed and thrum-eyed primrose.
(b) Primroses are pollinated by insects, which reach into the bottom of the flower to get nectar. Which part of the insect's body would pick up pollen in (i) a pin-eyed primrose, and (ii) a thrum-eyed primrose?
(c) Which part of the insect's body would touch the stigma in (i) a pin-eyed primrose, and (ii) a thrum-eyed primrose?
(d) Explain how this will help to ensure that cross-pollination takes place.
(e) Self-pollination does sometimes occur in primroses. Would you expect it to occur more often in pin-eyed or thrum-eyed flowers? Explain your answer.
(f) Why is cross-pollination usually preferable to self-pollination?

4 Use the table below to plot growth curves for (a) a human male, and (b) a human female. Plot both curves on the same axes.

(a) At which age does growth appear to stop?

Age in years	Height in cm	
	Male	Female
0	53.0	53.0
1	61.0	61.0
2	71.0	71.0
3	91.5	86.5
4	99.0	91.5
5	104.5	96.0
6	108.5	101.0
7	114.0	111.0
8	122.0	119.0
9	124.5	124.0
10	124.5	127.5
11	127.0	130.0
12	129.5	132.0
13	131.5	134.0
14	137.0	137.0
15	142.0	142.0
16	147.0	147.0
17	155.0	152.5
18	162.5	157.0
19	170.0	160.0
20	172.5	161.5
21	175.0	162.0
22	175.0	162.0
23	175.0	162.0
24	175.0	162.0

(b) At which age is the difference in height between male and female (i) least, and (ii) greatest?

(c) How much does the female grow between the ages of 9 and 17?

(d) What is the average rate of growth per year for the female between the ages of 9 and 17?

(e) Do you think that height is a good way of measuring human growth? Give reasons for your answer.

5 (a) Use the following table to plot a growth curve for a pea plant.

Time in weeks from planting of seed	Dry weight in g
0	1.4
0.5	0.8
1	1.6
1.5	2.5
2	5.2
3	21.5
4	31.6
5	41.3
6	49.0
7	53.2
8	61.1
9	63.4
10	66.5
11	65.2
12	67.4
13	66.5
14	66.4
15	67.2
16	66.0
17	53.2

(b) Explain exactly how these results would have been obtained.

(c) Explain the reasons for the shape of the curve.

9 Sensitivity and coordination

9.1 Organisms detect changes around them.

All living organisms are sensitive to their environment. This means that they can detect changes in their environment. The changes they detect are called **stimuli**.

The parts of the organism's body that detect stimuli are called **receptors**. In animals, the receptors are often part of a **sense organ**. For example, your eye is a sense organ and the rod and cone cells in the retina of your eye are receptors. They are sensitive to light.

Touch and taste

9.2 Skin contains receptive nerve endings.

One of the functions of skin is to pick up various kinds of information about your environment. If you look at Fig 10.3 you will see that there are several sorts of nerve endings in the dermis. These nerve endings are receptors for touch, heat, cold, pressure and pain.

If you do Practical 9.1, you can find out which parts of your skin contain the most touch receptors.

Practical 9.1 To find which part of the skin contains the most touch receptors

This experiment tests the skin on the back of the hand, the palm of the hand, and the forehead. You could try different parts of the body if you like.

Results table	Distance apart of pins			
	2 cm	1 cm	0.5 cm	0.2 cm
back of hand				
palm of hand				
forehead				

1 Copy out the results table, ready to fill in your results.
2 Set your two pins at exactly 2 cm apart. Keep checking that the points stay 2 cm apart all the time you use them.
3 Ask your partner to close his or her eyes. Touch your partner gently on the back of the hand with either one or two pins. Ask your partner to tell you how many pins are touching the hand. Put a tick in the first space in your table if your partner is right, and a cross if your partner is wrong.
4 Repeat this nine more times. You should now have ten ticks or crosses in the first space in the table.
5 Now repeat steps 3 and 4, still keeping the pins exactly 2 cm apart, but this time touching the skin on the palm of the hand.
6 Repeat on the forehead.
7 Now adjust the pins to 1 cm apart. Test the back of the hand, the palm of the hand and the forehead as before.

8 Adjust the pins to 0.5 cm apart, and test as before.
9 If there is time, test again with the pins 0.2 cm apart.
10 Use your results to draw a histogram. Fig 9.1 shows how you can do this.

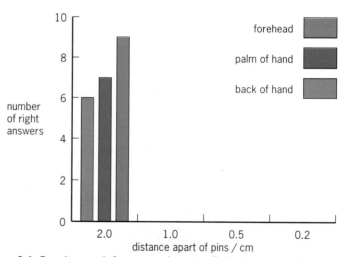

9.1 Results graph from experiment to find which part of the skin contains the most touch receptors

Questions

1 Why does it get more difficult to tell how many pins are touching your skin, as the pins get closer together?
2 Which of the three parts of the body you tested had the most touch receptors?
3 Why do you think this part of the body needs to be so sensitive?

9.3 Some receptors detect chemicals.

The nose and tongue both contain receptors which respond to chemical stimuli. They are sensitive to chemicals in the air, or in food.

On the tongue, these receptor cells are in small groups, called **taste buds** (Fig 9.2). The taste buds do not all respond to the same kinds of chemical. Try Practical 9.2, to find out which parts of your tongue can taste which kinds of flavour.

Fact!

The animal with the most acute sense of smell is the male Emperor moth. Using its antennae, it can detect a female Emperor moth 11 km upwind.

The biggest mammalian tongue that has ever been weighed belonged to a Blue whale caught by Russian trawlers in 1947. Its tongue weighed 4.3 tonnes.

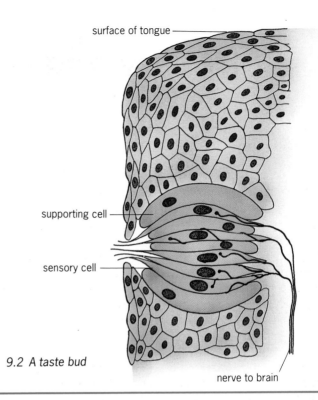

9.2 A taste bud

Practical 9.2 To find out which parts of the tongue can taste which flavours

The four tastes you are going to test are sweet, sour, bitter and salty.

1. Copy out the results table, ready to fill in your results.
2. Arrange a communications system between yourself and your partner, so that he or she can tell you which flavour can be tasted without moving the tongue.
3. Put a cotton wool stick into each of the four kinds of solution. Each piece of cotton wool must be put back into its own solution as soon as you finish using it.
4. Ask your partner to shut his or her eyes, and put out his or her tongue. Choose one piece of cotton wool, and touch it onto one of the areas of the tongue shown in Fig 9.3. *Do not* let your partner put his or her tongue back into the mouth yet.

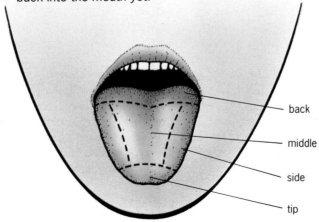

9.3 Testing the sensitivity of the tongue

5. Ask your partner to indicate what flavour has been put on their tongue. Your partner can now put his or her tongue back into his or her mouth and moisten it ready for the next test. Fill in the result in the appropriate space in the table, with a tick or a cross.
6. Repeat with each flavour on each part of the tongue, in a random order. If there is time, do each test twice.

Results table

Flavour	Part of tongue			
	front	centre	sides	back
sweet				
sour				
bitter				
salty				

Questions

1. Why must your partner not be allowed to put his or her tongue into his or her mouth before telling you what flavour they can taste?
2. Why is it best to do the tests in a random order?
3. Copy the drawing of the tongue, and show on it which parts of the tongue are most sensitive to sweet, sour, bitter and salty tastes.

133

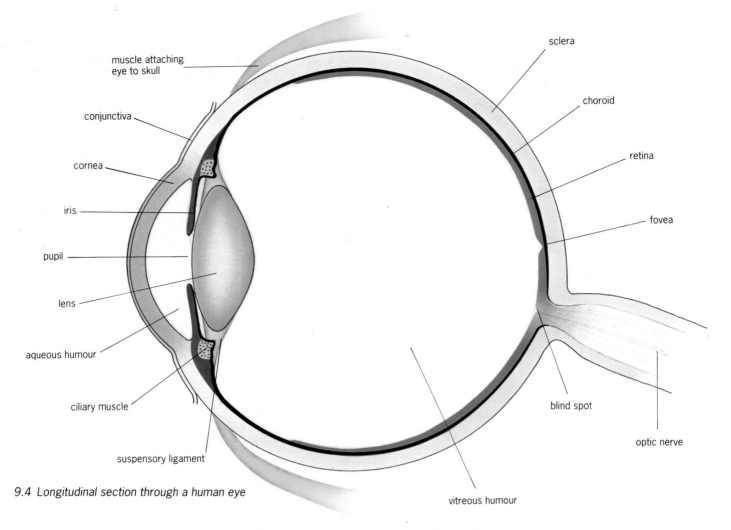

muscle attaching eye to skull

conjunctiva

cornea

iris

pupil

lens

aqueous humour

ciliary muscle

suspensory ligament

sclera

choroid

retina

fovea

blind spot

optic nerve

vitreous humour

9.4 Longitudinal section through a human eye

The eye

9.4 The eye is well protected.

The part of the eye which contains the receptor cells is the **retina** (Fig 9.4). This is the part which is actually sensitive to light. The rest of the eye simply helps to protect the retina, or to focus light onto it.

Each eye is set in a bony socket in the skull, called the **orbit**. Only the very front of the eye is not surrounded by bone.

The front of the eye is covered by a thin, transparent membrane called the **conjunctiva**, which helps to protect the parts behind it. The conjunctiva is always kept moist by a fluid made in the **tear glands**. This fluid contains an enzyme called **lysozyme**, which can kill bacteria.

The fluid is washed across your eye by your eyelids when you blink. The eyelids, eyebrows and eyelashes also help to stop dirt from landing on the surface of your eyes.

Even the part of the eye inside the orbit is protected. There is a very tough coat surrounding it called the **sclera**.

9.5 Cells in the retina are receptive to light.

The retina is at the back of the eye. It contains two sorts of receptor cell. **Rods** are sensitive to quite dim light, but only let you see in black and white. **Cones** give colour vision, but only in bright light.

When light falls on a receptor cell in the retina, the cell sends a message along the **optic nerve** to the brain. The brain sorts out all the messages from each receptor cell, and builds up an **image**.

The closer together the receptor cells are, the clearer the image the brain will get. The part of the retina where the receptor cells are packed most closely together is called the **fovea**. This is the part of the retina where light is focused when you look straight at an object. All the receptor cells in the fovea are cones. The rods are scattered further out on the retina.

There are no receptor cells where the optic nerve leaves the retina. This part is called the **blind spot**. If light falls on this place, no messages will be sent to the brain.

Behind the retina is a black layer called the **choroid**. The choroid absorbs all the light after it has been through the retina, so it does not get scattered around the inside of the eye.

Practical 9.3 Looking at human eyes

It is best to perform this experiment with a partner, although it is possible to use a mirror and look at your own eyes.

1. First identify all the following structures: eyebrows; eyelashes; eyelids; conjunctiva; pupil; iris; cornea; sclera; small blood vessels; openings to tear ducts. Fig 9.4 will help you to do this.

2. Copy the diagram below, and label each of these structures on it.

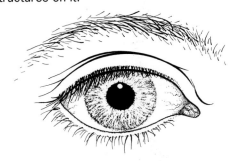

3. Use Sections 9.4 to 9.8 to find out the functions of each structure you have labelled. Write down these functions, as briefly as you can, next to each label or beneath your diagram.

4. Ask your partner to close their eyes, and cover them with something dark to cut out as much light as possible. (Alternatively, you may be able to darken the whole room.) After about 3 or 4 minutes, quickly remove the cover (or switch on the lights) and look at your partner's eyes as they adapt to the light. What happens? What is the purpose of this change?

5. Read Section 9.8, and then explain how this change is brought about.

9.6 How the eye focuses light.

For the brain to see a clear image, there must be a clear image focused on the retina. Light rays must be bent, or **refracted**, so that they focus exactly onto the retina.

The **cornea** is responsible for most of the bending of the light. The **lens** makes fine adjustments.

Figure 9.5 shows how these two parts of the eye focus light onto the retina.

The image on the retina is upside down. The brain interprets this so that you see it the right way up.

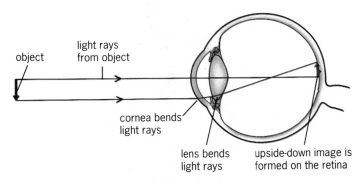

object
light rays from object
cornea bends light rays
lens bends light rays
upside-down image is formed on the retina

9.5 How an image is focused onto the retina

9.7 The lens adjusts the focusing.

Not all light rays need bending the same amount to focus them onto the retina. Light rays coming from a nearby object are going away from one another, or diverging. They will need to be bent inwards quite strongly.

Light rays coming from an object in the distance will be almost parallel to one another. They will not need bending so much.

The shape of the lens can be adjusted to bend light rays more. The fatter it is, the more it will bend them. The thinner it is, the less it will bend them. The adjustment in the shape of the lens, to focus light coming from different distances, is called **accommodation**.

Figures 9.6 and 9.7 show how the shape of the lens is changed. It is held in position by a ring of **suspensory ligaments**. The tension on the suspensory ligaments,

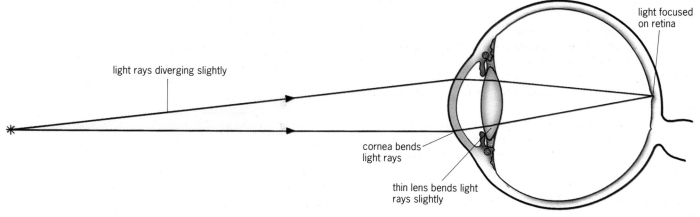

light rays diverging slightly
light focused on retina
cornea bends light rays
thin lens bends light rays slightly

9.6 Focusing on a distant object

135

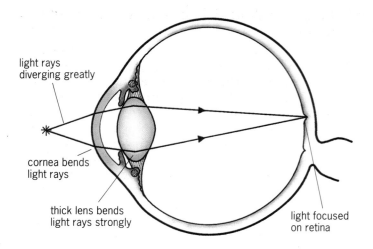

light rays diverging greatly

cornea bends light rays

thick lens bends light rays strongly

light focused on retina

9.7 Focusing on a nearby object

Distant object

ciliary muscles relax

suspensory ligaments pulled tight

lens pulled thin

Side view

Front view

Nearby object

ciliary muscles contract

suspensory ligaments slackened

lens allowed to bulge

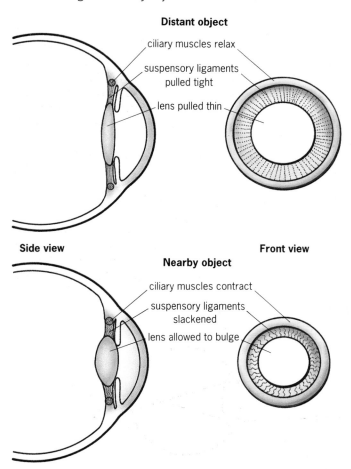

9.8 How the shape of the lens is changed

and thus the shape of the lens, is altered by means of the **ciliary muscle**. When it contracts, the suspensory ligaments are loosened. When it relaxes, they are pulled tight (Fig 9.8). When the suspensory ligaments are tight, the lens is pulled thin. When they are loosened, the lens get fatter.

Practical 9.4 Dissecting a sheep's eye

1 Carefully examine the eye. Using forceps and a scalpel (ask to be shown how to use them correctly), remove as much of the white **fat** as you can. Be careful, though, not to damage the brownish coloured **muscles** attached to the outside of the eye, or the white **optic nerve** which comes out at the back of it.

2 Draw the eye, and label: conjunctiva and cornea; iris; sclera; fat; eye muscles; optic nerve; pupil.

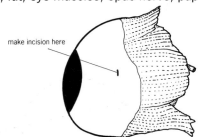

make incision here

3 Using sharp scissors, make a small incision into the eye as shown. What comes out? What happens to the shape of the eye? So what is one of the functions of this substance?

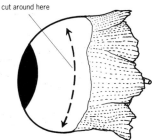

cut around here

4 Continue cutting around the eye until you have cut it completely in half.

5 First, look at the back half. The **retina** may have detached itself from here, and may have floated away in the fluid. The next layer in is the black **choroid**. Is it still there? What is the function of the choroid?

6 Behind the choroid is the **sclera**. What is it like? What is its function?

7 Now investigate the front half of the eye. The **lens** will probably be floating loose. What normally holds the lens in position? What does the lens look like? If the lens is not too cloudy, put it over some writing and look through it. What does it do?

8 Try to find other structures at the front of the eye, for example the **iris**. Identify and describe any structures you can find.

9.8 The iris adjusts how much light enters the eye.

In front of the lens is a circular piece of tissue called the **iris**. The iris contains pigments, which absorb light and stop it getting through to the retina.

In the middle of the iris is a gap, called the **pupil**. The size of the pupil can be adjusted. The wider the pupil is, the more light can get through to the retina. In strong light, the iris closes in, and makes the pupil small. This stops too much light getting in and damaging the retina.

To allow it to adjust the size of the pupil, the iris contains muscles. **Circular muscles** lie in circles around the pupil. When they contract, they make the pupil constrict, or get smaller. **Radial muscles** run outwards from the edge of the pupil. When they contract, they make the pupil dilate, or get larger.

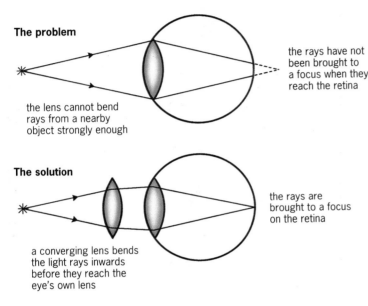

The problem

the rays have not been brought to a focus when they reach the retina

the lens cannot bend rays from a nearby object strongly enough

The solution

the rays are brought to a focus on the retina

a converging lens bends the light rays inwards before they reach the eye's own lens

9.9 Long sight

9.9 Long and short sight can be corrected with glasses.

Eyes do not always work perfectly. There are many different kinds of problem that people may have with their eyes, most of which are not serious. Two of the commonest problems are long sight and short sight.

Long-sighted people can see objects in the distance very clearly, but cannot focus on objects close to their eyes. So long-sighted people need to wear glasses for reading. The usual reason for this is that the eyeball is shorter than normal, so that even when the lens is at its fattest, it cannot bend diverging light rays sharply enough to focus them onto the retina (Fig 9.9).

Long sight can easily be corrected by wearing glasses or contact lenses with **converging lenses**. The lenses bend the light rays inwards, doing some of the work for the eye's own lens.

Short-sighted people have the opposite problem; their eyes can easily focus on nearby objects, but cannot see things in the distance. Short-sighted people need to wear glasses for seeing the blackboard or driving, but can read without glasses. In this case the cause is usually a long eyeball, so that the light from distant objects comes to a focus before it reaches the retina (Fig 9.10). It is as though the lens is too 'strong' for the eye.

Short sight is corrected by wearing **diverging lenses**. These bend the light outwards, before it reaches the eye's own lens.

Even if people have had good sight all their lives, they often need to wear glasses when they are older. This is because the lens gets stiffer, so that it cannot be pulled into different shapes to focus on objects at different distances. It often gets fixed into a shape which is good for focusing on distant objects, so many older people need to wear glasses for reading. This problem is called **old sight**.

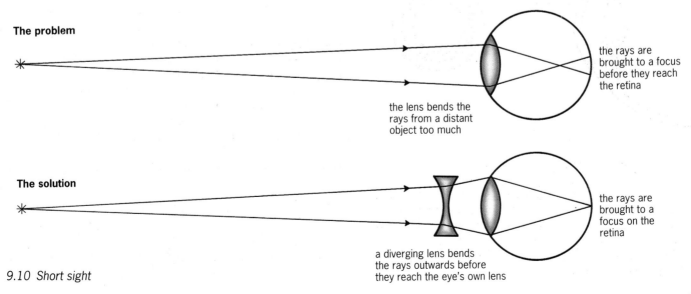

The problem

the rays are brought to a focus before they reach the retina

the lens bends the rays from a distant object too much

The solution

the rays are brought to a focus on the retina

a diverging lens bends the rays outwards before they reach the eye's own lens

9.10 Short sight

Questions

1 What is a stimulus?
2 Name two parts of the body which contain receptors of chemical stimuli.
3 Which part of the eye contains cells which are sensitive to light?
4 Your brain can build up a very clear image when light is focused onto the fovea. Explain why it can do this.
5 If you look straight at an object when it is nearly dark, you may find it difficult to see it. It is easier to see if you look just to one side of it. Explain why this is.
6 What is the choroid, and what is its function?
7 List, in order, the parts of the eye through which light passes to reach the retina.
8 Name two parts of the eye which refract light rays.
9 What is meant by accommodation?
10 (a) What do the ciliary muscles do when you are focusing on a nearby object?
(b) What effect does this have on (i) the suspensory ligaments, and (ii) the lens?

The ear

9.10 The structure of the ear.

The ear has two functions. Firstly, it is sensitive to sound. It also contains receptor cells which are sensitive to the position and movement of your head. These cells help with balance.

Figure 9.11 illustrates the structure of the human ear. The outer ear and middle ear both contain air. The inner ear though, is filled with two sorts of fluid, **perilymph** ('peri' means round the outside) and **endolymph** ('endo' means inside).

9.11 Hearing.

The cells which are sensitive to sound waves are inside the **cochlea**. Sound waves need to be made stronger, or amplified, before these cells will respond to them.

Firstly, the sound waves make the air in the outer ear vibrate. This makes the eardrum vibrate. Touching the eardrum is a tiny bone or ossicle, called the hammer or **malleus**. As the eardrum vibrates, the malleus vibrates too. The vibrations pass along the chain of ossicles. The malleus vibrates on the anvil or **incus**, and the incus vibrates on the stirrup or **stapes**.

The stapes lies against a membrane over the **oval window**. The oval window transmits the vibrations to the perilymph.

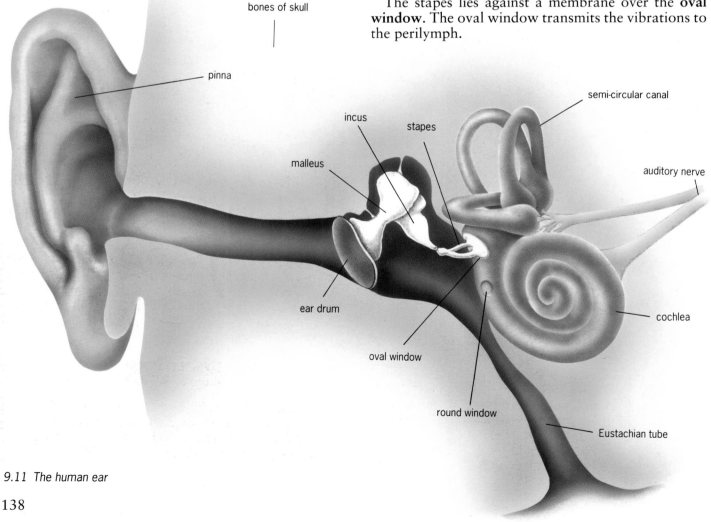

bones of skull
pinna
incus
stapes
malleus
semi-circular canal
auditory nerve
ear drum
oval window
cochlea
round window
Eustachian tube

9.11 The human ear

138

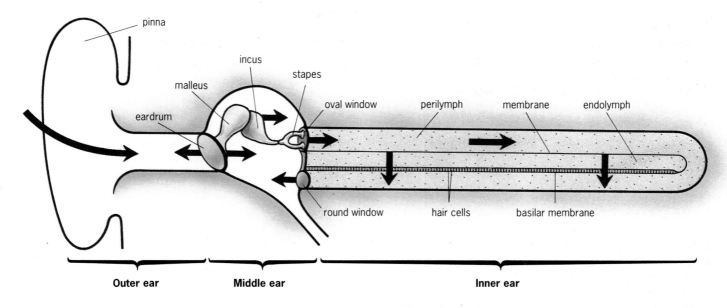

9.12 Diagrammatic section through the ear, with the cochlea unwound

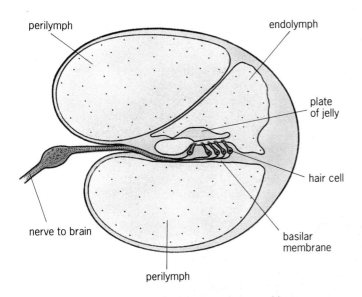

9.13 Transverse section through part of the cochlea

This chain of events helps to amplify the size of the vibrations. The vibrations in the perilymph are then passed into the cochlea. Fig 9.12 shows how the inside of the cochlea would look if it was uncoiled. Fig 9.13 shows a cross-section of the cochlea. As the perilymph vibrates, it makes the membrane in the cochlea move up and down. On the basilar membrane are **hair cells**. The hairs are embedded in a plate of jelly. As they move up and down, the hairs are pulled and pushed against the jelly plate. This makes the hair cells send messages along the auditory nerve to the brain.

The hair cells in different parts of the cochlea respond to different frequencies of vibration. The ones nearest to the oval window respond to high frequen-cies (high pitched sounds). Low frequency sounds are picked up by the cells nearest the middle of the coil.

9.12 Balance.

The three **semi-circular canals** are sensitive to movements of the head. They are filled with endolymph. Each semi-circular canal has a swelling near one end of it, called an **ampulla**.

Figure 9.14 shows part of the inside of an ampulla. Like the cochlea, it contains hair cells with their hairs embedded in a plate of jelly. The jelly is called the **cupula**. When you move your head, the cupula moves in the endolymph. It pulls on the hairs, so the hair cells send messages along a nerve to the brain.

Each ear has three semi-circular canals, all at right angles to one another. By comparing the messages from each one, your brain can tell exactly how your head is moving, and so enable you to keep your balance. Usually, messages from your eyes help with this as well. If the messages from your eyes and ears do not match, such as when you are reading a book while travelling in a car, then you may feel sick.

Fact!

High-pitched sounds are rapid vibrations of the molecules in air. Humans can hear sounds which vibrate at about 19 kHz. Some bats can hear ultrasonic sounds up to about 160 kHz.

139

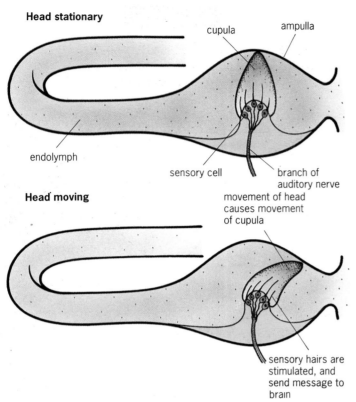

Head stationary

cupula
ampulla
endolymph
sensory cell
branch of auditory nerve

Head moving

movement of head causes movement of cupula

sensory hairs are stimulated, and send message to brain

9.14 Section through part of a semi-circular canal

9.13 The Eustachian tube prevents eardrum damage.

Both the outer and the middle ear are filled with air. They are separated by the eardrum. If there is a big difference in the air pressure on the two sides of the eardrum, it may burst.

To stop this happening, there is a tube leading from the middle ear to the back of the throat. It is called the **Eustachian tube.** Usually, it is kept closed by a sphincter muscle at the bottom. But when you swallow, it opens, so that air taken into your mouth can enter the Eustachian tube. This allows the air pressure in the middle ear to equalise with the air pressure outside.

Questions

1 In which part of the ear are the cells which are sensitive to sound?
2 Explain how sound brings about a response by these cells.
3 Which part of the ear helps with balance?
4 Name one other sense organ which helps with balance.
5 Where is the Eustachian tube?
6 As an aeroplane takes off, the air pressure inside it drops. Your ears will feel less uncomfortable if you suck a sweet. Explain why this is.

Coordination and response

9.14 Effectors respond when the body is stimulated.

Being able to detect stimuli is not much use to an organism unless it can respond to them in some useful way. The part of the body which responds to a stimulus is called an **effector.**

Muscles are effectors. For example, if you touch something hot, the muscles in your arm contract, so that your hand is quickly pulled away. Glands can also be effectors. If you smell food cooking, your salivary glands may react by secreting saliva.

To make sure that the right effectors respond at the right time, there needs to be some kind of communication system between receptors and effectors. The pain receptors on your fingertips need to send a message to your arm muscles to tell them to contract. The chemical receptors in your nose must communicate with your salivary glands, to make them secrete saliva. The way in which receptors pick up stimuli, and then pass messages on to effectors, is called **coordination.**

9.15 Hormones and nerves allow communication.

Animals need fast and efficient communication systems between their receptors and effectors. This is partly because most animals move in search of food. Many animals need to be able to respond very quickly to catch their food, or to avoid predators.

Most animals have two methods of sending messages from receptors to effectors. The fastest is by means of **nerves.** The receptors and nerves make up the animal's **nervous system.** A slower method, but still a very important one, is by means of chemicals called **hormones.** Hormones are part of the **endocrine system.**

Nervous systems

9.16 Neurones carry nerve impulses.

Nervous systems are made of special cells called **neurones.** Fig 9.15 illustrates a neurone from a mammal's body.

Neurones contain the same basic parts as any animal cell. Each has a nucleus, cytoplasm, and a cell membrane. But their structure is specially adapted to be able to carry messages very quickly.

To enable them to do this, they have long, thin fibres of cytoplasm stretching out from the cell body. They are called **nerve fibres.** The longest fibre is usually called an **axon.** Axons can be more than a metre long. The shorter fibres are called **dendrons** or **dendrites.**

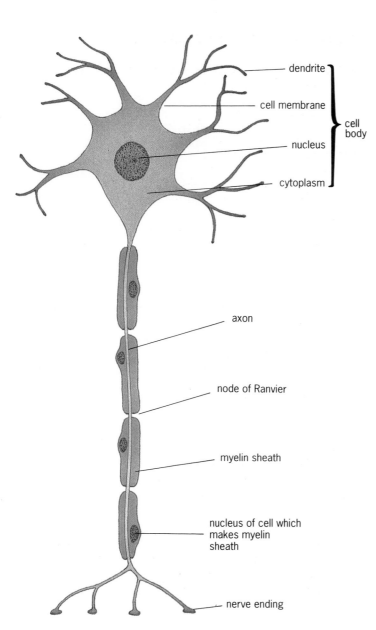

9.15 A neurone

Labels: dendrite, cell membrane, nucleus, cytoplasm, cell body, axon, node of Ranvier, myelin sheath, nucleus of cell which makes myelin sheath, nerve ending

nated nerve fibre in a cat's body can carry impulses at up to 100 metres per second. A fibre without myelin can only carry impulses at about 5 metres per second.

9.18 Most animals have a central nervous system.

The **brain** and **spinal cord** make up the **central nervous system**, or **CNS** (Fig 9.17). Like the rest of the nervous system, the CNS is made up of neurones. Its job is to coordinate the messages travelling through the nervous system.

When a receptor detects a stimulus, it sends a message to the brain or spinal cord. The brain or spinal cord receives the message, and 'decides' which effectors need to react to the stimulus. It then sends the message on, along the appropriate nerve fibres, to the appropriate effector.

9.19 Reflex arcs allow rapid response.

Figure 9.18 shows how these messages are sent. If your hand touches a hot plate, a message is picked up by a

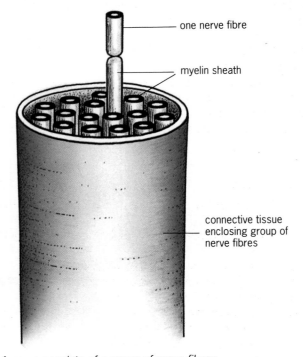

Labels: one nerve fibre, myelin sheath, connective tissue enclosing group of nerve fibres

9.16 A nerve consists of a group of nerve fibres

The dendrites pick up messages from other neurones lying nearby. They pass the message to the cell body, and then along the axon. The axon might then pass it on to another neurone.

9.17 Myelinated neurones carry impulses quickly.

Some of the nerve fibres of active animals like mammals are wrapped in a layer of fat and protein called **myelin**. Every now and then, there are narrow gaps in the myelin sheath.

The messages that neurones transmit are in the form of electrical impulses. Myelin insulates the nerve fibres, so that they can carry impulses much faster. A myeli-

141

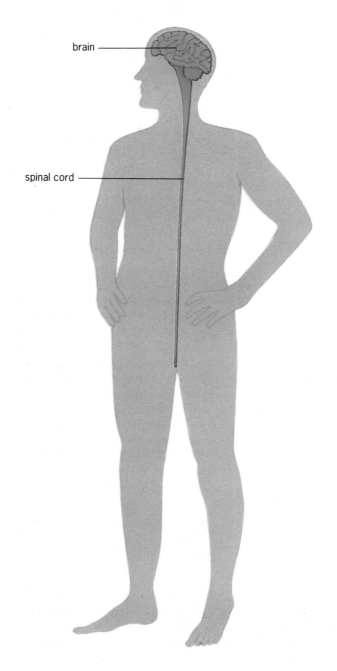

brain

spinal cord

9.17 The human central nervous system

In this case, the effectors are the muscles in your arm. The message travels to the muscle along the axon of a **motor neurone**. The muscle then contracts, so that your hand is pulled away.

This sort of reaction is called a **reflex action**. You do not need to think about it. Your brain is made aware of it, but you only consciously realise what is happening after the message has been sent on to your muscles.

Reflex actions are very useful, because the message gets from the receptor to the effector as quickly as possible. You do not waste time in thinking about what to do.

The arrangement of sensory neurone, relay neurones and motor neurone is called a **reflex arc**.

Practical 9.5 Measuring reaction time

The time taken for a message to travel from a receptor, through your CNS and back to an effector is very short. It can be measured, but only with special equipment. However, you can get a reasonable idea of the time it takes if you use a large number of people, and work out an average time.

1 Get as many people as possible to stand in a circle, holding hands.
2 One person lets go of his or her neighbour with the left hand, and holds a stopwatch in it. When everyone is ready, this person simultaneously starts the stopwatch, and squeezes their neighbour's hand with the right hand.
3 As soon as each person's left hand is squeezed, he or she should squeeze his or her neighbour with the right hand. The message of squeezes goes all round the circle.
4 While the message is going round, the person with the stopwatch puts it into the right hand, and holds his or her neighbour's hand with the left hand. When the squeeze arrives, he or she should stop the watch.
5 Keep repeating this, until the message is going round as fast as possible. Record the time taken, and also the number of people in the circle.
6 Now try again, but this time make the message of squeezes go the other way around the circle.

Questions

1 Using the fastest time you obtained, work out the average time it took for one person to respond to the stimulus they received.
2 Did people respond faster as the experiment went on? Why might this happen?
3 Did the message go as quickly when you changed direction? Explain your answer.

sensory receptor in your finger. It travels to the spinal cord along the axon from the receptor cell. This cell is called a **sensory neurone**, because it is carrying a message from a sensory receptor.

In the spinal cord, the neurone passes its message on to several other neurones. Only one is shown in Fig 9.18. These neurones are called **relay neurones**, because they relay the message on to other neurones. The relay neurones pass the message on to the brain. They also pass it on to an effector.

142

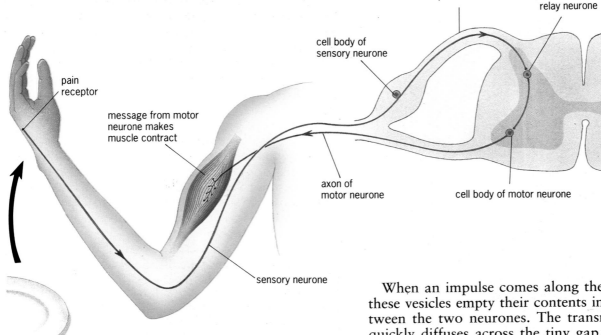

9.18 A reflex arc

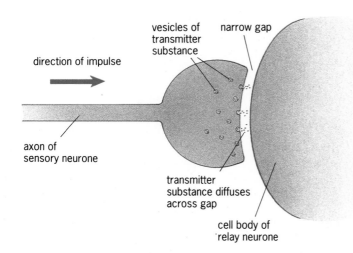

9.19 A synapse

9.20 Synapses connect neurones.

If you look carefully at Fig 9.18, you will see that the three neurones involved in the reflex arc do not quite connect with one another. There is a small gap between each pair. These gaps are called **synapses**.

Figure 9.19 shows a synapse in more detail. Inside the sensory neurone's axon are hundreds of tiny vacuoles, or **vesicles**. These each contain a chemical, called **transmitter substance**.

When an impulse comes along the axon, it makes these vesicles empty their contents into the space between the two neurones. The transmitter substance quickly diffuses across the tiny gap, attaches to the membrane of the relay neurone and triggers an impulse in the relay neurone. The relay neurone then sends the message onwards.

Synapses act like one-way valves. There is only transmitter substance on one side of the gap, so messages can only go across from that side. Synapses ensure that nervous impulses only travel in one direction.

9.21 A complex CNS allows complex behaviour.

Why is the central nervous system needed? Would it not be much quicker if pain receptors in your hand could just send a message straight to your arm muscles to tell them to move your hand away from the hot plate, rather than all the way to the spinal cord and back? Yes, it would, but that system would not be good enough for animals which need to be able to vary their behaviour under different circumstances.

With a central nervous system it is possible to give a modified, more 'intelligent' response. Say, for example, that you started to pick up the hot plate before you knew it was hot. If you just pulled your hand away, you would drop the plate and break it.

When the message from your fingers saying 'hot plate' arrives at your CNS, there is already another message there saying 'but don't drop it'.

The CNS will 'consider' the two messages together. It will probably send a message to your muscles to tell them to put the plate down gently, not to drop it.

The job of the CNS is to collect up all the information from all the receptors in your body. This information will be added together before messages are sent to effectors. In this way, the best action can be taken in a particular set of circumstances.

143

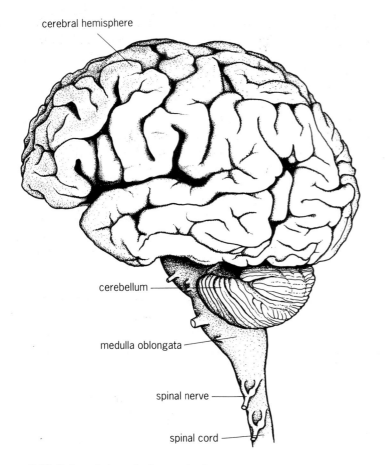

cerebral hemisphere

cerebellum

medulla oblongata

spinal nerve

spinal cord

9.20 External view of a human brain

9.22 Brain functions are localised.

The brain and spinal cord both help to receive impulses from receptors, and pass them on to effectors. But the brain does much more than this.

Figures 9.20 and 9.21 show the structure of the human brain. It is surrounded by three membranes or **meninges**, which help to protect it.

The **cerebrum** is the largest part of the brain. It is made of two **cerebral hemispheres**. Mammals have much larger cerebral hemispheres than any other kind of animal. Humans have the largest ones of all, compared with the size of the rest of the brain.

Conscious thought and memory take place in the cerebrum. Different parts of the cerebrum have different functions. For example, some areas deal with sight, others with speech. An area near the front determines some aspects of your personality.

The **hypothalamus** lies underneath the front part of the cerebrum. This is the part of the brain which controls osmoregulation and temperature regulation. The **cerebellum** is in control of coordination of body movements, and posture. The **medulla oblongata** controls heart beat and breathing.

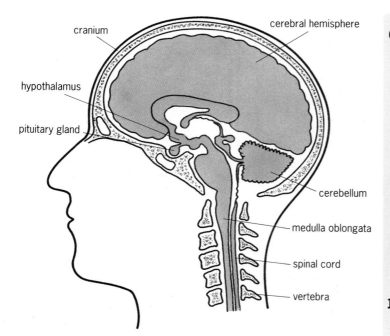

cranium

cerebral hemisphere

hypothalamus

pituitary gland

cerebellum

medulla oblongata

spinal cord

vertebra

9.21 Section through a human head, to show the brain

Questions

1 Give two examples of effectors.
2 What are the two main communication systems in an animal's body?
3 List three ways in which neurones are similar to other cells.
4 List three ways in which neurones are specialised to carry out their function of transmitting messages very quickly.
5 What is a nerve?
6 What is the function of the central nervous system?
7 Where are the cell bodies of each of these types of neurone found: (a) sensory neurone, (b) relay neurone, and (c) motor neurone?
8 What is the value of reflex actions?
9 Describe two reflex actions, other than the one described in Section 9.19.
10 How many synapses are there in the reflex arc shown in Fig 9.18?

The endocrine system

9.23 Endocrine glands make hormones.

Nerves can carry electrical messages very quickly from one part of an animal's body to another. But animals also use chemical messages.

The chemicals are called **hormones**. Hormones are made in special glands called **endocrine glands**.

Endocrine glands have a good blood supply. They have blood capillaries running right through them. When the endocrine gland makes a hormone, it releases it directly into the blood.

Other sorts of gland do not do this. The salivary glands, for example, do not secrete saliva into the blood. Saliva is secreted into the salivary duct, which carries it into the mouth. Endocrine glands do not have ducts, so they are sometimes called ductless glands.

Once the hormone is in the blood, it is carried to all parts of the body, dissolved in the plasma. Each kind of hormone only affects certain parts of the body.

Figure 9.22 shows the position of the main endocrine glands in the human body, while Table 9.1 summarises the hormones which they secrete, and their effects. The functions of adrenalin, thyroxine, and the male and female sex hormones are described in the next few pages. The functions of insulin, glucagon and ADH are described in Chapter 10.

9.24 Adrenalin prepares the body for action.

There are two adrenal glands, one above each kidney. They make a hormone called **adrenalin**. When you are frightened, excited or keyed up, your brain sends

Table 9.1 Mammalian endocrine glands and hormones

Hormone	Gland which secretes it	When secreted	Function	Other points
Adrenalin	adrenal gland	in small amounts all the time; in large amounts when frightened	prepares the body for fight or flight	
Thyroxine	thyroid gland	throughout life	controls metabolic rate, especially respiration in mitochondria	thyroxine contains iodine; lack of thyroxine in childhood causes cretinism
Insulin	islets of Langerhans in pancreas	when blood glucose level rises above normal	causes liver and muscles to take up glucose, so restoring blood glucose level to normal	lack of insulin causes diabetes
Glucagon	islets of Langerhans in pancreas	when blood glucose drops below normal	causes liver to release glucose into the blood	
Testosterone	testes	in small quantities throughout life; in larger quantities from puberty onwards	controls development of male sex organs and secondary sexual characteristics	
Oestrogen	ovaries	in small quantities throughout life; in larger quantities from puberty onwards, particularly when follicle is developing in ovary	controls development of female sex organs and secondary sexual characteristics; causes lining of uterus to get thick and spongy	
Progesterone	corpus luteum	after ovulation	maintains lining of uterus	if placenta does not secrete enough progesterone, a miscarriage may occur
	placenta	throughout pregnancy		
ADH (Anti-diuretic hormone)	pituitary gland	when quantity of water in blood gets too low	causes kidneys to reabsorb water from urine	
Thyroid stimulating hormone	pituitary gland	throughout life	causes thyroid gland to secrete thyroxine	
Growth hormone	pituitary gland	throughout life, especially during growing period	stimulates growth	lack of growth hormone causes dwarfism; too much causes gigantism

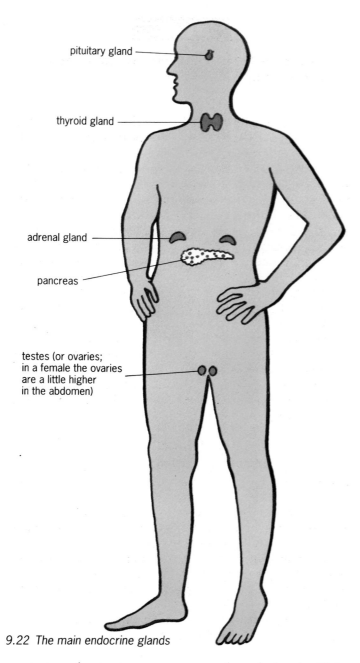

9.22 The main endocrine glands

pituitary gland

thyroid gland

adrenal gland

pancreas

testes (or ovaries;
in a female the ovaries
are a little higher
in the abdomen)

messages along a nerve to your adrenal glands. This makes them secrete adrenalin into the blood.

Adrenalin has several effects which are designed to help you to cope with danger. For example, it makes your heart beat faster, supplying oxygen to your brain and muscles more quickly. This gives them more energy for fighting or running away.

The blood vessels in your skin and digestive system contract right down so that they carry very little blood. This makes you go pale, and gives you 'butterflies in your stomach'. As much blood as possible is needed for your brain and muscles in the emergency.

All of this is very useful if you really have to fight an enemy. It is also useful if you are an athlete at the start of a race. But it does not help at all if you are on your way to the dentist, or watching a horror film.

Like most hormones, adrenalin breaks down very quickly after it is released, so its effects do not last long. If you need to go on feeling frightened, then your brain will keep telling the adrenal glands to secrete more adrenalin.

9.25 The thyroid regulates metabolism and growth.

The thyroid gland secretes **thyroxine**. Thyroxine is secreted almost all the time, but in quite small amounts. Thyroxine helps to control the metabolic rate, mostly by regulating the speed at which mitochondria break down glucose in respiration. This is particularly important in children. If a child does not have enough thyroxine, it will not grow properly, and its brain will not develop. A child like this is called a **cretin**. Cretinism can be cured by giving injections of thyroxine.

Adults who are short of thyroxine are sluggish, and tend to be overweight. Too much thyroxine makes a person overactive, thin and edgy.

Thyroxine contains iodine. A lack of iodine in the diet will mean that the thyroid gland cannot make enough thyroxine. To compensate for this, the thyroid gland may get bigger, forming a swelling or **goitre**.

9.26 Male sex hormones.

Male sex hormones are called **androgens**. The most important androgen is **testosterone**. Testosterone is made in the testes.

Testosterone and other androgens regulate the development of the male sex organs. They also control the development of the male secondary sexual characteristics (Section 8.22).

9.27 Female sex hormones.

Female sex hormones are called **oestrogens**. They regulate the development of the female sex organs, and the female secondary sexual characteristics.

Whereas male mammals make sperm all the time, females only produce eggs at certain times. In humans, ovulation (Section 8.11) happens once a month. Ovulation is part of the **menstrual cycle**. The menstrual cycle is controlled by hormones (Fig 9.23).

Figure 8.27 illustrates what happens during the human menstrual cycle. First, a follicle develops inside an ovary. The developing follicle secretes a hormone called **oestrogen**. The oestrogen makes the lining of the uterus grow thick and spongy.

When the follicle is fully developed, ovulation takes place. The follicle stops secreting oestrogen. It becomes a **corpus luteum**. The corpus luteum starts to secrete another hormone, called **progesterone**.

Progesterone keeps the uterus lining thick, spongy, and well supplied with blood, in case the egg is

146

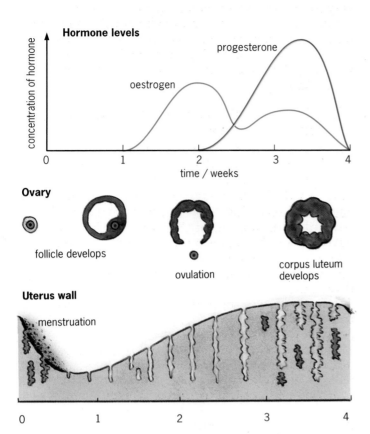

Hormone levels

concentration of hormone

progesterone

oestrogen

0　　　1　　　2　　　3　　　4
time / weeks

Ovary

follicle develops

ovulation

corpus luteum develops

Uterus wall

menstruation

0　　　1　　　2　　　3　　　4

9.23 Hormones and the menstrual cycle

fertilised. If it is not fertilised, then the corpus luteum gradually disappears. Progesterone is not secreted any more, and so the lining of the uterus breaks down. Menstruation happens. A new follicle starts to develop in the ovary, and the cycle begins again.

But if the egg is fertilised, the corpus luteum does not degenerate so quickly. It carries on secreting progesterone until the embryo sinks into the uterus wall, and a placenta develops. Then the placenta secretes progesterone, and carries on secreting it all through the pregnancy. The progesterone maintains the uterus lining, so that menstruation does not happen during the pregnancy.

9.28 Human sex hormones are used to treat infertility.

You may already know that oestrogen and progesterone are used in the contraceptive pill, to stop eggs being released from the ovaries. Hormones can also be used to *make* eggs be produced. They can be used to treat infertility.

Many couples who would like to have children find that the woman does not get pregnant. There are many possible reasons for this. For example, the woman may not be producing enough eggs, or her oviducts may be blocked so that the sperm and egg cannot meet, or her

partner's sperm may not be healthy enough to swim all that way. In all of these cases, the couple may decide to try to have a test-tube baby.

Test-tube babies are not made in test tubes, but they may begin their lives in a petri dish! First, the woman is given a course of hormones to make her produce eggs. The hormones are ones which are normally produced by the pituitary gland. Usually, enough hormones are given to her to make her produce quite a lot of eggs at once. She then has a small operation, in which the eggs are taken out of her ovaries.

The eggs are put into a petri dish, into a warm liquid with just the right concentration of salts and sugars in it. Everything has to be kept spotlessly clean and sterile. Then some of her partner's sperm are added, and allowed to fertilise the eggs. Lastly, two or three of the fertilised eggs are put into her uterus, where they may implant and grow into embryos. She may be given more hormones at this stage, to get her uterus in the right condition to accept the eggs.

9.29 The pituitary gland controls other glands.

The pituitary gland is in the centre of the head. It is attached to the part of the brain called the **hypothalamus**.

The pituitary gland secretes a large number of hormones. For example, when receptor cells in the hypothalamus sense that there is not enough water in the blood, they send messages along nerves to the pituitary gland. The pituitary gland then secretes ADH. ADH stops the kidneys allowing too much water to leave the body in the urine (Section 10.27).

Many of the hormones secreted by the pituitary gland control the other endocrine glands. **Thyroid**

Table 9.2 A comparison of the nervous and endocrine systems in a mammal.

Nervous system	Endocrine system
Made of neurones	Made of secretory cells
Messages transmitted in the form of electrical impulses	Messages transmitted in the form of chemicals called hormones
Messages transmitted along nerve fibres	Messages transmitted through the blood system
Messages travel very quickly	Messages travel more slowly
Effect of message usually only lasts a very short while	Effect of messages usually lasts longer

stimulating hormone, for example, makes the thyroid gland secrete thyroxine.

The pituitary gland also secretes **growth hormone**. Growth hormone stimulates the growth of the body, partly by causing proteins to be built up in cells. Sometimes, not enough growth hormone is secreted during childhood. If this happens, the child may develop into a dwarf. Section 19.17 describes how this hormone is now made by genetically engineered bacteria.

Questions

1 How do endocrine glands differ from other glands?
2 Describe three effects of adrenalin, and explain the value of each one.
3 Why is it important that adrenalin is broken down very quickly in your body?
4 Why do you need iodine in your diet?
5 Which female hormone is secreted by a follicle as it develops inside an ovary?
6 What effect does this hormone have?
7 Which hormone is secreted by a corpus luteum?
8 What effect does this hormone have?
9 Name one other structure which secretes this hormone.
10 The pituitary gland is sometimes called 'the master gland'. Suggest why this is.

9.30 Hormones are sometimes used in agriculture.

Farmers sometimes use hormones to make their animals grow faster, or to produce more of a particular product. One hormone used in this way is called **bovine somatotropin**, or **BST**.

BST is a hormone which is naturally produced by cattle. However, if cows are given *extra* BST, they make more milk. Some people think it would be a good idea to give cows BST, to get higher milk yields. You would need fewer cows to get the same amount of milk.

However, in the United Kingdom, people do not want BST to be used in this way, and it is not legal at the moment (1994). There are several reasons for this.

People are worried about drinking milk from cows treated with BST They think the BST might damage their health. In fact, this is very unlikely, because the hormone does not get into the milk in any significant quantity.

It is difficult to see why we need BST The European Union already produces more milk than it needs, so milk quotas have to be imposed, to stop farmers from producing too much milk.

There are concerns that the BST might harm the cows Cows treated with BST make very large amounts of milk, far beyond the 'natural' levels which they produce. This makes them more likely to get infections of their udders, and may make them feel less comfortable.

Coordination in plants

9.31 Tropisms are directional growth responses.

Most plants cannot respond to stimuli as quickly as animals can. They respond more slowly, usually by growing. They grow either towards or away from the stimulus. This sort of response is called a **tropism**.

Two important stimuli for plants are light and gravity. For example, the shoot of a plant grows towards light. This is called **phototropism** ('photo' means light). Because the shoot grows towards the light, the response is called **positive phototropism**.

Plants can respond to gravity by growing either towards or away from the centre of the Earth. This is called **geotropism**. Shoots tend to grow away from the pull of gravity. This is called **negative geotropism** because the shoot is growing away from the stimulus.

Roots are **positively geotropic** – they grow towards the pull of gravity (Fig 9.24). Some roots also respond to light by growing away from it, which means that they are **negatively phototropic**.

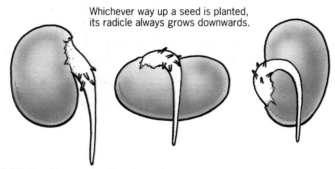

Whichever way up a seed is planted, its radicle always grows downwards.

9.24 Positive geotropism in roots

9.32 Tropisms aid plant survival.

It is very important to the plant that its roots and shoots behave like this. Shoots must grow upwards, away from gravity and towards the light, so that the leaves are held out into sunlight. The more light they have, the better they can photosynthesise. Flowers, too, need to be held up in the air, where insects or the wind can pollinate them.

Roots, though, need to grow downwards into the soil in order to anchor the plant in the soil, and to absorb water and minerals from between the soil particles.

Practical 9.6 To find out how shoots respond to light

1 Label three petri dishes A, B and C. Line each with moist cotton wool or filter paper, and sprinkle on some mustard seeds.
2 Leave all three dishes in a warm place for a day or two, until the seeds begin to germinate. Check that they do not dry out.
3 Now put dish A into a light-proof box with a slit in one side, so that the seedlings get light from one side only.
4 Put dish B onto a **clinostat** (Fig 9.25) in a light place. The clinostat will slowly turn the seedlings around, so that they get light from all sides equally.
5 Put dish C into a completely light-proof box.
6 Leave all the dishes for a week, checking that they do not dry out.
7 Make labelled drawings of one seedling from each dish.

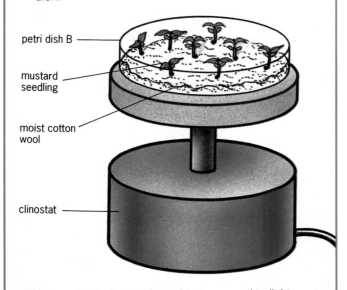

petri dish B
mustard seedling
moist cotton wool
clinostat

9.25 *Apparatus to find out how shoots respond to light*

Questions

1 How had the seedlings in A responded to light from one side? What is the name for this response?
2 Why was dish B put onto a clinostat, and not simply left in a light place?
3 Explain what happened to the seedlings in dish C.
4 What was the control in this experiment?

Practical 9.7 To find out how roots respond to gravity

1 Germinate several broad bean seeds. Leave them until their radicles are about 2 cm long.
2 Line the containers of two clinostats with blotting paper. Dampen the paper.
3 Cover the cork discs on the clinostats with wet cotton wool.
4 Choose about eight bean seeds with straight radicles. Pin four onto each disc, with their radicles pointing straight outwards (Fig 9.26). Put the containers lined with blotting paper over them.
5 Turn both clinostats on their sides. Switch on clinostat B.
6 Leave both clinostats for a few days. Check the beans occasionally to see that they have enough water.
7 Make labelled drawings of the bean seedlings from each clinostat.

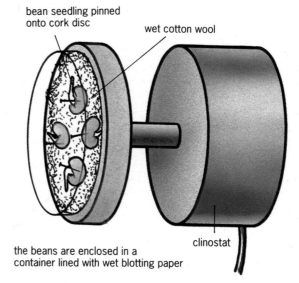

bean seedling pinned onto cork disc
wet cotton wool
clinostat
the beans are enclosed in a container lined with wet blotting paper

9.26 *Apparatus to find out how roots respond to gravity*

Questions

1 How had the seedlings in clinostat A responded to the pull of gravity? What is the name for this response?
2 What was the purpose of clinostat B?
3 Design an experiment to find out how shoots respond to gravity. Give full instructions for the method, including labelled diagrams. What results would you expect?

9.33 How a shoot responds to light.

For an organism to respond to a stimulus, there must be a **receptor** to pick up the stimulus, an **effector** to respond to it, and some kind of **communication system** in between. In mammals, the receptor is often part of a sense organ, and the effector is a muscle or gland. Messages are sent between them along nerves, or sometimes by means of hormones.

Plants, however, do not have complex sense organs, muscles or nervous systems. So how do they manage to respond to stimuli like light and gravity?

The part of a shoot sensitive to light is the tip. This is where the receptor is.

The part of the shoot which responds to the stimulus is the part just below the tip. This is the effector.

These two parts of the shoot must be communicating with one another somehow. They do it by means of **hormones**.

9.34 Changes in auxin concentration cause phototropisms.

One kind of plant hormone is called **auxin**. Auxin is being made all the time by the cells in the tip of a shoot. The auxin diffuses downwards from the tip, into the rest of the shoot.

Auxin makes the cells just behind the tip get longer. The more auxin there is, the faster they will grow. Without auxin, they will not grow.

When light shines onto a shoot from one side, the auxin at the tip concentrates on the shady side (Fig 9.27). This makes the cells on the shady side grow faster than the ones on the bright side, so the shoot bends towards the light.

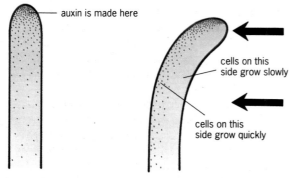

auxin is made here

cells on this side grow slowly

cells on this side grow quickly

Auxin made in the tip diffuses unevenly down the shoot, concentrating on the shady side.

The uneven concentration of auxin causes the shady side to grow faster than the light side, so the shoot bends towards the light.

9.27 Auxin and phototropism

9.35 Plant hormones are used in horticulture.

Gardeners and horticulturists often use plant hormones to improve the look of their gardens, to increase yields from plants, or to speed up the rate at which they can produce new plants.

Many people use weedkillers in their gardens. Most weedkillers contain plant hormones. These hormones are often a type of **auxin**. The weedkillers used to kill weeds in lawns are **selective weedkillers**. When they are sprayed onto the lawn, the weeds are affected by the auxin, but the grass is not. The weeds respond by growing very fast – so for a few days the lawn looks even weedier than it was before. Then the weeds die, leaving more space, nutrients and water for the grass to grow.

Fruit growers often use plant hormones to help the fruits to grow larger, or to ripen well. For example, many fruits produce the gas **ethene** when they are ripening. This encourages other fruits near them to ripen, as well. (There is no reason why a gas cannot be a hormone! Nevertheless, some people feel happier referring to plant hormones as 'plant growth substances' instead.) If tomatoes are picked while they are still green, they can be stored or transported without worrying about them going bad. When the suppliers want them to ripen, they can expose them to ethene.

Plant hormones are also used when propagating plants by cuttings or tissue culture. You can read about this on page 99.

Questions

1 What is a tropism?
2 Which parts of a plant show positive phototropism?
3 Which parts of a plant show positive geotropism?
4 Which part of a shoot is sensitive to light?
5 Which part of a shoot responds to light?
6 How do these parts communicate with one another?

Chapter revision questions

1 Explain the difference between each of the following pairs of terms, giving examples whenever they make your answer clearer.
   (a) cornea, conjunctiva
   (b) choroid, sclera
   (c) neurone, nerve
   (d) receptor, effector
   (e) endolymph, perilymph
   (f) sensory neurone, motor neurone
   (g) cerebrum, cerebellum
   (h) thyroxine, thyroid stimulating hormone
   (i) oestrogen, progesterone
   (j) negative geotropism, positive geotropism.
2 If you walk from a brightly lit street into a dark room, your pupil will rapidly dilate.
   (a) What type of action is this?
   (b) Using each of these words at least once, but not necessarily in this order, explain how this reaction is brought about.
   synapse, receptor, motor neurone, sensory neurone, relay neurone, radial muscles.
   (c) As well as the muscles in the iris, the eye also contains muscles in the ciliary body. What is their function?
3 (a) Make a large, labelled diagram of a nerve cell or neurone.
   (b) List three ways in which this cell is similar to other animal cells.
   (c) List three ways in which this cell differs from other animal cells, explaining how each of these differences enables it to perform its function efficiently.

10 Homeostasis and excretion

10.1 Homeostasis keeps the internal environment constant.

The environment (surroundings) of a living organism is always changing. Think about your own environment. The temperature of the air around you changes. For example, it might be −10 °C outside on a cold day in winter, and 23 °C indoors. The amount of water in the air around you changes. On a rainy day, the air could hold a lot of water, while on a hot, dry sunny day there could be very little water in the air.

The cells inside your body, however, do not have to put up with a changing environment. Your body keeps the environment *inside* your body almost the same, all the time. In the tissue fluid surrounding your cells, the temperature and amount of water are kept almost constant. So is the concentration of glucose. Keeping this internal environment constant is called **homeostasis.**

Homeostasis is very important. It helps your cells to work as efficiently as possible. Keeping a constant temperature of around 37 °C helps enzymes to work. Keeping a constant amount of water means that your cells are not damaged by absorbing or losing too much water by osmosis. Keeping a constant amount of glucose means that there is always enough fuel for respiration.

In this chapter, you will see how homeostasis is carried out in humans. Various endocrine glands are involved, and so are the kidneys.

10.2 Homeostasis involves negative feedback.

If you have studied any technology at school, you may know something about control systems. Fig 10.1 shows a simple control system to control the temperature of water being heated by a gas boiler.

A sensor constantly monitors the temperature of the water. When the water temperature drops below the temperature you want (you set this using a thermostat), the sensor makes the valve supplying gas to the boiler open. This makes the heater come on, which heats the water. The sensor senses the higher temperature of the water. When the water reaches the desired temperature, the sensor makes the valve supplying gas to the boiler close. The heater goes off, and the water gradually cools.

This kind of arrangement is called a **negative feedback loop.** When the sensor has done something, for example made the gas valve open, information about what has happened as a result of this – in this case a rise in temperature of the water – is **fed back** to the sensor. This makes the sensor change its message to the gas valve. It makes it close instead of open. This is why the feedback loop is a **negative** one. The information being fed back to the sensor makes it stop what it was just doing, and do the opposite.

What have boilers to do with living organisms? Quite a lot! In a way, your body is rather like this boiler system. Your cells are constantly generating heat, to keep you warm. You have sensors to monitor the

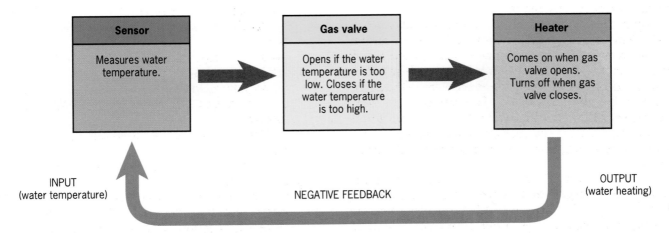

Fig 10.1 A negative feedback loop

temperature of your blood, and these can switch various processes on and off to keep your blood temperature constant.

This is not the only example of a negative feedback loop in your body. There are many others. In this chapter, you will find out more about the control of body temperature, and also the control of water content and of blood glucose levels. All of these involve negative feedback loops.

The control of body temperature

10.3 Mammals and birds are homeothermic.

Mammals and birds are able to keep their body temperature constant, no matter what the temperature of their environment is. They are **homeothermic.**

Being homeothermic has many advantages. You may have noticed that, in cold weather, invertebrate animals such as houseflies become very slow-moving. This is because they do not control their body temperature – they are **poikilothermic.** All invertebrates, and also all fish, amphibians and reptiles, are poikilothermic. Their body temperature is just the same as the temperature of the air or water around them. When this temperature is cold, their body temperature is cold. Cold temperatures slow down chemical reactions (this is explained in Section 3.5), which slows down the activity of the organism.

But homeothermic animals keep their body temperature warm even when the weather is very cold. Their enzymes can carry on working, and they remain active. So mammals and birds can keep active in winter, or during cold nights, when other animals are inactive.

There is a price to pay. The energy which homeothermic animals use to generate the heat to keep their bodies warm comes from food. This means that homeothermic animals have to eat much more food than poikilothermic ones.

10.4 How humans control their body temperature.

If you look back at Fig 9.21, you can see that there is an area at the base of the brain – almost in the middle of your head – called the **hypothalamus.** The hypothalamus keeps a constant check on the temperature of the blood flowing through it. The hypothalamus has the role of sensor in the negative feedback loop which controls your body temperature.

If the temperature is too low, the hypothalamus sends messages along nerves to various parts of your

Fact!

The domestic goat has the highest normal body temperature of any mammal, at about 39.9 °C.

At 0 °C, a poikilothermic animal's metabolic rate slows down, because its body temperature is also 0 °C. The animal is inactive.

At 20 °C, a poikilothermic animal's body temperature is also 20 °C. Its metabolic rate speeds up, and it becomes active.

At 0 °C, a homeothermic animal remains active. Its cells produce heat by breaking down food through respiration. Its body temperature stays high enough to keep its metabolism going.

At 20 °C, a homeothermic animal is no more active than at 0 °C, because its body temperature does not change. It may even be less active, to avoid overheating.

Fig 10.2 Poikilothermic and homeothermic animals

body to try to increase heat production, and reduce heat loss from your skin. If the temperature is too high, then messages are sent to reduce heat production, and increase heat loss. The system is very efficient, and – as long as you are well – your body temperature rarely varies by more than 0.5 °C or so.

10.5 The structure of human skin.

Figure 10.3 shows a section through a piece of human skin. Skin has many functions, one of which is varying the rate at which heat is lost from your body to the air.

Human skin is made up of two layers. The top layer is called the **epidermis**, and the lower layer is the **dermis.**

10.6 The epidermis protects the deeper layers.

All the cells in the epidermis have been made in the layer of cells at the base of it, called the **Malpighian layer**. These cells are always dividing by mitosis. The new cells which are made gradually move towards the surface of the skin. As they go, they die, and fill up with a protein called **keratin.** The top layer of the skin is made up of these dead cells. It is called the **cornified layer.**

The cornified layer protects the softer, living cells underneath, because it is hard and waterproof. It is always being worn away, and replaced by cells from beneath. On the parts of the body which get most wear, for example the soles of the feet, it grows thicker.

Some of the cells in the epidermis contain a dark brown pigment, called **melanin**. Melanin absorbs the harmful ultra-violet rays in sunlight, which would damage the living cells in the deeper layers of the skin.

Here and there, the epidermis is folded inwards, forming a **hair follicle**. A hair grows from each one. Hairs are made of keratin.

Each hair follicle has a **sebaceous gland** opening from the side of it. These glands make an oily liquid called **sebum**. Sebum keeps the hair and skin soft and supple.

10.7 The dermis has many functions.

Most of the dermis is made of **connective tissue**. This tissue contains elastic fibres. As a person gets older, the fibres lose their elasticity, so the skin becomes loose and wrinkled.

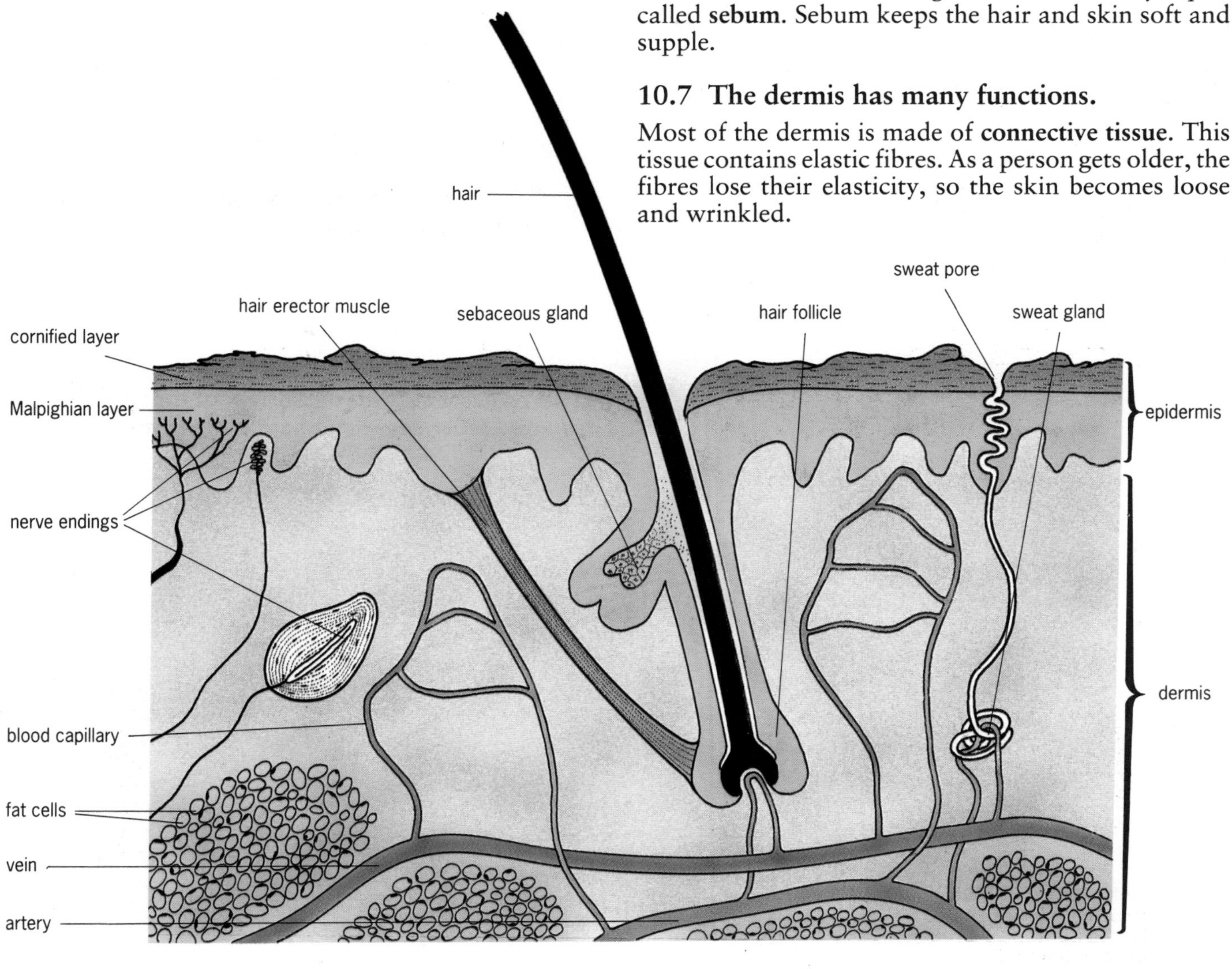

Fig 10.3 A section through human skin

153

The dermis also contains **sweat glands**. These secrete a liquid called **sweat**. Sweat is mostly water, with small amounts of salt and urea dissolved in it. It travels up the sweat ducts, and out onto the surface of the skin through the sweat pores. Sweat helps in temperature regulation.

The dermis contains **blood vessels**, and **nerve endings**. The nerve endings are sensitive to touch, pain, pressure and temperature, so they help to keep you aware of changes in your environment.

Underneath the dermis is a layer of **fat**. This is made up of cells which contain large drops of oil. This layer helps to insulate your body, and also acts as a food reserve.

10.8 How the skin reacts when you are too cold.

When your body temperature drops below 37 °C, messages from the hypothalamus cause your skin to cut down the rate of heat loss. Firstly, the messages make the **erector muscles** attached to your hair follicles contract, which makes the hairs stand on end. If you were a furry animal, this would provide you with a thick layer of hair, trapping air – which is an excellent insulator – next to your skin. As it is, you just get goose pimples, which don't help at all!

However, a second effect of the messages from the hypothalamus is more useful in conserving heat. The messages make the muscles around the **arterioles**, which supply blood to the capillaries near the surface of your skin, contract. This closes off these arterioles, and stops blood flowing along this pathway. Instead, it has to go through the capillaries which lie below the

fat layer. This reduces the amount of heat which is lost by radiation from your blood to the air. Your skin looks blue or white, and feels cold – but your blood will stay warm.

There are other responses, which do not involve your skin, which happen when your blood is too cold. You will probably **shiver**. Shivering is a very fast, random contraction and relaxation of muscles, which generates heat to warm your blood. Metabolic reactions in the liver may speed up, again generating extra heat. You may do something active like jumping up and down, which also increases the amount of heat generated in your body. You can also do things to decrease the amount of heat lost by your body, such as moving into a warmer place, or putting on more clothes.

10.9 How the skin reacts when you are too warm.

If your blood temperature rises much above 37 °C, the hypothalamus sends messages which cause a different set of responses by your skin.

The erector muscles relax, so that the hairs lie flat against the skin, no longer trapping as much air and so allowing more heat to be lost by radiation.

The muscles constricting the arterioles relax, so that the blood is free to flow through the surface capillaries. This brings it close to the surface of the skin, so that it can lose more heat by radiation.

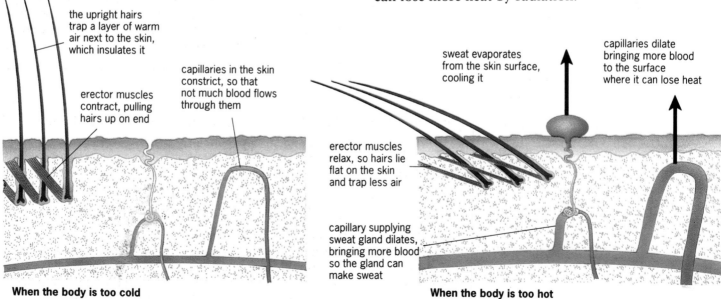

the upright hairs trap a layer of warm air next to the skin, which insulates it

erector muscles contract, pulling hairs up on end

capillaries in the skin constrict, so that not much blood flows through them

When the body is too cold

sweat evaporates from the skin surface, cooling it

capillaries dilate bringing more blood to the surface where it can lose heat

erector muscles relax, so hairs lie flat on the skin and trap less air

capillary supplying sweat gland dilates, bringing more blood so the gland can make sweat

When the body is too hot

Fig 10.4 How the skin helps in temperature regulation

The **sweat glands** begin to secrete **sweat**. This is a fluid made from blood plasma, containing mostly water and some salt and a little urea. It flows from the glands, through the sweat ducts and onto the surface of the skin. Here it evaporates, which cools the skin. This is a very important process, because it is the only way we have of making our body temperature *lower* than that of the temperature around us.

You can also purposefully do things which help you to keep cool. You can lie still, so generating less heat within your body. You can take off layers of clothes, or wear light, loose-fitting clothes. You can swim; when you get out of the water, the water evaporates from your skin and cools you down. You can move into the shade or a cool room.

Practical 10.1 Investigating the effect of size and covering on rate of cooling

1 Draw a results table.
2 Heat a beaker of water to about 80 °C.
3 While the water is heating, label 3 test tubes as follows:
   small tube A
   2 equal-sized large tubes B and C.
4 Wrap dry cotton wool around tube C, and hold in place with a rubber band.
5 When your water has reached 80 °C, pour it into the three tubes, to the same level in each one. *Immediately* take the temperature in each tube, and then put corks into each tube as quickly as you can. Record this initial temperature on the chart.
6 Take the temperature of the water in each tube every 5 minutes for the next 30 minutes. Each time, replace the corks in the tubes as quickly as possible.
7 Plot your results on graph paper, with time on the horizontal axis and temperature on the vertical one. Draw a separate line for each tube.

Questions

1 Which tube cooled fastest?
2 Did tube A cool faster or more slowly than tube B? Explain why.
3 Did tube B cool faster or more slowly than tube C? Explain why.
4 In cold climates, animals lose heat from their bodies just as the test tubes did. Would you expect a small animal to lose heat faster or more slowly than a large animal?
5 What do mammals have on their skin to help them to conserve heat?
6 Polar bears are the biggest of all the bears, whereas Malayan sun bears, which live in hot countries, are much smaller. Can you explain why this might be, using the results from this experiment?

Practical 10.2 Investigating the effect of evaporation on rate of cooling

When a liquid changes to a gas, it is said to **evaporate**. Evaporation uses heat energy, so when a liquid on your skin evaporates it takes heat energy from your skin, cooling it down.
1 Set up two stands with clamps and bosses, ready to hold thermometers. You will also need two pieces of cotton wool and two rubber bands. Soak one of the pieces of cotton wool in cold water.
2 Collect two thermometers which have been kept in a warm place. As quickly as possible, wrap dry cotton wool round the bulb of one of them, and wet cotton wool around the other. Support each thermometer in a clamp, and put them side by side on the bench in front of you.
3 Every two minutes, read the temperature on each thermometer, recording it in a results table. Do this for 20 minutes.
4 Draw graphs to show how each thermometer cooled.

Questions

1 Why were the two thermometers supported in clamps, rather than held in your hand or left lying on the bench?
2 Which thermometer cooled fastest? Explain why you think this was so.
3 If someone is rescued after falling into cold water, it is very important to get them into dry clothing as soon as possible. Why?
4 How do the following living organisms use evaporation to help them to cool their bodies:
   (a) a human
   (b) a dog
   (c) a tree?
5 Some of the hottest places in the world are dry deserts, such as the Sahara. What special problems would mammals have in using evaporation to keep cool if they lived in a desert?

10.10 Low temperatures make life difficult in winter.

In Britain, the most difficult time for any animal to survive is the winter, when temperatures fall, and food is in short supply.

Poikilothermic animals are so cold during the winter months that their metabolic rate is far too low for them to be active. Reptiles, amphibians and most invertebrates spend the winter in an inactive or dormant state.

Homeothermic animals can often remain active in the winter, providing they can get enough food to keep their bodies warm. Many birds, such as the robin, do this, and so do some mammals, such as rabbits.

Other mammals, though, eat the sort of food which is not available in winter. Hedgehogs, for example, feed on worms, slugs and beetles. They would not be able to find enough of this food during the winter to keep their body temperature high enough to be active. Because of this hedgehogs **hibernate**. Towards the end of the summer, when food is plentiful, they eat as much as they can, and build up large fat stores in their bodies. In autumn, they find a sheltered, well insulated place, such as a pile of dead vegetation, and make a nest. They curl into a small ball, to keep in as much body heat as possible, and go to sleep. (Fig 10.5).

It is not an ordinary sleep, however. The hedgehogs' metabolic rate slows right down, and their body temperature drops well below normal. The hedgehogs do not usually wake at all until spring comes.

10.11 Old people may get hypothermia in winter.

Hypothermia simply means having a body temperature well below normal. It happens when the body is no longer able to make enough heat to keep the temperature up. Old people spending long hours in very cold rooms may get hypothermia, especially if they do not eat well. The body's main way of making heat is by combining food with oxygen in the cells, so if the cells don't get a good food supply, they cannot make enough heat. Moving around and keeping active

Fig 10.5 A hibernating hedgehog

also helps to produce heat, but some old people cannot do this.

Even healthy, younger people may suffer from hypothermia if they spend a long time in very cold conditions, particularly if they are not able to keep active. Wet clothing makes things worse, as water evaporating from the clothes makes the temperature drop even faster.

People suffering from hypothermia should be wrapped in warm, dry clothing, moved to a warm place, and given hot, nourishing drinks. This will help the body temperature to rise again.

Questions

1 Explain what is meant by
  (a) homeothermic
  (b) poikilothermic
2 Outline the advantages and disadvantages of being homeothermic.
3 Draw a negative feedback loop, using the one in Fig 10.1 as a guide, to summarise how body temperature is controlled in humans.
4 Polar bears live in very cold climates. Using your general knowledge, and reference books, explain what special adaptations polar bears have to help them to keep warm.

The control of glucose content

10.12 Glucose is needed for respiration.

All cells in your body respire all the time. They must do this to provide themselves with a supply of energy. If they stop respiring, they die.

For many of your cells, the fuel they use in respiration is **glucose**. It is therefore very important that the concentration of glucose in your blood and tissue fluid is kept fairly constant, so your respiring cells do not run out. This is especially important for brain cells, which quickly die if they become short of glucose.

Glucose concentration in the blood is normally around 100 mg of glucose in every 100 cm³ of blood. This is controlled by the **pancreas** and the **liver**.

10.13 The pancreas secretes insulin and glucagon.

The pancreas is a soft, white structure which lies just below your stomach, on the left-hand side of the body below the ribs. It is an unusual organ because it has two very different functions. Most of the pancreas is made up of cells which secrete pancreatic juice, which flows along the pancreatic duct into the duodenum, where it helps in digestion (Section 4.38). But dotted around in the pancreas are groups of a different kind of cell; the groups are called **islets of Langerhans**. These cells secrete the hormones **insulin** and **glucagon**.

The cells in the islets of Langerhans constantly monitor the amount of glucose in the blood. If this level rises too high, then they secrete insulin. If the blood glucose level falls too low, they secrete glucagon.

10.14 The liver changes the amount of glucose in the blood.

Insulin and glucagon are carried around the body, in solution in blood plasma. Both of them affect the behaviour of the liver cells.

Insulin makes the liver remove glucose from the blood, so lowering the blood glucose level. The liver uses some of the glucose in respiration. It also changes some of it into the polysaccharide **glycogen**, which it stores inside its cells.

Glucagon makes the liver release glucose into the blood, so increasing the blood glucose level. The glucose that the liver releases is made by breaking apart the glycogen molecules stored in its cells.

10.15 Lack of insulin causes sugar diabetes.

Some people's pancreases do not produce enough insulin. If this happens, there is nothing to control the amount of glucose in the blood. This disease, called **diabetes**, can be very dangerous.

Imagine a person has eaten a meal containing a lot of sugar. In a normal person, the pancreas will respond by producing insulin, which will stop too much glucose being allowed into the blood. But if the person is diabetic, almost all the glucose will go into the bloodstream and be taken round the body.

This is dangerous. Very high blood glucose levels can damage brain cells, causing coma and possibly death.

The extra glucose in the blood is excreted by the kidneys. One way of diagnosing diabetes is to test urine for glucose. Healthy people have no glucose at all in their urine.

If there is no insulin in the body, then the liver and

Blood glucose above normal

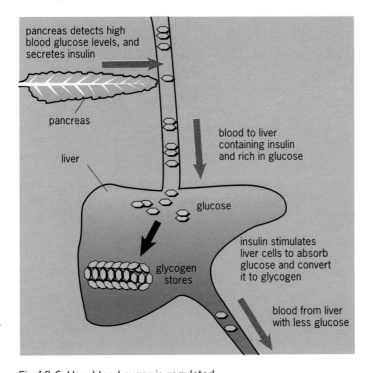

Blood glucose below normal

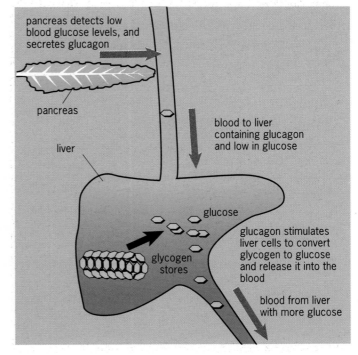

Fig 10.6 *How blood sugar is regulated*

muscles will not build up stores of glycogen. So later, when the blood glucose levels have dropped again, there will be no reserves to draw on. The blood glucose may drop to a very low level, again possibly causing coma and death.

Diabetes cannot be cured, but it can be controlled. Most diabetics can remain healthy by carefully controlling the amount of carbohydrate that they eat. Some, however, need daily injections of insulin.

Questions

1 Why is it important to control the concentration of glucose in the blood?
2 Draw a negative feedback loop to show how blood glucose levels are controlled.

Excretion

10.16 Excretion is the removal of waste substances.

Cells constantly produce waste products, such as carbon dioxide. Some of these waste products can damage the cells – they are **toxic**. Such toxic substances must be removed from the body. The removal of toxic waste substances which have been made by cells is called **excretion**.

Humans have three main excretory substances.

Carbon dioxide This is made by all cells, in respiration. It is transported in blood plasma to the alveoli of the lungs, where it is excreted in the air you breathe out.

Bile pigments These are made in the liver, from the haemoglobin in old red blood cells. They are carried in bile into the duodenum, and excreted in the faeces.

Urea This is made in the liver, from excess proteins. It is carried in blood plasma to the kidneys, where it is excreted in urine. It contains nitrogen, so it is a nitrogenous excretory product.

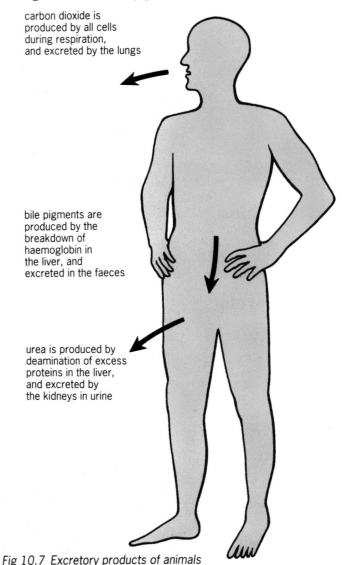

carbon dioxide is produced by all cells during respiration, and excreted by the lungs

bile pigments are produced by the breakdown of haemoglobin in the liver, and excreted in the faeces

urea is produced by deamination of excess proteins in the liver, and excreted by the kidneys in urine

Fig 10.7 Excretory products of animals

Table 10.1 Excretory products

| Excretory product | Where it is made | How it is made | Where it is excreted | |
			In animals	In plants
Carbon dioxide	in all living cells	by respiration	from lungs or other respiratory surface	from stomata, but only at night
Oxygen	in green plant cells	by photosynthesis		from stomata, but only in the daytime
Nitrogenous waste products, e.g. urea	in liver of mammals	by deamination	from kidneys, in urine	
Bile pigments	in liver and spleen of mammals	from haemoglobin	in bile, which flows into duodenum and out of the body in faeces	

10.17 Plants also have excretory products.

Plants have excretory products, too. Like animals, their cells are constantly respiring, and so produce carbon dioxide as a waste product. However, during the day their mesophyll cells photosynthesise faster than they respire, and so use up the carbon dioxide faster than they produce it. At night, when they are not photosynthesising, the carbon dioxide is excreted through their stomata. In the day, oxygen – a waste product of photosynthesis – is excreted through the stomata.

Plants do not produce excretory products from proteins, like urea, because they do not eat proteins! They make their own proteins, and can make just as many or as few as they need.

There are several other unwanted substances which plants make. These may accumulate in the leaves. When the leaves grow old and are dropped from the plant, these substances are lost.

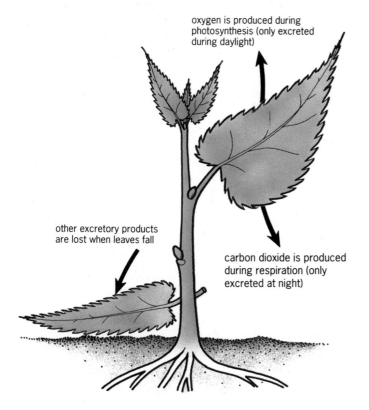

oxygen is produced during photosynthesis (only excreted during daylight)

other excretory products are lost when leaves fall

carbon dioxide is produced during respiration (only excreted at night)

Fig 10.8 Excretory products of plants

Excretion in animals

10.18 Excess proteins are converted to urea.

When you eat proteins, digestive enzymes in your stomach, duodenum and ileum break them down into amino acids. The amino acids are absorbed into the blood capillaries in the villi in your ileum (Section 4.41). The blood capillaries all join up to the hepatic portal vein, which takes the absorbed food to the liver.

The liver allows some of the amino acids to carry on, in the blood, to other parts of your body. But if you have eaten more than you need, then some of them must be got rid of.

It would be very wasteful to excrete the extra amino

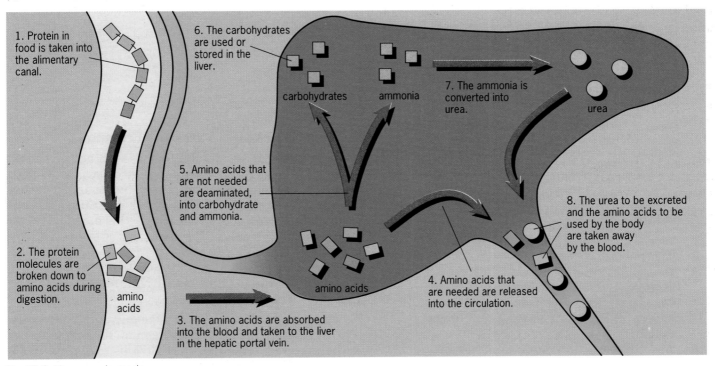

1. Protein in food is taken into the alimentary canal.

6. The carbohydrates are used or stored in the liver.

carbohydrates   ammonia

7. The ammonia is converted into urea.

urea

5. Amino acids that are not needed are deaminated, into carbohydrate and ammonia.

2. The protein molecules are broken down to amino acids during digestion.

amino acids

3. The amino acids are absorbed into the blood and taken to the liver in the hepatic portal vein.

amino acids

4. Amino acids that are needed are released into the circulation.

8. The urea to be excreted and the amino acids to be used by the body are taken away by the blood.

Fig 10.9 How urea is made

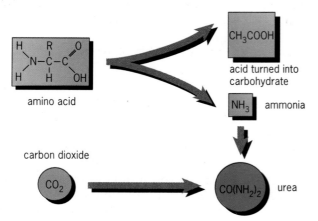

Fig 10.10 Deamination

acids just as they are. They contain energy which, if it is not needed straight away, might be needed later.

So enzymes in the liver split up each amino acid molecule (Figs 10.9 and 10.10). The part containing the energy is kept, turned into carbohydrate or fat, and stored. The rest, which is the part which contains nitrogen, is turned into urea. This process is called **deamination.**

The urea dissolves in the blood plasma, and is taken to the kidneys to be excreted. A small amount is also excreted in sweat.

The liver has many other functions, as well as deamination. Some of these are listed in Table 10.2.

Table 10.2   Some functions of the liver

1	Converts excess amino acids into urea and carbohydrate, in a process called deamination
2	Controls the amount of glucose in the blood, with the aid of the hormones insulin and glucagon
3	Stores carbohydrate as the polysaccharide glycogen
4	Makes bile
5	Breaks down old red blood cells, storing the iron, and excreting the remains of the pigments in bile
6	Breaks down harmful substances such as alcohol
7	Stores vitamins D and A
8	Makes cholesterol, which is needed to make and repair cell membranes
9	Produces heat as a result of the many metabolic reactions which take place in the liver cells

Questions

1   What is meant by an excretory product?
2   What are the two main excretory products of plants?
3   Through which part of the plant are these substances excreted?
4   Why is urea called a nitrogenous excretory product?
5   Why do plants not have nitrogenous excretory products?
6   What happens to excess amino acids in the liver?

The human excretory system

10.19   The kidneys are part of the excretory system.

Figure 10.11 illustrates the position of the two kidneys in the human body. They are near the back of the abdomen, behind the intestines.

Figure 10.12 illustrates a longitudinal section through a kidney. It has three main parts – the **cortex, medulla** and **pelvis.** Leading from the pelvis is a tube, called the **ureter.** The ureter carries urine that the kidney has made to the **bladder.**

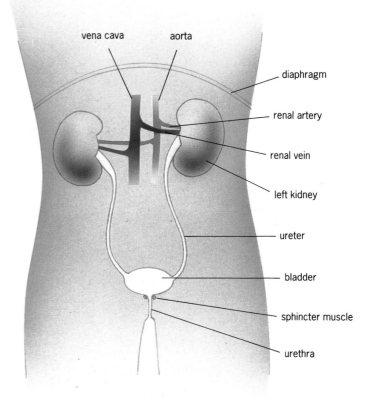

Fig 10.11 The human excretory system

10.20   The kidneys are full of tubules.

Although they seem solid, kidneys are actually made up of thousands of tiny tubules, or **nephrons** (Figs 10.13 and 10.14). Each nephron begins in the cortex, loops down into the medulla, back into the cortex, and then goes down again through the medulla to the pelvis. In the pelvis, the nephrons join up with the ureter.

10.21   Urine is made by filtration and reabsorption.

The job of the kidneys is to take unwanted substances from the blood and to pass them on to the bladder, to be excreted. The way they do this is shown in Fig 10.14.

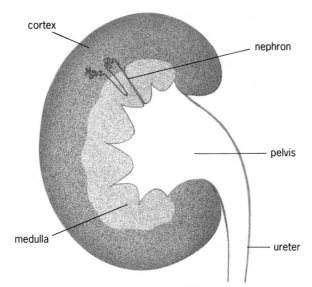

Fig 10.12 *A longitudinal section through a kidney*

blood again. The liquid left in the tubule, called **urine**, goes into the ureter and is taken to the bladder.

10.22 Filtration happens in Bowman's capsules.

There are thousands of Bowman's capsules in the cortex of each kidney. Each one is shaped like a cup. It has a tangle of blood capillaries, called a **glomerulus**, in the middle.

The blood vessel bringing blood to each glomerulus is quite wide, but the one taking blood away is narrow. This means that the blood in the glomerulus cannot get away easily. Quite a high pressure builds up, squeezing the blood in the glomerulus against the capillary walls.

These walls have small holes in them. So do the walls of the Bowman's capsule. Any molecules small enough to go through these holes will be squeezed through, into the space in the Bowman's capsule.

Only small molecules can go through. These include **water**, **salts**, **glucose** and **urea**. Most protein molecules are too big, so they stay in the blood, along with the blood cells.

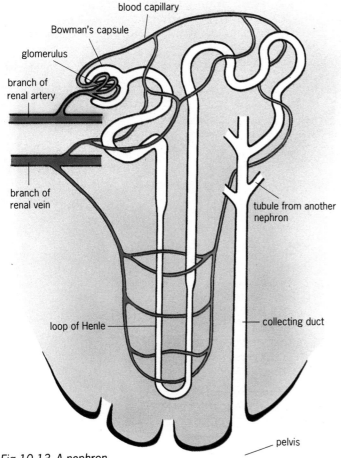

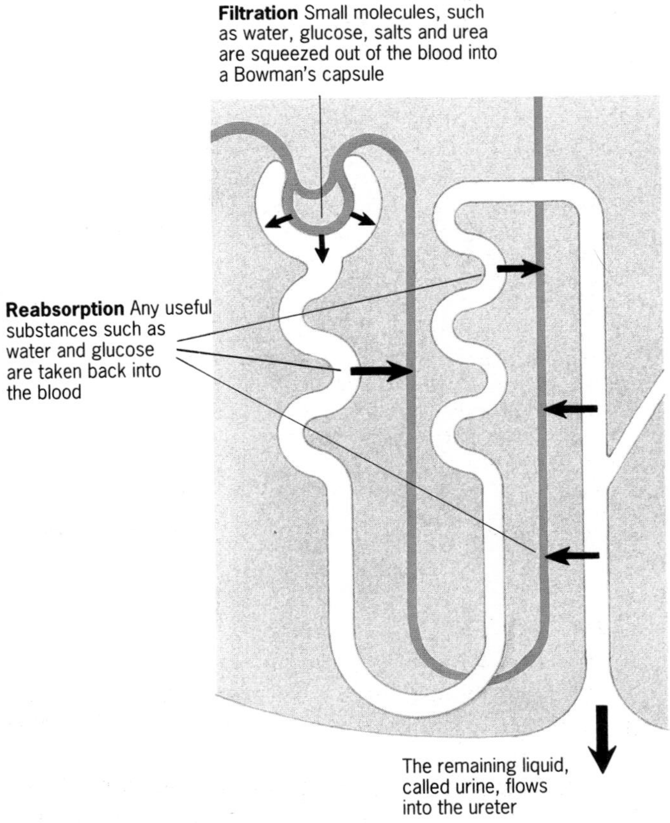

Fig 10.13 *A nephron*

Blood is brought to the Bowman's capsule in a branch of the renal artery. Small molecules, including water and most of the things dissolved in it, are squeezed out of the blood into the Bowman's capsule. Any useful substances are then taken back into the

Filtration Small molecules, such as water, glucose, salts and urea are squeezed out of the blood into a Bowman's capsule

Reabsorption Any useful substances such as water and glucose are taken back into the blood

The remaining liquid, called urine, flows into the ureter

Fig 10.14 *How urine is made*

161

10.23 Useful substances are reabsorbed.

The fluid in the Bowman's capsule is a solution of glucose, salts and urea, dissolved in water. Some of the substances in this fluid are needed by the body. All of the glucose, some of the water and some of the salts, need to be kept in the blood.

Wrapped around each kidney tubule are blood capillaries. They reabsorb these useful substances back from the fluid in the kidney tubule.

The remaining fluid continues on its way along the tubule. By the time it gets to the collecting duct, it is mostly water, with urea and salts dissolved in it. It is called urine.

10.24 The bladder stores urine.

The urine from all the nephrons in the kidneys flows into the ureters. The ureters take it to the bladder.

The bladder stores urine. It has stretchy walls, so that it can hold quite large quantities.

Leading out of the bladder is a tube called the **urethra**. There is a sphincter muscle at the top of the urethra, which is usually tightly closed. When the bladder is full, the sphincter muscle opens, so that urine flows along the urethra and out of the body.

Adult mammals can consciously control this sphincter muscle. In young mammals, it opens automatically when the bladder gets full.

10.25 Kidney machines can do the work of damaged kidneys.

Sometimes, a person's kidneys may stop working properly. This might be because of an infection in the kidneys. Complete failure of the kidneys allows urea and other waste products to build up in the blood. It also means that the amount of water in the body is not regulated. This will cause death unless the patient is given treatment.

If a transplant is not possible, then people with kidney failure are treated regularly on a **kidney machine**. Fig 10.15 shows one kind of kidney machine.

Blood from an artery in the patient's arm flows into the kidney machine. Here, it passes through a **dialyser**. The dialyser contains fluid containing water and other substances, such as salt.

As the patient's blood passes through the dialyser, it is separated from the fluid by a partially permeable membrane. As there is no urea in the fluid, most of the urea in the blood diffuses through the membrane into the fluid. The amount of other substances remaining in the blood can be regulated by controlling their concentrations in the fluid.

Patients have to be treated on a kidney machine two or three times a week. Each treatment lasts several hours.

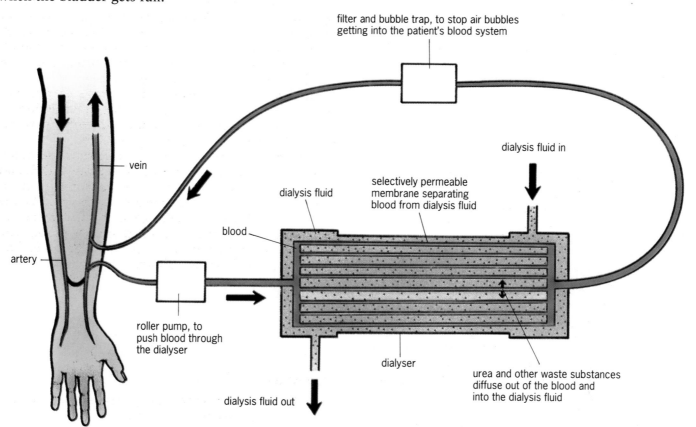

filter and bubble trap, to stop air bubbles getting into the patient's blood system

vein

dialysis fluid in

dialysis fluid

selectively permeable membrane separating blood from dialysis fluid

blood

artery

roller pump, to push blood through the dialyser

dialyser

urea and other waste substances diffuse out of the blood and into the dialysis fluid

dialysis fluid out

Fig 10.15 How a kidney machine works

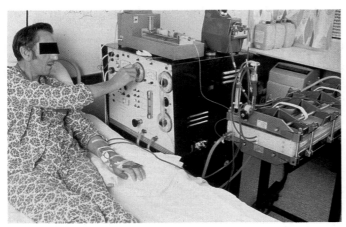
Fig 10.16 A kidney machine being used for dialysis. The man's blood will have to flow through the machine, back into his body and through the machine again many times before the treatment is complete.

Although treatment on a dialyser will keep a patient alive and well, it is not the ideal solution. Some people feel unwell during dialysis. It is also very inconvenient. Some patients have a dialyser at home, but many have to go into hospital for treatment, because kidney machines are expensive so there are not enough for all patients to have their own.

A better long-term solution for kidney failure is a kidney transplant. However, this has drawbacks as well. There are not enough donor kidneys available, and they are often rejected by the recipient even if the transplant operation is successful. You can read more about this in Chapter 18.

Questions

1 What is a nephron?
2 Which blood vessels bring blood to the kidneys?
3 What is a glomerulus?
4 How is a high blood pressure built up in a glomerulus?
5 Why is this high blood pressure needed?
6 Name two substances found in the blood which you would not find in the fluid inside a Bowman's capsule.
7 List three substances which are reabsorbed from the nephron into the blood.
8 What is urine?
9 Where are (a) ureters, and (b) the urethra found?
10 Look at Fig 10.15.
   (a) Why is the blood passed through the dialyser in many small channels instead of one large one?
   (b) Why might it be dangerous if an air bubble gets into the patient's blood?
   (c) Give two reasons why a successful kidney transplant is better than treatment on a kidney machine.

The control of water content

10.26 The kidneys help with osmoregulation.

The control of water content of the body is known as **osmoregulation**. The kidneys, acting together with the hypothalamus and pituitary gland, are responsible for osmoregulation in humans.

Osmoregulation is important because changes in the amount of water in the blood and tissue fluid can have great effects on body cells. If there is more water than there should be – that is, if the blood is too dilute – then water may move into cells by osmosis, causing them to swell and perhaps even burst. If the blood is too concentrated, water will move out of cells, causing them to shrink. In both of these cases, the reactions which go on inside the cells will be disrupted.

10.27 The hormone ADH regulates water loss in urine.

The hypothalamus continuously monitors the concentration of the blood. If there is too little water, it causes the hormone **ADH** (antidiuretic hormone) to be secreted from the **pituitary gland.** The ADH dissolves in the blood plasma, and is carried all over the body.

When it reaches the kidneys, it affects the walls of the collecting ducts in the nephrons. It makes them very permeable to water. As the urine flows down the collecting ducts, much of the water in it passes through the walls of the collecting ducts, and into the blood. So the maximum amount of water is kept in the blood, and the minimum amount is lost in the urine. The urine will be more concentrated than usual.

The hypothalamus also sends messages to the conscious areas of your brain, and makes you feel thirsty. You respond to this by drinking, which helps to increase the amount of water in your blood.

If the hypothalamus senses that there is too much water in your blood, then it stops secreting ADH, and stops you feeling thirsty. Now the collecting ducts in the kidneys become impermeable to water. As the urine flows down through them, the water can no longer go through their walls and into the blood. The water stays in the urine. More urine will be made than usual, and it will be very dilute.

Question

1 Draw a negative feedback loop to show how the water content of the blood is controlled.

Chapter revision questions

1 (a) Why do body cells need glucose?

(b) In healthy humans, the blood contains 60–110 mg of glucose per 100 cm³ of blood. Which gland secretes the hormones which are responsible for keeping this level fairly constant?

(c) The graph in Fig 10.17 shows the changes in blood glucose level after a meal. Explain the shape of the graph between (i) A and B, (ii) B and C, and (iii) C and D.

(d) People with the disease diabetes mellitus cannot make insulin. Why is it dangerous for diabetics to eat a meal containing a lot of sugar?

(e) The regulation of blood glucose levels is one example of homeostasis. What is homeostasis, and why is it important?

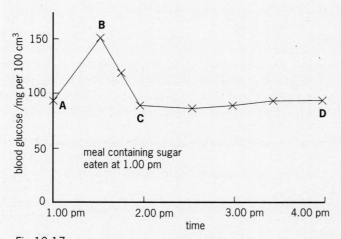

Fig 10.17

2 (a) What is the main nitrogenous waste product excreted by human kidneys?

(b) Where is this waste product formed?

(c) Briefly describe how this waste product is formed.

(d) Which blood vessels deliver this waste product to the kidneys?

(e) Name two substances found in the blood plasma which are not found in the urine of a healthy person.

(f) For each of these substances, explain how the structure and function of the kidney ensures that they are not lost in the urine.

3 An experiment was performed, to find how the rate of a chemical reaction was affected by temperature. The results are shown on the graph.

(a) Is this reaction catalysed by an enzyme? Give reasons for your answer.

(b) What is the optimum temperature for this reaction?

(c) Suggest one reaction which might give results like this.

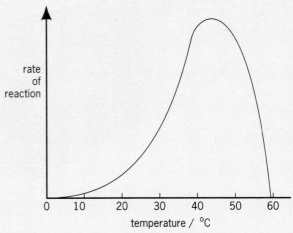

4 In an experiment, a number of newly-hatched sparrows were kept at a temperature of 20 °C. Each day, their body temperature and the amount of oxygen they used were measured. The average temperature and oxygen consumption for each day were plotted on a graph.

(a) What is (i) the body temperature, and (ii) the oxygen consumption of a three-day-old sparrow, when the air temperature is 20 °C?

(b) Adult sparrows are homeothermic, keeping their body temperature at around 38 °C. At what age do young sparrows become able to maintain this body temperature?

(c) Using the information provided by the graph, and your own knowledge of how homeothermic animals maintain their body temperature, explain why one-day-old sparrows consume less oxygen than seven-day-old sparrows.

(d) What would you expect to happen to (i) the body temperature, and (ii) the oxygen consumption of a one-day-old sparrow, if the air temperature was raised to 25 °C? Explain your answer.

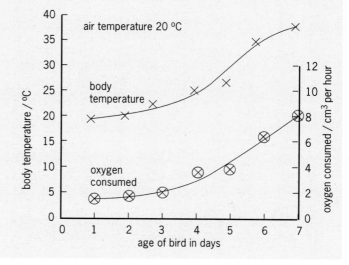

164

11 Support and movement

11.1 Skeletons support organisms.

All living organisms are held in shape, or supported, in some way. Many of them have special structures which do this. These structures are called **skeletons**.

The human skeleton, made of bone and cartilage, is only one kind of skeleton. Because it is inside the body, it is called an **endoskeleton** ('endo-' means inside). Earthworms and plants also have endoskeletons, although they are very different. Insects have a skeleton on the outside of their bodies, called an **exoskeleton** ('exo-' means outside).

Support and movement in mammals

11.2 Bone is made of protein and minerals.

Most of the human skeleton is made of **bone**. Bone is mostly made of mineral substances such as calcium phosphate, with small amounts of magnesium salts. This makes it very hard. Bone also contains **collagen fibres** (Fig 11.1) which give it elasticity. Collagen is a protein.

Bone is alive. It contains living cells, which are supplied with food and oxygen by blood vessels. The cells are arranged in rings around the blood vessels (Fig 11.2).

11.3 The structure of a bone.

Figure 11.3 shows a leg bone, cut in half lengthways. The hardest bone, called **compact bone,** is on the outside. Underneath this is a layer of **spongy bone,** which has spaces in it. This stops the bone from being too heavy.

In the centre is the **bone marrow**. This is very soft, and has a good supply of blood. Red blood cells, white blood cells and platelets are made here. The ends of the bone are covered with a layer of **cartilage**.

11.4 Cartilage contains less minerals than bone.

Cartilage (Fig 11.4) is much softer than bone. This is because it does not contain very many mineral salts, but like bone, it contains collagen.

Cartilage is found on the ends of bones, where they meet one another at a joint. It allows the bones to move easily over each other because it is smooth. There is also cartilage in the pinnae of your ears, and in the end of your nose.

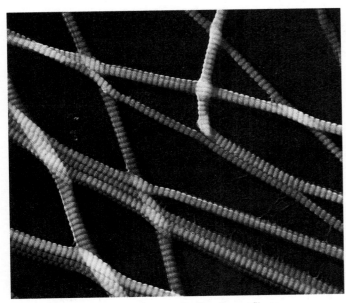

11.1 Scanning electron micrograph of collagen fibres

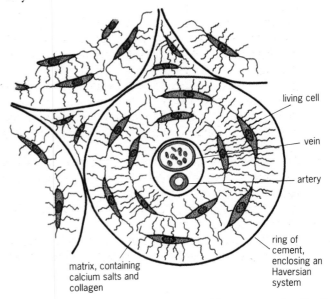

11.2 A piece of living bone as it would appear under the light microscope

165

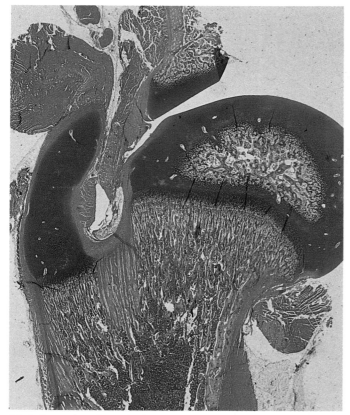

11.3 A section through the upper end of a femur (thigh bone), stained to show the cartilage blue and the bone red

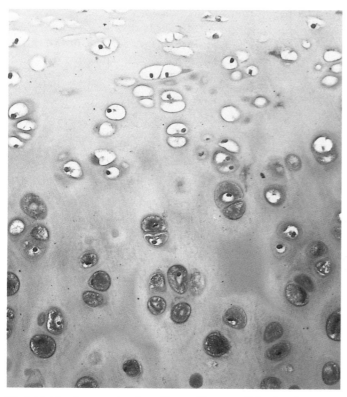

11.4 Light micrograph of cartilage. The roundish structures are cells, surrounded by a smooth-looking matrix which they have made.

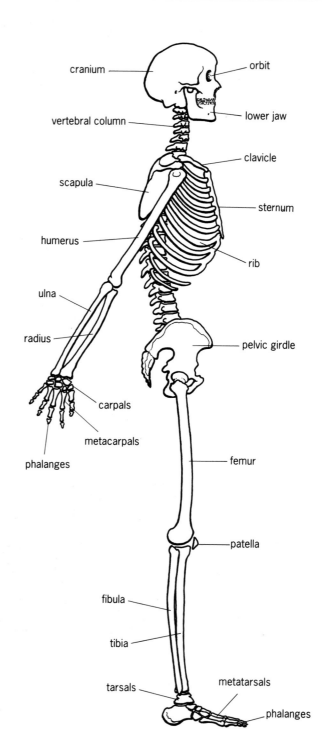

11.5 The human half-skeleton

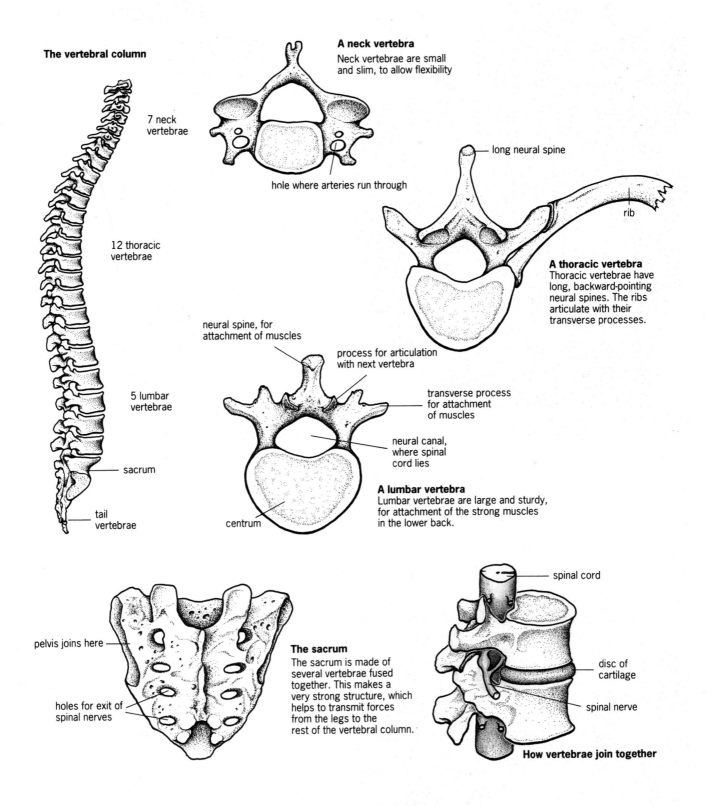

The vertebral column

7 neck vertebrae

12 thoracic vertebrae

5 lumbar vertebrae

sacrum

tail vertebrae

A neck vertebra
Neck vertebrae are small and slim, to allow flexibility

hole where arteries run through

long neural spine

rib

A thoracic vertebra
Thoracic vertebrae have long, backward-pointing neural spines. The ribs articulate with their transverse processes.

neural spine, for attachment of muscles

process for articulation with next vertebra

transverse process for attachment of muscles

neural canal, where spinal cord lies

A lumbar vertebra
Lumbar vertebrae are large and sturdy, for attachment of the strong muscles in the lower back.

centrum

pelvis joins here

holes for exit of spinal nerves

The sacrum
The sacrum is made of several vertebrae fused together. This makes a very strong structure, which helps to transmit forces from the legs to the rest of the vertebral column.

spinal cord

disc of cartilage

spinal nerve

How vertebrae join together

11.6 Vertebrae

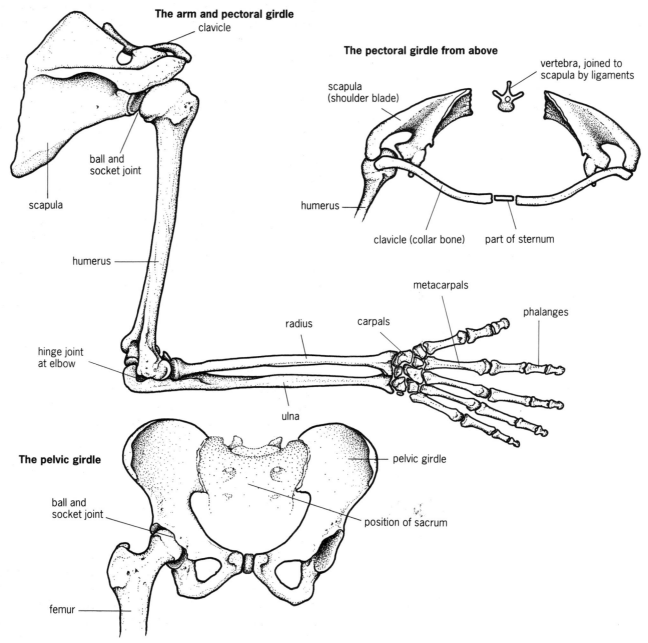

The arm and pectoral girdle
clavicle
ball and socket joint
scapula
humerus
hinge joint at elbow
radius
ulna
carpals
metacarpals
phalanges

The pectoral girdle from above
vertebra, joined to scapula by ligaments
scapula (shoulder blade)
humerus
clavicle (collar bone)
part of sternum

The pelvic girdle
ball and socket joint
femur
pelvic girdle
position of sacrum

11.7 Limbs and girdles

Questions

1 What runs through the centre of the vertebral column?
2 Why do vertebrae have transverse processes?
3 How can you tell the difference between a neck vertebra and a lumbar vertebra?
4 Which vertebrae have ribs joined to them?
5 Why does the sacrum need to be very strong?
6 What is the correct name for (a) the shoulder blade, and (b) the collar bone?

Table 11.1 Functions of the human skeleton

Function	Example
Support	vertebral column pectoral girdle pelvic girdle leg bones
Movement	leg and arm bones
Protection	skull (protects brain) ribs (protect heart and lungs)
Making red and white blood cells	marrow in leg bones and ribs

11.5 Bones are joined in different ways.

Wherever two bones meet each other, a **joint** is formed. There are two main kinds of joint.

Fibrous joints   Sometimes two bones are joined quite firmly together by fibres. The bones in the cranium of the skull are joined like this. The joins are called **sutures**. The bones are held so tightly together in an adult human that they cannot move at all.

There are also fibrous joints between the vertebrae. The bones are joined by pieces of cartilage with fibres in it, called **intervertebral discs**. The cartilage is quite soft in the middle, so the bones can move a little. Although any one joint between two vertebrae only allows a slight movement, the sum total of all these movements makes the backbone quite supple.

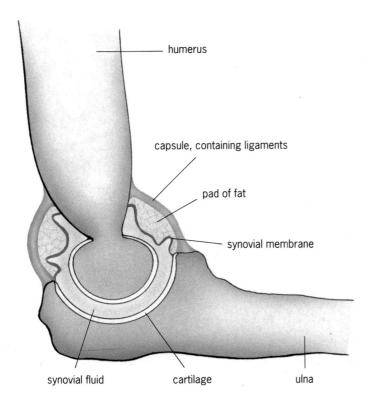

11.8 Section through the elbow joint

humerus

capsule, containing ligaments

pad of fat

synovial membrane

synovial fluid   cartilage   ulna

Synovial joints   **Synovial joints** are found where two bones need to move freely. The elbow joint and shoulder joint are examples of synovial joints.

Figure 11.8 shows the structure of a typical synovial joint. The two bones are held together by **ligaments**. Ligaments are very strong, but can stretch when the bones move.

If the two bones rubbed against one another when they moved, they would quickly be damaged. So the ends of the bones are covered with a layer of cartilage. Between the bones is a small amount of a thick liquid called **synovial fluid**. This lubricates the joint, so that it moves smoothly. The fluid is made and kept in place by the synovial membrane.

Synovial joints are given different names, depending on the kind of movement that takes place. The elbow joint is a **hinge joint,** because the bones can only move in one plane, like a door on hinges. The shoulder and hip joints are **ball and socket joints**. A ball at the end of one bone fits into a socket in the other. This allows a circular movement, or movement in all planes.

11.6 Replacement joints.

If the surfaces of the bones at a synovial joint are damaged, movement of that joint becomes very painful. It may eventually become impossible. The commonest cause of such problems is **arthritis**. In arthritis, the cartilage covering the surfaces of the bones at a joint is damaged. To relieve the pain, and make free movement possible again, a **replacement joint** can be put in.

The joints which are most often replaced are hips. Shoulder, knee and finger joints can also be replaced.

Figure 11.9 shows a replacement hip joint. The materials used to make the joint must be very carefully chosen. They must not corrode when in contact with body fluids. They must not cause the body to react to them, which could cause inflammation and pain. They must be very strong, and their surfaces must be very smooth, to allow easy movement. There are several different types of replacement joint, made from different combinations of materials, often using a metal alloy for the main parts, and a high density plastic or ceramic for the smooth joint surfaces.

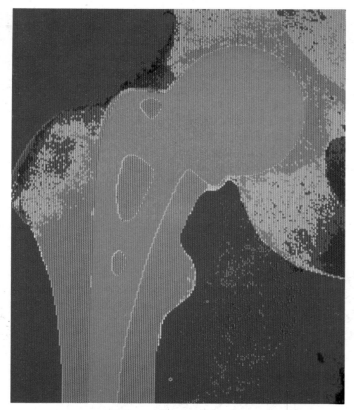

11.9 *An X-ray of an artificial hip joint. The colour has been added after the X-ray was taken. The metal part is shown in pink. The shaft of the femur (thigh bone), which is green in this photograph, was drilled out to make the space for the metal to be inserted.*

11.7 There are three kinds of muscle in mammals.

The three kinds of muscle in the human body (Fig 11.10) are listed below.

Cardiac muscle Cardiac muscle is only found in the heart. It makes up the walls of the atria and ventricles.

Smooth muscle Smooth muscle is found in organs such as the walls of the alimentary canal and the bladder. Smooth muscle is also called involuntary muscle, because you do not have conscious control over it.

Striated muscle All of the muscles attached to your bones are striated muscle. They are sometimes called skeletal muscles, or voluntary muscles, as they are normally under conscious control.

'Striated' means striped, and you can see why this kind of muscle has this name if you look at Fig 11.10.

11.8 Each kind of muscle contracts in a different way.

Muscles cause movement by getting shorter, or **contracting**. They need energy to do this. They get their energy from respiration, and so muscles must have a good blood supply, to bring food and oxygen to them. They also need plenty of mitochondria, to use these substances to make ATP.

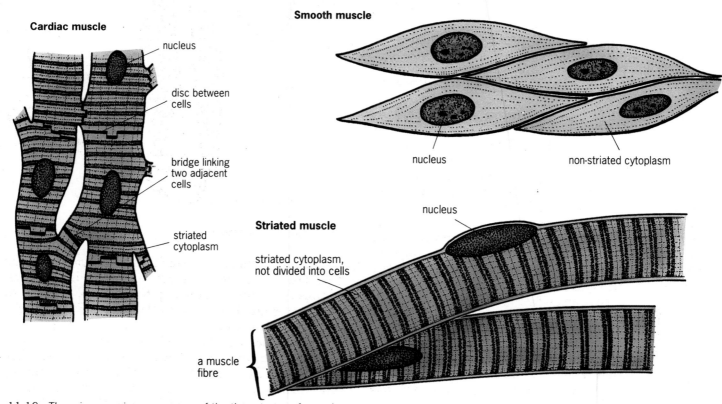

11.10 *The microscopic appearance of the three types of muscle*

Partially contracted

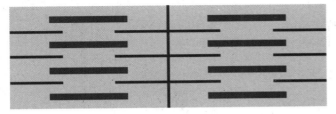

The actin and myosin molecules form filaments. The myosin filaments lie in between the actin filaments.

Fully contracted

myosin   actin

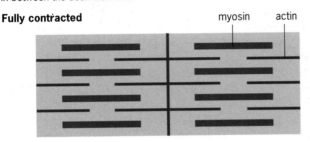

When a message comes to the muscle along a nerve, the actin and myosin filaments slide between each other. This makes the muscle shorter.

11.11 How actin and myosin make muscle contract

All of the three types of muscle can contract, but they do it in slightly different ways. Cardiac muscle contracts and relaxes rhythmically all through your life. It never tires. It does not need conscious messages from your brain to make it contract – it will do it anyway. Nervous impulses from the brain can, however, alter its rate of contraction.

Smooth muscle, too, can contract of its own accord. For example, the muscles in the wall of the alimentary canal do this during peristalsis. In other places, however, smooth muscle needs to be stimulated by nerves, in the same way as striated muscle.

The contractions of smooth muscle are much slower than those of cardiac muscle. Smooth muscle contracts and relaxes slowly and rhythmically.

Striated muscle only contracts when messages are sent to it along nerves. Striated muscle can contract quickly, and very strongly. But it gets tired more quickly than smooth or cardiac muscle.

All of the three types of muscle contain microscopic fibres, or **fibrils,** made of two kinds of protein. The proteins are **actin** and **myosin.** The actin and myosin molecules can slide past each other, which makes the muscle contract. Fig 11.11 shows how they do this. The process uses energy, which comes from ATP made in respiration.

11.9 Movements of the forearm.

Figure 11.12 shows the bones and two of the muscles in your arm. The arm can bend at the elbow, which is a hinge joint.

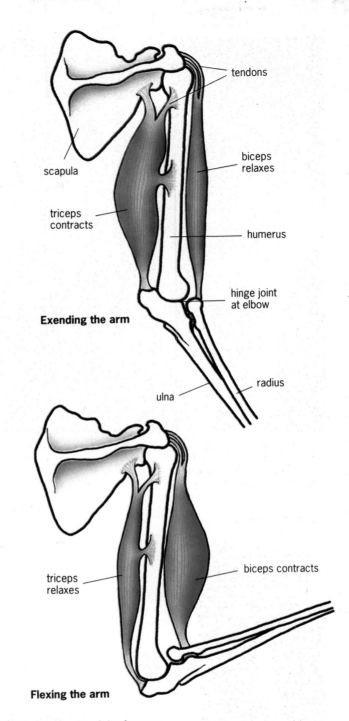

11.12 Movement of the forearm

The **biceps muscle** is attached to the scapula at the top, and the radius at the bottom. When it contracts, it pulls the radius and ulna up towards the scapula, so the arm bends. This is called **flexing** your arm, so the biceps is a **flexor muscle.**

But muscles can only pull, not push. The biceps cannot push your arm back down again. Another muscle is needed to pull it down. The **triceps muscle** does this. When it contracts, the triceps straightens or extends your arm. It is called an **extensor muscle.**

171

Practical 11.1 Using a model arm to investigate the action of the biceps muscle

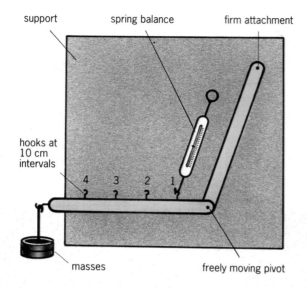

11.13 A model arm

1 Draw a results table.
2 Hang a 100 g mass on the hook at the end of the 'forearm' on the model.
3 Attach a spring balance to hook 1. Pull upwards with the spring balance, parallel to the 'humerus', until the 'forearm' is exactly horizontal. Take the reading on the spring balance, and fill it in on the results table.

4 Repeat with the balance pulling on hooks 2, 3 and 4.
5 Replace the 100 g mass with a 500 g mass, and repeat steps 3 and 4.

Questions

1 What does the spring balance represent?
2 At which position was the force needed to lift the weight greatest?
3 Which position most closely represents the actual position of attachment of the biceps to the radius?
4 Striated muscles are able to exert considerable forces, but they cannot shorten by a very large amount. Can you suggest why the biceps is attached in this position?

The forces acting on the forearm when lifting a weight can be shown diagrammatically like this.

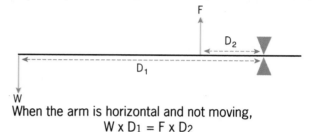

When the arm is horizontal and not moving,
$$W \times D_1 = F \times D_2$$

5 What does W stand for?
6 What does F stand for?
7 Use the equation to explain your answer to question 2.

The flexor and extensor muscles work together. When the biceps contracts, the triceps relaxes. When the triceps contracts, the biceps relaxes. The muscles are said to be **antagonistic muscles** because, in a way, they work against each other. There are many other examples of antagonistic muscles in your body.

11.10 Tendons are groups of collagen fibres.

Muscles are joined to bones by **tendons**. Tendons are very strong, and do not stretch. They are made of collagen fibres.

Some tendons are quite large. You can feel your Achilles tendon at the back of your ankle. It attaches your calf muscle to your heel bone.

11.11 Muscles, tendons and joints are easily damaged.

Most people will damage a muscle, tendon, ligament or bone at some time in their life. The damage most commonly occurs when a sudden, unexpected force acts at a joint. This might happen in a fall, or in an awkward movement or collision when taking part in

Fact!

Muscles make up about 40% of your body weight.

an active sport.

A sudden pull or twist on a joint can tear the ligaments and other tissues around the joint. This is called a **sprain**. Ankles and wrists are the most common joints to suffer from sprains. A sprained joint is painful, and swells up. The only treatment it needs, in order to heal itself, is rest. This can be helped by a carefully applied supportive bandage, which helps to make sure that no more strain will be put on the joint while it is healing, and also makes it feel more comfortable.

A more serious problem is **dislocation**. This is when a bone slips out of position at a joint (Fig 11.14). It most commonly happens at the shoulder joint, but some people are prone to dislocated knee joints. Dis-

172

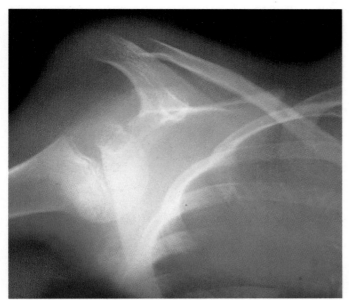

11.14 A false-colour X-ray of a dislocated shoulder. You can see the head of the humerus (upper arm bone) just left of centre of the picture, and the socket in the scapula (shoulder blade) it should fit into just above it. As you can imagine, this is very painful!

locations are very painful, and do not usually get better on their own. A skilled person, such as a doctor, will move the bone back into position again. This instantly eases the pain, but the joint will probably need some support until it has had time to settle back into its normal state.

A broken bone, or **fracture** (Fig 11.15), is almost always painful, and almost always needs treatment. Hairline fractures, in which a crack appears in a bone, but the bone remains in one piece, often simply heal themselves, and may need no more than a little support. If the bone – say an ulna – breaks right through, then the broken ends will need to be brought carefully together (a painful process for the patient, so done under anaesthetic) and then the limb held firmly by a plaster. This keeps the ends of the bone in position

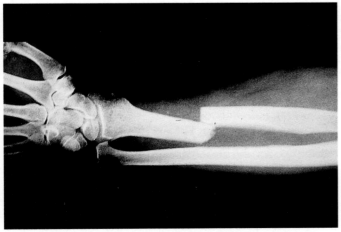

11.15 An X-ray of a broken arm. The broken bone is the radius.

while they grow together and heal. A really bad fracture, where the bone is too badly shattered to be able to heal itself, may need steel pins to be inserted to hold the remaining pieces of bone together.

Questions

1 Why do muscles contain many mitochondria?
2 Which kinds of muscle will contract without a conscious message from the brain?
3 What are the special features of striated muscle?
4 What is meant by (a) a flexor muscle, and (b) an extensor muscle? Give an example of each.
5 What are tendons? How do they differ from ligaments?

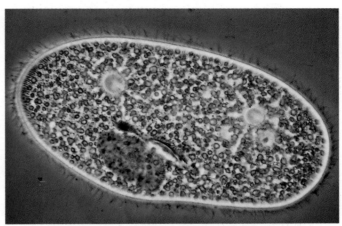

11.16 This microscopic protoctist, Paramecium, moves by means of its covering of cilia, which beat rhythmically to push it through the water

11.12 Cilia can cause movement.

Muscles are not the only things which can move in the human body. Some cells have microscopic threads on them, called **cilia**.

Ciliated cells are found in the tubes of the respiratory system. There are cilia in your trachea and bronchi, for example. They beat rhythmically, wafting mucus up towards the back of your mouth. The mucus traps bacteria and particles of dirt in the air you breathe in.

Many single-celled organisms also use cilia to move around. Fig 11.16 shows one of these. These organisms belong to the phylum Protoctista. Ciliated unicellular organisms like this often live in water, where they feed on bacteria and smaller protoctists.

11.13 Some cells use amoeboid movement.

Figure 11.17 shows a different kind of protoctist. This is a species of *Amoeba*. It, too, lives in water and feeds on bacteria and other smaller protoctists, but it has a different way of getting around. It is called **amoeboid movement**.

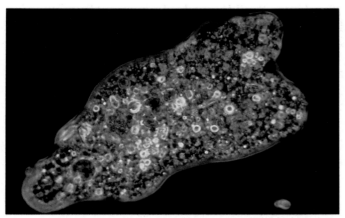

11.17 Amoeba, *also a protoctist, moves by means of pseudopodia, which it can push out in any direction*

change direction by putting out a pseudopodium in a different place. Amoeboid movement is slower than movement using cilia, but is useful for crawling over surfaces such as decaying leaves or the mud at the bottom of a pond.

White blood cells, inside the human body, also move in this way. They crawl into almost every corner of the body, searching for invading cells such as bacteria, or for your own old and damaged cells which need to be removed.

In amoeboid movement, the cytoplasm flows towards a particular part of the cell, which pushes outwards to produce a **pseudopodium**. The whole cell gradually flows in this direction. *Amoeba* can easily

Support and movement in birds

11.14 Birds are adapted for flight.

Figure 11.18 shows part of the skeleton of a bird. It is basically very similar to the human skeleton. But there are some important differences, which enable birds to fly.

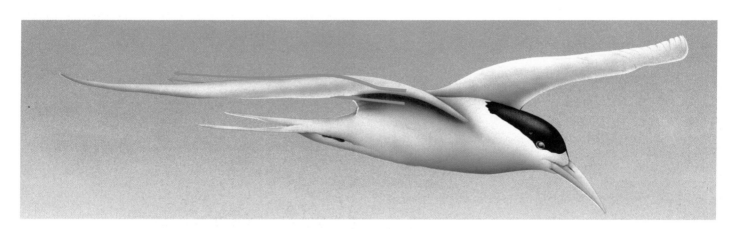

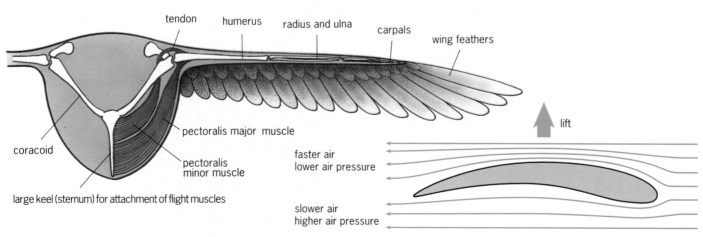

11.18(a) *Transverse section through the thorax of a bird*

11.18b *The wing acts as an aerofoil. When the bird is moving forwards, the shape of the wing causes air to flow faster over the top of the wing than over the lower surface. This makes the downward pressure on the top of the wing less than the upward pressure on the lower surface of the wing. There is a net upward force, providing lift.*

174

The bones contain large air spaces This makes them lighter. Think of the weight of a chicken bone, compared with the bone in a pork chop.

The forelimbs have become wings They have very strong muscles attached to them, which pull the wings up and down. The sternum is much larger than in other vertebrates, forming a **keel**. The keel is needed for the attachment of these strong flight muscles. You eat the flight muscles when you eat chicken breast.

The wing is an aerofoil. As the bird moves forward through the air, the air flows more quickly over the curved upper surface than over the flatter lower surface. This reduces the air pressure on the top of the wing, compared with the air pressure below the wing. There is therefore a net upward pressure on the wing. This gives the bird lift.

The body is covered with feathers These have two important functions. Firstly, birds, like mammals, are homeothermic. The feathers help to insulate their bodies, like hair on a mammal. Their bodies must be kept warm, so that they can produce enough energy to fly.

Secondly, the feathers on the tail and wings give a large surface area, which helps to keep the bird in the air.

The body is streamlined When a bird is flying, its body is shaped to cut cleanly through the air. The feathers lie smoothly against its body, so that the air can easily flow over them.

Support and movement in fish

11.15 Fish are adapted for swimming.

Swimming in water presents very different problems from walking on land like a human, or flying in air like a bird. Herrings, which are very active marine fish, have several adaptations which help them to swim.

They have a flexible vertebral column Most fish swim by moving their bodies from side to side. Fig 11.19 illustrates how this produces a forward movement. The vertebral column has to be able to bend, to allow the fish's body to curve like this.

They have a swim bladder This is an air-filled sac just below the vertebral column. It is found in all bony fish, such as herrings. The fish can adjust the amount of air in it. This helps to keep them afloat at the right depth in the water. The more air in the swim bladder, the nearer they will float to the surface.

Because the buoyancy of the water supports them, fish do not need such strong skeletons as mammals and birds.

They are streamlined This allows them to slide easily through the water. The scales overlap, and point backwards. The scales are covered by a thin, transparent skin. The skin secretes mucus, which makes a fish feel slimy to touch, and which reduces drag when swimming quickly.

They have fins which help them to balance in the water. The caudal fin helps with propulsion.

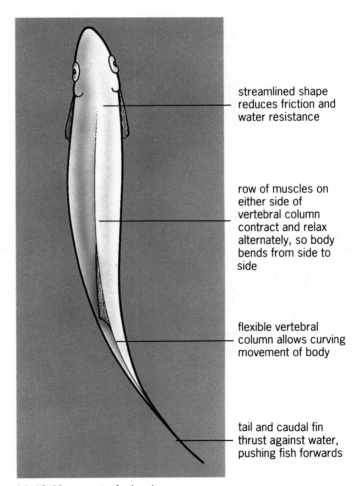

streamlined shape reduces friction and water resistance

row of muscles on either side of vertebral column contract and relax alternately, so body bends from side to side

flexible vertebral column allows curving movement of body

tail and caudal fin thrust against water, pushing fish forwards

11.19 Movement of a herring

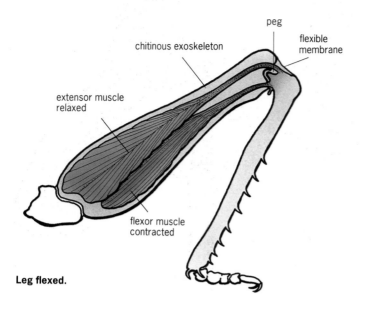

peg

flexible membrane

chitinous exoskeleton

extensor muscle relaxed

flexor muscle contracted

Leg flexed.

extensor muscle contracted

flexor muscle relaxed

Leg suddenly extended, pushing body upwards.

11.20 How a locust hops

Support and movement in insects

11.16 Insects have an exoskeleton of chitin.

An insect's skeleton is built on a completely different plan from a vertebrate's skeleton. Instead of being inside the body, it is on the outside of it. It is called an exoskeleton.

An insect's exoskeleton is mostly made of **chitin**. Chitin is quite a flexible substance, but when it combines with protein it becomes hard. Where the exoskeleton needs to be strong and rigid, it is made of chitin and protein. Where it needs to be flexible, such as at joints, or on the wings, it is made only of chitin.

The exoskeleton is covered with a layer of wax, called a **cuticle**. The cuticle stops water evaporating from the insect's body.

Figure 11.20 illustrates how an insect's muscles are attached to its exoskeleton, and how they cause movement.

Support and movement in earthworms

11.17 Earthworms have hydrostatic skeletons.

Earthworms have no hard parts to support their bodies. They are held in shape by the fluid inside them. The fluid presses out on the muscular body wall, keeping the earthworm's body firm. This is called a **hydrostatic skeleton**.

11.18 How an earthworm moves.

Earthworms are adapted for squeezing through burrows in the soil. Their long, cylindrical shape helps them to do this. The mucus on their skin helps them to slide past soil particles without damaging themselves. They have small bristles called **chaetae** on their underside, which help them to grip the sides of their burrow.

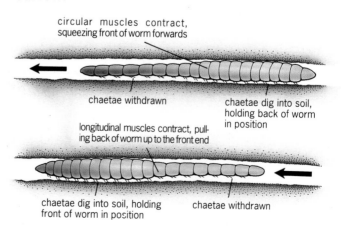

circular muscles contract, squeezing front of worm forwards

chaetae withdrawn

chaetae dig into soil, holding back of worm in position

longitudinal muscles contract, pulling back of worm up to the front end

chaetae dig into soil, holding front of worm in position

chaetae withdrawn

11.21 How an earthworm moves

Earthworms have two sets of muscles outside their fluid skeleton. **Circular muscles** run round the earthworm's body. When they contract, they make its body long and thin. **Longitudinal muscles** run lengthways. When they contract, they make the earthworm's body short and fat. These two sets of muscles work antagonistically (Section 11.9).

Figure 11.21 shows how an earthworm moves.

Support in plants

11.19 Plant skeletons.

All the skeletons so far described in this chapter have two main functions – support and movement. Plants, though, do not move very much. They only need to be supported, so they do not need elaborate skeletons.

11.20 Xylem forms wood and supports plants.

Plant stems, roots and leaves contain xylem (Section 7.27). Xylem is made of cells which have very strong walls containing lignin. These lignified xylem vessels help to support the stem.

The larger and taller the plant, the more support it needs. Trees are supported by the wood in their trunks and branches, which is made almost entirely of xylem.

11.21 Cell turgor supports herbaceous plants.

In parts of plants where there is not much xylem, another means of support is needed.

When a plant has plenty of water, the contents of each cell press outwards on the cell wall. This makes

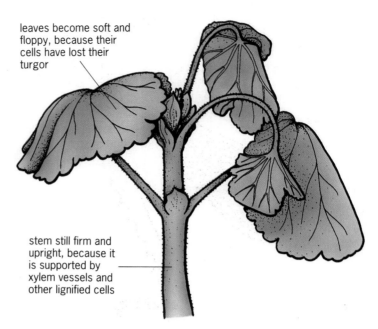

11.22 A wilting geranium shoot

the cells firm, or **turgid**. They press against each other, holding the plant firm and upright. This is particularly important in leaves, and in **herbaceous plants** which do not have woody stems.

Questions

1 List four ways in which birds are adapted for flight.
2 Look at Fig 11.18b. What will happen to the wing when (a) the pectoralis major contracts, and (b) the pectoralis minor contracts?
3 What is a swim bladder, and how it is used?
4 What is meant by a hydrostatic skeleton?
5 What is wood made of?
6 How does turgor help to support plants?

Table 11.2 Summary of the skeletons of different organisms

	Type of skeleton	Material skeleton is made of	Main functions
Mammal	endoskeleton	bone and cartilage	support, movement and protection
Bird	endoskeleton	bone and cartilage	support, movement and protection
Fish	endoskeleton	bone and cartilage	support, movement and protection
Insect	exoskeleton	chitin and protein	support, movement and protection
Earthworm	hydrostatic endoskeleton	fluid	support and movement
Plant	(a) hydrostatic skeleton and (b) endoskeleton	(a) fluid in cells (b) cellulose and lignin in cell walls	support

Chapter revision questions

1 Match each word below with its definition.

collagen, cartilage, ligament, tendon, flexor, extensor, keel, chitin, chaetae, lignin

(a) a structure which holds two bones together at a joint, allowing movement between them

(b) a muscle which pulls two bones closer together when it contracts

(c) a tough material from which an insect's exoskeleton is made

(d) the very large sternum of a bird, to which its flight muscles are attached

(e) small hair-like structures, which help an earthworm to grip the sides of its burrow.

(f) the protein found in bone

(g) a muscle which pulls two bones away from one another when it contracts

(h) the strong substance found in the walls of xylem vessels

(i) a strong but flexible substance, found on the ends of movable bones

(j) a structure which attaches a muscle to a bone

2 (a) What is meant by antagonistic muscles? Give one example.

(b) Make a large, labelled diagram to show the position of one pair of antagonistic muscles in a named mammal, including the structure of the joint whose movement they cause.

(c) Describe how these muscles cause flexing of the joint you have shown.

12   Living organisms in their environment

12.1 Organisms interact with their environment.

One very important way of studying living things is to study them where they live. Animals and plants do not live in complete isolation. They are affected by their surroundings, or **environment**. Their environment is also affected by them. The study of the interaction between living organisms and their environment is called **ecology**.

You cannot really learn about ecology without doing a lot of practical work outside. The information in this chapter and the next should help you to interpret what you find out from your practical work.

12.2 Some important words.

There are many words used in ecology with which you need to be familiar. The area where an organism lives is called its **habitat**. The habitat of a tadpole might be a pond. There will probably be many tadpoles in the pond, forming a **population** of tadpoles. A population is a group of organisms of the same species.

But tadpoles will not be the only organisms living in the pond. There will be many other kinds of animals and plants making up the pond **community**. A community is all the organisms, of all the different species, living in the same habitat.

The living organisms in the pond, the water in it, the stones and the mud at the bottom, make up an **ecosystem**. An ecosystem consists of a community and its environment.

Within the ecosystem, each living organism has its own life to live and role to play. The way in which an organism lives its life in an ecosystem is called its **niche**. Tadpoles, for example, eat algae and other weeds in the pond; they disturb pebbles and mud at the bottom of shallow areas in the pond; they excrete ammonia into the water; they breathe in oxygen from the water, and breathe out carbon dioxide. All these things, and many others, help to describe the tadpoles' role, or niche, in the ecosystem.

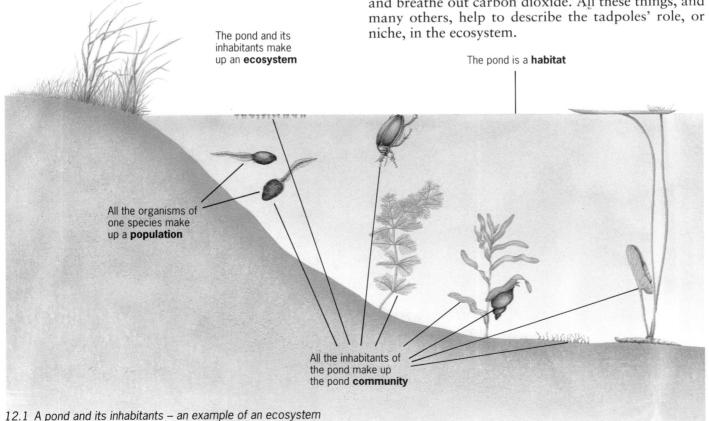

The pond and its inhabitants make up an **ecosystem**

The pond is a **habitat**

All the organisms of one species make up a **population**

All the inhabitants of the pond make up the pond **community**

12.1 A pond and its inhabitants – an example of an ecosystem

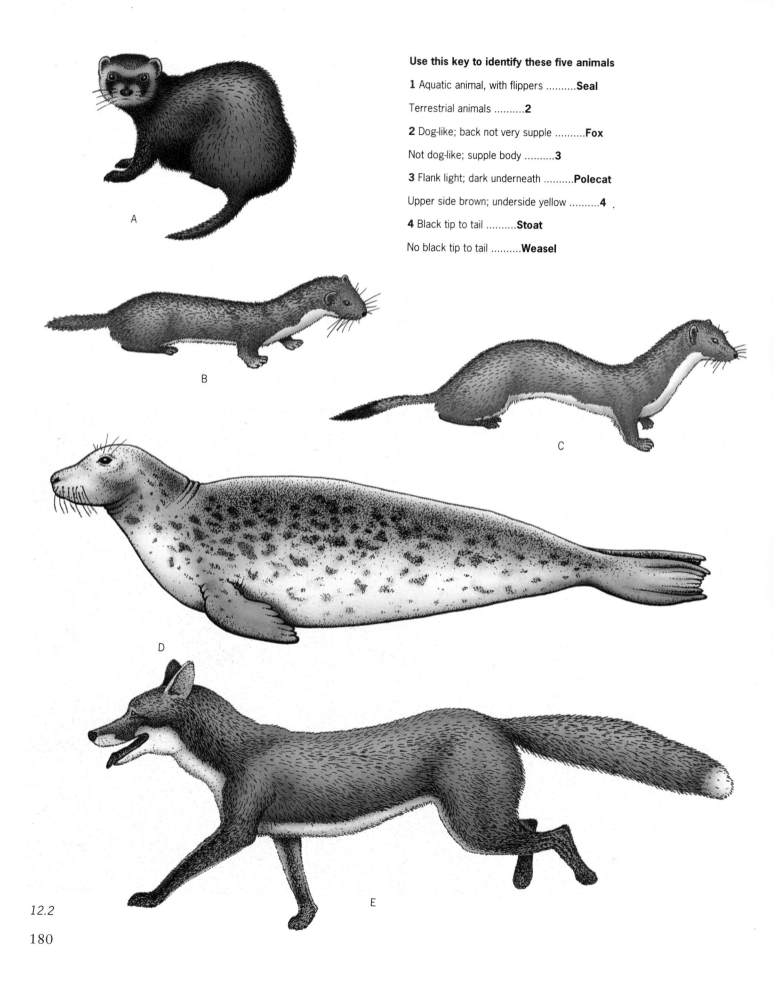

Use this key to identify these five animals

1 Aquatic animal, with flippers ....**Seal**

Terrestrial animals **2**

2 Dog-like; back not very supple ....**Fox**

Not dog-like; supple body **3**

3 Flank light; dark underneath ....**Polecat**

Upper side brown; underside yellow **4**

4 Black tip to tail ....**Stoat**

No black tip to tail ....**Weasel**

A

B

C

D

E

12.2

Questions
1 What is ecology?
2 What is a population?
3 Give two examples of an ecosystem, other than a pond.
4 What is a niche?

Studying ecosystems

12.3 Keys are used for identification.

There are many different ways of studying ecosystems. But whatever ecosystem you study, and however you decide to study it, you will have to begin by identifying the living organisms in it.

Some of them, particularly the bigger ones, you may be able to identify quite quickly from pictures in books. But there will almost certainly be many that you cannot find pictures of, or where you are not sure if the picture really is of your plant or animal.

When this happens, you will need to use a **key**. A key is a way of leading you through to the name of your organism by giving you two descriptions at a time, and asking you to choose between them. Each choice you make then leads you onto another pair of descriptions, until you end up with the name of your organism.

An example of a key like this is shown in Fig 12.2. It is called a **dichotomous key**, because each time you choose between *two* descriptions ('di' means two).

12.4 Sampling can estimate abundance.

When you have identified as many of the organisms as possible in your ecosystem, you can make a list of them, called a **species list**. The next job will probably be to try to find out how many of each species live there.

Sometimes, you can simply count them. You could find how many oak trees there were in a small wood just by counting them. Often it is not quite that easy.

12.3 Using quadrats to survey lichens growing on an old tennis court

If you are studying part of a field, for example, you could not possibly count every buttercup plant. You will have to take a **sample** of the field, and count the numbers of each species in that sample. If you work out the scale factor of the sample to the whole field, you could then get an indication of the numbers of each species in the field.

12.5 Quadrats are used to sample plant cover.

One very useful way of taking a sample is to use a **quadrat**. A quadrat is a square. It can be any size, but one with sides of about 0.5 m is a convenient size to use in a field.

The quadrat is put down onto the ground, and the numbers of each species of plant inside it are counted. With some species, like grasses, though, it is impossible to say where one plant stops and another begins. In this case, you can estimate what percentage of the quadrat area is covered by grass, and by other plants.

If the plants in your quadrat are quite tall, there may be more than one layer of plants. In this case, the total of all your percentages may be more than 100%.

12.6 Sampling should be random.

Your quadrat sample only gives you an idea of the numbers of plants in one small area. You cannot guarantee that that area is representative of the whole field. You will need to do many quadrats, and average your results from each, to be sure of getting a representative sample.

The placing of your quadrat is very important. If you just choose where to put it, the part of the field full of gorse bushes and nettles, with a bull standing behind them, will probably not get sampled very often! So you must use some way of placing your quadrats randomly in the field.

There are several ways of doing this. One way is to divide the piece of ground into squares and use pairs of random numbers as co-ordinates. These you can get from tables. If your numbers are 12,8 for example, you could go twelve squares forward from a corner along an edge, and then eight squares out into the field, and put your quadrat down at that point.

12.7 Transects sample changes between habitats.

Another way of sampling the distribution of organisms in your field is to use a **transect**. A transect is a line crossing the field. You can use a long tape measure to mark the transect. You then record the species of plants touching the tape.

Often, it would take far too long to record all the plants touching the tape. Instead, you might record them at intervals, say every 10 cm.

Transects are particularly useful where one kind of habitat is changing into another. You could use one, for example, where a grassy field merged into a wood, or into a stream. A transect will give you information about how the numbers and kinds of species change, as the environment changes.

12.8 Mark, release, recapture estimates numbers.

Quadrats and transects are very useful ways of finding out how many organisms of different species are living in a habitat. But they can only be used with organisms which stay in one place for most of the time. This usually means plants, though on a seashore you can also count limpets, barnacles, sea anemones and many other animals in this way.

You need a different method for estimating the numbers of animals that move around a lot. One method is the **mark, release, recapture technique**. It works so long as there are reasonable numbers of each kind of animal, and so long as they move around quite freely.

Suppose that you wanted to estimate the size of a population of woodlice. First, you need to capture a sample of perhaps 30 woodlice. Each woodlouse is marked with a small spot of waterproof paint, and then released.

The woodlice are then left alone for about a day, to give the marked ones a chance to become mixed up with any unmarked ones. You then capture a second sample, of as many woodlice as you can. Count the total number, and the number of marked ones.

Suppose that you caught 100 woodlice in your second sample, and 10 of them had been marked. You have recaptured 10 of the 30 you originally marked, or ⅓ of them. So it is probable that you have caught about ⅓ of the whole woodlouse population. The size of the population will therefore be about 3 x 100 woodlice, that is 300.

In general, the formula for working this out is

$$\text{number of animals caught the first time} \times \frac{\text{number of animals caught the second time}}{\text{number of marked animals caught the second time}}$$

Questions

1 When using a quadrat, how can you estimate the amount of a plant, such as grass, in your sample?
2 Why is it important to place quadrats randomly?
3 When might you use a transect?
4 50 water beetles were caught and marked, before being returned to their pond. The next day, another 50 water beetles were caught, 10 of which had been marked. About how many water beetles were in the pond altogether?

12.4 Using a transect to estimate how numbers of different species change between the upper and lower levels of a rocky shore

Diagram of area being studied

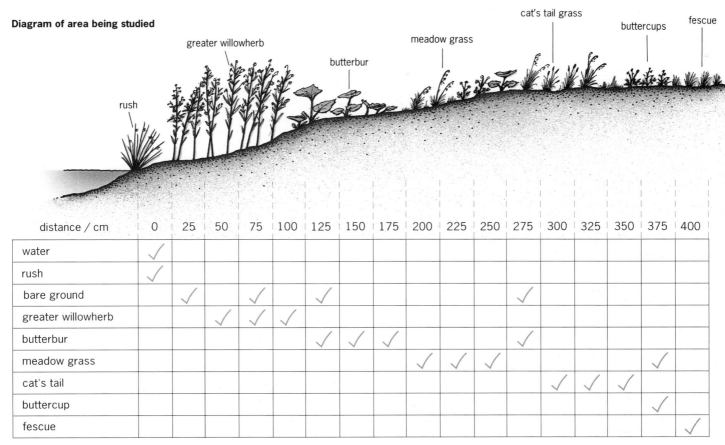

distance / cm	0	25	50	75	100	125	150	175	200	225	250	275	300	325	350	375	400
water	✓																
rush	✓																
bare ground		✓		✓		✓						✓					
greater willowherb			✓	✓	✓												
butterbur						✓	✓	✓				✓					
meadow grass									✓	✓	✓					✓	
cat's tail													✓	✓	✓		
buttercup																✓	
fescue																	✓

Record of transect

12.5 A transect recording changes in vegetation from wet to dry ground

Practical 12.1 Estimating the size of a bead population, using the mark, release, recapture technique.

1 Fill a bucket or large tray with a large number of beads, all the same colour and size.
2 Capture a sample of about 50 beads.
3 'Mark' the captured beads, by exchanging them for beads of a different colour. Return the marked beads to the population.
4 Thoroughly mix the marked beads with the rest of the population.
5 Capture a second, quite large but random, sample of beads. It may be best to use a blindfold for this sample to ensure that it is random.
6 Count (a) the number of marked beads in your second sample, and (b) the total number of beads in this sample.
7 Work out the estimated population of beads using the formula

$$\text{number of beads in first sample} \times \frac{\text{number of beads in second sample}}{\text{number of marked beads in second sample}}$$

8 Now count the actual number of beads in the population.

Questions

1 How close was your estimate to the actual number of beads in the population? Do you consider it was close enough for this to be a useful technique?
2 When using the technique in the field, how could you ensure that your estimate came as close as possible to the real size of the population?
3 For which of these populations would this method be suitable?
(a) snails in a small garden
(b) rabbits in a hedgerow
(c) dandelions in a lawn
(d) killer whales in the Atlantic Ocean
(e) lichens on a tree trunk
Give reasons for your answers, and suggest alternative methods if you do not think that mark, release, recapture would be suitable.

Food and energy in an ecosystem

12.9 Energy passes along food chains.

All living organisms need energy. They get energy from food, by respiration. All the energy in an ecosystem comes from the sun. Some of the energy in sunlight is captured by plants, and used to make food – glucose, starch and other organic substances such as fats and proteins. These contain some of the energy from the sunlight. When the plant needs energy, it breaks down some of this food by respiration.

Animals get their food, and therefore their energy, by eating plants, or by eating animals which have eaten plants.

The sequence by which energy, in the form of food, passes from a plant to an animal and then to other animals, is called a **food chain**. Fig 12.6 shows one example of a food chain.

12.10 Consumers use food made by producers.

Every food chain begins with green plants because only they can capture the energy from sunlight. They are called **producers**, because they produce food.

Animals are **consumers**. An animal which eats plants is a **primary consumer**, because it is the first consumer in a food chain. An animal which eats that animal is a **secondary consumer**, and so on along the chain.

12.11 Food chains are usually short.

As the energy is passed along the chain, each organism uses some of it. So the further along the chain you go, the less energy there is. There is plenty of energy available for producers, so there are usually a lot of them. There is less energy for primary consumers, and less still for secondary consumers. This means that towards the end of the food chain, the organisms get fewer in number, or smaller in total size.

The loss of energy along the food chain also limits the length of it. There are rarely more than five links in a chain, because there is not enough energy left to supply the next link. Many food chains only have three links.

12.12 Consumers feed at different trophic levels.

In Fig 12.8, the number of organisms in the food chain is shown as a pyramid. The size of each block in the pyramid represents the number of organisms. It is called a **pyramid of numbers**. Each level in the pyramid is called a **trophic level** ('trophic' means feeding).

The pyramid is this shape because there is less energy available as you go up the trophic levels, so there are fewer organisms at each level.

Fact!

Places where most sunlight energy is put into the ecosystem are estuaries, coral reefs and tropical rain forests, which are nearly twice as productive as fertilised agricultural land.

grass – a primary producer eaten by rabbit – a primary consumer eaten by fox – a secondary consumer

12.6 A food chain

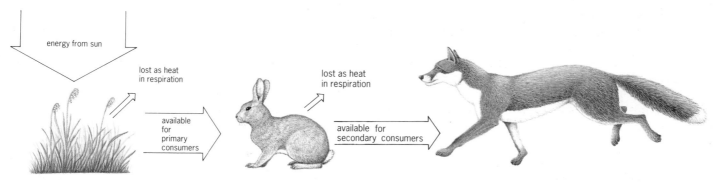

energy from sun

lost as heat in respiration

available for primary consumers

lost as heat in respiration

available for secondary consumers

12.7 Energy losses in food chain

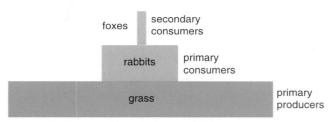

foxes	secondary consumers
rabbits	primary consumers
grass	primary producers

Each level in the pyramid is called a trophic level. The size of each level represents the numbers of organisms feeding at that level.

12.8 A pyramid of numbers

blue tits

caterpillars

oak tree

The pyramid is this shape because one oak tree provides food for hundreds of caterpillars.

12.9 An inverted pyramid of numbers

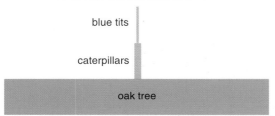

blue tits

caterpillars

oak tree

In this pyramid, the size of each box represents the mass of each kind of organism.

12.10 A pyramid of biomass

Many organisms feed at more than one trophic level. You, for example, are a primary consumer when you eat vegetables, a secondary consumer when you eat meat or drink milk, and a tertiary consumer when you eat a predatory fish such as a salmon.

12.13 Pyramids of numbers may be 'upside down'.

Figure 12.9 shows a different shaped pyramid of numbers. The pyramid is this shape because of the sizes of the organisms in the food chain. Although there is only a single oak tree, it is huge compared with the caterpillars which feed on it. If you make the size of the blocks represent the **mass** of the organisms, instead of their **numbers**, then the pyramid becomes the right shape again. It is called a **pyramid of biomass** (Fig 12.10), and gives a much better idea of the actual quantity of animal or plant material at each trophic level.

12.14 Understanding energy flow helps agriculture.

Understanding how energy is passed along a food chain can be useful in agriculture. We can eat a wide variety of foods, and can feed at several different

185

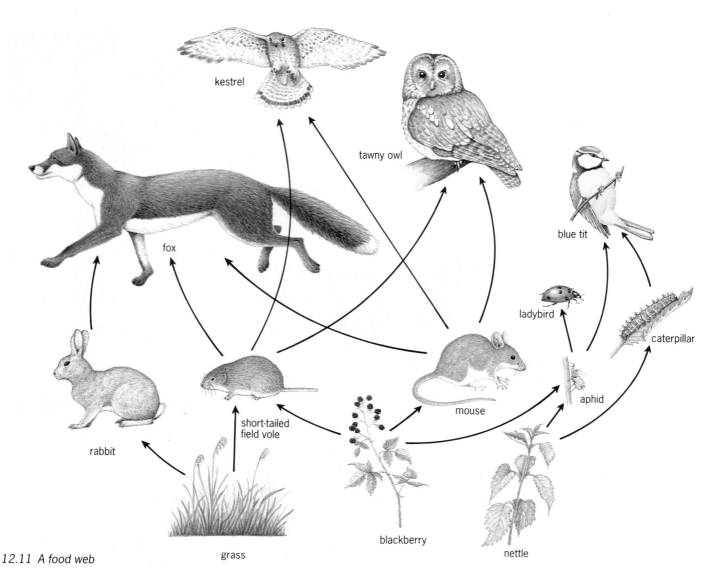

12.11 A food web

trophic levels. Which is the most efficient sort of food for a farmer to grow, and for us to eat?

The nearer to the beginning of the food chain we feed, the more energy there is available for us. This is why our staple foods, wheat, rice, potatoes, are plants.

When we eat meat, eggs or cheese or drink milk, we are feeding further along the food chain. There is less energy available for us from the original energy provided by the sun. It would be more efficient in principle to eat the grass in a field, rather than to let cattle eat it, and then eat them.

In fact, however, although there is far more energy in the grass than in the cattle, it is not available to us. We simply cannot digest the cellulose in grass, so we cannot release the energy from it. The cattle can; they turn the energy in cellulose into energy in protein and fat, which we can digest.

However, there are many plant products which we can eat. Soya beans, for example, yield a high amount of protein, much more efficiently and cheaply than cattle or other animals. A change towards vegetarianism would enable more food to be produced on the Earth, if the right crops were chosen.

Questions

1 Where does all the energy in living organisms originate from?
2 Write down a food chain
   (a) which ends with humans
   (b) in the sea
   (c) with five links in it.
3 Why are green plants called producers?
4 Why are there rarely more than five links in a food chain?
5 At which trophic level are you feeding when you eat (a) roast beef, (b) bread, (c) eggs, (d) an apple, (e) strawberries?

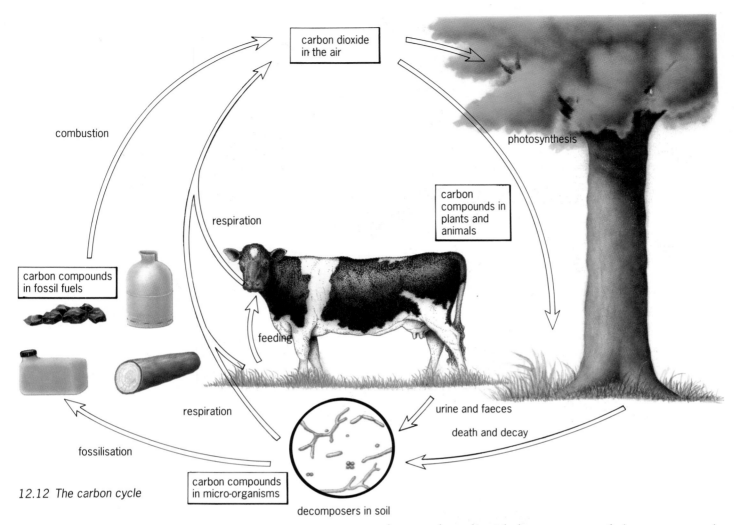

combustion

carbon dioxide in the air

photosynthesis

respiration

carbon compounds in plants and animals

carbon compounds in fossil fuels

feeding

respiration

urine and faeces

death and decay

fossilisation

12.12 The carbon cycle

carbon compounds in micro-organisms

decomposers in soil

Nutrient cycles

12.15 Decomposers release minerals from dead organisms.

One very important group of organisms which it is easy to overlook when you are studying an ecosystem, is the **decomposers**. They feed on waste material from animals and plants, and on their dead bodies. Many fungi and bacteria are decomposers.

Decomposers are extremely important, because they help to release substances from dead organisms, so that they can be used again by living ones. Two of these substances are carbon and nitrogen.

12.16 Carbon is recycled.

Carbon is a very important component of living things, because it is an essential part of carbohydrates, fats and proteins.

Figure 12.12 shows how carbon circulates through an ecosystem. The air contains about 0.03% carbon dioxide. When plants photosynthesise, carbon atoms from carbon dioxide become part of glucose or starch molecules in the plant.

Some of the glucose will be broken down by the plant in respiration. The carbon in the glucose becomes part of a carbon dioxide molecule again, and is released back into the air.

Some of the carbon in the plant will be eaten by animals. The animals respire, releasing some of it back into the air as carbon dioxide.

When the plant or animal dies, decomposers will feed on them. The carbon becomes part of the decomposers' bodies. When they respire, they release carbon dioxide into the air again.

12.17 Few organisms can use nitrogen gas.

Living things need nitrogen to make proteins. There is plenty of nitrogen around. The air is about 79% nitrogen gas. Molecules of nitrogen gas, N_2, are made of two nitrogen atoms joined together. These molecules are very inert, which means that they will not readily react with other substances.

So, although the air is full of nitrogen, it is in such an unreactive form that plants and animals cannot use

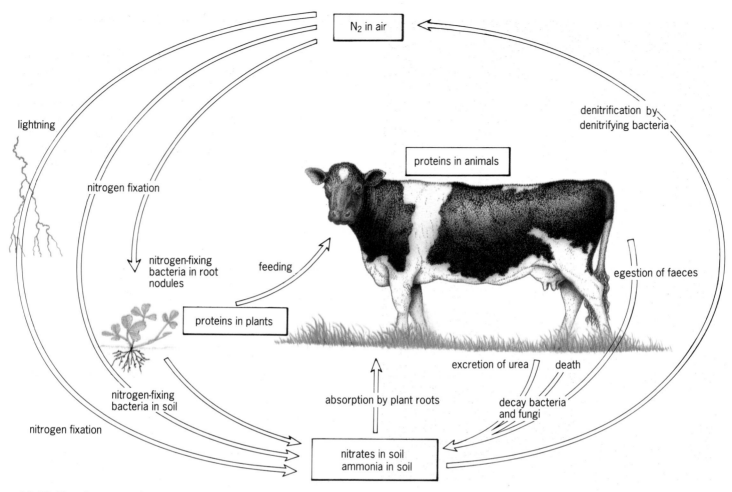

12.13 The nitrogen cycle

it at all. It must first be changed into a more reactive form, such as ammonia, (NH_3), or nitrates, (NO_3^-).

Changing nitrogen gas into a more reactive form is called **nitrogen fixation**. There are several ways that it can happen.

Lightning Lightning makes some of the nitrogen gas in the air combine with oxygen, forming nitrogen oxides. They dissolve in rain, and are washed into the soil, where they form nitrates.

Artificial fertilisers Nitrogen and hydrogen can be made to react in an industrial chemical process, forming ammonia. The ammonia is used to make ammonium compounds and nitrates, which are sold as fertilisers.

Nitrogen-fixing bacteria These bacteria live in the soil, or in root nodules (small swellings) on plants like peas, beans and clover. One kind is called *Rhizobium* ('rhizo' means root, 'bium' means living). They use nitrogen gas from the air spaces in the soil, and combine it with other substances to make nitrates and other compounds.

12.18 Fixed nitrogen moves round the nitrogen cycle.

Once the nitrogen has been fixed, it can be absorbed by the roots of plants, and used to make proteins. Animals eat the plants, so animals get their nitrogen in the form of proteins.

When an animal or plant dies, bacteria and fungi decompose the bodies. The protein, containing nitrogen, is broken down to ammonia and this is released. Another group of bacteria, called **nitrifying bacteria**, turn the ammonia into nitrates, which plants can use again.

Nitrogen is also returned to the soil when animals excrete nitrogenous waste material. It may be in the form of ammonia or urea. Again, nitrifying bacteria will convert it to nitrates.

12.19 Denitrifying bacteria make nitrogen gas.

A third group of bacteria complete the nitrogen cycle. They are called **denitrifying bacteria**, because they undo the work done by nitrifying bacteria. They turn nitrates and ammonia in the soil into nitrogen gas, which goes into the atmosphere.

12.14 *Insect-eating sundews live in boggy soils. You can find them growing on peat moorlands in Britain. This one has trapped a damselfly, which it will digest and absorb.*

12.20 Carnivorous plants get nitrogen from insects.

If the soil is waterlogged, nitrogen-fixing bacteria cannot live there, but denitrifying ones can. So boggy soil is usually very short of nitrates. Plants living in these places either have to manage with very little nitrogen, or get it from somewhere else. Some of them have become carnivorous. Plants like the Venus fly trap, or the sundews, supplement their diet with insects. They digest them with enzymes, and get extra nitrogen from the protein in the insects' bodies.

Questions

1 What is a decomposer?
2 Why are decomposers important?
3 Why do living organisms need carbon?
4 How do carbon atoms become part of a plant?
5 What happens to some of these carbon atoms when a plant respires?
6 How do decomposers help in the carbon cycle?
7 Why do living organisms need nitrogen?
8 Why can plants and animals not use the nitrogen in the air?
9 What is nitrogen fixation?
10 Where do nitrogen-fixing bacteria live?
11 How do animals obtain nitrogen?
12 What do nitrifying bacteria do?
13 Which type of bacteria return nitrogen to the air?
14 Why do you often find carnivorous plants growing in bogs?

Chapter revision questions

1 Explain the difference between each of the following pairs, giving examples where you can.
(a) habitat, niche
(b) community, population
(c) quadrat, transect
(d) primary consumer, secondary consumer
(e) nitrogen-fixing bacteria, nitrifying bacteria
2 Construct a dichotomous key, to enable someone to identify six people in your class.
3 Using the following list of words, in order, explain how
(a) a carbon atom in the air becomes part of a glucose molecule in your biceps muscle, and
(b) how that carbon atom might return to the air again.
broad bean plant, stomata, photosynthesis, glucose, sucrose, phloem vessel, bean seed, starch, feeding, amylase, maltose, maltase, glucose, ileum, hepatic portal vein, liver, hepatic vein, heart, aorta, subclavian artery, capillary, diffusion, muscle, respiration, carbon dioxide, diffusion, capillary, subclavian vein, heart, pulmonary artery, capillary, diffusion, alveolus, expiration

4 (a) Why is nitrogen important to living organisms?
(b) In what form do each of the following obtain their nitrogen?
(i) a green plant
(ii) nitrogen-fixing bacteria
(iii) a mammal
(c) In the sea, the main nitrogen-fixing organisms are blue-green algae, which float near the top of the water in the plankton. Construct a diagram or chart similar to Fig 12.13, showing how nitrogen is circulated amongst marine organisms.

continued

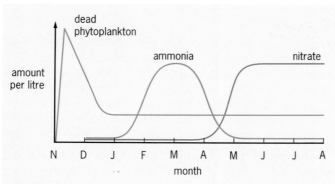

12.15

5 A fish tank was filled with water, and some bacteria were added. Some phytoplankton (microscopic plants) were then introduced. The tank was put into a dark place, and left for eight months.

At intervals, the water was tested to find out what it contained. The results are shown in the graph in Fig 12.15.

(a) Why did the phytoplankton die so quickly?

(b) The phytoplankton contain nitrogen in their cells. In what form is most of this nitrogen?

(c) Why does the quantity of dead phytoplankton decrease during the first two months of the experiment?

After one month, ammonia begins to appear in the water.

(d) Where has this ammonia come from?

(e) What kind of bacteria are responsible for its production?

(f) When does nitrate begin to appear in the water?

(g) What kind of bacteria are responsible for its production?

13 Environmental factors

13.1 Environmental factors partly determine organism distribution.

Why do living organisms live where they do? Why do polar bears live in the Arctic, and not in Africa? Why do poppies grow on recently disturbed grass verges or in cornfields, but not on lawns?

The simple answer is that organisms tend to live where the environment is suitable for them to live. Any feature of the environment which affects a living organism is called an **environmental factor**. Each kind of living organism is especially equipped, or adapted, to cope with a particular set of environmental factors.

13.1 A polar bear has a thick coat of insulating fur, which helps it to maintain its body temperature

Polar bears, for example, are adapted to live in the intense cold of the Arctic. They have thick fur and a thick layer of fat beneath their skin to insulate their bodies. Poppies grow where the ground has recently been disturbed, because this is where their seeds can germinate easily. They cannot cope with the constant mowing on a lawn. The cold of the Arctic, the disturbance of ground and the mowing of a lawn are all examples of environmental factors.

Environmental factors alone, however, cannot completely explain the distribution of living organisms. Sometimes, an environment may seem just right for an organism, and yet it is not found there. This may be because it has never been able to spread to that area.

13.2 Biotic and abiotic factors.

Because there are so many different environmental factors, it is useful to try to group them in some way. The two main groups are **biotic factors**, which are the influences of other living things, and **abiotic factors**, which are the influences of non-living parts of the environment.

Each of these main groups includes several kinds of environmental factor.

Abiotic factors These include **climatic** factors, such as sunlight, rainfall, humidity and temperature. Also important are **chemical** and **physical** factors, such as the amount of oxygen dissolved in a pond or stream, the amount of hydrogen sulphide gas in the air, or the pH of pond water. Factors caused by the soil are also very important. They are sometimes called **edaphic** factors.

Biotic factors These include availability of **food**, and how many **predators** there are. **Parasites** and **pathogens** (disease-causing organisms) are also important biotic factors. Another is the amount of **competition** with other organisms for food, shelter, or anything which an organism needs.

Environmental factors affect living organisms in many ways. For example, they affect their distribution, their size, their numbers, and their ability to reproduce. You will find many examples when studying any ecosystem. This chapter can describe only a few factors, and some of the effects they have on some organisms.

Questions

1 What is an environmental factor?
2 Describe at least four ways in which (a) a herring, and (b) a locust are adapted to their way of life.
3 What is meant by (a) a biotic factor, and (b) an abiotic factor?
4 What are edaphic factors?

Abiotic factors – climate

13.3 Climate influences natural vegetation.

On a world scale, climate has a great influence on the kinds of plants and animals which can live in different areas (Fig 13.2). The two most important factors are temperature and rainfall.

For example, in hot places with plenty of rainfall, a large variety of plants can thrive, and **tropical rain forest** is formed. This provides a very rich and varied environment for animals, and so the number and variety of animals is also large.

Dry or **desert** areas, whether hot or cold, are more difficult for both plants and animals, because they lose water by evaporation and cannot easily replace it.

Only a very few plants and animals are adapted to live in these conditions, so deserts are sparsely populated.

13.4 Microclimate is important to many organisms.

Climate is also important to living organisms on a much smaller scale. To a woodlouse, for example, the climate which immediately affects it is the climate where it lives, perhaps under a rotting log. The climate in a small space like this is called a **microclimate**.

Microclimates may be quite different from the general climate in that area. Beneath the log, for example, humidity will probably be nearly 100%, whereas the air outside might be quite dry. Woodlice are not well adapted to conserve water, so they tend to stay under cover during the day, and come out at night when the air is cooler and more humid. They are **cryptozoic** animals ('crypto' means hidden).

Fact!

In an Alaskan winter, it could be only –7 °C under 60 cm of snow at the soil surface, when the air above the snow is –57 °C. This allows small mammals like lemmings to live.

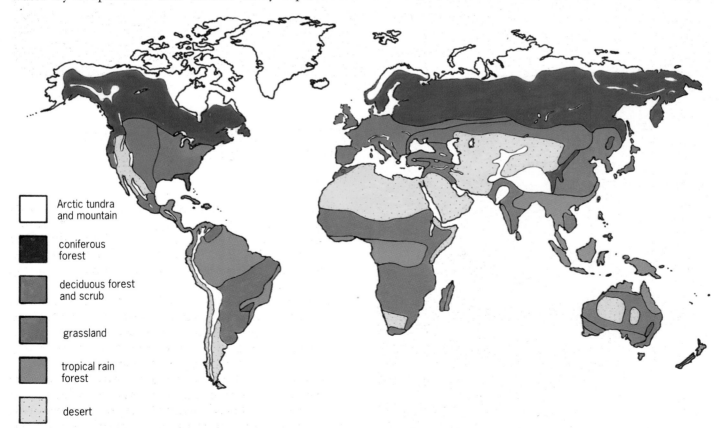

Arctic tundra and mountain

coniferous forest

deciduous forest and scrub

grassland

tropical rain forest

desert

13.2 World vegetation

13.3 *A great variety of plants grows densely where the climate is always warm and moist, as here on the Seychelles islands*

13.4 *In deserts such as the Namib, plants are few and far between*

Abiotic factors – chemical and physical factors

13.5 Oxygen.

Most living organisms need oxygen, for respiration. Usually, there is plenty of oxygen available in the air.

Aquatic organisms rely on oxygen which is dissolved in the water. Some of this will come from the air, and some from water plants which give off oxygen during photosynthesis.

Oxygen can quite often be in short supply in water. This is because oxygen is not very soluble in water, and does not diffuse through it very quickly. So the bottom of a deep lake may have little or no oxygen, especially as it will be too dark for plants to grow there.

Shallow, fast-flowing streams, however, always have plenty of oxygen. Trout and salmon, which swim very actively and need plenty of oxygen, may be found here. They are not found in deep, poorly oxygenated water.

193

13.5 Salmon will only breed in unpolluted fast-flowing rivers with plenty of dissolved oxygen

Pollution of streams and rivers by sewage causes the amount of oxygen dissolved in them to decrease. This is because the sewage provides food for bacteria. A large population of bacteria builds up. This uses up the oxygen in the water so fish and other organisms cannot live there (Fig 13.6 and Section 14.19).

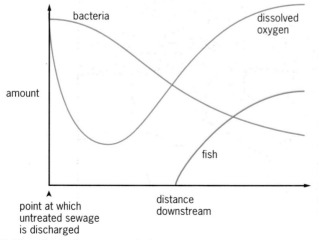

13.6 The effect of sewage pollution on a stream

13.6 Light.

Light is a very important environmental factor for plants, because they need it for photosynthesis. Many plants, such as poppies, need as much light as they can get. Others, such as dog's mercury (Fig 13.7) are adapted to live in more shady places. Dog's mercury is usually found in woodland, where it can tolerate the shade of the trees. By growing in the shade, it avoids competition with other plants which need more light.

Questions

1 What are the two most important factors influencing the type of vegetation found in an area?
2 What type of vegetation would you expect to find in an area with a mean annual temperature of 20 °C and a rainfall of 80 cm?
3 What is a microclimate?
4 Why are woodlice more active at night than in the daytime?
5 The River Thames used to contain salmon, but until recently there had been no salmon in it for many years. Why was this?

194

13.7 Dog's mercury is adapted to grow well in the shade of a wood

Abiotic factors – soil

13.7 Soil affects plants, and therefore animals too.

Soil is a very important environmental factor, because plants rely on it for many of their requirements.

Anchorage Soil provides an anchorage for plant roots. A thin or very loosely structured soil will not support many plants, because their roots will not be able to get a good grip.

Nutrient minerals Soil provides nutrients for plants, particularly minerals such as nitrates, potassium salts etc.

Water Plants obtain water from the soil.

Air Plant roots and other soil organisms need air, to provide them with oxygen for respiration. A good soil has plenty of air spaces.

So the type of soil in a particular area has a large effect on the plants growing in it. This in turn will affect the animals which live there.

13.8 Soil is slowly formed from rock.

Soil is formed from rock. When rocks are weathered by wind, freezing and thawing, or by water flowing over them, they are broken down into small particles, called **rock waste**.

These particles are gradually colonised by lichens and mosses and a few flowering plants. As the plants die and decay, their remains add organic materials to the mineral particles of the rock waste. Other plants and animals can then begin to colonise the soil. This takes a very long time. It probably takes thousands of years to form a good, deep soil suitable for agriculture.

13.9 Soil has several components.

Figure 13.8 shows a vertical section through a good agricultural soil. The top layers are called **topsoil**.

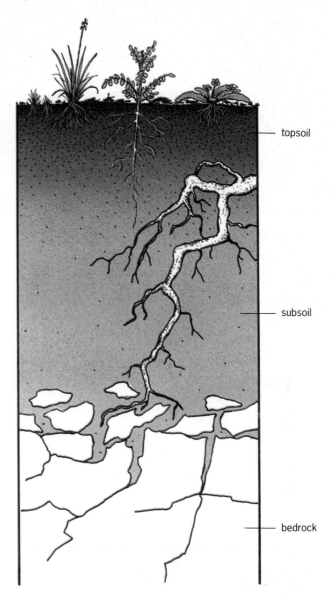

13.8 A vertical section through an agricultural soil

Topsoil has six main constituents. They are mineral particles, humus, water, nutrient ions, air and living organisms.

13.10 The size of soil particles is important.

Mineral particles are formed from rocks, by weathering. The size of the mineral particles in a soil is very important. Very small particles form a soil called **clay**, while larger ones form **sand**.

Clay soils   A clay soil contains very small soil particles, which can pack tightly together (Fig 13.9a). Because they are so closely packed, they tend to hold water between them, by **capillarity**. Capillarity is the tendency for water to move into very narrow spaces. Clay soils do not dry out quickly in dry weather.

However, this can be a disadvantage. In wet conditions, the small spaces between the soil particles fill up with water, so there is no room for air. The soil becomes waterlogged (Section 13.14).

Clay particles have a slight electrical charge, and so mineral ions like potassium (K^+) and calcium (Ca^{2+}) are attracted to them. This is useful, because the clay particles hold the ions, stopping them from being washed or **leached** out of the soil by rain water.

Sandy soils   A sandy soil contains larger soil particles (Fig 13.9b). The large particles cannot pack very closely together, so there are large air spaces between them. Sandy soils are usually well aerated.

The large spaces, however, mean that water is not held by capillarity. Sandy soils drain very quickly. Sand particles do not hold mineral ions in the same way that clay particles do. So minerals are leached out of a sandy soil more quickly.

Loam   A loam is a soil which contains a good mixture of sand and clay particles. If the balance is right, it will hold water and mineral ions, but will not get waterlogged too easily.

13.11 Remnants of decayed organisms form humus.

The dead bodies of animals and plants, and any other organic waste such as faeces, are decomposed by bacteria and fungi in the soil. They are slowly broken down to a dark, sticky material called **humus**.

Humus forms a coating over the mineral particles in soil. It sticks the soil particles together into small

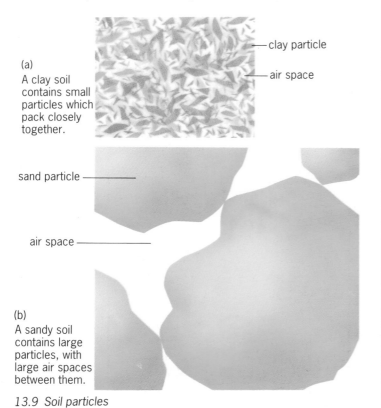

(a)
A clay soil contains small particles which pack closely together.

clay particle

air space

sand particle

air space

(b)
A sandy soil contains large particles, with large air spaces between them.

13.9 Soil particles

Practical 13.1 Making a rough estimate of the proportions of particles of different sizes in a soil sample

1   Put the soil sample into a gas jar.
2   Fill the gas jar to within 5 cm of the top with tap water.
3   Stir or shake the jar, to mix the soil and water completely.
4   Leave the jar undisturbed, until the particles have settled into layers (Fig 13.10).

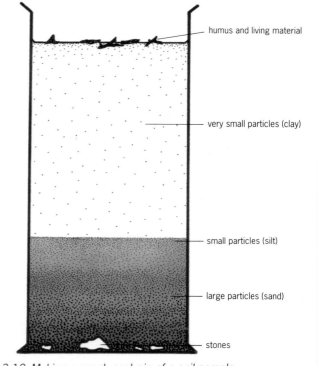

humus and living material

very small particles (clay)

small particles (silt)

large particles (sand)

stones

13.10 Making a rough analysis of a soil sample

Practical 13.2 To estimate the percentage of water in a soil sample

1 Weigh an evaporating dish.
2 Put your soil sample into the dish, and reweigh. Work out the weight of the soil sample, and record it.
3 Put the dish and soil into a cool oven. The warmth will dry out the soil. The oven must not be too hot, or the organic material in the soil will break down.
4 After a day or so, reweigh the dish and soil. Replace in the oven, and leave for a few hours more. Reweigh. If the two weights are the same, the soil is dry. If not, replace in the oven. This is called drying to constant weight.
5 Work out the weight of water in the soil, by subtracting the weight of the dried soil plus dish from the weight of the wet soil plus dish.
6 Work out the percentage of water in the soil like this.

$$\frac{\% \text{ water in}}{\text{soil sample}} = \frac{\text{weight of water in soil sample}}{\text{original weight of soil sample}} \times 100$$

Questions

1 Why must the oven not be hot enough to break down organic material in the soil?
2 What type of soil would you expect to contain the highest percentage of water?

Practical 13.3 To estimate the percentage of humus in a soil sample

1 Take the dried soil sample in its dish from Practical 13.2. Reweigh to check its weight. If necessary, dry to constant weight again.
2 Heat the soil strongly, either in a very hot oven, or over a Bunsen burner. The high temperature will oxidise the humus.
3 Allow the sample to cool, and reweigh.
4 Heat again, cool, and reweigh, until the weight is constant.
5 Work out the weight of humus in the soil, by subtracting the weight of heated soil plus dish, from the weight of dried soil plus dish.
6 Work out the percentage of humus in the soil like this.

$$\frac{\% \text{ humus in}}{\text{soil sample}} = \frac{\text{weight of humus in soil sample}}{\text{original weight of soil sample}} \times 100$$
$$\text{(before drying)}$$

Questions

1 Why was dried soil used for this experiment?
2 If the dried soil has been left for a while since the last experiment, you may find that its weight has increased slightly when you reweigh it at the beginning of this experiment. Explain this.
3 How could you use your results from Practicals 13.2 and 13.3 to calculate the % of minerals in the soil?

groups, called **crumbs**. A soil with a good crumb structure tends to be well drained and aerated, and yet holds water and minerals.

It takes a long time before bacteria and fungi can break humus down completely. So humus provides a long-term store of useful substances such as nitrogen, which plants can eventually use.

Humus also provides food for other living organisms in the soil, such as earthworms.

13.12 Water coats soil particles.

Plants obtain all their water from the soil. The water is absorbed by osmosis, through root hairs.

Even in dry weather, a good loam with plenty of humus will hold water. The water forms a film around each soil particle. Too much water in soil, however, causes waterlogging.

13.13 Minerals are dissolved in soil water.

Plants obtain nutrient or mineral ions from soil. They are absorbed by diffusion or active transport through root hairs. Table 5.2 lists the main mineral ions required by plants.

The mineral ions in soil are dissolved in the soil water. The kind and amount of ions depends partly on the kind of rock from which the soil was made, and partly on the activities of bacteria in the soil. For example, a soil with plenty of nitrogen-fixing and nitrifying bacteria will contain plenty of nitrate ions.

13.14 Organisms in soil need air.

Some of the spaces between the soil particles in soil are filled with air. If all the spaces are filled with water, so that there is no room for air, then the soil is said to be **waterlogged**.

Plant roots need oxygen from the air spaces for respiration. In a waterlogged soil, plant roots respire anaerobically. They make alcohol as a waste product, which may kill them. Some plants, though, such as the marsh ragwort (Fig 13.11) can tolerate the alcohol, and so are well adapted to live in boggy soils.

Soil animals also need oxygen for respiration. Nitrogen-fixing bacteria need nitrogen from the air in the soil.

13.15 Soil is a habitat for many organisms.

A good soil contains a large variety of living organisms. They include plant roots, earthworms, fungi and bacteria.

Earthworms can help to improve soil for plant growth. Their burrows help to aerate soil, and improve drainage. They also add humus to the soil by pulling in dead leaves, by excreting waste material, and from their decaying bodies after death. Earthworms feed by eating soil particles and extracting organic material

13.11 *Marsh ragwort tolerates boggy soils which kill other plants*

from them, and the remains which they egest improve the texture of the soil.

Bacteria occur in soil in huge numbers. These bacteria, along with other decomposers such as fungi, feed on the dead bodies and faeces of animals and plants. They form humus. They help to release nutrients into the soil so that these can be reused by other living organisms (Sections 12.15 and 12.16).

13.16 Acid soils can form peat.

Acid soils form where rainfall is very high and drainage is poor, such as on high ground in the north and west of Britain. Because there is so much water in the soil, bacteria are unable to get enough air from the soil to allow them to decay dead plants and animals. The partly decomposed remains of the plants and animals build up as **peat**. Peat has a very high capacity for holding water, so the ground becomes even more waterlogged.

The partly decomposed plant remains release acids, which lower the pH in the soil. Few bacteria can live in these acidic, airless conditions. Because there are not many bacteria there are not many nitrates available to plants.

It is not surprising that only a few types of plant, such as heather, sedges and sphagnum moss (Fig 13.13) are adapted to live in wet, acid, peat soils.

light and heat source drives animals downwards

soil sample

wire platform

animals drop down through funnel

funnel

alcohol kills and preserves animals, ready for identification and counting

13.12 *A Tullgren funnel – a method of collecting small soil animals*

13.13 *Heather-covered moorland occurs where the soil is wet and acid*

13.14 Clay soil is easily compacted by heavy machinery. You can see how water is trapped in the wheel ruts made by a tractor.

13.15 Clay soils may crack badly when dry

13.17 Clay soils are heavy and hard to cultivate.

A clay soil has the advantage that it holds water and mineral ions well. However, drainage and aeration are poor.

A clay soil is difficult to dig or plough. When wet, it is soft and sticky, and heavy farm machinery will compact it, squeezing out air from between the soil particles. When dry, it becomes very hard, and difficult to break up.

A clay soil may be made easier to work, and better for plants to grow in, by improving its crumb structure. There are two main ways that this can be done.

One way is by adding **lime** to the soil. Lime is calcium hydroxide. It reacts with the clay particles, making them clump together, or **flocculate**. The large crumbs improve the drainage and aeration of the soil.

Another way of improving the crumb structure is by adding humus to the soil, in the form of manure or compost. This also sticks the clay particles together to form crumbs. Other advantages of adding humus are that it adds nutrients to the soil, and encourages soil organisms.

A clay soil, if properly managed, can become an excellent agricultural soil.

13.18 Sandy soils are dry and poor in nutrients.

The natural advantage of a sandy soil is its good drainage. This makes it easy to work in winter or summer, because the large particles separate easily, and do not become compacted.

Sandy soils, though, lack nutrients and have poor water retentive properties. Both of these can be improved by the addition of humus.

13.19 Drainage improves acid soils.

It is not easy to convert a wet, acid peat soil into good agricultural land. The first step is to drain it. As the land becomes drier, it becomes better aerated, and bacteria and other organisms can colonise it. It may be ploughed, and sown with grass seed.

The main problem is that rainfall will still be high, and so it is very difficult to keep the land well drained.

Table 13.1 A comparison of clay and sandy soils

	Clay soil	Sandy soil
Particle size	Small	Large
Aeration	Spaces between particles are small, so soil is often poorly aerated	Spaces between particles are large, so soil is usually well aerated
Water holding capacity	Water is held in the small spaces by capillarity	Water is not held by capillarity, because the spaces are too large
Drainage	Water only drains slowly through the small spaces	Water drains quickly through the large spaces
Mineral ions	Many, because they are bound to the clay particles, slow drainage prevents them being leached out	Few, because they are quickly leached out as water drains through

199

Practical 13.4 To find the effect of lime on clay particles

1 Put a small amount of powdered clay into a container, and mix it up thoroughly with plenty of tap water. The fine clay particles will form a cloudy suspension in the water.
2 Now add a small amount of lime (calcium hydroxide or calcium oxide) to the clay suspension. Watch carefully to see what happens (a) immediately, and (b) after a few minutes.

Questions

1 What effect did the lime have on the clay particles?
2 What are the main problems that farmers have when trying to cultivate a clay soil?
3 How might the addition of lime improve such a soil?

Questions

1 List four reasons why soil is important to plants.
2 What is topsoil?
3 List the six constituents of topsoil.
4 Explain why a clay soil usually contains plenty of mineral ions.
5 Why are sandy soils better aerated than clay soils?
6 What is a loam?
7 What is humus?
8 List three advantages of having plenty of humus in a soil.
9 What is meant by a waterlogged soil?
10 Why do many plants die if their soil becomes water-logged?
11 How does a large earthworm population benefit a soil?
12 What is peat?
13 Why are peat soils acidic?
14 What are the problems of trying to cultivate a clay soil?
15 How may a sandy soil be improved?

The living environment

13.20 Relationships between living organisms.

Every living organism is affected by others in some way. Often these effects are harmful. Predators, parasites, pathogens (disease-causing parasites) and competitors all make life more difficult. But sometimes organisms may help each other out, as in mutualism. This chapter describes a few examples of these five kinds of relationship between living organisms.

Predators

13.21 Predators kill prey for food.

A **predator** is an animal which kills another living organism, called its **prey**, for food. An example of a predator is the nymph of a dragonfly (Fig 13.16). The nymph lives at the bottom of freshwater ponds, and feeds on any small living organisms that it can catch.

Predators need to be adapted to catch and kill their prey. But animals which are preyed on must also be adapted to protect themselves from their predators. Caddis fly larvae, for example, which may be attacked by dragonfly nymphs, build protective cases around their soft bodies (Fig 13.17).

Predators and prey sometimes have important effects on each others' population sizes. This is explained in Section 13.33.

mouthparts which can be thrown forwards quickly to catch prey

large compound eyes for detecting prey

13.16 A dragonfly nymph – an example of a predator

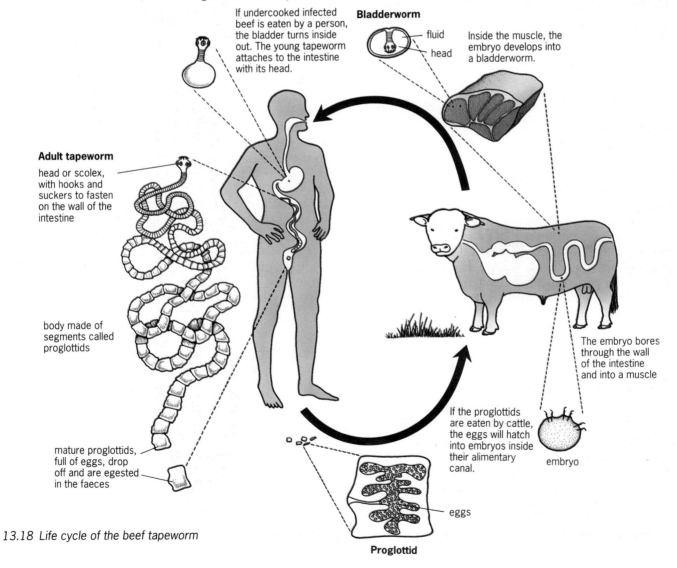

13.17 *A case made of leaves camouflages this caddis fly larva*

Parasites

13.22 Parasites harm their host.

A **parasite** is an organism which lives in close association with another organism, called its **host**. The parasite usually harms the host.

A **tapeworm** (Fig 13.18) is an example of a parasite. It lives inside the body of its host, so it is an endoparasite. The protoctist *Plasmodium* which causes malaria (Fig 18.8) is also an endoparasite. The **head louse** (Fig 13.19) lives on the outside of a person's body, so it is an ectoparasite.

13.23 Parasites have special adaptations.

Although parasites usually have plenty of food, their lives are not always easy ones. The tapeworm, for example, has to grip tightly to the wall of its host's alimentary canal, so that it is not swept away by peristalsis. To do this, it has hooks and suckers on its head.

It also has to protect itself from being digested by its

If undercooked infected beef is eaten by a person, the bladder turns inside out. The young tapeworm attaches to the intestine with its head.

Bladderworm

fluid

head

Inside the muscle, the embryo develops into a bladderworm.

Adult tapeworm

head or scolex, with hooks and suckers to fasten on the wall of the intestine

body made of segments called proglottids

mature proglottids, full of eggs, drop off and are egested in the faeces

The embryo bores through the wall of the intestine and into a muscle

If the proglottids are eaten by cattle, the eggs will hatch into embryos inside their alimentary canal.

embryo

eggs

13.18 *Life cycle of the beef tapeworm*

Proglottid

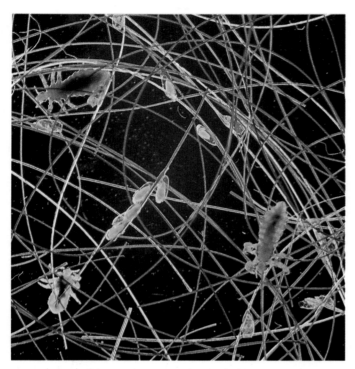

13.19 Head lice and their eggs on human hair

host's enzymes. An enzyme-resistant covering performs this function.

It is never easy for a parasite's offspring to find its way into a new host. The complicated life cycle of the tapeworm is designed to help with this. Nevertheless, most of the tapeworm's eggs will never develop into adults, so huge numbers have to be produced.

13.24 Parasites can be controlled by breaking their life cycles.

Pork and beef tapeworms are now very rare in Great Britain, because beef and pork are carefully inspected for bladderworms. For many years, any meat containing bladderworms has been banned from sale, so the tapeworm's life cycle has been broken.

Head lice, though, are still quite common. Like tapeworms, they are well adapted to cope with their parasitic life-style. Their flattened shape lets them lie close against the scalp or hair. Their eggs are cemented firmly to hairs, and the adults' legs are designed to be able to grip hair tightly, so that they are not dislodged even when you wash or comb your hair.

Head lice will live happily in any kind of hair. They get from one head to another by walking across when heads are in contact. Once a person realises that they have head lice, the lice can easily be killed by using a special lotion on the hair and scalp. This kills both eggs and adults.

The malarial parasite is also very common in some parts of the world. It can be controlled by reducing the population of mosquitoes. Mosquitoes need water in which to lay their eggs, so draining swamps will help to reduce their numbers. Insecticides may also be used to kill mosquitoes. Sleeping under a mosquito net will reduce the risk of being bitten and infected with the malarial parasite.

Pathogens

13.25 Pathogens cause disease.

A **pathogen** is an organism which causes disease. The most important pathogens are bacteria and viruses. Some fungi and protoctists may also be pathogens. You can read more about some human pathogens in Chapter 18.

Mutualism

13.26 In mutualism, both partners benefit.

Mutualism happens when two organisms of different species live in a close association with one another, and both organisms benefit.

One example of mutualism is the relationship between the nitrogen-fixing bacterium *Rhizobium*, and clover. The bacteria live in swellings or nodules on the clover roots. The plant benefits because the bacteria take nitrogen gas from the air spaces in soil, and convert it into nitrogen compounds which the plant can use to make proteins. The bacteria benefit because they obtain sugars from the plant.

Lichens (Fig 13.20) are another example of a very successful mutualistic partnership. A lichen consists of two types of organism – a fungus and a green alga. The partnership is so successful that lichens can colonise places where no other plant can grow, such as roofs of buildings, or the soil in Arctic regions. The alga photosynthesises, while the fungus extracts minerals from the roof or soil.

Competition

13.27 Organisms compete with each other.

Competition happens whenever two or more organisms need the same thing, which is in short supply. If the competition is between individuals belonging to the same species, it is called **intraspecific** competition. If it is between individuals belonging to different species, it is called **interspecific** competition.

Plants compete for light, root space, and sometimes for water and minerals from the soil. Animals compete for food, and a place to live and reproduce.

13.20 Lichens can grow in places that no other plant can tolerate; however, they grow slowly, as can be seen by the size of the patches on this tombstone.

13.28 Occupying different niches reduces competition.

Competition between living organisms only happens when their niches, or life styles, overlap. The more they overlap, the more likely it is that they will compete.

For example, black ants and yellow ants have quite similar niches. Both kinds of ant live in pastures in Britain. They both feed on aphids and other small insects. Because their niches overlap, competition occurs between the two species of ant. They compete for space and food. If the black ant colonies are destroyed, then the yellow ant colonies breed more rapidly than when the black ants are there. Therefore the competition has a harmful effect on the yellow ant colonies.

Although the niches of the yellow and black ants overlap enough to cause them to compete with one another, they do not overlap completely. Yellow ants, for example, always look for food under the surface of the ground, while black ants forage on the surface. Yellow ants build ant hills to breed in, while black ants breed under stones.

Because their niches do not overlap completely, it is possible for yellow and black ants to live in the same place at the same time. This seems to be true for almost all species of living organism. Although niches may sometimes appear to be identical, each type of organism does in fact have its own niche which is different from every other. The more different an organism's niche is from those of other organisms, the less it will be in competition with them.

13.21 Ant hills in Wytham Wood, near Oxford. These hills belong to yellow ants. Black ants also live in this area, but under stones rather than in ant hills. This reduces competition between the two species.

203

Competition is a very important factor in evolution. This is described in Chapter 16.

The effect of environmental factors on population size

13.29 Most populations stay about the same size.

This chapter has described some of the environmental factors that affect living organisms. Many of these factors affect the sizes of animal and plant populations.

Most populations tend to stay roughly the same size over a period of time. They may go and down, or fluctuate, but the average population will probably stay the same over a number of years. The population of greenfly in your garden, for example, might be much greater one year than the next. But their numbers will almost certainly be back to normal in a year or so. Over many years, the sizes of most populations tend to remain at around the same level.

Yet if all the offspring of one female greenfly survived and reproduced, she could be the ancestor of 600 000 000 000 greenfly in just one year! Why doesn't the greenfly population shoot upwards like this? Why isn't the world overrun with greenfly?

The answers to those questions are of great importance to human beings, because our own population is doing just that; it is shooting upwards at an alarming rate. Every hour, there are 9000 extra people in the world. We need to understand why this is happening, and what is likely to happen next. Can we slow down the increase? What happens if we don't?

13.30 Birth rate and death rate determine population size.

The size of a population depends on how many individuals leave the population, and how many enter it.

Individuals leave a population when they die, or when they migrate to another population. Individuals enter a population when they are born, or when they migrate into the population from elsewhere. Usually, births and deaths are more important in determining population sizes than immigration and emigration.

A population increases if new individuals are born faster than the old ones die, that is when the birth rate is greater than the death rate. If birth rate is less than death rate, then the population will decrease. If birth rate and death rate are equal, the population will stay the same size.

This explains why we are not knee-deep in greenfly. Although the greenfly population's birth rate is enormous, the death rate is also enormous. Greenfly are eaten by ladybirds and birds, and sprayed by gar-deners. Over a period of time, the greenfly's birth and death rates stay about the same, so the population doesn't change very much.

13.31 Yeast experiments give some clues about population growth.

By looking at changes in population sizes in other organisms, we can learn quite a lot about our own. Many experiments on population sizes have been done on organisms like bacteria and yeast, because they reproduce quickly and are easy to grow. Fig 13.22 shows the results of an experiment in which a few yeast cells are put into a container of nutrient broth. The cells feed on the broth, grow and reproduce. The numbers of yeast cells are counted every few hours.

At the beginning of the experiment, the population only grows quite slowly, because there are not many cells there to reproduce. But once they get going, growth is very rapid. Each cell divides to form 2, then 4, then 8, then 16... . There is nothing to hold them back except the time it takes to grow and divide.

But as the population gets larger, the individual cells can no longer reproduce as fast, and begin to die off more rapidly. This may be because there is not enough food left for them all, or it might be that they have made so much alcohol that they are poisoning themselves. The cells are now dying off as fast as new ones are being produced, so the population stops growing and levels off.

13.32 Environmental factors control population size.

Although the experiment with the yeast is done in artificial conditions, a similar pattern is found in the growth of populations of many species in the wild. If a few individuals get into a new environment, then their population curve may be very like the one for

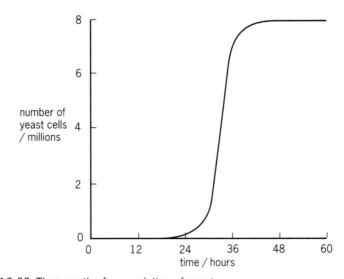

13.22 The growth of a population of yeast

yeast cells in broth. The population increases quickly at first, and then levels off.

The levelling off is always caused by some kind of environmental factor. In the case of the yeast, the factor may be food supply. Other populations may be limited by disease, or the number of nest sites, or the number of predators, for example.

13.33 Population sizes often oscillate.

It is usually very difficult to find out which environmental factors are controlling the size of a population. Almost always, many different factors will interact. A population of rabbits, for example, might be affected by the number of foxes, the amount of food available, the amount of space for burrows, and the amount of infection by the virus which causes myxomatosis.

Figure 13.23 shows an example of how the size of population of a predator may be affected by its prey. This information comes from the number of skins which were sold by fur traders in Northern Canada to the Hudson Bay Company, between 1845 and 1925. Snowshoe hares and northern lynxes were both trapped for their fur, and the numbers caught probably give a very good idea of their population sizes.

Snowshoe hare populations tend to vary from year to year. No-one is quite sure why this happens, but it may be related to their food supply. Whenever the snowshoe hare population rises, the lynx population also rises shortly afterwards, as the lynxes now have more food. A drop in the snowshoe hare population is rapidly followed by a drop in the lynx population.

The numbers tend to go up and down, or **oscillate**, but the average population sizes stay roughly the same over many years.

13.34 Age pyramids show whether a population is increasing or decreasing.

When scientists begin to study a population, they want to know whether the population is growing or shrinking. This can be done by counting the population over many years, or by measuring its birth rate and death rate. But often it is much easier just to count the numbers of individuals in various age groups, and to draw an **age pyramid**.

Figure 13.24 shows two examples of age pyramids. The size of each box represents the numbers of individuals of that age.

Figure 13.24a is a bottom-heavy pyramid, because there are far more young individuals than old ones. This indicates that birth rate is greater than death rate, so this population is increasing.

Figure 13.24b shows a much more even spread of ages. Birth rate and death rate are probably about the same. This population will remain about the same size.

If an age pyramid is drawn for the human population on Earth, it is bottom-heavy, like Fig 13.24a. Age pyramids for most of the world's developing countries are also this shape, showing that their populations are increasing. But an age pyramid for Great Britain looks more like Fig 13.24b. The human population in Great Britain is staying about the same.

13.35 The human death rate has decreased dramatically.

Figure 13.25 shows how the human population of the world has changed since about 3000 BC. For most of that time, human populations have been kept in check by a combination of disease, famine and war. Nevertheless, there has still been a steady increase.

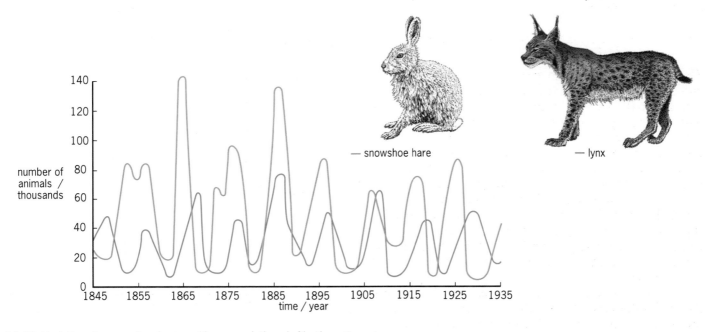

13.23 *Variations in snowshoe hare and lynx populations in Northern Canada*

(a) An increasing population
If all the organisms in the younger age groups grow up and reproduce, the population will increase.

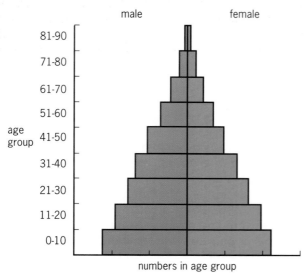

(b) A stable population
The sizes of the younger age groups are only a little larger than the older ones, so this population should not change much in size.

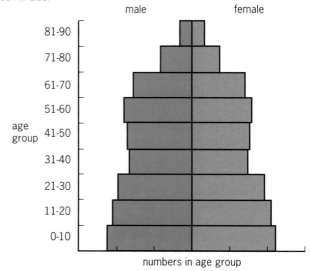

13.24 Age pyramids   (a) An increasing population   (b) A stable population

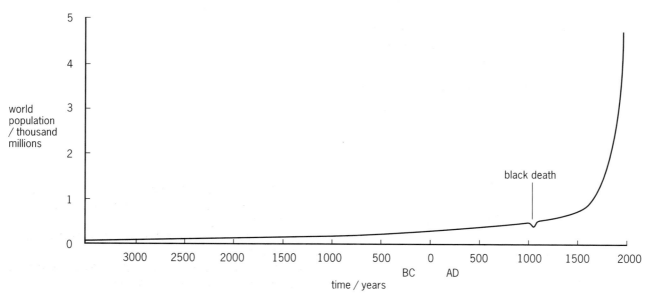

13.25 The growth of the human population

Twice there have been definite 'spurts' in this growth. The first was around 8000 BC, not shown on the graph, when people in the Middle East began to farm, instead of just hunting and finding food. The second began around 300 years ago, and is still happening now.

There are two main reasons for this recent growth spurt. The first is the **reduction of disease**. Improvements in water supply, sewage treatment, hygienic food handling and general standards of cleanliness have virtually wiped out many diseases in Great Britain, such as typhoid and dysentery. Immunisation against diseases such as polio has made these very rare

indeed. Smallpox has been totally eradicated. And the discovery of antibiotics has now made it possible to treat most diseases caused by bacteria.

Secondly, there has been an **increase in food supply**. More and more land has been brought under cultivation. Moreover, agriculture has become more efficient, so that each hectare of land is now producing more than ever before.

13.36 Birth rate now exceeds death rate.

The human population has increased dramatically because the death rate has been brought down. More and more people are now living long enough to reproduce.

If the birth rate doesn't drop by the same amount as the death rate, then the world population will continue to increase.

In developed countries, the dramatic fall in the death rate began in about 1700. To begin with, the birth rate stayed high, so the population grew rapidly. But since 1800, there has been a marked drop in birth rate. In 1870, for example, the 'average' British family was 6.6 children, but by 1977 it was only 1.8. In these countries, birth rate and death rate are now about equal, so the population is staying the same.

However, in many of the developing countries, the fall in the death rate only began about 50 years ago. As yet, the birth rates have not dropped, and so the populations are rising rapidly.

13.37 Birth rate must be reduced to slow population growth.

The human population could be brought back under control in two ways – increasing the death rate or decreasing the birth rate. There is no question as to which of these is the best.

In the developed countries, the single largest factor which brought down the birth rate was the introduction of contraceptive techniques. Considerable efforts are being made to introduce these to people in the developing countries, with some success. But many people are suspicious of contraceptive methods, or barred from using them by their religion, or simply want to have large families. It looks as though the population will go on rising for at least another 200 years.

If we do not control the overall human birth rate, then it may happen that famine, war or disease will increase the death rate. This cannot be the best thing for the human race. We must do our best to stabilise the world population at a level at which everyone has a fair chance of a long, healthy life.

Chapter revision questions

1 (a) List the components of topsoil.
   (b) What problems are associated with the cultivation of (i) clay soil, (ii) sandy soil, and (iii) acid soil?
   (c) Explain how each of the following can improve the properties of a clay soil.
   (i) earthworms
   (ii) addition of humus
   (iii) addition of lime
2 (a) What is a parasite?
   (b) List four problems faced by most parasites.
   (c) For one named parasite, describe how it overcomes these difficulties.
3 The graph in Fig 13.26 shows the changes in the size of a population of primary producers (plants) and primary consumers (herbivorous animals) in a lake, during one year.
   (a) At what time of year is the amount of producers (i) lowest, and (ii) highest?
   (b) How can the information about light and temperature given on the graph help to explain your answer to (a)?
   (c) The population of primary consumers begins to increase about one month later than the increase in producers. Suggest why.
   (d) Why does the population of producers begin to decrease in April?
   (e) Why does the population of primary consumers begin to decrease in May and June?

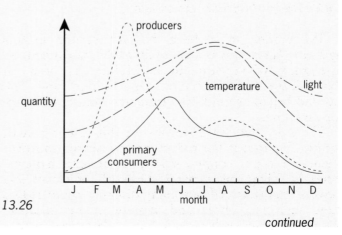
13.26

continued

4 The graph in Fig 13.27 shows population changes over one summer, for two insects. One is a type of greenfly, and the other is a ladybird which feeds on it.
(a) Which curve represents the ladybird population, and which the greenfly population?
(b) Give a reason for your answer to part (a).
(c) Explain why the two curves are similar shapes.
(d) Why do the two curves rise and fall at slightly different times?

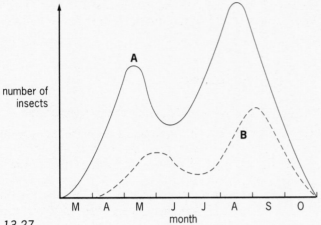

13.27

5 The figures in the table below show the changes in population size of a culture of bacteria, grown in a culture vessel in a laboratory at 20 °C.
(a) Use these results to plot a population growth curve for these bacteria.
(b) Explain the reasons for the shape of the curve (i) between 2 and 10 hours, and (ii) between 14 and 18 hours.
(c) Draw another line to show the results you would expect if the population had been kept at 30 °C.

Time in hours	Number of bacteria in population
0	0
2	70
4	162
6	280
8	455
10	735
12	897
14	980
16	1032
18	1050

6 The chart shows the birth rates and death rates in three countries between 1932 and 1972. The number in the 'birth rate' line is the number of births per 1000 people in the population. The number in the 'death rate' line is the number of deaths per 1000 people in the population.
(a) Which of these three countries had the greatest birth rate in (i) 1932 (ii) 1972?
(b) How have the birth rates changed in each of these three countries between 1932 and 1972?
(c) How have the death rates changed in each of these countries between 1932 and 1972?

		1932	1960	1972
Great Britain	birth rate	15.8	16.9	14.9
	death rate	12.3	11.7	11.9
Chile	birth rate	34.0	35.4	29.6
	death rate	22.7	12.5	9.4
Japan	birth rate	32.9	17.5	19.2
	death rate	17.7	7.4	6.6

(d) Were the populations in these countries increasing or decreasing in each of these three years?
(e) What happened to the *rate* of increase between 1932 and 1972?

14 Humans and the environment

14.1 All organisms affect their environment.

All living things affect the living and non-living things around them. For example, earthworms make burrows and wormcasts, which affect the soil, and therefore the plants growing in it. Rabbit fleas carry the virus which causes myxomatosis, so they can affect the size of a rabbit population, and perhaps the size of the fox population if the foxes depend on rabbits for food.

Perhaps the biggest ever effect which living organisms have had on the environment happened about 1500 million years ago. At this time, the first living cells which could photosynthesise evolved. Until then, there had been no oxygen in the atmosphere. The photosynthetic organisms began to produce oxygen, which gradually accumulated in the atmosphere. Almost all the oxygen in the air which we now breathe has been produced by photosynthesis. The appearance of oxygen in the air meant that many anaerobic organisms could no longer survive, or could only live in particular parts of the Earth which were oxygen-free, such as in deep layers of mud. It meant that many other kinds of organism could evolve, which used the oxygen for respiration. The excretion of all this oxygen by photosynthetic organisms could be considered to be the biggest pollution incident of all time!

14.2 Humans affect the environment.

Within the past 10 000 years or so, another organism has had an enormous impact on the environment. Ever since humans learnt to hunt with weapons, to domesticate animals and to farm crops, we have been changing the environment around us in a very significant way. We kill wild animals for food, decreasing their populations and making some species extinct. We cut down forests. We build cities, roads and dams. We release harmful substances into the water, air and soil.

As the human population continues to increase, and expectations of living standards become higher, the effects which we have on the environment become ever greater. It is very important that we do our best to understand what we are doing, and what the effects might be. The more we understand, the more we can do to prevent too much damage before it happens, and keep the Earth a pleasant place for humans, plants and other animals to live.

Table 14.1 summarises some of the damaging effects we have had on our environment. The rest of this chapter describes each one in more detail, and explains what we can do to limit further damage.

The ozone layer

14.3 Most ozone is high in the atmosphere.

High up in the Earth's atmosphere, between about 12 and 50 km above the ground, is a layer of the gas **ozone**. An ozone molecule contains three oxygen atoms, so its formula is O_3.

The ozone in this layer is constantly being formed, broken down and reformed. It is formed when ultraviolet light (short wavelength light) hits an oxygen molecule. The two oxygen atoms break apart, forming separate and very reactive individual oxygen atoms. Each of these can then combine with an oxygen molecule to form an ozone molecule:

$$\text{UV light}$$
$$O_2 \rightarrow O + O$$
$$O_2 + O \rightarrow O_3$$

14.1 The ozone layer. It is closer to the Earth's surface over the poles than over the equator.

Table 14.1 A summary of the harmful effects of humans on the environment

Type of damage	Example	Main causes	Possible solutions
Air pollution	Damage to the ozone layer	CFCs.	Stop using CFCs; find harmless alternatives.
	Global warming	Enhanced greenhouse effect, caused by release of carbon dioxide, methane, CFCs and nitrogen oxides.	Reduce use of fossil fuels. Stop using CFCs. Produce less organic waste and/or collect and use methane produced from landfill sites.
	Acid rain	Sulphur dioxide and nitrogen oxides from the burning of fossil fuels.	Burn less fossil fuel.
Habitat destruction	Deforestation	Destruction of forests, especially rainforests, for wood and for land for farming, roads and houses.	Provide alternative sources of income for people living near rainforests.
	Loss of wetlands	Draining wetlands for housing and land for farming.	Protect areas of wetland.
Water pollution	Eutrophication	Sewage and fertilisers running into streams.	Treat all sewage before discharge into streams. Use fewer inorganic fertilisers.
Species destruction	Loss of habitat	See deforestation and wetlands above.	See above.
	Damage from pesticides	Careless use of insecticides and herbicides.	Development of more specific and less persistent pesticides. More use of alternative control methods, such as biological control.
	Damage from fishing	Overfishing, greatly reducing populations of species caught for food. Accidental damage to other animals, such as dolphins.	Impose controls on methods and amount of fishing.

This reaction happens at these high levels in the atmosphere because this is where the most ultraviolet light is present. The ultraviolet light comes from the Sun. Most of it is absorbed by the ozone layer, so there is much less of it in the lower layers of the atmosphere.

What breaks the ozone down? This happens quite naturally. For example, one of the three oxygen atoms in an ozone molecule may separate from the others, and then combine with another ozone molecule to form oxygen:

$$O_3 \rightarrow O_2 + O$$
$$O_3 + O \rightarrow 2O_2$$

Until quite recently, the rates at which ozone formed and broke down in the high levels of the atmosphere were about equal. The amount of ozone stayed about the same. But since the 1970s, the amount of ozone has been decreasing. Why has this been happening? And why does it matter?

14.4 Ozone is broken down by CFCs.

Chlorofluorocarbons, or **CFCs**, are very stable, unreactive, non-poisonous chemicals. They have had a

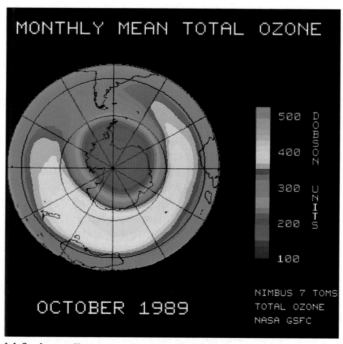

14.2 A satellite map showing the hole in the ozone layer of Antarctica, in October 1989. Dobson units are a measure of ozone concentration.

wide variety of uses. They have been used as coolants in fridges, and in air conditioning. They have been used as aerosol propellants, and for filling the spaces in foam used to make packaging or furniture. It was a long time before anyone realised the harm that these seemingly harmless chemicals were doing.

When CFCs escape from fridge cooling systems, from foam packaging or from aerosols, they go into the atmosphere. Because they are very unreactive, they stay there for a very long time. They gradually find their way up to the level of the ozone layer.

Here, at last, the large amounts of ultraviolet light begin to break their molecules apart. Chlorine is released from the CFC molecules. The chlorine reacts with ozone molecules, speeding up the rate at which they break down. The CFCs speed up the breakdown of the ozone molecules, but have no effect on the rate at which they reform. Therefore, CFCs reduce the amount of ozone in the atmosphere.

Why does this matter? The ozone layer is very important to all living things on Earth, because it absorbs a lot of the ultraviolet rays hitting the atmosphere. Ultraviolet light is very damaging. One effect it can have is to damage DNA in cells, causing mutations.

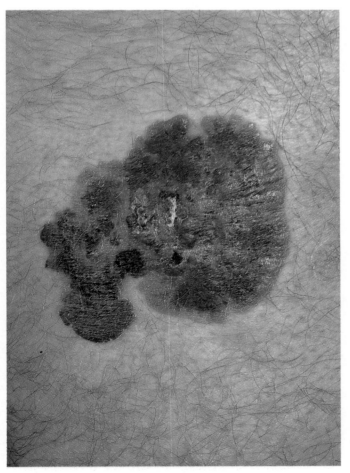

14.3 This type of skin cancer, called melanoma, can be caused by ultraviolet radiation from the Sun damaging the DNA in skin cells

This can lead to skin cancer. If the ozone layer is lost, then we will have no natural protection from this harmful ultraviolet radiation. High levels of ultraviolet radiation would also damage crops.

14.5 We can save the ozone layer.

Now that people understand what is happening to the ozone layer, we can begin to do something to save it. We must stop using CFCs.

Unfortunately, this will not be an immediate and complete solution to the problem. Firstly, many countries, especially developing countries, want to go on using CFCs. Although alternative chemicals have been developed, they are more expensive. Also, it is now realised that these alternative chemicals, although they may not do any damage to the ozone layer, may contribute to the greenhouse effect! We need to try to develop even better alternatives to CFCs.

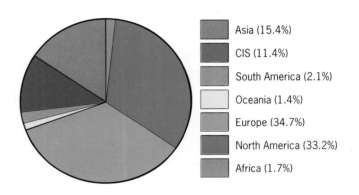

Asia (15.4%)

CIS (11.4%)

South America (2.1%)

Oceania (1.4%)

Europe (34.7%)

North America (33.2%)

Africa (1.7%)

14.4 Use of CFCs in different parts of the world in the early 1990s

Secondly, you may remember that CFCs are very stable substances. The CFCs already in the atmosphere will stay there for a long time. Even if everyone stopped producing and using CFCs immediately, it would take about 100 years for the amount of ozone to get back to anything like 'normal'.

Questions
1 What is ozone?
2 Why is most ozone found in a layer high in the Earth's atmosphere, rather than close to the ground?
3 What are CFCs, and what are they used for?
4 Explain how CFCs are damaging the ozone layer.
5 Describe the harmful effects which might occur if the ozone layer is destroyed.
6 How can we save the ozone layer?

211

Global warming

14.6 The greenhouse effect is essential to life.

The Earth's atmosphere contains several different gases which act like a blanket, keeping the Earth warm. The most important of these gases is **carbon dioxide**.

Carbon dioxide is transparent to shortwave radiation from the Sun. The sunlight passes freely through the atmosphere (Fig 14.5), and reaches the ground. The ground is warmed by the radiation, and emits longer wavelength, infrared radiation. Carbon dioxide does not let all of this infrared radiation pass through. Much of it is kept in the atmosphere, making the atmosphere warmer.

This is called the **greenhouse effect**, because it is just the same as the effect which keeps an unheated greenhouse warmer than the air outside. The glass around the greenhouse behaves like the carbon dioxide in the atmosphere. It lets shortwave radiation in, but does not let out the longwave radiation. The longwave radiation is trapped inside the greenhouse, making the air inside it warmer.

We need the greenhouse effect. If it did not happen, then the Earth would be frozen and lifeless. The average temperature on Earth would be about 33 °C lower than it is now.

14.7 The enhanced greenhouse effect may cause global warming.

Although we need the greenhouse effect, people are worried that it may be increasing. The amount of carbon dioxide and other greenhouse gases in the

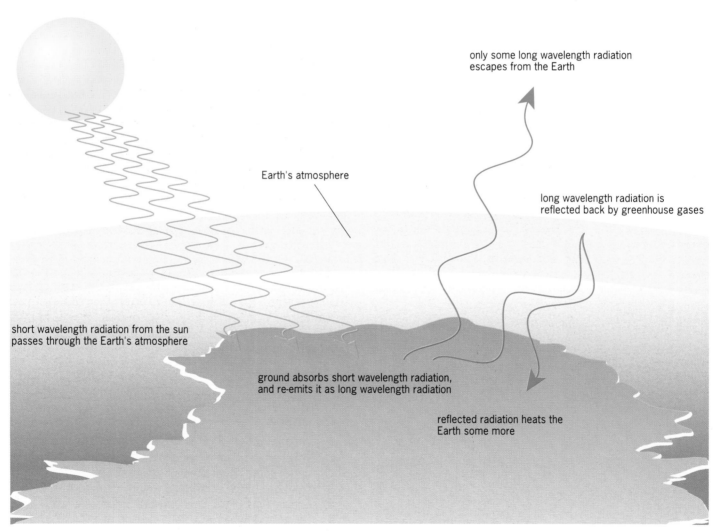

only some long wavelength radiation escapes from the Earth

Earth's atmosphere

long wavelength radiation is reflected back by greenhouse gases

short wavelength radiation from the sun passes through the Earth's atmosphere

ground absorbs short wavelength radiation, and re-emits it as long wavelength radiation

reflected radiation heats the Earth some more

14.5 *The greenhouse effect. Short wavelength radiation from the Sun passes through the atmosphere and reaches the ground. Some of it is absorbed by the ground, and is re-emitted as longwave radiation. Much of this cannot pass through the blanket of 'greenhouse gases' in the atmosphere. It is reflected back towards the Earth, warming the atmosphere.*

atmosphere is getting greater. This may trap more infrared radiation, and make the atmosphere warmer. This is called the **enhanced greenhouse effect**, and its possible effect on the Earth's temperature is called **global warming**.

Over recent years, the amount of fossil fuels which have been burnt by industry, and in engines of vehicles such as cars, trains and aeroplanes, has increased greatly. This releases carbon dioxide into the atmosphere. Fig 14.6 shows what has happened to the amount of carbon dioxide in the atmosphere since 1750.

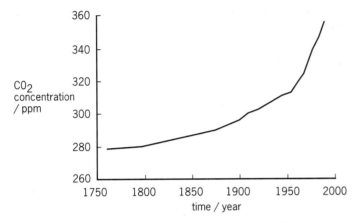

14.6 How carbon dioxide concentrations in the atmosphere have changed since 1750

Other gases which contribute to the greenhouse effect have also been released by human activities. These include **methane, nitrous oxide** and **CFCs**. Table 14.2 shows where these gases come from. The concentrations of all of these gases in the atmosphere is steadily increasing.

Some scientists think that, as the concentration of these gases increases, the temperature on Earth will also increase. At the moment, however, no-one is quite

sure whether this will happen or not. There are all sorts of other processes, many of them natural, which can cause quite large changes in the average temperature of the Earth, and these are not fully understood. For example, every now and then the Earth has been plunged into an Ice Age. Perhaps we are due for another Ice Age soon. Perhaps the enhanced greenhouse effect might help to delay this!

But most people think that we should be very worried about the enhanced greenhouse effect and global warming. If the Earth's temperature did rise significantly, there could be big changes in the world as we know it. For example, the ice caps might melt. This would release a lot more water into the oceans, so that sea levels would rise. Many low-lying areas of land might be flooded. This could include large parts of countries like Bangladesh, almost the whole of the Maldive islands, and major cities such as London.

A rise in temperature would also affect the climate in many parts of the world. No-one is sure just what would happen where – there are too many variables for scientists to be able to predict the consequences. It would probably mean that some countries which already have low rainfall might become very dry deserts. Others might have more violent storms than they do now. This would mean that animals and plants living in some areas of the world might become extinct. People in some places might not be able to grow crops.

There might be some beneficial effects, too. For example, extra carbon dioxide in the atmosphere and higher temperatures might increase the rate of photosynthesis in some parts of the world. This could mean that higher yields could be gained from crops. It might mean that, in countries like Britain, we could grow crops which need warmer temperatures than we have at the moment.

14.8 Can we avoid global warming?

The fact is that, although we know for sure that the levels of greenhouse gases are increasing, we do *not* know for sure whether this will cause global warming. Nor do we know for sure what effects global warming would have. But, for the very reason that we do not know these things, we need to take great care with our atmosphere. We cannot afford to do this enormous experiment with our planet!

It is important that we cut down the emission of greenhouse gases. One obvious way to do this is to reduce the amount of **fossil fuels** which are burnt. This would reduce the amount of **carbon dioxide** we pour into the air. Agreements have been made between countries to try to do this, but they are proving very difficult to implement.

Deforestation has also been blamed for increasing the amount of carbon dioxide in the air. (You can read more about deforestation on pages 216 to 218.) It has

Table 14.2 Gases contributing to the greenhouse effect

Gas	% estimated contribution	Main sources
Carbon dioxide	55	Burning fossil fuels
Methane	15	Decay of organic matter, e.g. in waste tips and paddy fields; waste gases from digestive processes in cattle and insects; natural gas leaks
CFCs	24	Fridges and air conditioning systems; plastic foams
Nitrous oxides	6	Fertilisers; burning fossil fuels, especially in vehicles

been argued that, by cutting down rainforests, there are fewer trees to photosynthesise and remove carbon dioxide from the air. However, this is not strictly true. A mature forest tree gives out almost as much carbon

14.7 Large amounts of methane are produced by microorganisms living in paddy fields, such as these in Thailand

14.8 The blue and yellow pipes are collecting methane from this landfill site in Leicestershire. The methane is used to fuel an electricity generator.

dioxide from respiration as it takes in by photosynthesis! Also, when the tree has been cut down, other plants grow in its place – either naturally, or planted for crops by farmers. These probably take as much carbon dioxide from the air as the tree did.

However, if the tree is burnt or left to rot when it is chopped down, then carbon dioxide will be released from it. So just chopping down trees does not increase the amount of carbon dioxide in the air, but burning them or letting them decay does.

Farming can add **nitrous oxide** to the air. This is because nitrogen-containing fertilisers can release this gas. Nitrous oxide also comes from burning fossil fuels. We could reduce the amount of nitrous oxide which we release by reducing the usage of fertilisers, as well as cutting down the use of fossil fuels.

CFCs have been discussed on page 210. There are already agreements to stop using CFCs. However, the new products which have been developed to replace them, called HFCs, do still contribute to the greenhouse effect. Even better replacements need to be found.

Methane, like nitrous oxide, is produced by farming activities. It is released by bacteria which live on organic matter, such as in paddy fields (flooded fields which are used for growing rice), by animals which chew the cud, such as cattle, and by some insects, such as termites. There is probably not much that we can do about this. Methane is also produced by decaying rubbish in landfill sites. We can help this problem by reducing the amount of rubbish which we throw away, and by collecting the methane from these sites. It can be used as fuel. Although burning it for fuel does release carbon dioxide, this carbon dioxide does not trap so much infrared radiation as the methane would have done.

Questions

1 Explain the difference between *the greenhouse effect*, *the enhanced greenhouse effect* and *global warming*.
2 Copy Table 14.2, adding a large fourth column. In this column, write short summaries of what we can do to reduce our emissions of each gas. (Have a look at question 3, which might give you some extra ideas!)
3 Each of the following has been suggested as a way of reducing global warming. For each suggestion, explain why it would work, and discuss the problems which would probably occur in trying to implement it.
(a) reducing the top speed limit for cars and lorries
(b) improving traffic flow in urban areas
(c) insulating houses
(d) increasing the number of nuclear power stations
(e) encouraging people to recycle more of their rubbish

Acid rain

14.9 Burning fossil fuels releases sulphur and nitrogen oxides.

Fossil fuels, such as coal, oil and natural gas, were formed from living organisms. They all contain sulphur; coal contains the most. When they are burnt, the sulphur combines with oxygen in the air and forms sulphur dioxide. Nitrogen oxides are also formed.

Sulphur dioxide is a very unpleasant gas. If people breathe it in, it can irritate the linings of the breathing system. If you are prone to asthma or bronchitis, sulphur dioxide can make it worse. Sulphur dioxide is also poisonous to many kinds of plants, sometimes damaging their leaves so badly that the whole plant dies.

14.10 Sulphur and nitrogen oxides produce acid rain.

Rain is usually slightly acid, with a pH a little below 7. This is because carbon dioxide dissolves in it to form carbonic acid.

Sulphur dioxide and nitrogen oxides also dissolve in rain. They form an acidic solution, called **acid rain**. The pH of acid rain can be as low as 4.

Acid rain damages plants. Although the rain usually does not hurt the leaves directly when it falls onto them, it does affect the way in which plants grow. This is because it affects the soil in which the plants are growing. The acid rain water seeps into the soil, and washes out ions such as calcium, magnesium and aluminium. The soil becomes short of these ions, so the plant becomes short of nutrients. It also makes it more difficult for the plant to absorb other nutrients from the soil. So acid rain can kill trees and other plants.

The ions which are washed out of the soil by the acid rain often end up in rivers and lakes. Aluminium, in particular, is very poisonous to fish, because it affects their gills. Young fish are often killed if the amount of aluminium in the water is too great. Other freshwater organisms are often killed, too. At the same time, the water itself becomes more acidic, which means that many kinds of plants and animals cannot live in it.

14.11 Sulphur dioxide is carried long distances.

One of the biggest problems in trying to do anything about the problems of acid rain is that it does not usually fall anywhere near the place which is causing it. A coal-burning power station might release a lot of sulphur dioxide, which is then carried high in the air for hundreds of miles before falling as acid rain. Sulphur dioxide produced in England might fall as acid rain in Norway.

14.12 Sulphur dioxide emissions are being reduced.

Acid rain is, in many ways, a much easier problem to solve than the damage to the ozone layer or the greenhouse effect. The answer is simple – we must cut down emissions of sulphur dioxide and nitrogen oxides.

Coal-burning power stations have been the worst

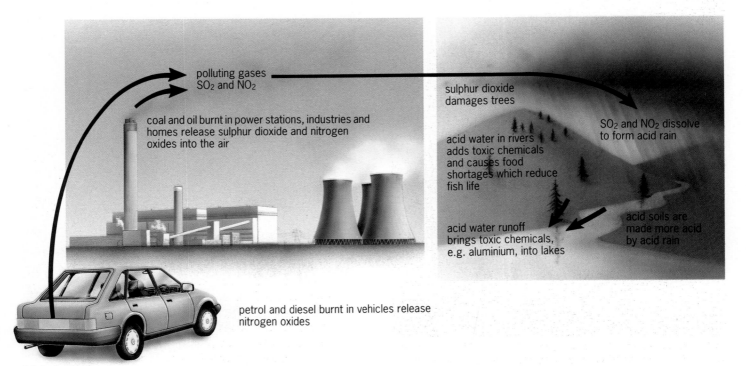

polluting gases SO_2 and NO_2

coal and oil burnt in power stations, industries and homes release sulphur dioxide and nitrogen oxides into the air

petrol and diesel burnt in vehicles release nitrogen oxides

sulphur dioxide damages trees

SO_2 and NO_2 dissolve to form acid rain

acid water in rivers adds toxic chemicals and causes food shortages which reduce fish life

acid water runoff brings toxic chemicals, e.g. aluminium, into lakes

acid soils are made more acid by acid rain

14.9 Acid rain

culprits. The number of coal-burning power stations in Britain has been going down – more because of the cost of coal than to try to stop pollution – and more of them are burning oil which produces less sulphur dioxide. However, this has meant a reduction in the demand for coal, which has been part of the reason for the closure of many coal mines, and the loss of jobs for many miners.

Whatever kind of fossil fuel is burnt in power stations or other industries, the waste gases can be 'scrubbed' to remove sulphur dioxide. This often involves passing the gases through a fine spray of lime.

The burning of petrol in car engines also produces sulphur and nitrogen oxides. These can be removed by catalytic convertors fitted to the exhaust system. All new petrol-burning cars now have to have catalytic convertors.

Questions

1. What causes acid rain?
2. How does acid rain damage trees?
3. How does acid rain damage fish?
4. Summarise what is being done to try to reduce the production of acid rain.

Deforestation

14.13 People cut down trees for fuel and farmland.

Humans have always cut down trees. Wood is an excellent fuel and building material. The land on which trees grow can be used for growing crops for food, or to sell. One thousand years ago, most of Europe was covered by forests. Now, most of them have been cut down. The cutting down of large numbers of trees is called **deforestation**.

14.14 Rainforests are special places.

Recently, most concern about deforestation has been about the loss of **rainforests**. In the tropics, the relatively high and constant temperatures, and high rainfall, provide perfect conditions for the growth of plants. A rainforest is a very special place, full of many different species of plants and animals. More different species live in a small area of rainforest than in an equivalent area of any other habitat in the world. We say that rainforest has a high **species diversity**.

When an area of rainforest is cut down, the soil under the trees is exposed to the rain. The soil of a rainforest is very thin. The soil is quickly washed away once it loses its cover of plants. This soil erosion may

14.10 When rainforest is cut down and burnt, as here in Brazil, large amounts of carbon dioxide are released to the atmosphere

14.11 Unspoilt tropical rain forest in Venezuela

216

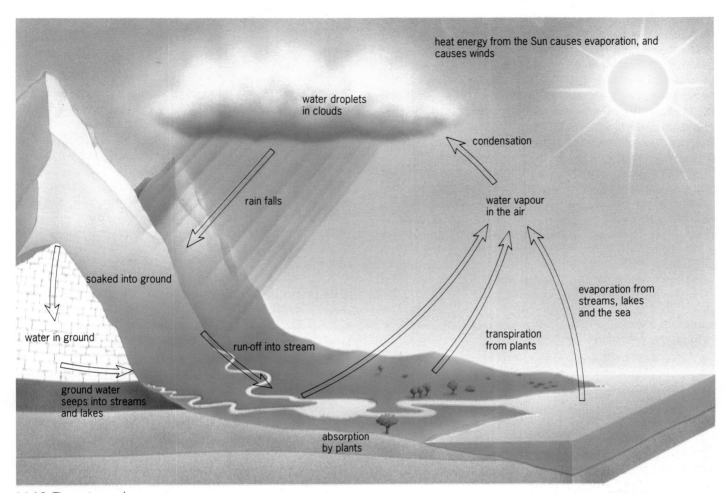

14.12 The water cycle

make it very difficult for the rainforest to grow back again, even if the land is left alone. The soil can also be washed into rivers, filling up the river bed and causing flooding.

The loss of part of a rainforest means a loss of a habitat for many different species of animals. Even if small 'islands' of forest are left as reserves, these may not be large enough to support a breeding population of the animals. Deforestation threatens many species of animals and plants with extinction.

The loss of so many trees can also affect the water cycle (Fig 14.12). With the trees growing, when rain falls a lot of it is taken up by the trees and taken up to their leaves. It then evaporates, and goes back into the atmosphere in the process of transpiration. If the trees have gone, then the rain simply runs off the soil and into rivers. Much less goes back into the air as water vapour. The air becomes drier, and less rain falls.

14.15 Developing countries need help to conserve rainforests.

When we get concerned about the rate at which some countries are cutting down their forests, it is very important to remember that we have already cut down most of ours!

No-one is quite sure how fast the rainforests are being cut down. In the early 1990s, it was thought that tropical rainforest was being cut down at a rate of about 10 or 11 hectares per minute! It is now thought that this was an overestimate – the rate is probably quite a lot less than this. But it is still great enough that we should be very concerned about it.

Most rainforests grow in developing countries, where many of the people are very poor. The people may cut down the forests to clear land on which they can grow food. It is difficult to expect someone who is desperately trying to produce food, to keep their family alive, not to do this, unless you can offer some alternative. International conservation groups such as the World Wide Fund for Nature, and governments of the richer, developed, countries such as the USA and the UK, can help by providing funds to the people or governments of developing countries to try to help them to provide alternative sources of income for people. Many of the most successful projects involve showing how the people can actually make use of the rainforest in a sustainable way.

217

The greatest pressure on the rainforest may come from the country's government in the big cities, rather than the people living in or near the rainforest. For example, Cameroon in West Africa still has a lot of rainforest. The government of Cameroon desperately needs more money, partly to pay off debts to developed countries. France has offered Cameroon large amounts of money in return for being allowed to harvest large areas of rainforest for timber. It is difficult for a country like Cameroon to refuse such an offer. It is important that developed countries should not put these pressures onto them. Instead, the developed countries should try to help the developing countries to conserve their natural resources such as rainforests. In Cameroon, conservation groups are working with local people to help them to live with the rainforest without destroying it. Most local people very much want to do this; they love their forest, and do not want to see it destroyed.

Destruction of wetlands

14.16 Wetlands are important habitats.

A wetland is an area where relatively shallow water lies for at least part of the year. The water may be fresh, forming bogs, marshes or swamps for example. The flood-plains of rivers may also contain areas of land which become very wet for part of most years. Or the water may be salt water, as in mangrove swamps or salt marshes.

Wetlands provide habitats for many species which cannot live anywhere else. Some live there all the time, while others – such as frogs and newts – may only need them at breeding times. If wetlands are destroyed, then these species will have nowhere to live or breed, and will become extinct.

14.17 Wetlands are destroyed by drainage and dams.

Wetlands are rapidly disappearing. In the USA, almost half of the wetlands have been destroyed. In the 20 years between 1950 and 1970, about three million hectares of wetlands were destroyed in the USA alone. Similar destruction is happening all over the world.

Wetlands are usually destroyed by drainage. People drain the land so that they can use it, either for farming or for building.

Wetlands may also be destroyed by the building of dams. For example, a natural river may carry a lot of water in winter and less in summer. In winter, it floods. If a dam is built to make a reservoir, then the amount

14.13 The Kafue Flats in Zambia are an internationally important wetland – you can read about conservation there in Section 14.18

218

of water flowing in the river will be controlled by people, who operate gates on the dam to let out the water. The river will no longer flood, so the wetlands in its flood-plain will no longer exist.

14.18 The Kafue Flats in Zambia are an important wetland.

In 1971, an international convention, called the Ramsar convention, put forward proposals for the protection of wetlands all over the world. Seventy-four nations have signed the convention. In 1994, 582 sites are being protected under the Ramsar convention.

One such project is in Zambia, where 6 % of the land is wetlands. The conservation project covers about one third of all of these wetlands. The project is run by the World Wide Fund for Nature, the World Conservation Union and the Government of the Republic of Zambia. It is a good illustration of how conservation projects work best when the people who traditionally live in the conservation area are themselves involved in the project.

Part of the conservation area in Zambia is called the Kafue Flats (Figs 14.13 and 14.14). The Kafue River runs through this region. There is also a small national park here, the Lochinver National Park, which was already in existence before the wetlands project began.

The Kafue Flats are rich in wildlife. There are large herds of a kind of antelope which lives nowhere else, as well as many other large mammals such as zebras and wildebeest. There are many species of birds, including some which are very rare and threatened with extinction. Many birds use the Kafue Flats as a stop-over site when they are migrating. There is a human population of about 120 000, many of whom own cattle, while others make a living from fishing. Maize is farmed here.

Conservationists were worried that, if care was not taken, the Kafue Flats would be damaged by the activities of people. For example, extensive irrigation for agriculture was using up water from the Kafue Flats wetlands, as were water supplies to towns. Uncontrolled hunting was destroying wildlife. A hydroelectric power station was affecting the flow of water in the Kafue River.

The National Park was first set up in 1972, to try to conserve wildlife which was rapidly disappearing because of hunting and cattle ranching. However, the people who lived there were not consulted. They were simply told that they could not hunt, or graze their animals in the Park. Not surprisingly, they did not support the Park, and some of them became poachers.

Now it is realised that it is important that local communities must be considered. In 1988, when the Kafue Flats project was set up, meetings were held with local people and their chiefs, so that they had a say in the conservation decisions. Most of them are now very supportive of the aims of the project. They feel that the project is theirs. Training regularly takes place, both to tell the people about the conservation project, and to help them in various ways, such as teaching them how to protect their cattle from disease. Some local people now work as 'scouts', helping with the

14.14 *In the Kafue Flats conservation area, domestic cattle and wild animals, such as these lechwe, graze side by side*

219

management of the area and stopping poachers from killing animals.

The managers of the Kafue Flats project try to make sure that local communities and government share the costs and benefits of the conservation of the wetlands. Fishing, cattle grazing and hunting is still allowed, but attempts are being made to control them. The hunting is paid for by people who come from other countries, to kill animals such as antelope. Although this may seem wrong, only a small percentage of the population is killed, and the money which is paid is important for helping to pay for the conservation measures. Tourists coming to the National Park also bring in money.

Questions

1 What is a wetland?
2 Why is the conservation of wetlands an important issue?
3 Some people think that 'conservation' should mean stopping any human activities in an area. How does the Kafue Flats project suggest that this is not always the best thing to do?

14.15 *The thick, green water in this pond is a sign of eutrophication. The green colour is caused by small photosynthetic organisms which thrive in the high concentration of nutrients in the water. Eventually, large populations of bacteria may develop, using up the oxygen in the water and stopping most other organisms from being able to live there.*

Water pollution

14.19 Aquatic organisms need clean water.

Many organisms live in water. They are called **aquatic** organisms. Aquatic habitats include fresh water, such as streams, rivers, ponds and lakes; and also marine environments – the sea and oceans.

Most organisms which live in water respire aerobically, and so need oxygen. They obtain their oxygen from oxygen gas which has dissolved in the water. Anything which reduces the amount of oxygen available in the water can make it impossible for fish or other aquatic organisms to live there.

In the UK, there are two main sources of pollution which can reduce oxygen levels in fresh water. They are **fertilisers** and **untreated sewage**.

Farmers and horticulturalists use fertilisers to increase the yield of their crops. The fertilisers usually contain **nitrates** and **phosphates**. Nitrates are very soluble in water. If nitrate fertiliser is put onto soil, it may be washed out in solution when it rains. This is called **leaching**. The leached nitrates may run into streams and rivers.

Algae and green plants in the river grow faster when they are supplied with these extra nitrates. They may grow so much that they completely cover the water. They block out the light for plants growing beneath them, which die. Even the plants on the top of the water eventually die. When they do, their remains are

Water with few nutrients is rich in oxygen, and supports a variety of animal life.

clear water

sunlight can penetrate deep in the water, allowing water plants to grow

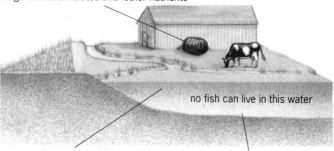

Water with high concentrations of nutrients is low in oxygen, so few animals can live in it.

run-off from fertilisers, animal waste and silage contains nitrates and other nutrients

no fish can live in this water

large populations of algae and bacteria grow

no light gets through the water, so no water plants grow

14.16 *Eutrophication. Plant nutrients flowing into the water increase plant and bacterial growth. This reduces oxygen levels, killing fish.*

220

a good source of food for **bacteria**. The bacteria breed rapidly. The large population of bacteria respires, using up oxygen from the water. Soon, there is very little oxygen left for other living things. Those which need a lot of oxygen, such as fish, have to move to other areas, or die.

This whole process is called **eutrophication**. It can happen whenever food for plants or bacteria is added to water. As well as fertilisers, other pollutants from farms, such as slurry from buildings where cattle or pigs are kept, or from pits where grass is rotted down to make silage, can cause eutrophication. Untreated sewage can also cause eutrophication. Sewage provides a good food source for many kinds of bacteria. Once again, their population grows, depleting the oxygen levels.

14.20 Nitrate use must be carefully controlled.

Eutrophication is not the only problem caused by the leaching of nitrate fertilisers. Some of the nitrates are carried deep into the soil, where they find their way into water in rocks deep underground, called **aquifers**. Water in aquifers may be extracted to use as drinking water. There is some concern that, if people drink water containing a lot of nitrate, they may become ill.

Could we stop using nitrate fertilisers? It is not really sensible at the moment to suggest that we could. People expect to have plentiful supplies of relatively cheap food. Although fertilisers are expensive, by using them farmers get so much higher yields that they make more profit. If they did not use fertilisers at all, their yields would be much lower and they would have to sell their crops for a higher price, in order to make any profit at all.

Some farmers are doing just this. They do not use **inorganic** fertilisers, such as ammonium nitrate, at all. Instead, they use **organic** fertilisers, such as manure. Organic fertilisers are better than inorganic ones in that they do not contain many nitrates which can easily be leached out of the soil. Instead, they release their nutrients gradually, over a long period of time, giving crops time to absorb them efficiently. Nevertheless, manures *can* cause pollution, if a lot is put onto a field at once, at a time of year when there is a lot of rain or when crops are not growing and cannot absorb the nutrients from them.

The yields obtained when using organic fertilisers are not usually as great as when using inorganic ones, so the crops are usually sold for a higher price. Many people are now prepared to pay this extra money for food from crops grown in this way, but many cannot afford to.

If nitrate fertilisers *are* used, there is much which can be done to limit the harm they do. Care must be taken not to use too much, but only to apply an amount which the plants can take up straight away. Fertilisers should not be applied to empty fields, but only when plants are growing. They should not be applied just before rain is forecast. They should not be sprayed near to streams and rivers. In some parts of England, which have been designated as **nitrate sensitive areas**, very strict controls have been laid down restricting farmers in their use of nitrate fertilisers, and also in the use of organic fertilisers such as manure.

14.21 Crop rotation can reduce the use of fertilisers.

Before inorganic fertilisers were widely available, farmers used **crop rotation** to maintain the fertility of the soil. This means growing different crops in a field each year, perhaps in a four-year cycle. Fig 14.18 shows one example of a crop rotation.

Each kind of crop – cereals such as wheat, root crops such as sugar beet, legumes such as peas and so on – takes its own particular requirements from the soil. If you grow the same crop year after year, then the particular nutrients needed by this crop are quickly removed from the soil, and you must keep replacing them with fertilisers. If you grow different crops, however, which have slightly different needs for nutrients, then nutrients are not removed so rapidly. Legumes are especially useful in a crop rotation because they

14.17 What is the cost of 100 g of organically produced mushrooms? What would it have been if they were not on special offer? What is the cost of 100 g of 'ordinary' mushrooms? (1 lb is about 455 grams).

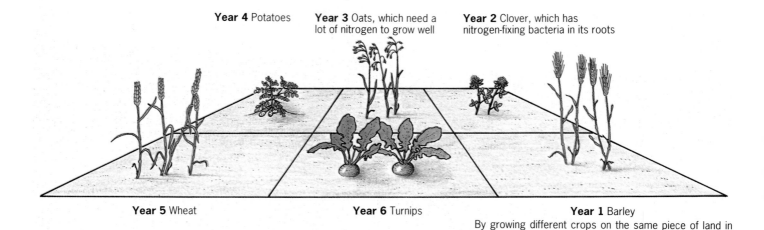

Year 4 Potatoes

Year 3 Oats, which need a lot of nitrogen to grow well

Year 2 Clover, which has nitrogen-fixing bacteria in its roots

Year 5 Wheat

Year 6 Turnips

Year 1 Barley

By growing different crops on the same piece of land in successive years, a farmer can gain several benefits. For example, crops like clover may provide nitrogen for the following crop. Also, a disease of one crop will not get the chance to infect that crop in the following year, and may die out before the same crop comes round again.

14.18   One type of crop rotation

actually *add* nitrates to the soil. They contain nitrogen-fixing bacteria in their root nodules. If the roots are left in the ground when the crop is harvested, there is nitrate available in the soil next year for the next crop which is planted.

Crop rotation also has another benefit – it can reduce the problems caused by pests, and so reduce the amount of pesticides which need to be used. This is because most pests will only feed on one particular crop. If the same crop is grown year after year, the pest population builds up. If different crops are grown, any particular kind of pest will only have food for one year at a time, and will have to move to another area to feed. Populations will probably stay quite low.

14.22   Sewage can be treated before releasing into streams.

As well as eutrophication, untreated sewage can cause other problems. It contains urine and faeces, both of which may contain harmful bacteria. If a person swims in, or drinks, water contaminated with untreated sewage, they run the risk of catching a wide variety of diseases, some of which – such as poliomyelitis – are very serious.

In Britain, most sewage is now treated to remove these harmful bacteria, and most of the nutrients which could cause eutrophication, before it is released into rivers. Sewage treatment is described in Section 19.6.

Questions
1   Explain what is meant by *eutrophication*.
2   How can crop rotation help to avoid water pollution?

Pesticides

14.23   Pesticides help to increase crop yields.

A pesticide is a substance which kills organisms which damage crops. Insects which eat crops can be killed with **insecticides**. Fungi which grow on crops are controlled with **fungicides**. Weeds which compete with crop plants for water, light and minerals can be controlled with **herbicides**. Pesticides may also be used to control organisms which transmit disease, such as mosquitoes (page 269).

In a natural ecosystem, a wide variety of plant species will probably grow in a particular habitat. A wide variety of animals will live in that habitat too, feeding on different plants and on each other. A natural ecosystem often has a large species diversity. Factors such as predation or food supply will prevent the population of any one species from growing too large (page 205).

On a farm, only a few plant species are allowed to grow in many of the fields. One field might contain nothing but wheat, for example. This is called a **monoculture**. Insects or fungi which can feed on the wheat have an almost inexhaustible food supply. The usual limits on their population growth do not apply. The populations of the insects or fungi may grow very rapidly, until they are so big that they cause extensive damage to the crop.

If nothing is done about this, then crop yields can be very badly reduced. It has been estimated that, in developing countries, at least one third of potential crops are destroyed by pests. If they did not use pesticides, then this would be even worse. In Britain, most farmers use pesticides.

14.19 Spraying pesticides onto a wheat crop. Farmers take care to spray only when the air is still, so that the spray does not drift away from the crop. How does the design of the sprayer help to prevent too much spray drift?

An investigation in the 1970s showed that, although the DDT levels in the water of an estuary were only 0.00005 parts per million (ppm), the amounts in the animals feeding in the estuary were much greater.

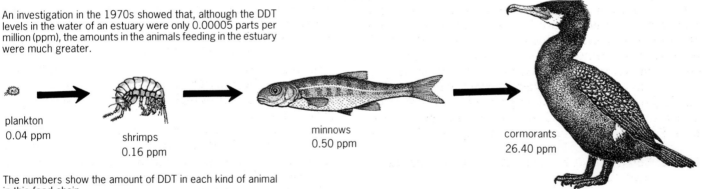

plankton
0.04 ppm

shrimps
0.16 ppm

minnows
0.50 ppm

cormorants
26.40 ppm

The numbers show the amount of DDT in each kind of animal in this food chain.

14.20 DDT accumulates along a food chain

14.24 Pesticides can harm the environment.

By definition, a pesticide is a harmful substance. In the 1950s and 1960s, some of the pesticides used did a lot of damage to the environment. One of these was **DDT**. DDT was used to kill insects. People did not realise that DDT is a **persistent** insecticide, which means that it does not break down, but remains in the bodies of the insects or in the soil. When a bird or other organism ate the insects, they ate the DDT too. The DDT stayed in their bodies; each time they ate an insect, more DDT accumulated in their tissues. If a bird of prey ate the insect-eating bird, it too began to accumulate DDT. Birds and other animals near the end of food chains built up very large concentrations of DDT in their bodies.

Unfortunately, as well as being persistent, DDT is also **nonspecific**. This means that it not only harms the insects it is meant to kill, but is also harmful to other living things. It is very harmful to birds, for example. In Britain, it affected the breeding success of peregrine falcons, by making their egg shells very weak, so that they very rarely hatched. The peregrine falcon population dropped very rapidly.

Once it was realised that DDT was doing so much harm, its use in Britain was stopped. Now DDT is not used in Britain or the rest of Europe. However, it is still used in many developing countries, such as much of Africa. This is because, without it, insects would be such a problem that more people would starve or die of diseases like malaria. It is also argued that DDT does break down in the higher temperatures of these countries.

223

14.25 Pesticide use can be reduced.

Since the scare about DDT, new kinds of pesticide have been introduced which are less persistent. However, even these have caused problems to other living organisms. For example, a group of insecticides called organophosphates, which are used to kill pests living on sheep, appear to have caused illness in farmers who use them frequently. A constant search goes on for pesticides which are only harmful to the organisms we want to kill.

No-one really wants to use pesticides unnecessarily. They are expensive to buy, take time to apply, and all farmers are aware of the damage they can do. Research is always going on to try to find ways of reducing the amount of pesticides which we use.

14.26 Pesticide use can be timed and targeted efficiently.

One way of reducing the use of pesticides is only to use them when the particular pest we want to get rid of is likely to be a problem. At the moment, many farmers simply spray insecticides or fungicides on their crops every year, to stop an infestation before it begins. If researchers could forecast when and if a particular pest was likely to appear, then farmers would only need to apply the pesticide when a problem was likely to occur.

For example, aphids (greenfly) are an important pest of many crops. Not only do they feed on the crops, but they can also transmit virus diseases to them. The Institute of Arable Crops Research now provides farmers with a forecast of when particular kinds of aphids are likely to infest their crops. They have set up a network of traps all over Britain, which suck in flying insects. The traps are emptied every day between April and November. The aphids migrate in spring, which is when they are most likely to infest crops. The researchers have found that the exact time when the aphids migrate depends on the temperatures in January and February. By keeping a record of this, and of the number of aphids trapped, the researchers can give farmers information about exactly when the aphids are likely to appear on their crops. The farmers can use this information to spray pesticide at exactly the right time – or not at all, if the aphid numbers are low that year.

14.27 Biological control is an alternative to pesticides.

In some situations, pests can be controlled without using pesticides at all. Instead, a natural predator or parasite can be used to keep the numbers of the pest down to a reasonable level. Another approach is to find a pesticide-free way to stop the pests from breeding. These methods are called **biological control**. Table 14.3 lists a few examples of biological control methods.

One example of a pest which can be controlled by a predator is the greenhouse whitefly. This tiny fly is an important pest of many glasshouse crops. It breeds rapidly, living and feeding on leaves, and badly damaging the plants. It can be controlled by introducing a very small wasp, called *Encarsia formosa*, into the glasshouse. This wasp lays its eggs inside the body of the larva of the whitefly. The wasp egg hatches into a larva which lives and feeds inside the whitefly larva, eventually killing it.

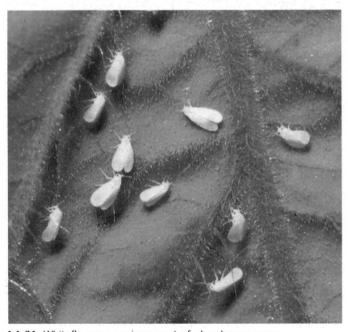

14.21 *Whitefly are a serious pest of glasshouse crops*

14.22 *The wasp* Encarsia *can be used to control whitefly numbers*

Table 14.3 Some examples of biological control

Problem	Control organism	How it works	Comments
Whitefly feeding on glasshouse crops, such as tomatoes	*Encarsia formosa*	Wasp larvae feed on whitefly larvae	Only works well in glasshouses, not outside
Aphids feeding on cereal crops	Hoverflies	Hoverfly larvae feed on aphids	Adult hoverflies feed on pollen and nectar, so allowing wildflowers to grow along field margins can increase the hoverfly population
River blindness, a disease spread by flies in West Africa	A bacterium, *Bacillus thuringiensis*	Bacterium infects and kills the flies which spread the disease	Different strains of this bacterium can be used against many insect pests
House mice in Australia	A parasitic worm	The worm infects the mice and reduces the fertility of the females	This control method is still being tested before it is widely used
Screw worms (larvae of flies, which eat the flesh of living animals) in Northern Africa	Sterilised male flies	The sterile males mate with female flies, so the eggs do not hatch	The screw worms originally came from Mexico, and this is where the sterile male flies are being produced

The wasp will probably not kill absolutely all of the whitefly. A small whitefly population will remain, kept in check by the wasps. The two populations may continue to oscillate at low levels for quite some time. Usually, however, more wasps will have to be introduced to the glasshouse at some stage.

Biological control is very useful because it is **specific**. The wasp only kills the whitefly – it does not harm useful insects such as bees. There is no pollution. Biological control is usually much cheaper than using pesticides, which are expensive and have to be applied over and over again.

Another advantage of biological control is that the pests are less likely to become **resistant** to the control organism than they are to a pesticide. The way in which pests develop resistance to pesticides is described in Chapter 16.

Genetic engineering is also being used to breed crop plants which have their own built-in resistance to pests. You can read more about this in Chapter 19.

14.28 Biological control needs careful research.

Even biological control is not without its dangers to the environment. If a predator is introduced to try to control a pest, great care must be taken to make sure that the predator does not become a pest itself.

This has happened in several parts of the world. In Australia, for example, there was a problem in the 1930s with beetles feeding on sugar cane crops. To try to control the beetles, a large toad from central America, called the cane toad (Fig 14.23) was introduced. It did its job well. However, the toad found Australia to its liking, and bred rapidly. In the north east of the country, there are now so many cane toads that almost all the native amphibians have been driven out. Moreover, the cane toad secretes a poison on its skin. Other animals which try to bite or lick the toad can be poisoned. The toad also eats native animals, and is threatening several species with extinction in some parts of Australia.

14.23 Biological control gone wrong – this cane toad is eating a pygmy possum, a native species of Australia which is under threat of extinction

Overfishing

14.29 Fishing is threatening fish species.

Humans have probably always used fish as a source of protein-rich food. However, in recent years there has been increasing concern about the threat to fish populations from the large numbers of fish which are being caught. Fig 14.24 shows how fish catches have increased since 1950. The figures on this graph only include fish caught by people who then sell their catch. There are probably another 24 million tonnes of fish caught each year by people who then eat it within their own family or community, especially in developing countries.

As a result of the great numbers of fish being caught, the populations of most of the species which are used for food are getting less and less. If we are not careful, the populations will get so small that there will not be enough adult fish left to breed. As it is, fishermen are having to work harder to catch enough fish to make a living.

14.30 Fish catches must be reduced.

The only way to ensure that we do not destroy fish populations is to reduce the number of fish which are caught. However, this is not easy. Each country wants to make sure that it gets a fair share of the fish catch,

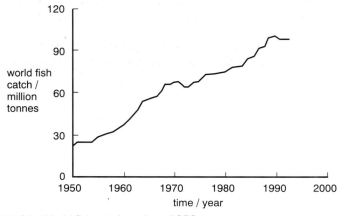

14.24 World fish catches since 1950

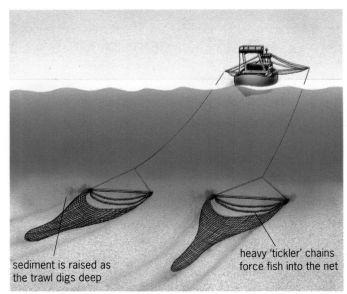

14.25 Beam trawling. The net may be up to 100 m long. As it scrapes along the sea bed, all the bottom living species such as starfish and flatfish – which the fishermen do not want and cannot sell – are caught in the net. All the fish which are caught die. For every 1 kg of commercial fish caught, 2–4 kg of dead fish are returned to the sea (data from World Wide Fund for Nature UK) .

sediment is raised as the trawl digs deep

heavy 'tickler' chains force fish into the net

so any international decision is very difficult to make. Everyone is worried that the other countries are getting more fish than they are. Moreover, fish do not stay in one place in the sea. Even if a country manages to reduce fishing to reasonable levels around its own shores, the same fish may be under threat when they move to the seas around other countries.

In 1982, the European Community agreed on a Common Fisheries Policy, to manage fish resources in the seas around Europe. This policy was concerned not only with conserving fish stocks, but also with making sure that European fishermen could compete with fishing industries in other parts of the world, and that there was a plentiful supply of fish for people to buy, at reasonable prices. Many people felt that the policy should have put more emphasis on conservation. It resulted in an *increase* in fishing, because it helped people to replace their old fishing boats with new, more efficient ones. As a result, overfishing actually got worse.

In 1992, the Common Fisheries Policy was reviewed. There was great concern that there would soon be no fish left to catch. A system of control is now used called *Total Allowable Catches*. This means that fishing fleets are given a maximum amount of fish that they are allowed to catch. Once they have caught this amount, they must stop fishing. Only certain species of fish are allowed to be caught, and only fish over a certain size. This, in theory, leaves the young fish to grow and reproduce. To help to stop small fish being caught, the mesh size of the nets must be above a certain size.

14.26 A salmon farm in a sea loch in Scotland. The fish are kept in underwater cages, with walkways above them to give people access for feeding the fish.

There are still many problems with this policy. Firstly, how do you decide what the Total Allowable Catch should be? The size of existing fish populations must be estimated, which is very difficult to do. Then someone must calculate the probable effects on the populations of different amounts of fishing, and decide on a Total Allowable Catch which will allow the population to stay the same, or grow. No-one can be sure exactly what this should be. There is constant pressure from fishermen to increase the Total Allowable Catch, because this is how they earn their living. If it is too low, then fishermen and other people who work in the fishing industry lose their jobs. Consumers also want the amount of fish caught to be as high as possible, because this keeps fish prices down.

Another problem is policing the amount of fish which is caught. It is obviously impossible for every catch from every fishing boat to be checked. Fishermen are mostly responsible for reporting their own catch. It is easy for them to say they have caught less than they really have.

Although only certain species of fish are supposed to be caught in certain seasons (to allow them to breed), the 'wrong' sort of fish can easily be caught along with the 'right' ones. These are often put back into the sea, but it is unlikely that they will live.

Could the Common Fishing Policy be improved? Most conservationists think that it could, and that it is essential that we make more effort to conserve fish stocks, unless we want to have no fish left in a few years' time. They suggest that the size of fishing fleets must be reduced, even though this would mean many people losing their jobs. But this is a very difficult political decision for a government to take.

14.31 Fish farming can provide more fish.

If overfishing is threatening wild fish populations, could we provide the fish which people want to eat by farming it?

Fish farming has increased greatly over the last twenty or so years. In Scotland, for example, there are now a large number of salmon farms. Salmon are kept in cages in sheltered sea lochs. They are fed well, and grow quickly. Fish farming has brought employment to remote parts of the country where it is very difficult for people to find jobs. It has increased the supply of fish, so that the prices of salmon and other farmed fish have dropped.

However, this, too, has caused problems. The food added to the water to feed the salmon, and the faeces from the salmon, are polluting the water. Another source of pollution is pesticides used to stop the farmed fish becoming infected with parasites and pathogens. Because the fish farms are usually in enclosed, sheltered waters, these pollutants build up, rather than being washed away. Other species of fish and invertebrates are being damaged by the pollution.

Questions

1 Summarise *three* aims of the Common Fisheries Policy of 1982.

2 Outline the ways in which the policy of 1992 has tried to solve the problem of overfishing.

3 Why is the 1992 policy still not successful in its aim of conserving fish stocks?

4 Make your own suggestions as to how the problem of overfishing in the seas around Europe could be solved. Remember to take into account the views of people such as fishermen, as well as those of conservationists.

5 What are (a) the benefits, and (b) the problems associated with farming fish, rather than catching wild ones?

15 Genetics

15.1 Nuclei contain chromosomes carrying genes.

In the nucleus of every cell there are a number of **chromosomes**. Chromosomes are long threads made of DNA and protein.

Most of the time, the chromosomes are too thin to be seen except with an electron microscope. But when a cell is dividing, they get shorter and fatter, so they can be seen with a light microscope.

Chromosomes contain **genes**. It is the genes on the chromosomes which determine all sorts of things about you – what colour your eyes or hair are, whether you have a snub nose or a straight one, and whether you have a genetic disease such as cystic fibrosis.

15.2 Each species has its own set of genes.

Each species of organism has its own number and variety of genes. This is what makes their body chemistry, their appearance and their behaviour different from those of other organisms.

Humans have a large number of genes. You have 46 chromosomes inside each of your cells, all with many

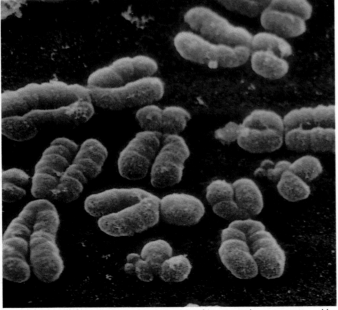

15.1 A scanning electronmicrograph of human chromosomes. You can see that each one is made of two chromatids, linked at a point called the centromere.

genes on them. Every cell in your body has an exact copy of all your genes. But, unless you are an identical twin, there is no-one else in the world with exactly the same combination of genes that you have. Your genes make you unique.

15.3 Genes describe how to make particular proteins.

Genes provide information about making proteins. Sections 15.23 to 15.26 explain how they do this.

Every chemical reaction inside a living organism is catalysed by **enzymes**. Enzymes are proteins. So, by providing information for making enzymes, genes affect all the chemical reactions in an organism's body.

Each cell contains many genes which carry the information for making many proteins. But not all of these genes are used by any one cell. Just a few genes will be 'switched on' in any one cell at any one time. If you have red hair, for example, you must have a red hair gene in all of your cells. But this gene will only have an effect in cells where hair grows, such as on your scalp. In heart cells, this gene will be switched off.

15.4 Most cells contain pairs of homologous chromosomes.

Figure 15.1 is a photograph of some chromosomes from a human cell which is about to divide.

In Figs 15.2 and 15.3 photographs of the chromosomes have been rearranged. You can see that there are, in fact, 23 pairs of chromosomes. The two chromosomes in a pair are the same size and shape.

The two chromosomes of a pair are called **homologous chromosomes**. One came from the person's mother, and the other from the father.

Each chromosome of a homologous pair carries genes for the same characteristic in the same place (Fig 15.4). Because there are two of each kind of chromosome, each cell contains two of each kind of gene. Let us look at one kind of gene to see how it behaves, and how it is inherited.

15.5 Cystic fibrosis is caused by an unusual protein.

In humans, cells in the lungs make mucus. The kind of mucus which is made partly depends on a **protein** in

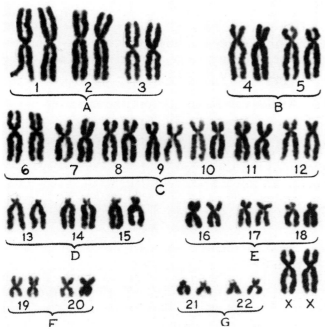

15.2 Chromosomes from a normal female, arranged in order

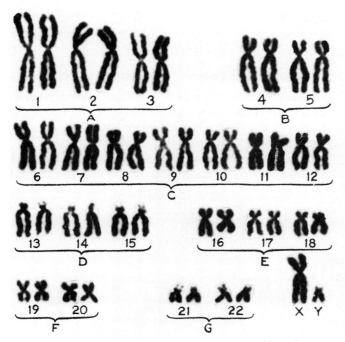

15.3 Chromosomes from a normal male, arranged in order

duct. This prevents pancreatic juice, containing digestive enzymes, from flowing into the duodenum, so food cannot be digested properly.

Instructions for making the protein are given by genes. There are two varieties of the gene for this protein – one for making the normal protein, and one for making the incorrect one. Different varieties of a gene are called **alleles**. We can give letters to alleles to use as symbols. So we can call the normal allele of the gene F, and the one which makes the abnormal protein f.

a pair of homologous chromosomes

two chromatids of one homologous chromosome

centromere

position of cystic fibrosis genes

15.4 Homologous chromosomes have genes for the same characteristic in the same position

15.5 People with cystic fibrosis have to have frequent therapy to clear mucus from their lungs. This girl's mother pummels her back to dislodge the thick mucus, which the girl can then remove from her lungs by coughing.

the cell membrane of some of the cells in the lungs. In some people, this protein is made incorrectly. This causes the disease **cystic fibrosis**. The lungs of a person with this disease make too much mucus, which is thicker than usual. The mucus collects in the lungs, making it difficult to get enough oxygen into the blood. The mucus makes a good breeding ground for bacteria, so infections can build up. The thick mucus is also made in the pancreas, where it blocks the pancreatic

229

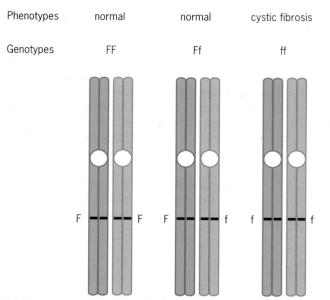

Phenotypes	normal	normal	cystic fibrosis
Genotypes	FF	Ff	ff

15.6 Genotypes for the cystic fibrosis gene

15.6 Each cell has two genes for any characteristic.

In each of your cells, there are two genes giving instructions about which of these two kinds of protein to make. This means that there are three possible combinations of alleles. You might have two F alleles, FF. You might have one of each, Ff. Or you might have two f alleles, ff.

If the two alleles for this gene in your cells are the same, that is FF or ff, you are said to be **homozygous**. If the two alleles are different, that is Ff, then you are **heterozygous**.

15.7 Genotype can determine phenotype.

The genes that you have are your **genotype**. Your genotype could be FF, Ff or ff.

The genotype determines the kind of protein you have, and therefore whether you will have cystic fibrosis or not. If your genotype is FF, then your protein is normal, and you will not have the disease. If your genotype is ff, then your protein is the incorrect one, and you will have cystic fibrosis. If your genotype is Ff, some of your protein is the incorrect one, and some of it is normal. You will have enough normal protein to ensure that the right sort of mucus is made, and you will not suffer from cystic fibrosis.

The features you have are called your **phenotype**. This can include what you look like – for example, what colour your hair is, or how tall you are – as well as things which we cannot actually see, such as what kind of protein you have in your cell membranes. In our example, your phenotype is either being normal or having cystic fibrosis.

You can see that, in this example, your phenotype depends entirely on your genotype. This is not always true. Sometimes, other things, such as what you eat, can affect your phenotype. However, for the moment, we will only consider the effect which genotype has on phenotype, and not worry about effects which the environment might have.

15.8 Alleles can be dominant or recessive.

You have seen that there are three different possible genotypes for the cell surface membrane protein, but only two phenotypes. We can summarise this as follows:

genotype	phenotype
FF	normal
Ff	normal
ff	cystic fibrosis

This happens because the allele F is **dominant** to the allele f. A dominant allele has just as much effect on phenotype when there is one of it as when there are two of it. A person who is homozygous for a dominant allele has the same phenotype as a person who is heterozygous.

The allele f is **recessive**. A recessive allele only affects the phenotype when there is no dominant allele present. Only people with the genotype ff – homozygous recessive – have cystic fibrosis.

15.9 Some alleles show codominance.

Sometimes, neither of a pair of alleles is dominant or recessive. Instead, both of them have an effect on the phenotype of a heterozygous organism. This is called **codominance**.

You will have noticed that, when we were dealing with dominant and recessive alleles, we used a capital letter for the dominant allele and a small letter for the recessive allele. We cannot do that with codominant alleles, because it might give the impression that one was dominant and the other recessive. Instead, we use a capital letter to represent the gene, and then small letters written just above and to the right of it to represent the alleles of that gene.

For example, imagine a kind of flower which has two alleles for flower colour. The allele C^W produces white flowers, while the allele C^R produces red ones. The possible genotypes and phenotypes are:

genotype	phenotype
$C^W C^W$	white
$C^W C^R$	pink
$C^R C^R$	red

Most people do not like writing alleles like this – it is much easier to try to get away with just writing a single letter! But it is very important that you *do* use the correct kind of symbols, or people will not understand that the alleles are codominant.

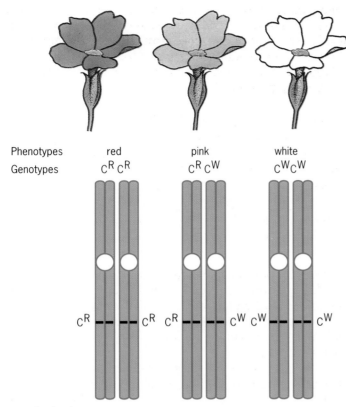

Phenotypes	red	pink	white
Genotypes	$c^R c^R$	$c^R c^W$	$c^W c^W$

c^R — — c^R c^R — — c^W c^W — — c^W

15.7 Codominance

Questions

1 What are chromosomes made of?
2 Why can you see chromosomes most easily when a cell is dividing?
3 Explain how genes affect all the chemical reactions in an organism's body.
4 What are homologous chromosomes?
5 What are alleles?
6 (a) The allele for brown eyes is dominant to the allele for blue eyes. Write down suitable symbols for these alleles.
   (b) What will be the phenotype of a person who is heterozygous for this characteristic?
7 What is codominance?

Inheritance

15.10 Gametes have only one gene for any characteristic.

All of the cells in your body have come from one original cell. This first cell, the zygote, was made when a sperm fertilised an egg. The sperm and the egg each contained chromosomes with a certain set of genes on them, which have since been copied exactly into all your body cells.

To study inheritance, you need to understand how the sperm and the egg get their genes. Gametes, such as eggs and sperm, are made by meiosis. Fig 8.10 shows how meiosis happens. During the first division of meiosis, the chromosomes come together in their homologous pairs, and then separate from each other. In the second division, each of the chromosomes separates into its two chromatids, which are exact copies of each other. These identical chromatids are now called chromosomes from the moment they separate. They have a centromere, and are now independent of each other.

So, whereas normal cells have two of each kind of chromosome, gametes only have one of each kind. This also means that they only have one of each pair of alleles.

15.11 Alleles are separated in meiosis.

Figure 15.8 shows some of the stages in meiosis, to show what happens to one pair of genes when a sperm is made.

In this example, the person is a carrier of cystic fibrosis, genotype Ff. For simplicity, only the chromosomes carrying this gene are shown. The other 44 have been left out.

During the first division of meiosis, these chromosomes come together and then separate. Two cells are made, one carrying the F allele and the other carrying the f allele.

In the second division of meiosis, the chromosome in each cell splits into its two identical chromatids. These identical chromatids become full chromosomes during the development of the sperm. So at the end of meiosis there are four cells, which will all grow into sperm cells. Half of them have the F allele and half have the f allele.

15.12 Genes and fertilisation.

If this man marries a woman with the genotype ff, will their children have cystic fibrosis or not?

The eggs that are made in the woman's ovaries are also made by meiosis. If you use Fig 15.8 to see what happens to her chromosomes during meiosis, you will see that she can only make one kind of egg. All of the eggs will carry an f allele.

During sexual intercourse, hundreds of thousands of sperm will begin a journey towards the egg. About half of them will carry an F allele, and half will carry an f allele. If there is an egg in the woman's oviduct, it will probably be fertilised. There is an equal chance of either kind of sperm getting there first.

If a sperm carrying an F allele wins the race, then the zygote will have an F allele from its father and an f allele from its mother. Its genotype will be Ff. After

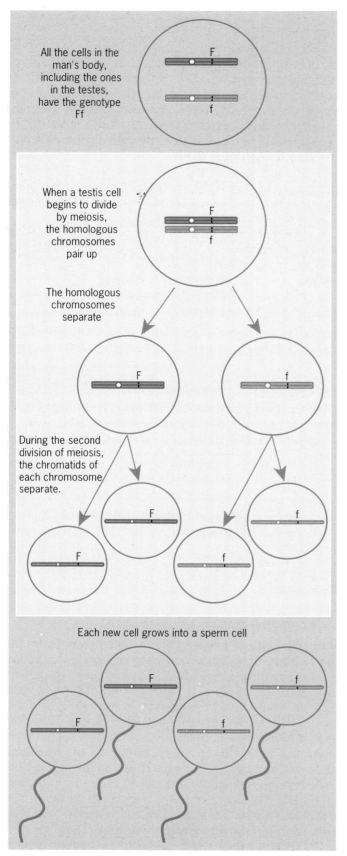

15.8 *What happens to the genes of a heterozygous man during meiosis*

All the cells in the man's body, including the ones in the testes, have the genotype Ff

When a testis cell begins to divide by meiosis, the homologous chromosomes pair up

The homologous chromosomes separate

During the second division of meiosis, the chromatids of each chromosome separate.

Each new cell grows into a sperm cell

nine months, a baby will be born with the genotype Ff.

But if a sperm carrying an f allele manages to fertilise the egg, then the baby will have the genotype ff, like its mother (Fig 15.9).

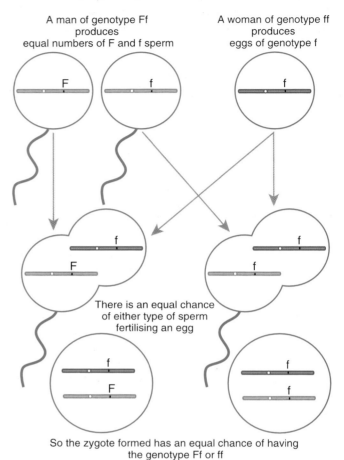

A man of genotype Ff produces equal numbers of F and f sperm

A woman of genotype ff produces eggs of genotype f

There is an equal chance of either type of sperm fertilising an egg

So the zygote formed has an equal chance of having the genotype Ff or ff

15.9 *Fertilisation between a heterozygous man and a woman with cystic fibrosis*

15.13 Genetic crosses must be written clearly.

There is a standard way of writing out all of this information. First, write down the phenotypes and genotypes of the parents. Next, write down the different types of gametes they can make, like this.

parents' phenotypes	normal	cystic fibrosis
parents' genotypes	Ff	ff
gametes	Ⓕ or Ⓕ	Ⓕ

The next step is to write down what might happen during fertilisation. Either kind of sperm might fuse with an egg.

gametes   Ⓕ or Ⓕ   Ⓕ

offspring genotypes

gametes	Ⓕ
Ⓕ	Ff
Ⓕ	ff

offspring phenotypes   Ff = normal (carrier for cystic fibrosis) $^1/_2$
                   ff = cystic fibrosis $^1/_2$

To finish your summary of the genetic cross, write out in words what you would expect the offspring from this cross to be.

'Approximately half of the children would be heterozygous carriers of cystic fibrosis, and half would be homozygous, with cystic fibrosis.'

15.14 Another example.

What happens if both parents are carriers?

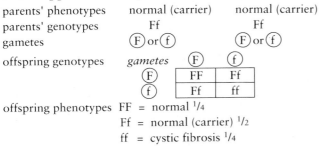

parents' phenotypes	normal (carrier)	normal (carrier)
parents' genotypes	Ff	Ff
gametes	F or f	F or f

offspring genotypes

gametes	F	f
F	FF	Ff
f	Ff	ff

offspring phenotypes FF = normal $1/4$
Ff = normal (carrier) $1/2$
ff = cystic fibrosis $1/4$

About one quarter of the children would be expected to have cystic fibrosis, and three quarters to be normal. However, half of the children would be expected to be carriers.

15.15 Probability in genetics.

In the last example, there were four offspring at the end of the cross. This does not mean that the man and woman will have four children. It simply means that each time they have a child, these are the possible genotypes that it might have.

When they have a child, there is a 1 in 4 chance that its genotype will be FF, and a 1 in 4 chance that its genotype will be ff. There is a 2 in 4, or rather 1 in 2, chance that its genotype will be Ff.

However, as you know, probabilities do not always work out. If you toss a penny up four times you might expect it to turn up heads twice and tails twice. But does it always do this? Try it and see.

With small numbers like this, probabilities do not always match reality. If you had the patience to toss your coin up a few thousand times, though, you will almost certainly find that you get much more nearly equal numbers of heads and tails.

The same thing applies in genetics. The offspring genotypes which you work out are only probabilities. With small numbers, they are unlikely to work out exactly. With very large numbers of offspring from one cross, they are more likely to be accurate.

So, if the man and woman in the last example had eight children, they might expect six of them to be normal and two to have cystic fibrosis. But they should not be too surprised if they have three normal children and five with cystic fibrosis.

15.16 Solving genetics problems.

Here is a typical question that you might be given to answer. Follow the steps you would use to answer it.

The seeds resulting from a cross between a tall pea plant and a dwarf one produced plants all of which were tall. When these plants were allowed to self-pollinate, the resulting seeds produced 908 tall plants and 293 dwarf plants. Account for these results. What would be the results of interbreeding the dwarf plants?

Firstly, work out whether or not one allele is dominant over the other. Next, decide on symbols. Then write a list of possible genotypes and phenotypes. Your answer might go like this.

There must be two alleles, one producing tallness and the other dwarfness. The plants are all either tall or dwarf, and no medium-sized ones are mentioned. So one allele must be completely dominant over the other.

When a tall plant is crossed with a dwarf plant, all the offspring are tall. This shows that it is the tall allele which is dominant.

Therefore, let us use the symbol T for the allele for tall plants, and the symbol t for the allele for dwarf plants. The allele T is dominant over the allele t, which is recessive.

The possible genotypes and phenotypes are these.

genotype	phenotype
TT	tall
Tt	tall
tt	dwarf

Now you are ready to begin explaining the first cross.

The first cross is between a tall pea plant and a dwarf one. The possible genotypes of the tall pea plant are TT or Tt. The dwarf plant must have the genotype tt.

If the tall plant is heterozygous, Tt, then half of its gametes would contain the t allele. During fertilisation, zygotes would be formed with the genotype tt, which would appear dwarf. But as none of the offspring of this cross are dwarf, the tall parent must be TT.

The first cross is therefore as follows.

parents' phenotypes	tall	dwarf
parents' genotypes	TT	tt
gametes	T	t

offspring genotypes

gametes	t
T	Tt

offspring phenotypes Tt = tall

This has explained the first sentence of the question. Next, these tall plants self-pollinate, in other words, they cross with themselves.

The offspring from the first cross are all heterozygous, Tt. When they self-pollinate, the results would be expected to be as follows.

parents' phenotypes	tall	tall
parents' genotypes	Tt	Tt
gametes	T or t	T or t

offspring genotypes

gametes	T	t
T	TT	Tt
t	Tt	tt

offspring phenotypes TT = tall $1/4$
Tt = tall $1/2$
tt = dwarf $1/4$

Approximately three quarters of the offspring would be expected to be tall and one quarter short. This fits in well with the figures of 908 tall, and 293 dwarf, which is a ratio of approximately 3 tall : 1 dwarf.'

Now all that is left to do is to answer the last sentence of the question.

> The dwarf plants all have the genotype tt. All of the gametes they produce will carry a t allele. Therefore all of their offspring will also be tt, that is homozygous dwarf plants.

15.17 Test crosses help to determine genotype.

In the last example, there were two kinds of pea plant, tall and dwarf. Once you have decided that the allele for dwarfness, t, is recessive, then you know that the genotype of any dwarf plants must be tt. But a tall plant could be either Tt or TT.

If you had a tall pea plant, and wanted to know its genotype, how could you find out? The best way would be to cross the plant with a dwarf plant, and then see what kind of offspring you got from the cross. If your original plant was homozygous, TT, then all the offspring would have the genotype Tt, and be tall (see the first cross in Section 15.16).

But if your plant was heterozygous, Tt, then not all the offspring will be tall. Try working it out. You will find that half of the offspring would have the genotype tt, and be dwarf.

By crossing a plant showing the dominant characteristic (in this case tallness) with a homozygous recessive plant (in this case, a dwarf one) you can find out the genotype of the plant with the dominant characteristic. This cross is called a **test cross**.

15.18 'Pure-breeding' means homozygous.

Some populations of animals or plants always have offspring just like themselves. For example, a rabbit breeder might have a strain of rabbits which all have brown coats. If he interbreeds them with one another, all the offspring always have brown coats as well. He has a **pure-breeding** strain of brown rabbits. Pure-breeding strains are always homozygous for the pure-breeding characteristic.

15.19 Sex is determined by X and Y chromosomes.

If you look carefully at Figs 15.2 and 15.3 you will see that the last pair of chromosomes is not the same in each case. In the first photograph, of a woman's chromosomes, the last pair are alike. In the second photograph, which is of a man's chromosomes, the last pair are not alike. One is much smaller than the other.

This last pair of chromosomes is responsible for determining what sex a person will be. They are called the **sex chromosomes**. A woman's chromosomes are

Questions

1. If a normal human cell has 46 chromosomes, how many chromosomes are there in a human sperm cell?
2. Using the symbols W for normal wings, and w for vestigial wings, write down the following.
   (a) the genotype of a fly which is heterozygous for this characteristic
   (b) the possible genotypes of its gametes.
3. Using the layout shown in Section 15.16, work out what kind of offspring would be produced if the heterozygous fly in question 2 mated' with one which was homozygous for normal wings.
4. In humans, the allele for red hair, c, is recessive to the allele for brown hair, C. A man and his wife both have brown hair. They have five children, three of whom have red hair, while two have brown hair. Explain how this may happen.
5. In Dalmatian dogs, the allele for black spots is dominant to the allele for liver spots. If a breeder has a black-spotted dog, how can she find out whether it is homozygous or heterozygous for this characteristic?

both alike and are called X chromosomes. She has the genotype XX.

A man, though, only has one X chromosome. The other, smaller one, is a Y chromosome. He has the genotype XY.

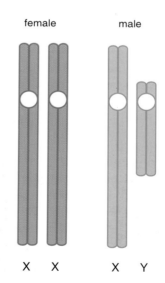

15.10 The sex chromosomes

15.20 Sex is inherited.

You can work out sex inheritance in just the same way as for any other characteristic, but using the letter symbols to describe whole chromosomes, rather than individual alleles.

parents' phenotypes	female	male
parents' genotypes	XX	XY
gametes	(X)	(X) or (Y)

offspring genotypes

	gametes	(X)
	(X)	XX
	(Y)	XY

offspring phenotypes XX = female ¹/₂
XY = male ¹/₂

Half the children will probably be male, and half female.

15.21 Some genes are sex linked.

The X and Y chromosomes do not only determine sex. They have other genes on them as well.

If you look back to Fig 15.4, you will remember that a pair of homologous chromosomes always carry genes for the same characteristic at the same place on the chromosome. This means that you have two genes for every characteristic in your cells.

However, most parts of the X and Y chromosomes do not carry the same genes. So a man has only one of most of the genes which are carried on the X chromosome. A woman, though, has two, just as for any other kind of gene.

We know quite a few of the genes which are carried on the X chromosome. One of them is a gene for blood clotting. The dominant allele of this gene, H, allows your blood to clot normally. But the recessive allele, h, causes **haemophilia**, a disease where even a bruise or small scratch will go on bleeding for a very long time.

There are three possible genotypes that a woman might have for the haemophilia characteristic (Fig 15.11).

genotype	phenotype
X^HX^H	normal
X^HX^h	carrier
X^hX^h	haemophiliac

A **carrier** is someone who has a recessive gene in their cells, but has a normal phenotype. A woman with the genotype X^HX^h seems perfectly normal. Her blood clots in the usual way.

There are only two possible genotypes for a man. This is because the Y chromosome does not have a haemophilia or blood clotting gene of any kind.

genotype	phenotype
X^HY	normal
X^hY	haemophiliac

A gene such as this, which is carried on the non-homologous part of a sex chromosome, is called a **sex-linked gene**. This is because the way it is inherited is linked with a person's sex. You will see how this happens in the next section.

15.22 Women can pass sex-linked genes to their sons.

What would happen if a carrier woman married a normal man and produced children?

parents' phenotypes	normal man	carrier woman
parents' genotypes	X^HY	X^HX^h
gametes	(X^H) or (Y)	(X^H) or (X^h)

offspring genotypes

gametes	(X^H)	(Y)
(X^H)	X^HX^H	X^HY
(X^h)	X^HX^h	X^hY

offspring phenotypes
X^HX^H = normal woman = ¹/₄
X^HY = normal man = ¹/₄
X^HX^h = carrier woman = ¹/₄
X^hY = man with haemophilia = ¹/₄

About half of the male children will probably be haemophiliacs.

Queen Victoria was a carrier for haemophilia. Her husband, Prince Albert, was normal. Fig 15.12 shows Queen Victoria's family tree.

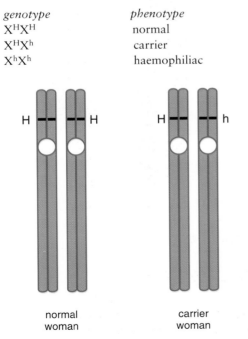
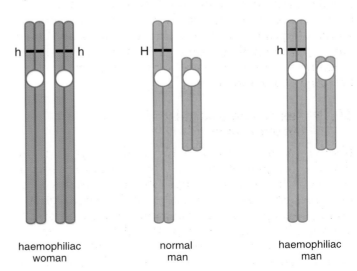

normal woman   carrier woman   haemophiliac woman   normal man   haemophiliac man

15.11 Haemophilia genotypes and phenotypes

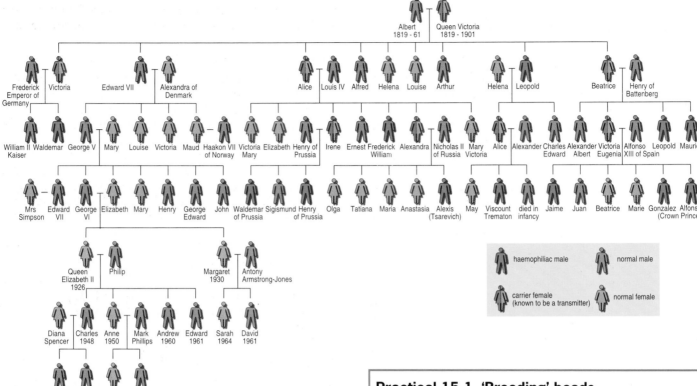

15.12 Queen Victoria's family tree

Questions

1 On which chromosome are most sex-linked genes carried?
2 What is a carrier?
3 The allele for colour-blindness, c, is a recessive allele, carried on the non-homologous part of the X chromosome.
(a) Write down the genotype of a colour-blind man.
(b) A man and his wife both have normal vision. They have three sons, two of whom are colour-blind. Explain how this may happen.

Fact!

If a colour-blind man married a normal woman none of his children would be colour-blind. But if one of his daughters marries a normal man the chances are that half their sons will be colour-blind. Can you explain this?

An isolated group of people living in the Zambesi river valley in Africa have only two toes on each foot. This mutation occurred several generations ago, and there are now dozens of these two-toed people.

Practical 15.1 'Breeding' beads

In this experiment, you will use two containers of beads. Each container represents a parent. The beads represent the gametes they make. The colour of a bead represents the genotype of the gamete. For example, a red bead might represent a gamete with genotype A, for dark hair. A yellow bead might represent a gamete with the genotype a, for fair hair.

1 Put 100 red beads into the first beaker. These represent the gametes of a person who is homozygous for dark hair, AA.
2 Put 50 red beads and 50 yellow beads into the second beaker. These represent the gametes of a heterozygous person with the genotype Aa.
3 Close your eyes, and pick out one bead from the first beaker, and one from the second. Write down the genotype of the 'offspring' they produce. Put the two beads back.
4 Repeat step 3 one hundred times.
5 Now try a different cross, for example Aa crossed with Aa.

Questions

1 In the first cross, what kind of offspring were produced, and in what ratios?
2 Is this what you would have expected? Explain your answer.
3 Why must you close your eyes when choosing the beads?
4 Why must you put the beads back into the beakers after they have 'mated'?

DNA and protein synthesis

15.23 A DNA molecule is a double helix.

Chromosomes are made of protein, and a substance called **DNA**. It is the DNA which carries the instructions for the proteins that the cell is to make.

DNA is short for **deoxyribonucleic acid**. Fig 15.13 shows a short length of DNA. It is made of two strands, twisted together into a spiral or helix. The two strands are linked together through the bases.

There are four kinds of base in DNA. They are adenine (**A**), thymine (**T**), cytosine (**C**) and guanine (**G**). The bases are different sizes and shapes, so that **A** will only fit next to **T**, and **C** will only fit next to **G**.

15.24 Each protein has its own amino acid sequence.

A protein is a long chain of amino acids. There are about twenty different amino acids, and there may be hundreds or thousands of them in one protein. The order in which the different amino acids are linked together determines what kind of protein is made. There are usually plenty of amino acids of each kind, in solution in the cytoplasm. They are linked together,

one by one, to make protein molecules. Proteins are made in the cytoplasm of every cell, on the ribosomes.

15.25 Three bases name an amino acid.

The amino acids are not joined together haphazardly. The order in which they are joined, and so the kind of protein they make, is very carefully organised. The instructions for this are kept in the DNA, in the nucleus.

The sequence of the bases in the DNA is a code for the sequence of amino acids in the proteins to be made. A row of three bases codes for one amino acid. Each amino acid has a different code 'word' of three 'letters'. For example, the sequence CCG on DNA represents the amino acid glycine. CAG means valine. So if a section of a DNA molecule runs CCGCAG, then glycine will be joined to valine when a protein is made.

There is a three-letter 'word' for each amino acid, and also for beginning and ending a protein molecule. A length of DNA which codes for one protein is called a **gene**.

15.26 Messenger RNA copies the genetic code.

Although DNA is found in the nucleus, proteins are made in the cytoplasm. A messenger molecule is used to carry the information from the nucleus to the ribosomes in the cytoplasm.

The messenger is a molecule called messenger RNA, or **mRNA**. It copies the instructions from DNA, and then takes them out to the ribosomes (Fig 15.14).

15.27 Accidental changes in DNA produce mutations.

DNA is a very important material. Almost everything that happens in a living organism is controlled by it. So all of the processes that DNA is involved in – mitosis, meiosis and protein synthesis – are very carefully controlled. The working of the cell is designed to ensure that the instructions carried on the DNA molecules are never damaged.

But occasionally things do go wrong. One time that this can happen is during meiosis. Sometimes, instead of homologous chromosomes separating perfectly, one may go the wrong way. Gametes will then be formed with the wrong number of chromosomes.

This sometimes happens when eggs are being made in a woman's ovaries. The chromosome 21s may fail to separate. Eggs are made with two chromosome 21s instead of one. If such an egg is fertilised by a normal sperm, the child which results will have three chromosome 21s in every cell. It will have **Down's syndrome**.

Another type of change that may occur is in the DNA molecule itself. Normally, the sequence of bases in DNA never changes. It is copied very carefully, and passed on unchanged from parent to offspring. But

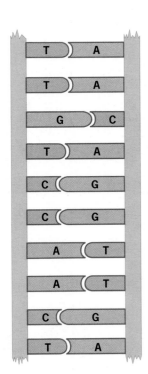

A DNA molecule is made of two strands, linked through the bases.

The two strands twist round each other, forming a double helix.

15.13 Part of a DNA molecule

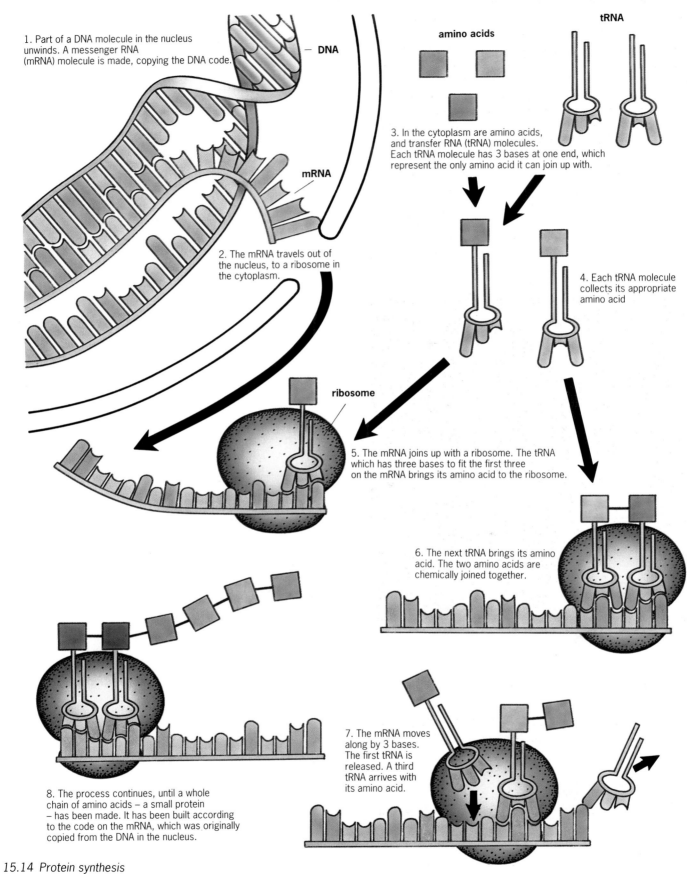

1. Part of a DNA molecule in the nucleus unwinds. A messenger RNA (mRNA) molecule is made, copying the DNA code.

— DNA

mRNA

2. The mRNA travels out of the nucleus, to a ribosome in the cytoplasm.

amino acids

tRNA

3. In the cytoplasm are amino acids, and transfer RNA (tRNA) molecules. Each tRNA molecule has 3 bases at one end, which represent the only amino acid it can join up with.

4. Each tRNA molecule collects its appropriate amino acid

ribosome

5. The mRNA joins up with a ribosome. The tRNA which has three bases to fit the first three on the mRNA brings its amino acid to the ribosome.

6. The next tRNA brings its amino acid. The two amino acids are chemically joined together.

7. The mRNA moves along by 3 bases. The first tRNA is released. A third tRNA arrives with its amino acid.

8. The process continues, until a whole chain of amino acids – a small protein – has been made. It has been built according to the code on the mRNA, which was originally copied from the DNA in the nucleus.

15.14 Protein synthesis

sometimes, one or more bases in the DNA may be altered, or moved out of sequence. This changes the sequence of amino acids in the protein molecule that is made, which may affect the phenotype (Fig 15.15).

Changes like this are called **mutations**. Most mutations are harmful, but just occasionally a mutation may turn out to produce a better characteristic than the original. An example of this is the mutation of the pale form of the peppered moth to a dark form in some parts of Great Britain. This is described in Chapter 16.

15.28 Radiation can increase mutation rate.

Mutations often happen for no apparent reason. However, we do know of many factors which make mutation more likely. One of the most important of these is **radiation**. Radiation can damage the bases in DNA molecules. If this happens in the ovaries or testes, then the altered DNA may be passed on to the offspring.

15.15 A mutation has caused the normal black skin colour to be missing in this African boy

Questions

1   One strand of DNA molecule has bases in the sequence **ACCGATAG**. What will be the sequence on the other strand?
2   Where is DNA found?
3   Where are proteins made?
4   What is a gene?
5   How is the information on DNA transferred to the ribosomes?
6   What is a mutation?

16 Evolution

16.1 Organisms have changed through time.

One of the questions which has always interested people is 'Where did all the different kinds of living organisms come from?' Were they all created at the same time, or have they gradually changed, or evolved, to become what they are now?

Most cultures, all around the world, have some kind of creation story, which describes how the world was made, and all the animals and plants created. Up until the nineteenth century, most people in Europe and America believed that the creation story described in Genesis, the first book of the Bible, was literally true. Some people still believe this today.

Today, the generally accepted idea is that the forms of life that now exist have gradually developed from much simpler ones. We think that life began on Earth about 4000 million years ago. Since then, more complex and varied organisms have developed – and are still developing. This is the process of evolution.

Evidence for evolution – fossils

16.2 Fossils provide evidence for evolution.

A **fossil** is the remains or impression of a living organism which have become preserved in rock. Fig 16.1 illustrates how a fossil can be formed.

It is usually possible to work out the age of the rock, and so we know roughly how long ago the fossil was formed. Some of the oldest fossils that have been found are about 3000 million years old. They are fossils of very simple organisms, rather like bacteria. No other kinds of living things seem to have existed at this time. It is not until 1200 million years ago that simple protoctists like *Amoeba* came into existence.

As we look at fossils from more recently formed, younger, rocks, more complex kinds of organism begin to appear. Fig 16.2 shows the age of the rocks in which the fossils of various kinds of plants and animals have first been found.

One way of explaining this sequence is to suggest that the more recent organisms such as mammals have developed from earlier forms such as reptiles. We can find more convincing evidence for this by looking at a small section of the fossil record in detail (Fig 16.5).

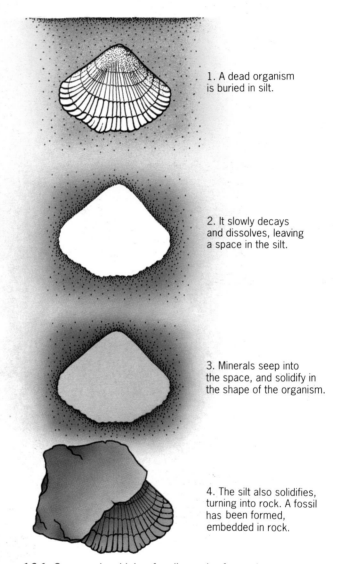

1. A dead organism is buried in silt.

2. It slowly decays and dissolves, leaving a space in the silt.

3. Minerals seep into the space, and solidify in the shape of the organism.

4. The silt also solidifies, turning into rock. A fossil has been formed, embedded in rock.

16.1 One way in which a fossil may be formed

In fact, it is only very rarely that enough fossils have been found for us to be able to 'see' one kind of organism evolving from another. Usually, there are big gaps in the fossil record, and we can only guess how the changes took place. The formation of a fossil is a rare event, and so it is not surprising that not enough fossils have yet been found for us to see exactly what happened to each kind of organism that lived in the past.

millions of years
before the present

50

100

150

200

250

300

350

400

450

500

550

600

650

900

1200

4000

flowering plants

monkeys and apes

birds

mammals

reptiles

conifers

insects

amphibians

fish

land plants

spiders and scorpions

fungi

seaweeds

molluscs

worms

trilobites

jellyfish

sponges

protoctista

bacteria

16.2 The ages of some of the earliest fossils of some types of organism

16.3 *These fossil bones of a 9-metre whale were found lying in a desert in Peru. This must once have been part of the floor of an ocean, where the dead whale became buried in sediment.*

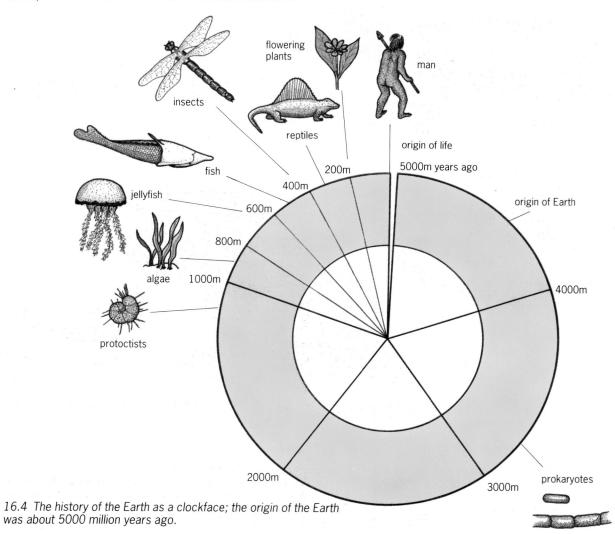

16.4 *The history of the Earth as a clockface; the origin of the Earth was about 5000 million years ago.*

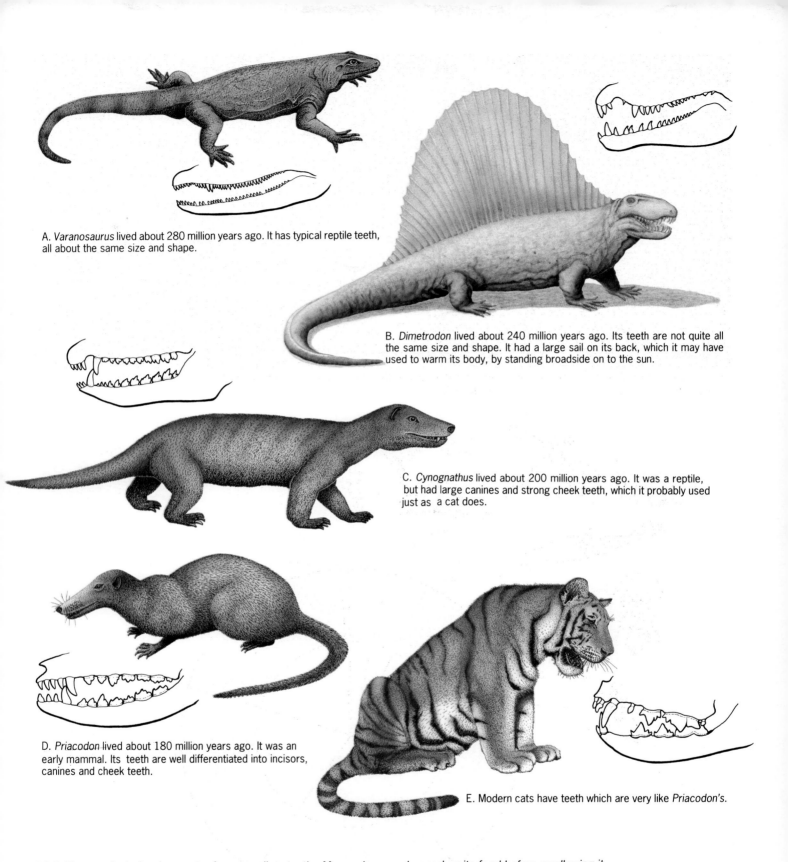

A. *Varanosaurus* lived about 280 million years ago. It has typical reptile teeth, all about the same size and shape.

B. *Dimetrodon* lived about 240 million years ago. Its teeth are not quite all the same size and shape. It had a large sail on its back, which it may have used to warm its body, by standing broadside on to the sun.

C. *Cynognathus* lived about 200 million years ago. It was a reptile, but had large canines and strong cheek teeth, which it probably used just as a cat does.

D. *Priacodon* lived about 180 million years ago. It was an early mammal. Its teeth are well differentiated into incisors, canines and cheek teeth.

E. Modern cats have teeth which are very like *Priacodon's*.

16.5 *The gradual development of mammalian teeth. Mammals evolved from reptiles. Skulls A, B and C are of reptiles belonging to the groups which were the ancestors of mammals. In the first two, the teeth were probably only used for catching and holding their prey, which was swallowed almost whole. Cynognathus, though, probably chopped up its food before swallowing it.*
Skulls D and E are of mammals. Mammals need specialised teeth to help them to digest their food really efficiently. This is because they are homeothermic. They need a lot of food to produce heat energy to keep their bodies warm.

Evidence for evolution – homologous structures

16.3 Vertebrate limb bones show homology.

Although the fossil record strongly suggests that evolution has happened, it does not actually prove it. What other evidence is there to support the theory of evolution?

If we look at the way in which living organisms are made, we can often see quite striking similarities in their construction. Fig 16.6 shows the limb bones of several different kinds of vertebrate. Although their limbs are used for many different purposes, they all seem to be built to the same basic design. Structures like this are called **homologous** structures.

One way to explain the existence of these homologous bones is to suggest that all of these animals have evolved from an ancestral animal which had a 'basic design' limb.

The most likely ancestors for the amphibians, birds, reptiles and mammals are fish. One group of fish seem particularly likely candidates. These are the lobe-finned fishes, which first appear in the fossil record about 350 million years ago. In fact, one species of these fish is still alive today. This is the coelacanth (Fig 16.7), which lives in deep water off Madagascar.

The arrangement of the bones in the pectoral fin of a lobe-finned fish is very similar to the arrangement of the bones in Fig 16.6. It is quite easy to imagine that a fish like this could have been the ancestor of the amphibians, reptiles, birds and mammals.

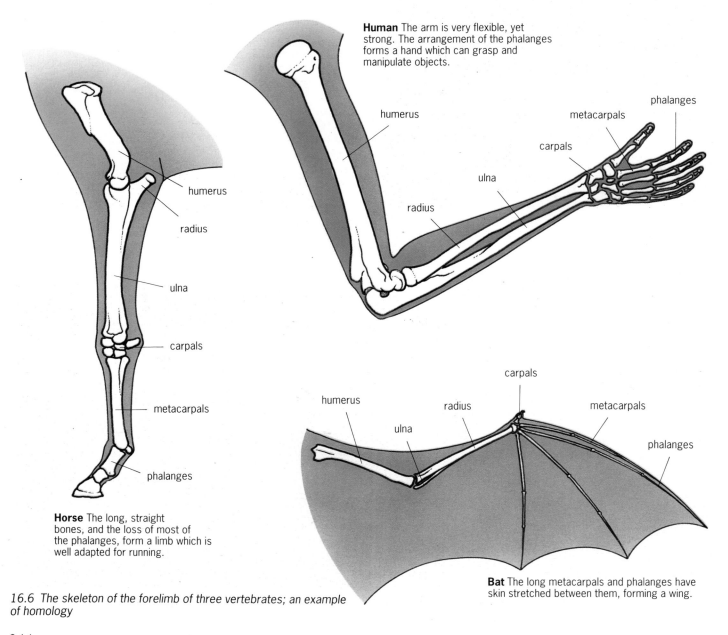

Human The arm is very flexible, yet strong. The arrangement of the phalanges forms a hand which can grasp and manipulate objects.

humerus
radius
ulna
carpals
metacarpals
phalanges

Horse The long, straight bones, and the loss of most of the phalanges, form a limb which is well adapted for running.

humerus
radius
ulna
carpals
metacarpals
phalanges

Bat The long metacarpals and phalanges have skin stretched between them, forming a wing.

humerus
ulna
radius
carpals
metacarpals
phalanges

16.6 The skeleton of the forelimb of three vertebrates; an example of homology

16.4 Vestigial structures have no obvious function.

Another example of the way in which homologous structures provide evidence for evolution is given by animals or plants which possess structures which do not seem to be used for anything. Structures like this are called **vestigial**. One example is the small limb bones of some snakes, such as pythons (Fig 16.8).

Snakes are reptiles. A logical way of explaining the presence of these bones is to suggest that snakes have evolved from other reptiles which used their limbs for walking. The limb bones have gradually become smaller. In most snakes, there is no longer any trace of them.

16.7 Coelacanths, which live deep in the Indian Ocean, have existed almost unchanged for 350 million years. Humans have existed for only about 4 million years.

Questions

1 About how long ago did life probably begin on Earth?
2 In what way do fossils suggest that evolution has happened?
3 How long ago did the first of each of these organisms appear?
   (a) bacteria
   (b) land plants
   (c) land animals
   (d) mammals
   (e) birds
4 What is meant by homologous structures?
5 How are (a) a horse's forelimb, and (b) a bat's forelimb adapted for their way of life?
6 What is meant by vestigial structures?
7 In what way are vestigial structures evidence for evolution?

Fact!

There are about 1 million species of insects (Class Insecta) living in the world today, and about 8000 new species are discovered each year.

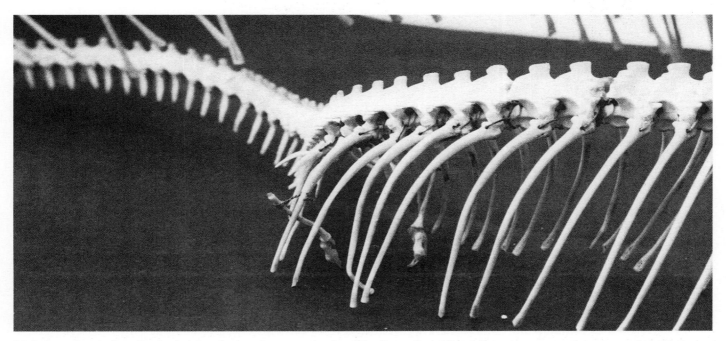

16.8 A small part of a python's skeleton; the long bones are its ribs. Near the centre of the picture, you can see the very small hind limb bones, which are not used at all. They are vestigial structures.

The theory of natural selection

16.5 Natural selection can cause gradual change.

The evidence for evolution has been known for a very long time. Yet until the second half of the nineteenth century, most people believed that all the different species of living organism had been created at the same time, when the world began. Some people still believe this.

One of the reasons why many people were reluctant to accept the idea of evolution was that they could not see why or how it could happen. In the nineteenth century, several ideas were put forward. One, still widely accepted today, was suggested by Charles Darwin. He put forward his theory in a book called *The Origin of Species*, which was published in 1859.

Darwin's theory of how evolution could have happened can be summarised like this.

Variation Most populations of organisms contain individuals which vary slightly from one another. Some slight variations may better adapt some organisms to their environment than others.

Over-production Most organisms produce more young than will survive to adulthood.

16.9 *A portrait of Charles Darwin at the age of 76*

16.10 *When large numbers of organisms, such as these wildebeest of the East African plains, live together, there is competition for food, and a tendency for the weaker ones to be killed by predators. The organisms best adapted to their environment survive.*

246

Struggle for existence Because populations do not generally increase rapidly in size there must therefore be considerable competition for survival between the organisms.

Survival of the fittest Only the organisms which are really well adapted to their environment will survive.

Advantageous characteristics passed on to offspring Only these well adapted organisms will be able to reproduce successfully, and will pass on their advantageous characteristics to their offspring.

Gradual change In this way, over a period of time, the population will lose all the poorly adapted individuals. The population will gradually become better adapted to its environment.

This theory is called the **theory of natural selection,** because it suggests that the best adapted organisms are selected to pass on their characteristics to the next generation.

Darwin proposed his theory before anyone understood how characteristics were inherited. Now that we know something about genetics, his theory can be stated slightly differently. We can say that natural selection results in the genes producing advantageous phenotypes being passed on to the next generation more frequently than the genes which produce less advantageous phenotypes.

Variation

16.6 Variation can be continuous or discontinuous.

Variation is the raw material for natural selection to act on. To understand how natural selection might work, we must try to understand how and why organisms vary.

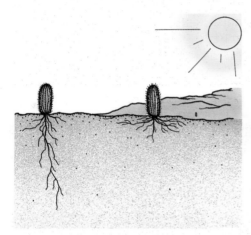

1 Genetic variation In a population of cacti, some have longer roots than others.

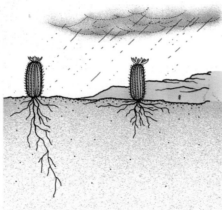

In the wet season they flower.

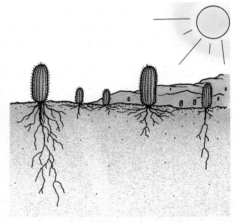

2 Overproduction The cacti produce large numbers of offspring.

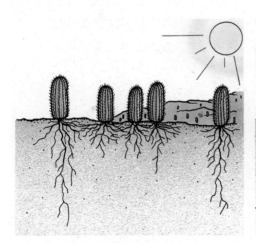

3 Struggle for existence During the dry season, there is competition for water.

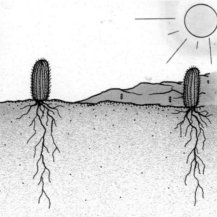

4 Survival of the fittest The cacti with the longest roots are able to obtain water, while the others die from dehydration.

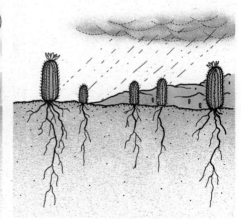

5 Advantageous characteristics passed on to offspring When conditions are suitable, the long-rooted cacti reproduce, producing long-rooted offspring.

16.11 An example of how natural selection might occur

247

You have only to look around a group of people to see that they are different from one another. Some of the more obvious differences are in height or hair colour. We also vary in intelligence, blood groups, whether we can roll our tongues or not, and in many other ways.

There are two basic kinds of variation. One kind is **discontinuous variation**. Tongue rolling is an example of discontinuous variation. Everyone fits into one of two definite categories – they either can or cannot roll their tongue. There is no in between category.

The other kind is **continuous variation**. Height is an example of continuous variation. There are no definite heights that a person must be. People vary in height, between the very lowest and highest extremes.

You can try measuring and recording discontinuous and continuous variation in Practical 16.1. Your results for continuous variation will probably look similar to Fig 16.13. This is called a **normal distribution**. Most people come in the middle of the range, with fewer at the lower or upper ends.

16.7 What causes variation?

By describing variation as continuous or discontinuous, we can begin to explain how organisms vary. But the cause of the variation is another question altogether.

Genetic variation One reason for the differences between individuals is that their **genotypes** are different. Blood groups, for example, are controlled by genes. There are also genes for hair colour, eye colour, height and many other characteristics.

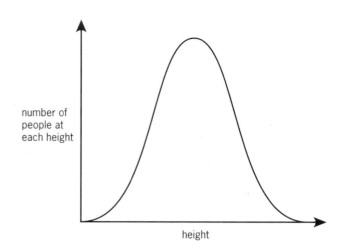

16.13 A normal distribution curve – a graph showing the numbers of people of different heights

Environmental variation Another important reason for variation is the difference between the **environments** of individuals. Scots pine trees possess genes which enable them to grow to a height of about 35 m. But if a Scots pine tree is grown in a very small pot, and has its roots regularly pruned, it will be permanently stunted (Fig 16.14). The tree's genotype gives it the potential to grow tall, but it will not realise this potential unless its roots are given plenty of space and it is allowed to grow freely.

Characteristics caused by an organism's environment are sometimes called acquired characteristics. They are not caused by genes, and so they cannot be handed on to the next generation.

16.12 Human height shows continuous variation. What characteristic here shows discontinuous variation?

Practical 16.1 Measuring variation

1 Make a survey of at least 30 people, to find out whether or not they can roll their tongue. Record your results.
2 Measure the length of the third finger of the left hand of 30 people. Take the measurement from the knuckle to the finger tip, not including the nail.
3 Divide the finger lengths into suitable categories, and record the numbers in each category, like this.

length/cm	number
8.0 – 8.4	2
8.5 – 8.9	4 and so on

4 Draw a histogram of your results.

Questions

1 Which of these characteristics is an example of continuous variation, and which shows discontinuous variation?
2 Your histogram may be a similar shape to the curve in Fig 16.13. This is called a **normal distribution**. The class which has the largest number of individuals in it is called the **modal class**. What is the modal class for the finger lengths of your samples?
3 The **mean** or average finger length is the total of all the finger lengths, divided by the number of people in your sample. What is the mean finger length of your sample?

A bonsai pine tree is dwarfed by being grown in a very small pot, and continually pruned.

A Shetland pony's genes are responsible for its small size.

Variation caused by the environment is not inherited

A cutting from a bonsai pine would grow into a full size tree, if given sufficient space.

16.14 The inheritance of variation

Variation caused by genes is inherited

The offspring of Shetland ponies are small like their parents, no matter how well they are fed and cared for.

16.8 Genetic variation arises in several ways.

Meiosis During sexual reproduction, gametes are formed by meiosis. In meiosis, homologous chromosomes exchange genes, and separate from one another, so the gametes which are formed are not all exactly the same.

Fertilisation Any two gametes of opposite types can fuse together at fertilisation, so there are many possible combinations of genes which may be produced in the zygote. In an organism with a large number of genes the possibility of two offspring having identical genotypes is so small that it can be considered almost impossible.

Mutation Sometimes, a gene may suddenly change. This is called mutation. Most mutations are harmful, but occasionally one may happen which gives the mutant organism an advantage in the struggle for existence. It will then survive to pass its new characteristic on to the next generation. The mutant may even replace the normal form over a period of time.

Questions

1 When was the idea of natural selection first suggested?
2 Using the six points listed in Section 16.5, explain how giraffes may have evolved from a short-necked ancestor by natural selection.
3 Give one example of discontinuous variation.
4 Give one example of continuous variation.
5 What is a normal distribution?
6 Explain the difference between genetic variation and environmental variation, giving examples of each.

Evidence for natural selection

16.9 Melanic moths are selected near cities

Darwin's theory of natural selection provides a good explanation for our observations of the many types of animals and plants. It could explain what we see in the fossil record, and it could explain the presence of homologous structures. But it is almost impossible to prove that these were produced by natural selection. The only way we can really be sure that natural selection works is if we can watch it happening.

The peppered moth, *Biston betularia*, lives in most parts of Britain. It flies by night, and spends the daytime resting on tree trunks. It has speckled wings, which camouflage it very effectively on lichen-covered tree trunks (Fig 16.15).

People have collected moths for many years, so we know that up until 1849 all the moths in collections

16.15a *Lichen-covered bark hides a speckled moth perfectly*

16.15b *Dark moths are better camouflaged on lichen-free trees*

were speckled. Can you see the speckled form in Fig 16.15a? But in 1849, a black or **melanic** form of the moth was caught near Manchester. By 1900, 98% of the moths near Manchester were black.

The distribution of the black and speckled forms in 1958 is shown in Fig 16.17.

How can we explain the sudden rise in numbers of the dark moths, and their distribution?

We know that the black colour of the moth is caused by a single dominant gene. The mutation from a normal to a black gene happens fairly often, so it is reasonable to assume that there have always been a few black moths around, as well as pale speckled ones. Up until the beginning of the Industrial Revolution, the pale moths had the advantage, as they were better camouflaged on lichen-covered tree trunks.

But in the middle of the nineteenth century, some areas became polluted by smoke. As the prevailing

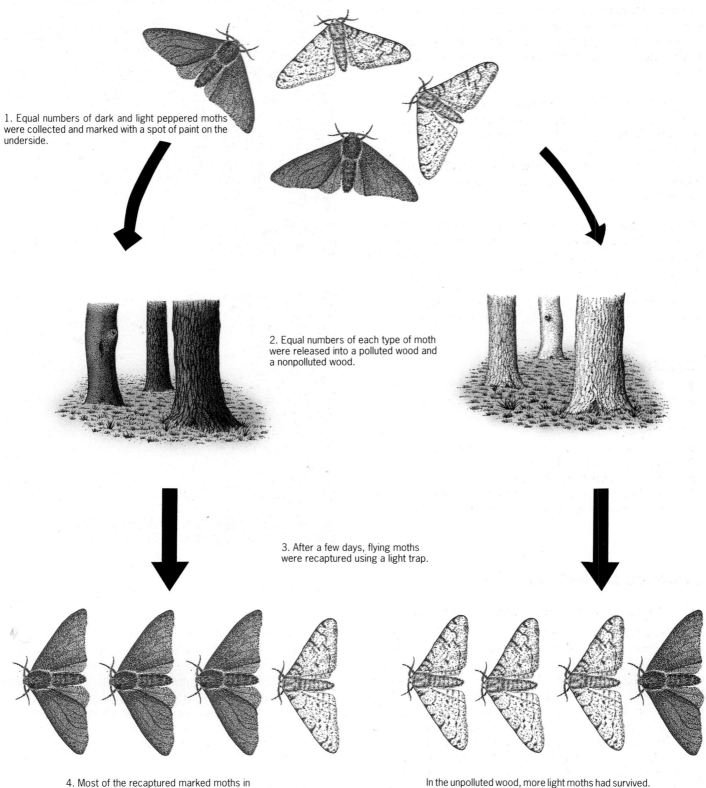

1. Equal numbers of dark and light peppered moths were collected and marked with a spot of paint on the underside.

2. Equal numbers of each type of moth were released into a polluted wood and a nonpolluted wood.

3. After a few days, flying moths were recaptured using a light trap.

4. Most of the recaptured marked moths in the polluted wood were dark, suggesting that the light ones had been eaten by birds.

In the unpolluted wood, more light moths had survived.

16.16 An experiment to measure the survival of dark and light peppered moths in polluted and unpolluted environments

The proportion of dark/light areas in each circle shows the proportion of dark/light moths in that part of the country.

Manchester

Birmingham

London

prevailing winds

16.17 The distribution of the pale and dark forms of the peppered moth, Biston betularia, in 1958. Since then, the number of dark moths has been decreasing, because there is now less air pollution.

winds in Britain blow from the west, the worst affected areas are to the east of industrial cities like Manchester and Birmingham. The polluted air prevents lichens from growing. Dark moths are better camouflaged than pale moths on trees with no lichens on them.

Proof that the dark moths do have an advantage in polluted areas has been supplied by several experiments. Fig 16.16 summarises one of them.

The factor which confers an advantage on the dark moths, and a disadvantage on the light moths in polluted areas, is predation by birds. This is called a **selection pressure**, because it 'selects' the dark moths for survival. In unpolluted areas, the pale moths are more likely to survive.

16.10 Antibiotic resistance in bacteria is selected.

Another example of natural selection can be seen in the way that bacteria may become resistant to antibiotics, such as penicillin. Penicillin works by stopping bacteria from forming cell walls. When a person infected with bacteria is treated with penicillin, the bacteria are unable to grow new cell walls, and they burst open.

However, the population of bacteria in the person's body may be several million. The chances of any one

of them mutating to a form which is not affected by penicillin is quite low, but because there are so many bacteria, it could well happen. If it does, the mutant bacterium will have a tremendous advantage. It will be able to go on reproducing while all the others cannot. Soon, its descendants may form a huge population of penicillin-resistant bacteria.

This does, in fact, happen quite frequently. This is one reason why there are so many different antibiotics available – if some bacteria become resistant to one, they may be treated with another.

The more we use an antibiotic, the more we are exerting a selection pressure which favours the resistant forms. If antibiotics are used too often, we may end up with resistant strains of bacteria which are very difficult to control.

16.11 People heterozygous for sickle cell anaemia are selected for.

Sickle cell anaemia is an inherited disease. You can read more about it in Chapter 18. It is caused by a recessive allele, h. People with the genotye HH or Hh are normal, while people with the genotype hh have sickle cell anaemia. It is an unpleasant disease, and many people with it die before they can have children.

For some time, people were puzzled why sickle cell anaemia is common in some parts of the world. In some parts of Africa, for example, as many as 14 % of the babies born have sickle cell anaemia. Why has natural selection not eliminated the h allele from the population?

If you look at the maps in Fig 16.18, you can see that the places where sickle cell anaemia is found match quite closely with the distribution of another disease – malaria. Malaria is another potentially fatal disease, which you can read more about in Chapter 18.

It was found that people with the genotype Hh were far less likely to suffer and die from malaria than people with the genotype HH. So there are different selection pressures acting on people with the three different genotypes. People with the genotype HH are at risk of dying from malaria if they live in certain parts of the world. People with the genotype hh are at risk of dying from sickle cell anaemia. People with the genotype Hh have a strong selective advantage in areas where malaria is present, because they are more likely to live and reproduce than people with the other two genotypes.

Therefore, in each generation, the people most likely to reproduce are heterozygous people. Some of their children will also be heterozygous, but some will be homozygous dominant, and some homozygous recessive. This will continue generation after generation – until someone finds a really good cure or prevention for malaria, or a really successful treatment for sickle cell anaemia.

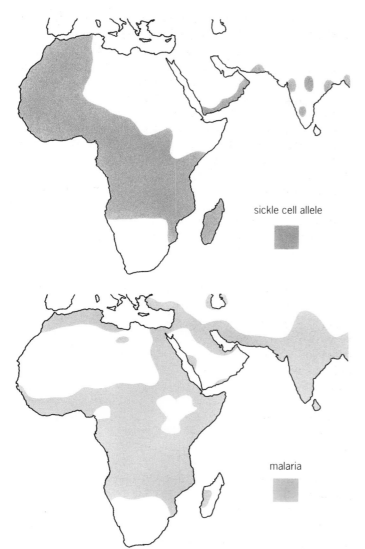

(a) Crab apple

(b) James Grieve apple

16.19 Wild and cultivated apples

16.18 The distribution of (a) the sickle cell allele and (b) malaria

16.20(a) Longhorn cattle are a very old breed. They are thought to be quite similar to the original, wild cattle.

(b) Limousin cattle have been bred to have heavy, muscular bodies, to give a high yield of beef. What other differences between the Longhorn and the Limousin do you think might have been produced by artificial selection?

16.12 Artificial selection.

Humans can also bring about changes in living organisms, by selecting certain varieties for breeding. Figs 16.19 and 16.20 show examples of the results of this kind of selection. From the varied individuals amongst a herd of cattle, the breeder chooses the ones with the characteristics he wants to appear in the next generation. He then allows these individuals, and not the others, to breed. Over many generations, these characteristics will become the commonest ones in the population.

This process is called **artificial selection**. It has been going on for thousands of years, ever since humans first began to cultivate plants and to domesticate animals. It works in just the same way as natural selection. Individuals with 'advantageous' characteristics breed, while those with 'disadvantageous' ones do not.

However, what humans think are desirable characteristics would often not be at all advantageous to the plant or animal if it was living in the wild. Modern varieties of cattle, for example, selected over hundreds of years for high milk yield or fast meat production, would stand little chance of surviving for long in the wild.

Some farmers are now beginning to think differently about the characteristics they want in their animals and plants. Instead of enormous yields as their first priority, they are now looking for varieties which can grow well with less fertiliser or pesticide in the case of food plants, and with less expensive housing and feeding in the case of animals. Luckily, many of the older breeds which had these characteristics have been conserved, and can now be used to breed new varieties with 'easy-care' characteristics.

Practical 16.2 The results of artificial selection

For this investigation, you will need a fruit of a wild crab apple, and of a cultivated apple.
1 Make large, labelled drawings of each apple. Draw each apple to the same scale. Fig 16.19 may help you, but don't copy it – draw your own apples.
2 Make a list of important differences between the crab apple and the cultivated apple.
3 Which of the features of the cultivated apple do you think have been selected for by humans?

16.13 Natural selection does not always cause change.

Natural selection does not always produce change. Natural selection ensures that the organisms which are best adapted to their environment will survive. Change will only occur if the environment changes, or if a new mutation appears which adapts the organism better to the existing environment.

For example, in the south-west of Britain the environment of the peppered moth has never changed very much. The air has not become polluted, so lichens have continued to grow on trees. The best camouflaged moths have always been the pale ones. So selection has always favoured the pale moths in this part of Britain. Any mutant dark moths which do appear are at a disadvantage, and are unlikely to survive.

Most of the time, natural selection tends to keep populations very much the same from generation to generation. It is sometimes called **stabilising selection**. If an organism is well adapted to its environment, and if that environment stays the same, then the organism will not evolve. Coelacanths, for example, have remained virtually unchanged for 350 million years. They live deep in the Indian Ocean which is a very stable environment.

Questions

1 Using the six points listed in Section 16.5, explain why the proportion of dark peppered moths near Manchester increased at the end of the nineteenth century.
2 Why is it unwise to use antibiotics unnecessarily?
3 Imagine you are a farmer with a herd of dairy cattle. You want to build up a herd with a very high production of milk. You have access to sperm samples from bulls, for each of which there are records of the milk production of his offspring. What will you do?
4 Wheat is attacked by many different pests, including a fungus called yellow rust.
   (a) Describe how you could use artificial selection to produce a new variety of wheat which is naturally resistant to yellow rust.
   (b) How could the growing of resistant varieties reduce pollution?
   (c) When resistant varieties of wheat are produced, it is found that after a few years they are infected by yellow rust again. Explain how this might happen.

Chapter revision questions

1 Match each term with its definition.
   evolution   homologous structures
   natural selection   species
   (a) parts of different kinds of organisms, which seem to have a similar basic design
   (b) a group of organisms which are very similar to one another, and can breed with each other
   (c) gradual changes in the types of living things over a long period of time
   (d) a process which selects only the fittest organisms to survive and reproduce.
2 Make a short summary of the evidence that suggests that
   (a) evolution has happened in the past,
   (b) evolution is happening now,
   (c) evolution happens by means of natural selection.
3 Natural selection causes living organisms to become well adapted to their environment. The best adapted organisms are the most successful. Explain each of the following.
   (a) A population of organisms which can reproduce sexually can often become adapted to a new environment faster than a population of organisms which can only reproduce asexually.
   (b) Evolution does not come to a halt once organisms have become well adapted to their environment.

17 The diversity of life

17.1 Classification.

Classification means putting things into groups. Biologists classify living organisms according to how closely they think they are related to one another.

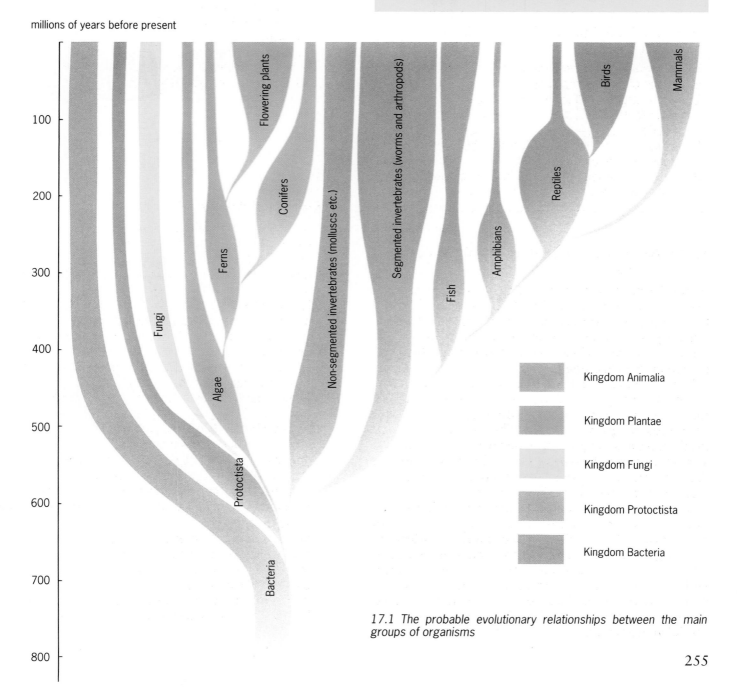

millions of years before present

17.1 The probable evolutionary relationships between the main groups of organisms

255

pony

wolf

jackal

dog

zebra

The animals can be sorted like this:-

Dog-like animals

Genus *Canis*

familiaris

lupus

mesomeles

Horse-like animals

caballus

burchelli

Genus *Equus*

Each large group is a genus.   Each small group is a species

To name an animal, you write the name of its genus and the name of its species. A wolf, for example, is called *Canis lupus*.

17.2 Sorting and naming living things

17.2 Homologies help to classify organisms.

The first person to try to classify living things in a scientific way was a Swedish naturalist called **Linnaeus**. He introduced his system of classification in 1735.

Linnaeus grouped living organisms according to how similar they are. He looked for **homologies** (Section 16.3). He lived a century before Darwin, so he did not realise that the different groups of living organisms he studied were actually related to one another. Today, we know that homologies are a result of evolution. The more homologies different kinds of living things share, the more closely they are related to one another.

17.3 The species is the basic group in classification.

Linnaeus divided all the different kinds of living things into groups called **species**. He recognised 12 000 species.

Linnaeus' species were groups of organisms which had a lot of features in common. Today we look even more closely at a group of organisms to decide whether or not it is a species. Organisms belonging to the same species can breed with each other, but not with members of other species.

17.4 The classification system.

Species are grouped into **genera** (singular **genus**). Each genus contains several species with similar characteristics (Fig 17.2).

Several genera are then grouped into a **family**, families into **orders**, orders into **classes**, classes into **phyla** and finally phyla into **kingdoms**. Some of the more important ones are described in this chapter.

17.5 Each species has two Latin names.

Linnaeus gave every kind of living organism two names. The first name is the name of the genus it belongs to, and always has a capital letter. The second name is the name of its species, and always has a small letter.

For example, a wolf belongs to the genus *Canis* and the species *lupus*. Its Latin name is *Canis lupus*. These names are printed in italics. When you write one, you cannot really write in italics, so you should underline any Latin names.

When Linnaeus was alive, Latin was a language that every scientist used and understood. He therefore chose Latin names, not Swedish ones, because everyone who was interested would understand them. We still use Latin names today. Although Latin is no longer used as a language, it is very useful if all scientists use exactly the same name for a particular kind of living organism. Any language would do, but as Linnaeus began with Latin, we continue to use it today. Many of the scientific names for animals and plants that are used today are the same ones that Linnaeus gave them over 250 years ago.

Kingdom Bacteria

These are the bacteria and blue-green algae. The oldest fossils belong to this kingdom, so we think that they were the first kind of organisms to evolve.

Characteristics
unicellular (single-celled) organisms,
have no nucleus,
have a cell wall.

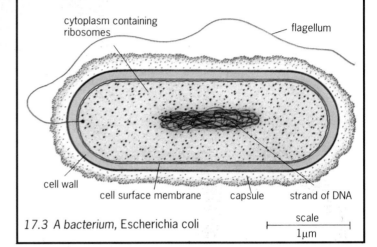

17.3 A bacterium, Escherichia coli

scale
1μm

Kingdom Protoctista

These are simple organisms. Unlike bacteria, they have a nucleus. Some are unicellular. Others, such as seaweeds, are made of many cells.

Almost all the protoctists live in water, because they have no protection against drying out. Some, like *Chlorella*, are plant-like, and feed by photosynthesis. Others, like *Amoeba*, are animal-like, feeding on other living things (see Figs 17.4, 17.5, 17.6 and 17.7).

Characteristics
simple organisms,
cells have nuclei.

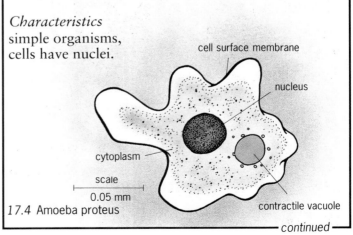

scale
0.05 mm

17.4 Amoeba proteus

— continued —

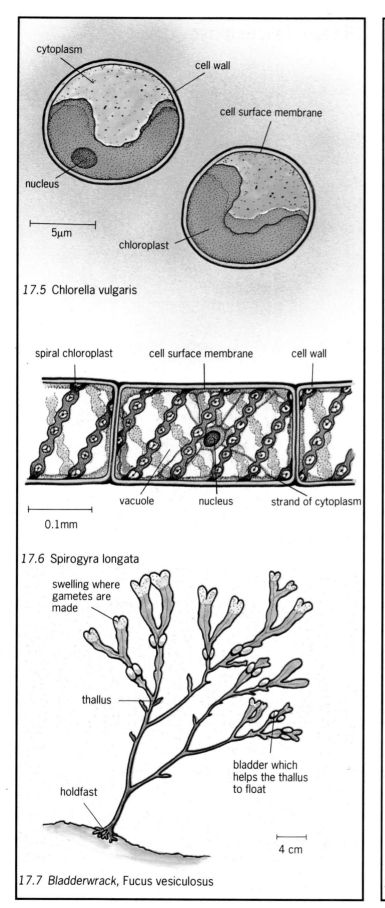

cytoplasm

cell wall

cell surface membrane

nucleus

chloroplast

5μm

17.5 Chlorella vulgaris

spiral chloroplast   cell surface membrane   cell wall

vacuole   nucleus   strand of cytoplasm

0.1mm

17.6 Spirogyra longata

swelling where
gametes are
made

thallus

holdfast

bladder which
helps the thallus
to float

4 cm

17.7 Bladderwrack, Fucus vesiculosus

Kingdom Fungi

Fungi do not have chlorophyll, and do not photosynthesise. Instead, they feed saprophytically, or parasitically, on organic material like faeces, bread and dead
plants and animals.

Characteristics
multicellular (many-celled),
cells have nuclei,
have cell walls,
do not have chlorophyll,
feed saprophytically or parasitically.

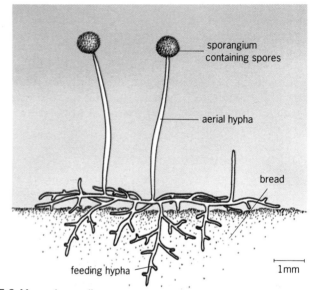

sporangium
containing spores

aerial hypha

bread

feeding hypha

1mm

17.8 Mucor haemalis

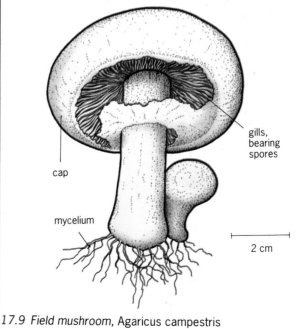

gills,
bearing
spores

cap

mycelium

2 cm

17.9 Field mushroom, Agaricus campestris

258

Kingdom Plantae

Almost all plants are green, because they contain chlorophyll which they use for photosynthesis.

Characteristics
multicellular,   have chlorophyll,
cells have nuclei,   feed by photosynthesis.
have cell walls,

Phylum Bryophyta

These are the mosses and liverworts. Although they live on land, they can only grow successfully in wet places. One reason for this is that they have no xylem to carry water. Another reason is that the male gametes have to swim in water to fertilise the female gametes.

Characteristics
simple stems and leaves,
single-celled rhizoids (rootlets),
no xylem or phloem,
reproduce by means of spores.

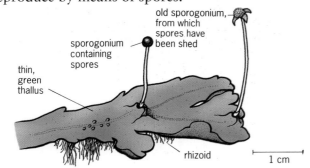

17.10 Liverwort, Pellia epiphylla

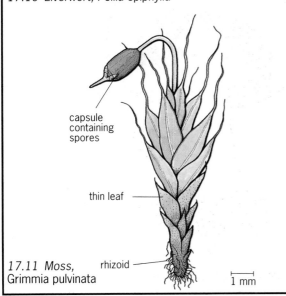

17.11 Moss,
Grimmia pulvinata

Phylum Filicinophyta

These are the ferns. Like bryophytes, they need water for fertilisation. However, they do have xylem and phloem, so they can live in slightly drier places than the bryophytes.

Characteristics
have roots, stems and leaves,
have xylem and phloem,
reproduce by means of spores, which grow on the backs of the leaves,
young leaves coiled in bud.

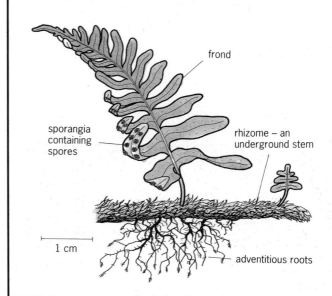

17.12 Common polypody, Polypodium vulgare

17.13 Bracken is a very common fern, covering large areas of land in some parts of Britain

259

Phylum Coniferophyta

These are the conifers. Their male gametes are contained inside pollen grains, which can be carried to the female gametes by the wind. This means that they do not need water for the male gamete to swim in, so they are able to live even in very dry places like deserts. These plants all have cones, in which seeds develop.

Characteristics
have roots, stems and leaves,
have xylem and phloem,
reproduce by seeds,
have cones.

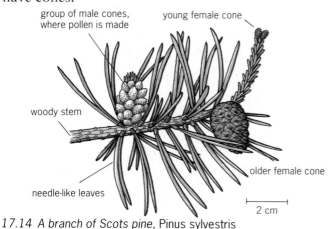

17.14 A branch of Scots pine, Pinus sylvestris

17.15 A group of Scots pine trees

Phylum Angiospermophyta

These are the flowering plants. The seeds grow inside a fruit which developed from an ovary, inside a flower.

Characteristics
have roots, stems and leaves,
have xylem and phloem,
seeds produced inside ovary, inside flower.

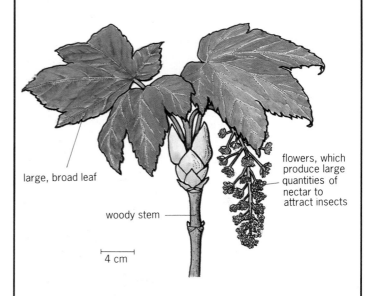

17.16 Twig of sycamore, Acer pseudoplatanus

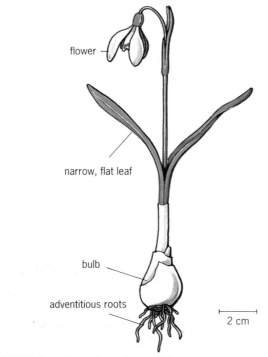

17.17 Snowdrop, Galanthus nivalis

260

Kingdom Animalia

Animals do not photosynthesise, so they never have chlorophyll. They eat other living organisms, so they are usually able to move, to find their food. They do not have cell walls as this would make it difficult for them to move easily.

Characteristics
multicellular,
do not have cell walls,
do not have chlorophyll,
feed heterotrophically.

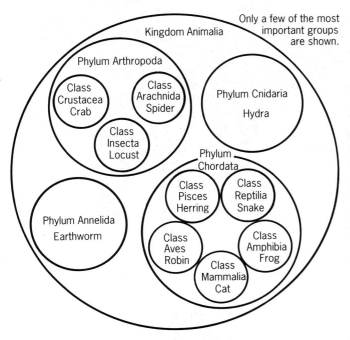

17.18 Classification of the Animal Kingdom

Phylum Annelida

These are worms, with bodies made up of ring-like segments. Most of them live in water, though some, like the earthworm, live in moist soil.

Characteristics
animals with bodies made up of ring-like segments,
no legs,
have chaetae (bristles).

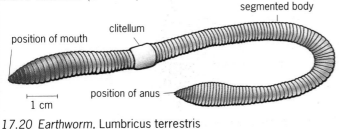

17.20 Earthworm, Lumbricus terrestris

Phylum Cnidaria

These are the jellyfish and sea anemones. They all live in water, because their soft bodies would dry out very quickly on land. They have a ring of tentacles surrounding a mouth. The mouth is the only opening in their digestive system – they have no anus.

Characteristics
animals made of only two layers of cells,
have a ring of tentacles, with a mouth in the centre,
only one opening to gut.

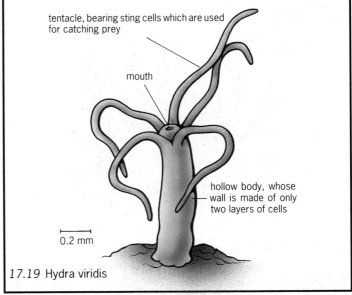

17.19 Hydra viridis

Phylum Mollusca

These are soft-bodied animals, sometimes with a shell, like snails, or sometimes without, like slugs. Octopuses are also molluscs.

Characteristics
animals with soft, unsegmented bodies,
may have a shell.

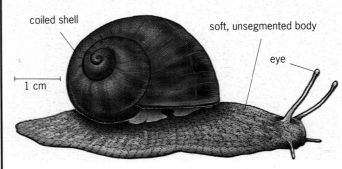

17.21 Garden snail, Helix aspersa

Phylum Arthropoda

Arthropods are animals with jointed legs, but no backbone. They are a very successful group, because they have a waterproof exoskeleton which has allowed them to live on dry land. There are more kinds of arthropod in the world than all the other kinds of animals put together.

Characteristics
animals with several pairs of jointed legs,
have an exoskeleton.

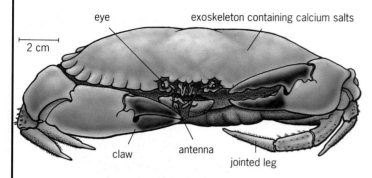

17.22 *Edible crab*, Cancer pagurus

Class Crustacea

These are the crabs, lobsters and woodlice. They breathe through gills, so most of them live in wet places.

Characteristics
arthropods with more than four pairs of jointed legs,
breathe through gills,
two pairs of antennae.

17.23 *A spiny lobster*, Palinurus vulgaris

Class Arachnida

These are the spiders, ticks and scorpions.

Characteristics
arthropods with four pairs of jointed legs,
breathe through gills called book lungs.

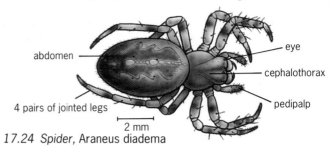

17.24 *Spider*, Araneus diadema

Class Insecta

Insects are a very successful group of animals. This is mostly because their exoskeleton and tracheae are very good at stopping water from evaporating from the insects' bodies, so they can live even in very dry places.

Characteristics
arthropods with three pairs of jointed legs,
two pairs of wings (one or both may be vestigial),
breathe through tracheae,
three body regions.

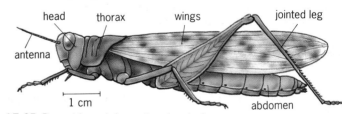

17.25 *Desert locust*, Locusta migratoria

Class Chilopoda

These are the centipedes. Centipedes are fast-moving carnivores.

Characteristics
arthropods with a pair of appendages
on each segment.

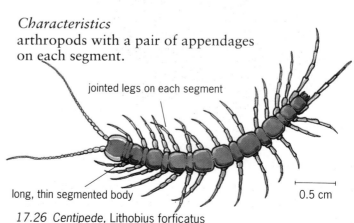

17.26 *Centipede*, Lithobius forficatus

Phylum Chordata

These are animals with a supporting rod running along the length of the body. The most familiar ones have a backbone, and are called vertebrates.

Class Pisces

The fish all live in water, except for one or two like the mud skipper, which can spend short periods of time breathing air.

Characteristics
vertebrates with scaly skin,
have gills,
have fins.

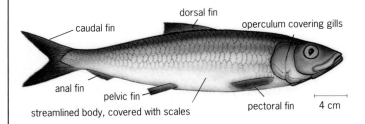

17.27 *Herring*, Clupea harengus

Class Amphibia

Although most adult amphibians live on land, they always go back to the water to breed.

Characteristics
vertebrates with moist, scale-less skin,
eggs laid in water,
larva (tadpole) lives in water, but adult often lives on land,
larva has gills, adult has lungs.

17.28 *Frog*, Rana temporaria

Class Reptilia

Reptiles do not need to go back to the water to breed, because their eggs have a waterproof shell which stops them from drying out.

Characteristics
vertebrates with scaly skin,
lay eggs with shells.

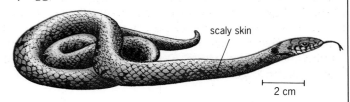

17.29 *Grass snake*, Natrix natrix

Class Aves

The birds, like reptiles, lay eggs with waterproof shells.

Characteristics
vertebrates with feathers,
forelimbs have become wings,
lay eggs with hard shells,
homeothermic,
have a beak.

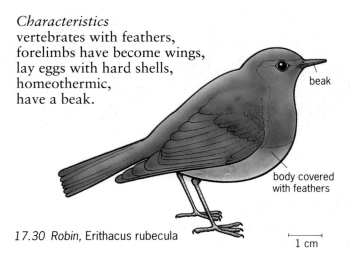

17.30 *Robin*, Erithacus rubecula

Class Mammalia

This is the group to which humans belong.

Characteristics
vertebrates with hair,
have a placenta,
young fed on milk from mammary glands,
homeothermic,
have a diaphragm,
heart has four chambers,
have different types of teeth (incisors, canines, premolars and molars),
cerebral hemispheres very well developed.

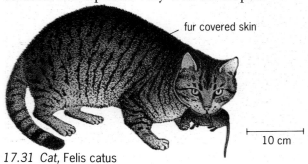

17.31 *Cat*, Felis catus

Chapter revision questions

1 Put these words into the correct order, beginning with the largest group and ending with the smallest:
   species   phylum   genus   kingdom
   order   class   family

2 What is the Latin name for a horse? (Fig 17.2).

3 List three similarities and two differences between annelids and cnidarians.

4 List five differences between birds and mammals.

18 Health, disease and medicine

18.1 There are many causes of disease.

People often think of a disease as being something caused by bacteria or viruses, like flu (influenza) or AIDS. While many diseases *are* caused by microorganisms, there are many other causes of disease. The most important ones are:

1 Inherited diseases, caused by **genes**. These include cystic fibrosis, sickle cell anaemia, Huntington's chorea and some kinds of diabetes.
2 Infectious diseases caused by other living organisms, which are called **pathogens**. These include influenza, AIDS, malaria, cholera, poliomyelitis and many others.
3 Autoimmune diseases, in which a person's own **immune system** begins to attack their own cells. These include some kinds of diabetes, some kinds of arthritis, and muscular dystrophy.
4 Self-inflicted diseases, where a person damages their health by a poor **life-style**. These include alcoholism and most cases of lung cancer.
5 Deficiency diseases, caused by a lack of a particular nutrient in a **diet**. These include scurvy and anaemia, caused by a lack of vitamin C and iron respectively.
6 Degenerative diseases, caused by natural **ageing** processes. These include most heart disease, and some kinds of arthritis.

With so many kinds of disease, you might wonder how anyone ever manages to stay well! However, many of these diseases are avoidable or treatable – or both. In this chapter, we will look briefly at three genetic diseases, and then concentrate on diseases caused by pathogens. We will also consider how your life-style affects your chances of suffering from serious diseases.

Genetic diseases

18.2 Huntington's chorea is caused by a dominant allele.

Huntington's chorea is quite a rare disease, suffered by only about 5 people in every 100 000 in Britain. People with Huntington's chorea are quite normal until they reach the age of about 40 or 50, when their symptoms first begin to show. The disease affects the nervous system. Symptoms include uncontrollable muscle movements, and gradual mental deterioration.

Question

1 Huntington's chorea is caused by a dominant allele (Section 15.8). If a person with the disease, and a normal person, have a child, what is the chance that this child will inherit the disease?
2 Many people with a genetic disease choose not to have children. However, many people with Huntington's chorea *do* have children. Why do you think this is?

18.3 Sickle cell anaemia and cystic fibrosis are caused by recessive alleles.

Sickle cell anaemia is caused by an allele of the gene which codes for the production of haemoglobin. The sickle cell allele is recessive, so only people who are homozygous for this allele have the disease.

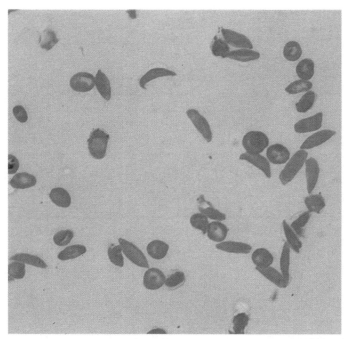

18.1 *This sample of blood contains some normal, round red blood cells, and some which have 'sickled'. You can imagine how easily the sickle-shaped ones could get stuck in a narrow capillary.*

The sickle cell allele causes the production of abnormal haemoglobin, which does not carry oxygen very well. When the concentration of oxygen in the blood becomes low – for example, if the person is doing exercise – the sickle cell haemoglobin forms a precipitate inside the red blood cells. It pulls the red cells into a curved, sickle shape instead of their normal round shape (Fig 18.1). The cells get stuck in capillaries, which is very painful and stops blood flowing through them. Cells get starved of oxygen, which is why the disease is called 'anaemia'.

If you look back at page 253, you will see that sickle cell anaemia is most common in parts of Africa where malaria is present. Sickle cell anaemia is now also found in other parts of the world, such as Britain and the USA, because people whose ancestors came from malarial regions now live there.

Cystic fibrosis is another disease caused by a recessive allele. It is the commonest inherited disease in Britain; about 1 in 1600 babies are born with cystic fibrosis. The allele causes an incorrect version of a protein in cell surface membranes to be made. The effects of this are described in Section 15.5.

Question

1 If two people with sickle cell anaemia have children, what is the chance of their first child having sickle cell anaemia?

Infectious diseases

18.4 A pathogen is an organism which causes disease.

Many diseases are caused by other living organisms, which get into our bodies and breed there. These organisms are called **pathogens**. Pathogens may damage our cells directly, by living in them and feeding on them. They may produce waste products called **toxins**, which spread around the body in the blood and cause symptoms such as high temperature and rashes. Some

Table 18.1

Group to which pathogen belongs	Examples of diseases which they cause
Viruses	Influenza, common cold, poliomyelitis, AIDS
Bacteria	Cholera, syphilis, whooping cough, tuberculosis, tetanus
Protoctists	Malaria, amoebic dysentery
Fungi	Athlete's foot, ringworm

toxins – such as the one caused by the bacterium *Clostridium botulinum* – are amongst the most dangerous poisons in the world.

Pathogens may belong to one of four different groups of organisms – viruses, bacteria, protoctists and fungi. Table 18.1 shows some diseases caused by organisms from each of these groups.

18.5 Pathogens get into the body in different ways.

There are several ways in which pathogens can get into your body.

Through the skin The skin usually makes a very good protective barrier around your body, stopping most pathogens from gaining entry. However, there are a few bacteria and viruses which can get through undamaged skin. One of these is the virus which causes warts. The bacterium *Staphylococcus* can get in through a cut, turning it septic.

Through the respiratory passages Cold and influenza viruses are carried in the air in tiny droplets of moisture. Every time someone with these illnesses speaks, coughs or sneezes, millions of viruses are propelled into the air. If you breathe in the droplets, you may become infected.

In food or water Bacteria such as *Salmonella* can enter your alimentary canal with food you eat. If you eat a large amount of them, you will get food poisoning. Many pathogens, including the virus which causes polio and the bacterium which causes cholera, are transmitted in water. If you drink untreated water, you run the risk of catching these diseases.

By vectors In Biology, a vector is an organism which carries a pathogen from one host to another. One example of a vector is the mosquito which transmits malaria. The mosquito injects the malarial pathogen (which is a protoctist) into a person's blood when it bites.

18.6 Influenza is caused by a virus.

Influenza is a very infectious disease – this means that it can easily be passed from one person to another. The virus which causes it is usually breathed in in tiny droplets of moisture.

Viruses are very strange organisms. Indeed, some people think they should not be classified as living things at all! They are not made of cells, but just some protein molecules around some DNA or RNA (Fig 18.2). They cannot do any of the things which living things are supposed to be able to do, such as respire or grow. They cannot do anything at all until they get inside another living cell – when they begin to reproduce.

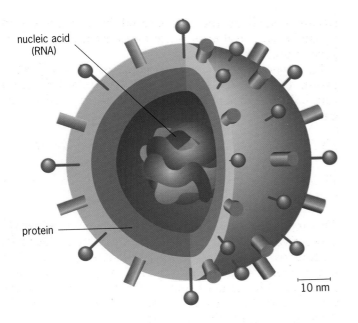

nucleic acid
(RNA)

protein

10 nm

18.2 A flu virus

Flu viruses get into the cells lining your respiratory passages. They take over your cells, and instruct them to make more flu viruses. So many new viruses are made that the cell is destroyed. The new flu viruses burst out of the cell, ready to infect more of your cells, or to be breathed out in droplets of moisture, ready to infect someone else's cells.

Not surprisingly, you feel rather ill while this is happening. For the first three days after **infection** – the time when you first breathed the viruses in – nothing very much happens. This is called the **incubation period**. Then your temperature starts to go up, and you will probably get aching muscles, a headache, a sore throat and perhaps a cough.

If you are relatively fit and healthy, your immune system will quite quickly destroy all the infected cells and the viruses, so that you will recover within about one or two weeks. The way the immune system does this is described on page 274. However, if someone has a weak immune system, then other pathogens may take advantage of the viral infection to get a toehold in the respiratory system. They can cause **secondary infections**, producing bronchitis and pneumonia. These can be fatal. Major outbreaks of influenza often cause death in some old people.

18.7 Cholera is caused by a bacterium.

Cholera is a disease which is most commonly found in places where clean drinking water is not available. It is caused by a bacterium called *Vibrio cholerae* (Fig 18.4). This bacterium is passed out of the body of an

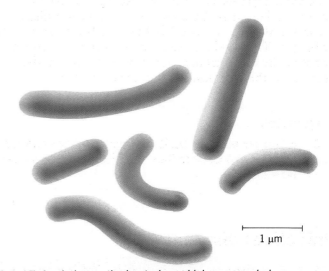

1 μm

18.4 Vibrio cholerae, *the bacterium which causes cholera*

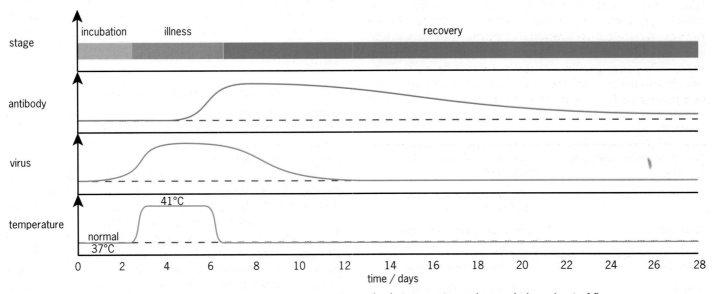

18.3 *How the numbers of viruses and antibodies in your body, and your body temperature, change during a bout of flu*

infected person in their faeces. If these faeces contaminate water which is used for drinking, or for washing food, then the bacterium can get into another person's body and cause cholera.

As with influenza, there is an incubation period of a few days before a person infected with cholera has any symptoms. But once the symptoms *do* begin, they rapidly become very severe. The bacteria produce a toxin, which affects the digestive system, and causes severe diarrhoea. So much water may be lost in this way that the patient often dies of dehydration within a day, unless **oral rehydration therapy** is given. This consists of lots of drinks of water in which glucose and salts have been mixed. This works better than just water on its own, because the glucose and salts speed up the rate at which the water is absorbed into the blood from the intestine.

Cholera is a very, very rare disease in Britain, but it can occur in developing countries, or anywhere where water supplies become contaminated. Sometimes major outbreaks occur, which spread quickly. These are called **epidemics**. There was a cholera epidemic in Peru in 1993.

18.8 Amoebic dysentery is caused by a protoctist.

Amoebic dysentery is a disease in which a protoctist called *Entamoeba histolytica* (Figs 18.6 and 18.7) lives and breeds in the large intestine, especially the colon. A person with this disease may have pain in their abdomen, and produce faeces containing blood. This is because the protoctist damages the lining of the colon. However, many people have *E. histolytica* in

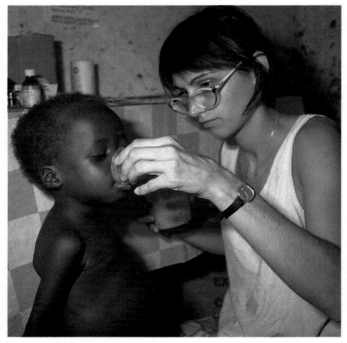

18.5 Oral rehydration

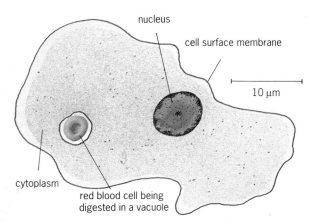

18.6 Entamoeba histolytica, a protoctist which causes dysentery

their digestive system without suffering from any symptoms.

You catch amoebic dysentery by eating food, or drinking water, which contains **cysts** of *E. histolytica*. The cyst is a living *E. histolytica* surrounded by a protective covering. The cysts are passed out of the body in the faeces of an infected person. If the faeces contaminate water, then this water or food which is washed in it can cause infection. The transmission of amoebic dysentery can be prevented by providing people with clean water.

Amoebic dysentery occurs all over the world. However, it is commonest in tropical and subtropical countries, especially developing countries. It is most likely to occur where sanitation is poor. In the USA, about 1 % to 2 % of people are probably infected with *E. histolytica*. In some tropical developing countries, as many as 50 % may be infected. However, many of these people will have no symptoms at all.

If someone with amoebic dysentery suffers from bad diarrhoea, then they may need oral rehydration therapy (Section 18.7) to stop them becoming dehydrated. The disease can be cured with drugs which kill the *E. histolytica*.

18.9 Malaria is transmitted by a vector.

The pathogen which causes malaria is a protoctist called *Plasmodium* (Fig 18.8). Malaria is one of the world's biggest killers. Up to 500 million people have

Fact!

Of all the animal-borne diseases, one of the most devastating for a time has been bubonic plague, or the black death, which has killed more than 50 million humans in recorded times. The disease is a bacterial infection injected into the blood by infected fleas from rats.

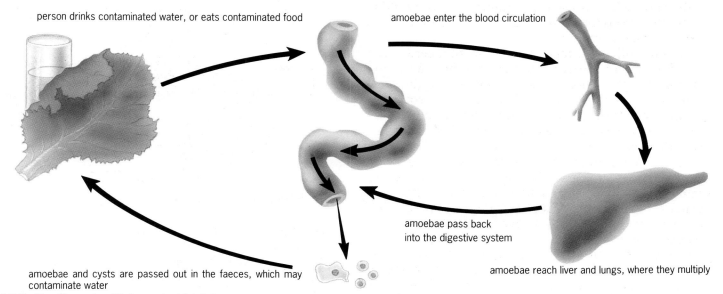

person drinks contaminated water, or eats contaminated food

amoebae enter the blood circulation

amoebae pass back into the digestive system

amoebae and cysts are passed out in the faeces, which may contaminate water

amoebae reach liver and lungs, where they multiply

18.7   The life cycle of Entamoeba histolytica

malaria every year. The distribution of malaria in Africa is shown in Fig 16.18.

You get malaria by being bitten by a female mosquito belonging to the genus *Anopheles* if she is carrying *Plasmodium* in her saliva. The mosquito has a long proboscis, which she pushes through the skin into a blood vessel. She sucks up blood through the proboscis. To stop the blood clotting, she injects some saliva. If her saliva contains *Plasmodium*, then she injects *Plasmodium* as well. The mosquito is a **vector** for the disease. This explains the distribution of malaria in the world – you find malaria where you find the mosquitoes which transmit it.

The *Plasmodium* get into your liver cells. They breed and, after a few days, leave the liver and enter some of your red blood cells. This is when you first feel ill, feeling a bit as though you have flu.

The organisms breed even faster when they are in the red blood cells. When a red cell becomes full of young organisms, it bursts, releasing them into your blood so that they can infect other red blood cells. This happens at regular intervals – say every two days. The exact interval depends on the species of *Plasmodium* with which you are infected.

Every time the red cells burst, your temperature goes up and you feel ill. This stage of the disease can be very

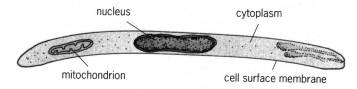

nucleus   cytoplasm

mitochondrion   cell surface membrane

18.8 Plasmodium, *the protoctist which causes malaria*

dangerous, and many people die. Body temperature may go up to 40 °C. The burst blood cells may block blood vessels, stopping oxygen supplies getting to many parts of the body.

18.10 Malaria is difficult to control.

Malaria has proved very difficult to control. There are several different lines of attack which have been tried.

Destroy the mosquitoes which transmit the disease The life cycle of the mosquito which transmits malaria is shown in Fig 18.10. If mosquitoes can be killed at any stage of this life cycle, then the number of mosquitoes available to transmit malaria should be reduced.

Insecticides   Adult mosquitoes are active at night, and rest in places such as houses during the day. **Insecticides**, including DDT, have been used to spray their resting places. This has been very effective in some areas, but in many places the mosquitoes have now evolved to become resistant to insecticides.

You can see from Fig 18.10 that mosquitoes lay their

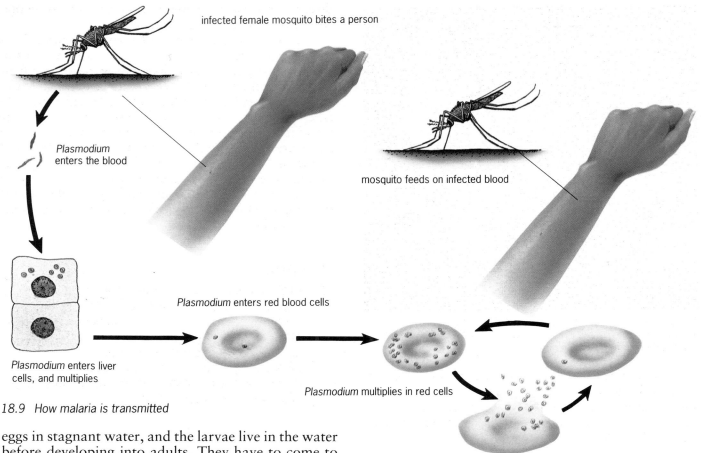

infected female mosquito bites a person

Plasmodium enters the blood

Plasmodium enters liver cells, and multiplies

Plasmodium enters red blood cells

mosquito feeds on infected blood

Plasmodium multiplies in red cells

18.9   How malaria is transmitted

eggs in stagnant water, and the larvae live in the water before developing into adults. They have to come to the surface to get oxygen from the air. In some places, swamps and open water have been **drained**, to reduce the amount of water available for mosquitoes to breed. People take care not to leave containers of water, or even puddles, near their houses. **Oil** can be sprayed onto open water to make a film on the surface, preventing the larvae from coming to the surface to get air. All of these methods have had some success, but they are often too expensive to carry out often enough to destroy all the larvae, and they also harm the environment.

Biological control has also been tried. Fish have been put into ponds where mosquitoes breed, to eat the larvae. Bacteria which infect the larvae have been put into the water. These methods do less harm to the environment, but they do not kill all of the larvae.

Malaria can only be transmitted if female mosquitoes bite an infected person, and then an uninfected one. People should sleep under a **mosquito net**, so that they cannot be bitten. Insect-repellent creams put onto the skin can also help, but they do not completely prevent you being bitten.

Drugs Another approach is to use **drugs** to kill the *Plasmodium* inside an infected person's body. There are several different drugs available. There are also

Plasmodium bursts out of red cells, and infects others

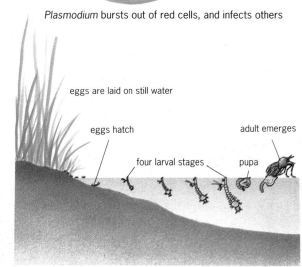

eggs are laid on still water

eggs hatch

four larval stages

pupa

adult emerges

18.10   The life cycle of Anopheles, *a mosquito which transmits malaria*

drugs which you can take to prevent the *Plasmodium* ever infecting you, even if you are bitten by a mosquito carrying *Plasmodium*. People visiting a country where malaria is present should always take these drugs. However, *Plasmodium* appears to be able quickly to become resistant to them, and new drugs are always having to be developed.

270

18.11 *Sleeping under a mosquito net is a good protection against malaria. The mosquitoes which are vectors for the disease are most active after dark.*

Until recently, there was no **vaccine** available for malaria. However, in 1994, a new vaccine has proved successful in trials in South America and Africa. You can read about the way in which vaccines work on pages 275–276.

18.11 Athlete's foot is caused by a fungus.

Athlete's foot is a skin infection caused by a fungus called *Tinea*.

It most commonly occurs between the toes, where it causes the skin to flake and crack. Occasionally, it can spread across the foot and cause quite bad skin damage. The mild form of athlete's foot is a very common

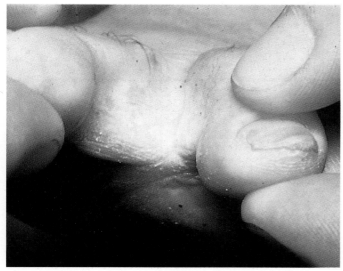

18.12 *Athlete's foot fungus growing between the toes*

disease, and it is estimated that up to 50 % of people will have it at some time in their life.

Athlete's foot gets its name because it is most likely to occur on feet which have been confined inside sweaty shoes, and is most likely to be picked up from floors of communal showers and swimming baths. Washing these floors with disinfectant will reduce the risk of people catching the disease. The best way to avoid it is good foot hygiene – making sure that your shoes are large enough to allow your feet to 'breathe', changing your socks regularly, and washing and drying your feet thoroughly. If you *do* get athlete's foot, there are lotions which can be prescribed to kill the fungus, although these do not always do their job very quickly.

Questions

1 Explain whether each of the following procedures could help to prevent the spread of any of these diseases: influenza, cholera, amoebic dysentery, athlete's foot, malaria.
    (a) spraying houses with insecticide
    (b) providing everyone with clean water
    (c) not swimming in water contaminated with sewage
    (d) draining wet areas near towns

Body defences against infectious disease

18.12 Blood clotting stops pathogens entering through cuts.

Normally, your skin provides a very effective barrier stopping pathogens getting into your blood. However, if you cut yourself, there is a chance for them to get in through the cut. **Blood clotting** helps to stop this happening, as well as stopping you from losing too much blood.

Figure 18.13 summarises what happens when your blood clots. **Platelets** are very important in this process. Normally, blood vessel walls are very smooth. When a blood vessel is cut, the platelets bump into the rough edges of the cut, and react by releasing a chemical. The damaged tissues around the blood vessel also release chemicals.

In the blood plasma, there are always two soluble proteins – **prothrombin** and **fibrinogen**. The chemicals released by the platelets and the damaged tissues set off a chain of reactions, which cause the prothrombin to be changed into a different protein called **thrombin**. Thrombin is an enzyme. It acts on the fibrinogen to change it into **fibrin**.

271

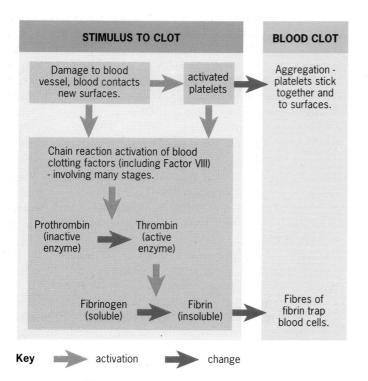

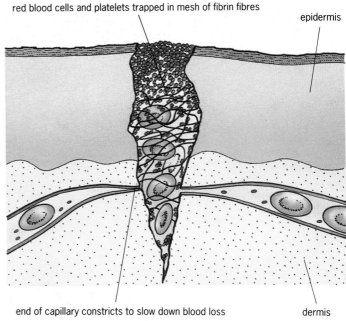

STIMULUS TO CLOT

Damage to blood vessel, blood contacts new surfaces. → activated platelets

BLOOD CLOT

Aggregation - platelets stick together and to surfaces.

Chain reaction activation of blood clotting factors (including Factor VIII) - involving many stages.

Prothrombin (inactive enzyme) → Thrombin (active enzyme)

Fibrinogen (soluble) → Fibrin (insoluble)

Fibres of fibrin trap blood cells.

Key → activation → change

18.13 The sequence of events which occurs as blood clots

Unlike all the other proteins involved in this process, fibrin is insoluble. As its name suggests, it forms fibres. These fibres form a mesh across the wound. Red blood cells and platelets get trapped in the tangle of fibrin fibres, forming a **blood clot**.

18.13 White blood cells destroy pathogens.

There are many different kinds of white blood cells. They all have the function of destroying pathogens in your body, but they do it in different ways.

Phagocytes are cells which can move around the body, engulfing and destroying pathogens (Figs 18.15 and 18.16). They also destroy any of your own cells which are damaged or worn out. Phagocytes often

have lobed nuclei. If you damage your skin, perhaps with a cut or graze, phagocytes will collect at the site of the damage, to 'mop up' any microorganisms which might possibly get in.

Lymphocytes have a quite different method of attacking pathogens. They produce chemicals called **antibodies**, which are carried in the blood and tissue fluid to almost every part of the body.

18.14 Antibodies are specific.

In your body, you have thousands of different kinds of lymphocytes. Each kind is able to produce a different sort of antibody.

An antibody is a protein molecule with a particular shape. Rather like an enzyme molecule, this shape is

red blood cells and platelets trapped in mesh of fibrin fibres

epidermis

end of capillary constricts to slow down blood loss

dermis

18.14 Vertical section through a blood clot

Table 18.2 **How the body prevents infection**

Method of entry	Example	Natural defences
Through skin	*Staphylococcus* bacterium	1 Epidermis is a barrier between pathogens and body 2 When skin is damaged, blood clots seal wound and prevent entry of pathogens 3 Tears contain lysozyme, which helps to prevent eye infections
Into respiratory system	Influenza virus	1 Cilia and mucus in respiratory passages trap dust particles which may carry pathogens, and sweep them upwards
In food or water, into alimentary canal	*Salmonella*	1 Distaste for food which looks or smells bad 2 Hydrochloric acid in stomach kills many bacteria
Injection into body by a vector	*Plasmodium*	None
By sexual intercourse	Virus causing AIDS	None

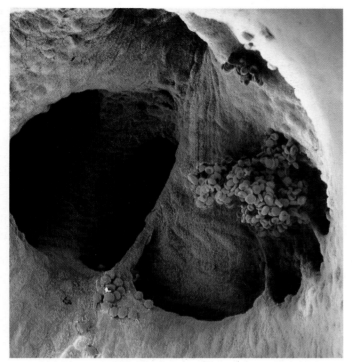

18.15 *A scanning electron micrograph of a blood clot – made up of a mass of red blood cells – in the entrance to an artery in the heart. This is a coronary thrombosis.*

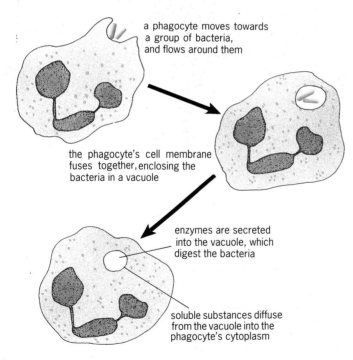

a phagocyte moves towards a group of bacteria, and flows around them

the phagocyte's cell membrane fuses together, enclosing the bacteria in a vacuole

enzymes are secreted into the vacuole, which digest the bacteria

soluble substances diffuse from the vacuole into the phagocyte's cytoplasm

18.16 *A white cell destroying bacteria by phagocytosis*

just right to fit into another molecule. To destroy a particular pathogen, antibody molecules must be made which are just the right shape to fit into molecules on the outside of the pathogen. These pathogen molecules are called **antigens**.

When antibody molecules lock onto the pathogen, they kill the pathogen. There are several ways in which they do this. One way is simply to alert phagocytes to the presence of the pathogen, so that the phagocytes will come and destroy them. Or they may start off a series of reactions in the blood which produce enzymes to digest the pathogens.

18.15 Lymphocytes multiply when 'their' pathogen is present.

Most of the time, most of your lymphocytes do not produce antibodies. It would be a waste of energy and materials if they did. Instead, each lymphocyte waits for a signal that a pathogen which can be destroyed by its particular antibody is in your body.

If a pathogen enters your body, it is likely to meet a large number of lymphocytes. One of these may recognise the pathogen as being something that its antibody can destroy. This lymphocyte will start to divide rapidly by mitosis, making a whole clone of lymphocytes just like itself. These lymphocytes will all begin to secrete their antibody, which will destroy the pathogen.

This takes time. It may take a while for the 'right' lymphocyte to recognise the pathogen, and then a few days for it to produce a big enough clone to make enough antibody to kill it. In the meanwhile, the pathogen breeds, making you ill. Eventually, however, the lymphocytes get the upper hand, and you get better.

18.16 B and T lymphocytes act in different ways.

Lymphocytes are divided into two groups, called **B cells** and **T cells**. They look just the same as each other. The difference is in the way they attack pathogens.

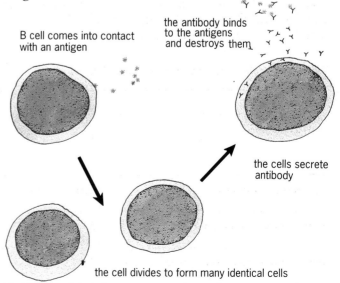

B cell comes into contact with an antigen

the antibody binds to the antigens and destroys them

the cells secrete antibody

the cell divides to form many identical cells

18.17 *How B lymphocytes respond to antigen*

273

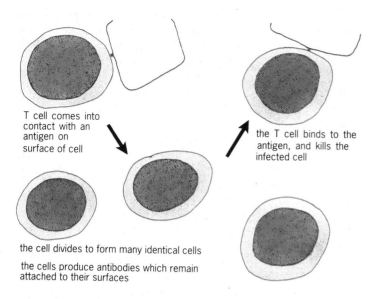

T cell comes into contact with an antigen on surface of cell

the T cell binds to the antigen, and kills the infected cell

the cell divides to form many identical cells

the cells produce antibodies which remain attached to their surfaces

18.18   How T lymphocytes respond to antigen

B cells are made in **bone marrow**. They behave just as described in section 18.14, secreting their antibody into the blood. B cells are most active against bacteria, but some of them also kill viruses.

T cells are made in the thymus gland. Like B cells, they only start to act when they meet an antigen which matches the antibody they can make.

However, T cells only recognise 'their' antigen when it is attached to the outside of one of your own cells. So they do not respond to bacteria living in your body fluids. Instead, T cells notice when one of your cells is infected with viruses. Cells infected with viruses usually put some pieces of the virus's protein coat on their outer surfaces, to signal to the T cells that they need help. These bits of virus protein are antigens.

If a T cell finds a body cell with a strange protein on its outer surface, and if this protein matches the antibody it can produce, it divides rapidly, forming a clone. However, instead of secreting their antibodies into the blood or tissue fluid, T cells keep them attached to their surfaces. The T cell then binds to the infected body cell, because its antibodies stick to the antigens. Finally, the T cell secretes a chemical which kills the infected cell, so stopping viruses from multiplying inside it. T cells which do this are called **killer T cells**.

18.17 Memory cells make you immune.

The response to the presence of pathogens in your body, described in Sections 18.15 and 18.16, is called the **immune response**. The first time a pathogen enters your body, it takes a little while for the immune response to swing fully into action. This gives the pathogen a chance to breed, so you get ill.

However, when the lymphocytes multiply to form clones, not all of the cells in the clone take on the job

of making antibodies. Some of them remain inactive. They are called **memory cells**. Both B and T cells produce memory cells. Memory cells stay in your blood for a very long time after an infection.

If the same pathogen gets into your body again, it is likely to be recognised by a memory cell almost straight away. The immune response to the pathogen is immediate, killing it before it has any chance to breed. You are now immune to that disease.

18.18 Cold viruses keep changing.

For many diseases, immunity lasts all your life. If you have mumps or measles once, you will probably never have it again. However, this is not true for one of the commonest diseases – the common cold.

Colds are caused by a virus. The special feature of cold viruses which helps them to win the battle against our immune response is that they keep changing the proteins in their outer coat. If you get a cold, the lymphocytes which make an antibody against the particular antigens of the cold virus which is infecting you form memory cells. But then along comes another cold virus with a slightly different protein coat. The memory cells do not recognise it. You get a cold all over again, and produce another set of memory cells. Then along comes another virus … You can't win!

18.19 AIDS is caused by a virus which attacks lymphocytes.

The disease **AIDS**, or autoimmune deficiency syndrome, is caused by **HIV**. HIV stands for **human immunodeficiency virus**. Fig 18.19 shows this virus.

HIV infects lymphocytes, in particular T cells. Over a long period of time, HIV slowly destroys T cells. Several years after infection with the virus, the level of

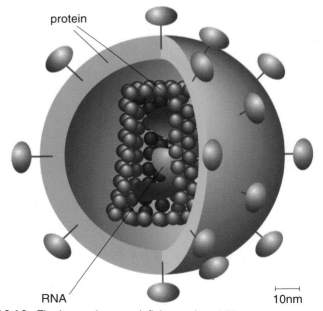

protein

RNA

10nm

18.19   The human immunodeficiency virus, HIV

274

certain kinds of T cells is so low that they are unable to fight against other pathogens effectively. Because HIV attacks the very cells which would normally kill viruses – the T cells – it is very difficult for someone's own immune system to protect them against HIV.

About ten years after initial infection with HIV, a person is likely to develop symptoms of AIDS. They become very vulnerable to other infections, such as pneumonia. They may develop cancer, because one function of the immune system is to destroy body cells which may be beginning to produce cancers. Brain cells are also quite often damaged by HIV. A person with AIDS usually dies of a collection of several illnesses.

There is still no cure for AIDS. Researchers are always trying to develop new drugs, which will kill the virus without damaging the person's own cells. As yet, no vaccine has been produced either, despite millions of pounds being spent on research.

18.20 HIV is transmitted in body fluids.

The virus which causes AIDS cannot live outside the human body. In fact, it is an especially fragile virus – much less tough than the cold virus, for example. You can only become infected with HIV through direct contact of your body fluids with those of someone with the virus. This can be in one of the following ways:

Through sexual intercourse HIV can live in the fluid inside the vagina, rectum and urethra. During sexual intercourse, fluids from one partner will come into contact with fluids of the other. It is very easy for the virus to be passed on in this way.

The more partners a person has, the more the chance of them becoming infected with HIV. In some parts of the world, where it is common practice for men to have many different sexual partners, extremely high percentages of people have developed AIDS. This is so in some parts of Africa, and also amongst some homosexual communities in parts of Britain and the USA.

The best way of avoiding AIDS is never to have more than one sexual partner. If *everyone* did that, then AIDS would immediately stop spreading. Using condoms is a good way of lowering the chances of the viruses passing from one person to another during sexual intercourse – though it does not rule out the possibility altogether.

Through blood contact Many cases of AIDS have been caused by HIV transferred from one person's blood to another. In the 1970s and 1980s, when AIDS first appeared, and before anyone knew what was causing it, blood containing HIV was used in transfusions. People being given the transfusions were infected with HIV, and later developed AIDS. Now all blood used in transfusions in Britain is screened for HIV before it is used.

Blood can also be transferred from one person to another if they share hypodermic needles. This most commonly happens in people who inject drugs, such as heroin. Many drug users have died from AIDS. In many parts of Britain, there are now schemes to provide people with sterile needles – even if they are using drugs illegally – to reduce the risk of them catching AIDS.

People who have to deal with accidents, such as police and ambulance attendants, must always be on the guard against AIDS if there is blood around. They often wear protective clothing, just in case a bleeding accident victim is infected with HIV.

However, in general, there is no danger of anyone becoming infected with HIV from contact with someone with AIDS. You can quite safely talk to them, shake hands with them, drink from cups which they have used and so on. In fact, there is far more danger to the person who *has* AIDS from such contacts, because they are so vulnerable to any bacterium or virus which they might catch from you.

18.21 Natural immunity can be active or passive.

You have seen how being infected with a particular pathogen can make you immune to the disease which it causes, by causing you to produce memory cells. This sort of immunity is called **natural active** immunity. It is 'natural' because it happens naturally, and it is 'active' because your body has made memory cells for itself.

Another sort of natural immunity is passed on from mothers to their babies. When a baby is first born, its immune system is not very well developed, and it cannot easily fight off infections. To help it through the first few months after birth, it is provided with antibodies from its mother. These pass across the placenta from the mother's blood into the embryo's blood. There are also antibodies in the mother's milk, so a breast-fed baby gets extra antibodies in this way. This is called **natural passive** immunity. 'Passive' means that the baby is not making its own antibodies – it is just 'borrowing' its mother's. Passive immunity does not last very long, because the antibodies soon disappear.

18.22 Vaccinations can provide you with active or passive immunity.

Vaccinations can also make you immune to a disease. There are several sorts of vaccination.

You can be injected with **live bacteria** *or* **viruses**. These are of a strain bred specially so that they do not actually give you the disease. This is done to immunise you against tuberculosis (caused by a bacterium) and rubella (caused by a virus). You will probably have

18.20 *Almost every country has vaccination programmes for young children, to protect them against common infectious diseases. This doctor is working in India.*

been given a TB vaccination by the time you read this – if not, look forward to it soon! Some people already have natural immunity to TB, so you will be tested to check this, to see if you need the vaccination.

Rubella vaccinations are normally only given to girls, because the disease is not dangerous except to an unborn child. The vaccination is usually given to teenage girls, to give them immunity before they may become pregnant later in their life.

*You can be injected with **killed bacteria** or **viruses**.* This is done for whooping cough. The vaccination is usually given when a child is very young. Whooping cough is a very unpleasant disease, which causes thick, sticky mucus to be produced, making it difficult to breathe. Small children may suffer permanent brain damage after a bad case of whooping cough, which is why the vaccination is given very early in life. However, some parents have decided not to let their children have this vaccination, because there have been a very few cases where the child has reacted badly to the vaccine, and brain damage has been caused.

*You can be injected with a **toxin** produced by a pathogen.* You may remember that a **toxin** is a poisonous chemical produced by bacteria. It can act as an antigen, stimulating your immune system just as a bacterium might. In vaccinations for diphtheria, an altered toxin is used – it is modified so that it does not make you ill. Diphtheria is another vaccination which is given to young children.

*You can be injected with just **parts** of a virus, which act as antigens.* This is done with flu vaccinations. The flu viruses are separated into bits, and the injection contains just part of the protein coat. A similar method is used for vaccinations against hepatitis B, a viral disease of the liver. However, in this case the antigen is produced by genetic engineering (you can read about this on pages 295–298). People are not usually given flu or hepatitis B vaccinations unless they really need them. For example, old people may have flu jabs if an epidemic is expected, and people travelling to developing countries where hygiene is not very good should have hepatitis B vaccinations.

All of the methods described above put an antigen into your body, which makes you produce antibodies and memory cells. They are all examples of **artificial active** immunity.

Vaccinations can also produce **artificial passive** immunity. This is done when it is thought that you might already be infected with a pathogen, and need instant antibodies to help you to fight it off. For example, if you get a bad cut, you might be given an antitetanus jab. This will contain antibodies against the tetanus bacterium. The antibodies are produced by injecting weakened tetanus bacteria into horses, and then separating the antibodies the horse produces from a sample of its blood. The antibodies will not last long in your body, but hopefully long enough to kill any tetanus bacteria which got in through the cut. You will probably be asked to go back to the doctor later, to be given some weakened tetanus bacteria to begin to develop your own, active immunity – just in case you cut yourself again.

18.23 The immune system can reject transplants.

People suffering from serious diseases affecting a particular organ may be given a **transplant**. Many different organs can now be transplanted. Some of the commonest transplants are kidney transplants and bone marrow transplants. Heart transplants are also given quite frequently.

The person receiving the transplant is the **recipient,** and the person from whose body the organ was taken is the **donor**. Often, the donor is someone who died in an accident. Many people carry donor cards with them all the time, stating that they are happy for their organs to be used in a transplant operation. Organs for transplants must be removed quickly from a body and kept cold, so that they do not deteriorate. Sometimes, however, the donor may be alive. A brother or sister may donate a kidney to someone who needs one urgently. You can manage perfectly well with just one kidney.

Surgeons now have very few problems with transplant operations – they can almost always make an excellent job of removing the old organ and replacing

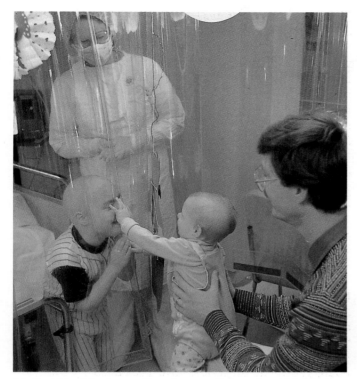

18.21 *This little boy suffers from a disease in which his bone marrow does not make enough red blood cells. He was given a 'transplant' of blood taken from the umbilical cord of his baby sister, which contains many of the cells normally found in bone marrow. Because she is closely related to him, there is less chance that his body will reject the cells. However, he still has to be treated with immunosuppressant drugs, and is kept in a sterile room for some time after the operation.*

it with a better one. The big problem comes afterwards. The recipient's immune system recognises the donor organ as being foreign, and attacks it. This is called **rejection**.

The cells which attack the transplanted organ are mostly T cells. The recipient is given drugs which stop them working efficiently, to decrease the chances of rejection. These drugs are called **immunosuppressants**. The trouble with immunosuppressants is that they stop the immune system from doing its normal job, and so the person is more likely to suffer from all sorts of infectious diseases. The drugs have to be taken for the rest of the recipient's life.

The chances of rejection are less if the donor is a close relative of the recipient. This, of course, can only be considered when the organ for donation is one which can be given by a living person, such as a kidney or some bone marrow. Closely-related people are more likely to have antigens on their cells which are similar to each other, so the recipient's immune system is less likely to react to the donated organ as if it was 'foreign'. If there is not a relative who can donate an organ, then a search may be made world-wide, looking for a potential donor with similar antigens to the recipient.

18.24 Monoclonal antibodies may prove useful in medicine.

In the late 1970s, scientists found a way to produce clones of B cells which all produced identical antibodies. These antibodies are called **monoclonal antibodies**. ('Mono' means 'one', so this means one clone of antibodies.)

The way they did this was to start with a single B cell. You may remember that each B cell secretes just one kind of antibody. However, B cells which secrete antibodies do not divide, so this cell could not produce a clone. To get round this, the scientists fused the B cell with a cancer cell. Cancer cells divide over and over again. The fused B cell and cancer cell divided to form thousands of cells, which all produced antibodies. The antibodies can then be extracted from the culture of cells.

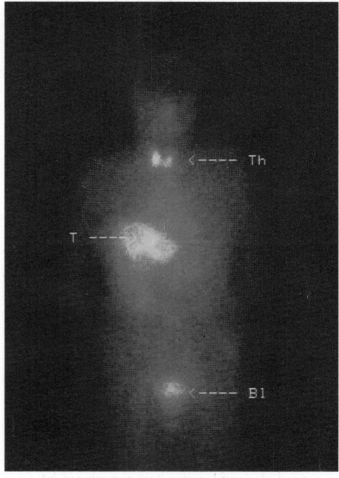

18.22 *Monoclonal antibodies have been used to detect tumours in this patient. He has been injected with monoclonal antibodies which react with antigens on tumour cells. Radioactive iodine has been attached to the antibodies, so that they show up on photographic film. Here, you can see how the radioactive iodine has been taken up in the thyroid gland (Th) and is being excreted through the bladder (Bl). However, the reason for doing this investigation was to detect the tumour (T) in the liver, where the antibodies have collected in large quantities.*

Monoclonal antibodies are useful in diagnosing diseases. For example, herpes viruses cause cold sores and other painful skin conditions. There are two sorts of herpes viruses, which are best treated with different drugs. To find out which virus was causing someone's illness used to take a long time – up to 3 or 6 days. Now monoclonal antibodies can do the job in 15 to 20 minutes. Two sorts of monoclonal antibodies have been produced to react with the antigens on the two types of herpes virus. By seeing which antibody reacts with the virus, the type of virus is quickly identified, and can be immediately treated with the right drug.

In the future, monoclonal antibodies may be useful in curing cancer. Cancer cells sometimes have proteins on their surfaces which differ from those on normal body cells. Monoclonal antibodies could be developed which latch onto the antigens on the cancer cells, but not to other cells. The antibodies themselves might kill the cancer cells. Another possibility is that cell-killing drug molecules could be attached to the antibody molecules. The monoclonal antibodies would deliver the drug to the cancer cells, so that it would not damage other healthy cells. Both of these methods have already been tried, with some success.

18.25 Antibiotics can kill bacteria in the body.

Sometimes, a person's body needs help in its fight against a bacterial infection. Until 1944, there was little help which could be given. People died from diseases which we now consider quite harmless, such as infected cuts.

Then a discovery was made which has had a tremendous effect on our ability to treat diseases. **Antibiotics**

were discovered. You can read about how this happened on page 312.

Antibiotics are substances which kill bacteria, but do not harm living cells. Most of them are made by fungi. It is thought that the fungi make antibiotics to kill bacteria living near them – bacteria and fungi are both saprophytes, so they might compete for food. We use the chemical warfare system of the fungus to wage our own war against bacteria.

The first antibiotic to be discovered was **penicillin**. It is made by the fungus *Penicillium*, which you might sometimes see growing on decaying fruit. Penicillin kills bacteria by stopping them making their cell walls. Since the introduction of penicillin, many more antibiotics have been found.

We have to go on trying to find more and more antibiotics, because bacteria evolve to become resistant to them, as described in Section 16.10. The more we use antibiotics, the more selection pressure we put on bacteria to evolve resistance. People did not realise this when antibiotics were first discovered, and used them for all sorts of diseases where they did not help at all, such as diseases caused by viruses. Now doctors are much more careful about the amount of antibiotics which they prescribe. We should only use antibiotics when they are really needed – then there is more chance that they will work when we need them to.

Life-style and disease

18.26 Life-style affects health.

In the nineteenth century, infectious diseases were a major cause of illness and death. Now, this is not so in the United Kingdom. We still get infectious diseases, but we rarely die from them. The discovery, by Joseph Lister, of the effectiveness of antiseptics in reducing infection of wounds, greatly reduced the number of deaths following operations. Edward Jenner's introduction of vaccination against smallpox was the beginning of a series of successful inoculations to prevent a whole range of infectious diseases. The discovery of penicillin and its mass production, by Fleming, Florey and Chain, gave us highly efficient weapons in the fight against bacterial diseases. You can read about these three discoveries on pages 311 to 312.

In Britain today, the main cause of death is **coronary heart disease**. **Cancer** and **strokes** are also important. To some extent, these diseases are all caused by natural ageing processes. However, they are also affected by life-style. Your diet, whether you smoke or not, the amount of exercise you get, and stress can all make a big difference to when and if you suffer from any of these diseases.

We all have to die of something, eventually. However, with a little care in your life-style you can reduce

18.23 *The production of antibiotics is now a major industry*

the risk of suffering from some diseases early in your life, and have a better chance of feeling healthy and living for a long time.

18.27 Coronary heart disease and strokes.

Coronary heart disease is often abbreviated to **CHD**. It is a disease which affects the coronary vessels which supply oxygen and nutrients to the heart muscles. In this disease the walls of the coronary arteries are gradually damaged by deposits of lipids and cholesterol. These are laid down in the artery wall. The wall becomes stiff which is why the term 'hardening of the arteries' is sometimes used to describe this disease. The medical term meaning 'hardening of the arteries' is **atherosclerosis**.

Although CHD is called a disease, it is probably a natural process of ageing. However, it progresses more slowly in women and some people develop it more than others. A number of factors indicate the possible risk of early development of CHD. The most important ones are genetic factors, high blood cholesterol levels and aspects of a person's life-style.

The genetic factor is particularly important. If a person has a father, mother, brother or grandparents who died early of CHD, there is a possibility that the person will also suffer CHD at an early age. If a person has a very high cholesterol level in the blood, that person can be at risk of CHD. Several life-style factors have been linked to CHD, including a high fat diet – especially one rich in saturated fat from animals – lack of exercise, smoking and leading a stressful life.

There are several possible consequences of the damage done to coronary arteries in CHD. The most common effect is that at some point the wall cracks on the inside, the platelets get caught on it and a blood clot starts to form inside the artery. Because of the speed of flow of the blood the clot can be swept off the artery wall and down the coronary artery. The artery divides into smaller and smaller arterioles. Eventually, the blood clot gets stuck and blocks the blood vessel. This stops blood from reaching an area of cardiac muscle. The lack of oxygen will stop these muscle cells contracting properly. If the area of muscle affected is big enough the regular beating of the heart is interrupted and we say that the person has suffered a **heart attack**.

Another consequence of the hardening of an artery is that the artery is more likely to burst at the peak of pressure when a pulse of blood is expelled from the heart. Blood leaks out of the damaged vessel. The result of this is most severe in the brain where an area of brain tissue can be killed. This is a **stroke**.

18.28 Regular exercise can reduce the risk of CHD.

In the past twenty years or so, the amount of exercise which people take has decreased. This is partly because of the kind of work they do. Fewer people now do hard, physical work. More time is spent in offices, doing sedentary jobs. Another reason is the change in the way in which people relax, especially young people. Fewer young people now spend much time doing energetic activities such as sport. They spend more time watching television, listening to music or playing computer games.

Exercise has many beneficial effects on health.

Exercise improves the efficiency of the heart Regular exercise improves the strength of the heart muscle. The heart of someone who exercises regularly is likely to be able to pump more blood with each beat than the heart of someone who does not take exercise. The amount of blood pumped in one beat is called the **stroke volume**. An increased stroke volume means that the heart can pump enough blood to the body with fewer beats per minute, so the **resting pulse rate** is lower. Overall, the heart does not have to work so hard. Regular exercise can greatly decrease the risk of suffering from CHD.

Aerobic exercise improves lung capacity Exercising muscles need extra oxygen, which is supplied to them by breathing faster and more deeply. If you regularly do exercise which makes your muscles demand extra oxygen, called **aerobic exercise**, this helps your respiratory system to become efficient at getting oxygen into your blood.

Aerobic exercise improves the oxygen-carrying capacity of the blood If your muscles constantly demand a lot of oxygen, the number of red blood cells in your blood increases. This makes your blood more efficient at carrying oxygen, so your heart does not have to beat as fast or as hard to supply your muscles.

Exercise improves the strength of your muscles The blood supply to muscles increases, so that they are less likely to have to respire anaerobically and produce lactic acid (Section 6.23). The muscles get stronger, and can work for longer without tiring.

Exercise affects the development of bones The way in which bones grow partly depends on the forces which act on them, and a person who regularly exercises may end up with stronger bones than a person who does not. Exercise can also make sure that joints stay flexible.

Exercise can make you feel good Many people get a lot of pleasure from exercise. Exercise may cause your brain to secrete chemicals which make you feel happy. Exercise also gives you a break from your work, and helps you to feel less stressed and more relaxed.

18.29 You can reduce the risk of getting cancer.

Cancer is a very important cause of death in all developed countries, including the United Kingdom. Cancer is a disease in which cells divide uncontrollably, forming a tumour. If detected early, this tumour can often be completely removed or destroyed, and the patient makes a complete recovery. However, often the tumour is not found until some cells have broken away from it and begun to form new tumours in other parts of the body. These secondary tumours are more difficult to destroy, and it is these which often cause death.

What causes cancer? When you began life, you were a single cell – a zygote – which divided to form two cells, and then four and so on. Cells normally divide until you are fully grown, and then stop. They have inbuilt control mechanisms which make them do this. However, if the control mechanism breaks down, a cell may start to divide again, when it should really have stopped.

A lot of research is being done into just what these control mechanisms are, and what makes them break down. The control mechanisms depend on genes, which are made of **DNA**. Damage to parts of the DNA which are involved in controlling cell division can result in cancer.

We now know that there are many things which can cause such damage to DNA. They include viruses, chemicals, and ionising radiation.

Viruses are now known to cause several kinds of cancer. One is **cervical cancer**, affecting the cells lining the cervix. Not everyone who has the virus, however, gets cervical cancer – there seem to be many other factors involved as well. For example, people who smoke are more likely to suffer from this cancer than people who do not. The virus is passed on during sexual intercourse, so women who have a lot of sexual partners are more likely to get cervical cancer than those who do not. Cervical cancer can be cured if it is detected early. Screening programmes are carried out, in which a small sample of cells is taken from the cervix (called a cervical smear) and examined for early stages of the disease. The cure rate is over 90 %.

Chemicals are probably one of the most important causes of cancer. A chemical which can cause cancer is called a **carcinogen**.

Chemicals in **cigarette smoke**, especially tar, are almost always the cause of **lung cancer**. People who smoke just a few cigarettes a day are ten times as likely to get lung cancer as people who do not smoke at all, while heavy smokers are twenty-five times as likely to get it. In Britain, it is a very common cause of death, with up to one in every eighteen deaths being caused by lung cancer. Only 0.3 % of people with lung cancer are people who have been non-smokers all their lives. The chemicals in cigarette smoke damage the DNA

in the cells lining the respiratory passages. If this damage affects the control mechanisms for cell division, then a tumour develops. Lung cancer is a very difficult cancer to treat, unless it is detected early enough for the tumour to be removed by surgery.

Smoking not only increases the risk of developing lung cancer, but also almost every other kind of cancer. Many of the chemicals in cigarette smoke get into the blood, and so can be taken all over the body.

Chemicals in food may also increase the risk of cancer, although this is not well understood at the moment. On the other hand, some foods can actually protect against cancer. One group of chemicals in food which may damage DNA are called **free radicals**, and free radicals can be stopped from doing too much damage by another group of chemicals called **antioxidants**. Vitamins A, C and E all act as antioxidants in the body. If you eat a diet with plenty of these vitamins, you may reduce your risk of getting cancer.

Ionising radiation damages DNA. Ionising radiation includes alpha, beta and gamma radiation, which come from **radioactive chemicals**. The accident at the nuclear power station at Chernobyl, which released large quantities of radioactive chemicals into the air, has greatly increased the incidence of thyroid cancer in countries across which the pollutants drifted.

Another form of radiation is **ultraviolet radiation** from the Sun. This is most likely to damage DNA in skin cells, causing skin cancer. In recent years, the incidence of skin cancers has greatly increased. This is because more people have been able to afford the money and time to go abroad for holidays. Skin which has not had much sun on it for most of the year, and then is roasted in the sun for two weeks with little protection, may develop cancer many years afterwards. Now that the danger is realised, people are taking much more care to protect their skin from this damage.

18.30 Alcohol is a commonly-used drug.

A drug is a substance which changes the way the body works. Many drugs are used in medicine, such as antibiotics and painkillers. Most of us take some drugs every day – for example, caffeine in coffee or tea. However, there are some drugs which can cause great harm if they are not used properly.

Alcohol is a very commonly-used drug in Britain. People often drink alcoholic drinks because they enjoy the effect that alcohol has on the brain. Alcohol can make people feel more relaxed and release their inhibitions, making it easier for them to enjoy themselves.

Alcohol is quickly absorbed through the wall of the stomach, and carried all over the body in the blood. It is eventually broken down by the liver, but this takes quite a long time.

Drinking fairly small quantities of alcohol is not

18.24 Alcohol abuse can cause misery both to the abuser and to their friends and family

dangerous, but alcohol does have many effects on the body which can be very dangerous if care is not taken.

It lengthens reaction time Even small amounts of alcohol reduce the rate at which messages travel in the nervous system, so alcohol lengthens the time you take to respond to a stimulus. This can mean the difference between life and death – often someone else's death – if the affected person is driving a car. A very high proportion of road accidents involve people who have recently drunk alcohol – either drivers or pedestrians. There are legal limits on how much alcohol you are allowed to have in your blood when you are driving. However, most people now think that, because even very small quantities of alcohol increase the risk of an accident, the only safe rule is not to drink alcohol at all if you are going to drive.

It can increase aggression in some people Different people react differently to alcohol. In some people, it increases their feelings of aggression, and releases their inhibitions so that they are more likely to be violent or commit other crimes. They may be violent towards members of their family. Research has shown that at least 50 % of violence in the home is related to drunkenness, and that alcohol has played a part in the criminal behaviour of around 60 % of people in prison.

Large intakes of alcohol can kill Every year, people die as a direct result of drinking a lot of alcohol over a short period of time. Alcohol is a poison. Large intakes of alcohol can result in unconsciousness, coma and even death. Sometimes, death is caused by a person vomiting when unconscious, and then suffocating because their airways are blocked by vomit.

18.31 Alcoholism is a dangerous disease.

Alcoholism is a disease in which a person cannot manage without alcohol. The cause of the disease is not fully understood. Although it is obvious that you cannot become an alcoholic if you never drink alcohol, many people regularly drink large quantities of alcohol, but do not become alcoholics. Probably, there are many factors which decide whether or not a person becomes alcoholic. They may include a person's genes, their personality, and the amount of stress in their lives.

An alcoholic needs to drink quite large quantities of alcohol regularly. This causes many parts of the body to be damaged, because alcohol is poisonous to cells. The **liver** is often damaged, because it is the liver which has the job of breaking down alcohol in the body. One form of liver disease resulting from alcohol damage is **cirrhosis**, where fibres grow in the liver. In Britain, about 2000 people a year die from cirrhosis of the liver.

Excessive alcohol drinking also damages the **brain**. Over a long period of time, it can cause loss of memory and confusion. One way in which the damage is done is that alcohol in the body fluids draws water out of cells by osmosis. When this happens to brain cells, they shrink, and may be irreversibly damaged. This osmotic effect is made worse because alcohol inhibits the release of **ADH**, which is a hormone which stops the kidneys from allowing too much water to leave the body in the urine. So drinking alcohol causes a lot of dilute urine to be produced, resulting in low levels of water in the blood.

Chapter revision questions

1 For each of the following types of disease (i) name one example, (ii) briefly describe the cause of your example, and (iii) briefly describe the symptoms of your example:

(You may have to use the index to find information for some of your answers to part (iii).)

(a) a deficiency disease

(b) an inherited disease

(c) a degenerative disease

(d) an infectious disease.

2 Distinguish between each of the following pairs of terms:

(a) phagocytes and lymphocytes

(b) T cells and B cells

(c) antibody and antibiotic

(d) passive immunity and active immunity

(e) vector and pathogen.

3 Explain why:

(a) you can normally get measles only once, but you can get a cold over and over again

(b) babies fed on breast milk are less likely to get an infectious disease than babies fed on bottled milk

(c) transplants are more likely to be successful if the donated organ comes from a close relative of the recipient

(d) it is no use trying to treat a cold with antibiotics.

4 Discuss the ways in which life-style can affect a person's health.

19 Making use of microorganisms

19.1 Biotechnology is not new.

Today, many industrial processes use **biotechnology**. Biotechnology means using living organisms to carry out processes which make substances which we want. The term is normally only used when *micro*organisms are used, or when plants or animals are used to produce something other than food. So most people would not include farming animals and crops for food as biotechnology.

Although the word 'biotechnology' only began to be widely used in the 1970s, we have been using organisms to make things for us for thousands of years. Yeast has been used to make alcoholic drinks, and to make bread, yoghurt and cheese. Bacteria and other organisms have been used to make compost. More recently, we have learned how to use bacteria and protoctists to make waste substances such as sewage harmless. Useful fuels such as biogas may be made by these processes, too.

Even more recently, in the last twenty years or so, genetic engineering has opened up a whole new world of possibilities for biotechnology. With genetic engineering, we can introduce almost any gene we like into microorganisms or other living things. The organisms may then make the protein for which the gene codes. This allows us to grow bacteria which make human hormones, or plants which produce drugs, for example.

19.2 Microorganisms include viruses, bacteria, some fungi and protoctists.

A microorganism is any organism which is too small to be seen without a microscope. Fig 19.1 shows examples of the four groups of microorganisms.

As you probably know, some microorganisms are harmful. Bacteria and fungi may make food go bad. This is described in Sections 4.53 to 4.57. All four of these groups may cause diseases in humans or in crop plants. This is described in Chapter 18.

However, many microorganisms are very useful to us. Bacteria and fungi, in particular, have essential roles to play in the carbon and nitrogen cycles (Sections 12.15 to 12.19). In this chapter, we will look at many other ways, both old and new, in which we make use of microorganisms.

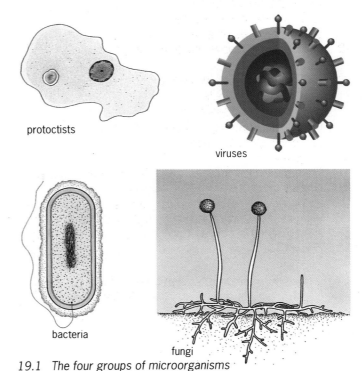

protoctists

viruses

bacteria

fungi

19.1 *The four groups of microorganisms*

Growing microorganisms

19.3 Viruses can only be grown in living cells.

You will not be able to do any experiments with viruses. This is because viruses are very difficult to grow. Viruses can only be grown inside living cells.

Figure 19.2 shows the life cycle of a virus. You can see that it reproduces only when it is inside another living cell. This particular virus reproduces inside a bacterium. Even bacteria can get ill!

Scientists do sometimes need to grow viruses. They may need, for example, to grow viruses which they have taken from someone who is ill, to find out exactly what sort of virus it is. They normally do this by injecting the viruses into hen's eggs, or into a culture of human cells. It takes quite a long time for the viruses to reproduce enough for the scientists to get a large sample of them.

Another reason for wanting to grow viruses is in genetic engineering. Viruses which infect bacteria, like

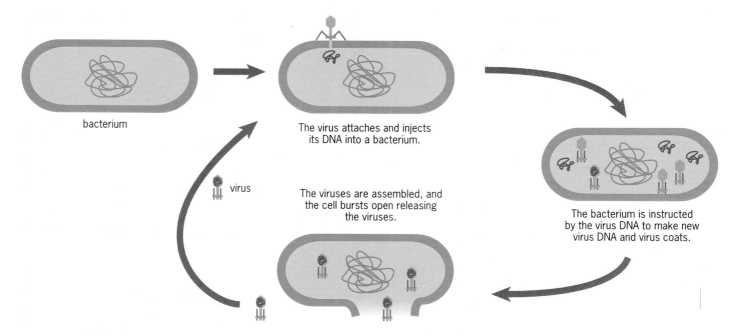

19.2   The life cycle of a virus which infects bacteria

the ones in Fig 19.2, are often used to introduce new genes into the bacteria. You can read about this in Section 19.15.

19.4   Bacteria and fungi can be grown on agar jelly.

Bacteria and fungi are quite easy to grow. You can try one way of growing them in Practical 19.1.

Bacteria and fungi need three things – water, a food source and a warm temperature – if they are to grow and reproduce quickly. Most of them also need oxygen. If we want to grow a large culture of bacteria or fungi, we need to give them good supplies of these four things. When these microorganisms are grown on a large scale, they are often grown in a **fermenter**, which is designed to supply all of their needs. You can see one example in Fig 19.14.

If we want to *stop* them growing, then we need to deprive them of one or more of these things. We do this when we preserve food. Table 4.9 on page 47 gives some examples of how this can be done.

Fact!

Some species of bacteria are the toughest living organisms known. One species of bacterium can survive 10 000 times the human lethal dose of ionising radiation. Another has been found growing in sulphurous sea bed vents in the East Pacific Rise, where the temperature is recorded at 306 °C.

Practical 19.1   Growing bacteria and fungi on agar jelly

In this practical, you are going to grow microorganisms from two different sources, pond water and tap water.

You need to keep all of your apparatus **sterile**. This means that no living microorganisms must be on it. This is because you want to be sure that any bacteria or fungi which you grow have come from the pond water or the tap water.

You will grow the microorganisms on agar jelly. This is made from seaweed. It is bought as a powder, which is mixed with water and then heated to boiling point. This kills any living organisms. The mixture is then allowed to cool to just below 60 °C. It is then poured into a sterile petri dish. It sets in the dish to form a layer of jelly, containing nutrients and water for bacteria and fungi to feed on.

The petri dishes you will use will probably be made of plastic. These are sterilised by the manufacturers (you cannot sterilise them in school by heating them, because they would melt!). When you handle them, you must make sure that you do not allow any microorganisms to get *inside*, except the ones in the pond water or tap water. For example, when the hot agar jelly is poured in, the top of the dish must only be lifted just a little way, and the jelly poured in quickly. Otherwise, microorganisms might drop in from the air.

1   Collect three petri dishes containing sterile agar jelly. Just by handling the dishes, you will get microorganisms on the outside of them – but this does not matter, so long as you do not let any microorganisms get

continued

inside. Use a glass marking pen to label the dishes by writing on the lid. Label one of them **pond water**, another one **tap water**, and the third one **control**. Write your name on the dishes, too.

2 Using Sellotape, tape down the lid of the **control** dish as shown in Fig 19.3. This is done so that the lid cannot accidentally be removed, which could let microorganisms in. Don't tape all around the dish, because air needs to be able to get in.

3 Collect a small container of pond water, and an **inoculating loop**. This is a piece of looped wire attached to a handle. You will use it to spread some pond water onto the agar jelly in the **pond water** dish.

   Before you do this, you need to get rid of any microorganisms on the loop. Fig 19.3 shows you how to do this, and how to spread some pond water onto the agar jelly. When you have done this, tape down the lid as before.

4 Repeat Step 3 using tap water instead of pond water, and spreading in on to the petri dish labelled tap water.

5 Now put the three petri dishes into an incubator at about 25 °C. This temperature is warm enough to let any microorganisms grow quite quickly, but not warm enough to encourage the growth of the sort of microorganisms which might make you ill. (At what temperature do you think such pathogenic microorganisms would grow best?) Put your petri dishes upside down, so that any condensation in the dish does not fall on to the surface of the agar jelly.

6 After a day or so, look at your three dishes to see if anything has grown on them, and make labelled diagrams of each of them. Fig 19.4 shows what a dish might look like. You may see **colonies** of bacteria and fungi on the surface of the agar. Although a single bacterium is much too small to see, if one breeds and forms a colony of many thousand, then they become visible. Each colony on your dish probably grew from just a single microorganism which was in the water which you spread on the agar.

Questions

1 Apart from stopping microorganisms from getting in, can you suggest another reason for taping down the lids of the petri dishes?

2 What was the purpose of the control petri dish?

3 Was there any difference in the numbers or kinds of microorganisms which came from the pond water and the tap water?

4 You have no idea what sort of microorganisms you have grown on your agar jelly. Some of them might be harmful to humans. What do you think should be done with all of the petri dishes once you have finished with them?

(a) Pouring the agar plate

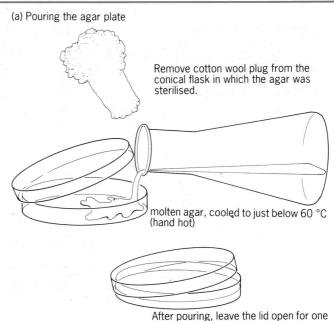

Remove cotton wool plug from the conical flask in which the agar was sterilised.

molten agar, cooled to just below 60 °C (hand hot)

After pouring, leave the lid open for one or two minutes to release steam, and then gently tip the lid down.

(b) Using an inoculating loop

First dry the loop by holding it in hot air *above* the bunsen flame.
Flame the loop by putting it into the flame at an angle. Let the loop and wire get red hot

Dip the loop into your pond water.

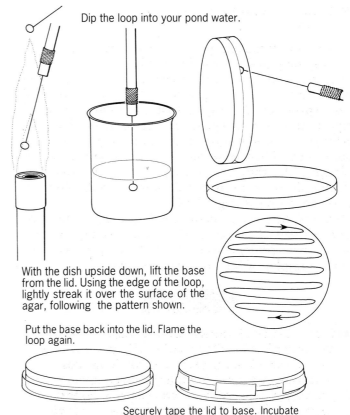

With the dish upside down, lift the base from the lid. Using the edge of the loop, lightly streak it over the surface of the agar, following the pattern shown.

Put the base back into the lid. Flame the loop again.

Securely tape the lid to base. Incubate upside down.

19.3 Growing bacteria on agar

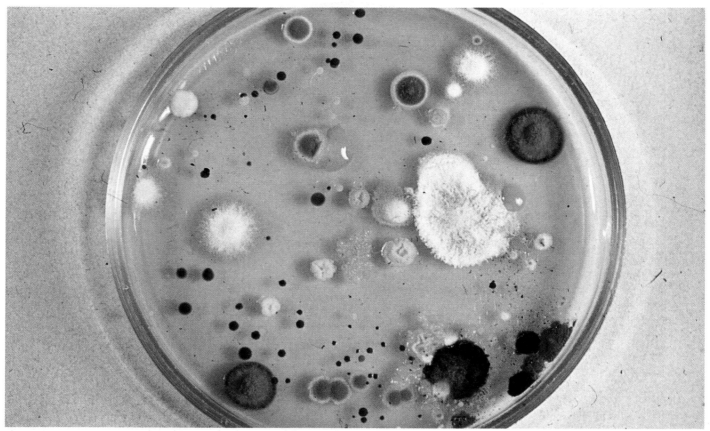

19.4 *Bacteria and fungi growing on agar jelly in a petri dish, which had been left open to the air. The 'furry' colonies are fungi, and the smoother ones bacteria. Each colony probably grew from a single organism which landed on the agar.*

Compost

19.5 Microorganisms and other decomposers make compost.

Most gardeners have a compost heap in their garden. Making compost is a way of recycling garden and kitchen waste. Weeds, old cabbage leaves, tea bags, apple cores, lawn mowings – anything organic – can be put on to the compost heap instead of being thrown away. These organic waste materials gradually rot down to form a dark brown, fibrous material. The compost is an excellent material to put on to soil. It adds nutrients to the soil. It adds humus, which improves the texture of the soil, and helps water retention and aeration.

To make compost, the waste material is piled into a heap, and left for decomposers and saprophytes to rot it down. Large organisms such as earthworms and millipedes are an important part of the process. However, the main workers are microorganisms, mostly bacteria and fungi.

The microorganisms make the best compost if they have three things – air, moisture, and a supply of fixed nitrogen (for example, nitrates or ammonium salts). The process goes faster if the temperature is kept quite high. So a good compost heap is built to supply the microorganisms with all of these things.

Figure 19.5 shows a compost heap. The gaps in the sides and underneath allow air to circulate through. This allows the microorganisms to respire aerobically, rather than anaerobically. If they respire anaerobically, the compost becomes slimy, sticky and smelly, instead of fibrous and pleasant to handle.

Moisture can be provided by leaving the top of the heap uncovered, so that rain falls onto it. However, this may not be necessary if the plant material put into the heap is already quite wet, for example grass mowings. Fixed nitrogen can be provided by adding anything which contains it, such as a sprinkling of ammonium nitrate fertiliser.

The high temperature builds up by itself. As all the microorganisms in the heap feed on the rotting plant material, they respire. They generate a lot of heat in this process. The heap can get so hot that it steams – sometimes, it gets so hot that you cannot hold your hand inside it for more than a second or two. These high temperatures not only help to speed up the rotting process, but they also kill most weed seeds. So you can safely put the compost onto the garden, even if you put a lot of weeds onto the heap, knowing that you are not putting even more weeds back into your soil.

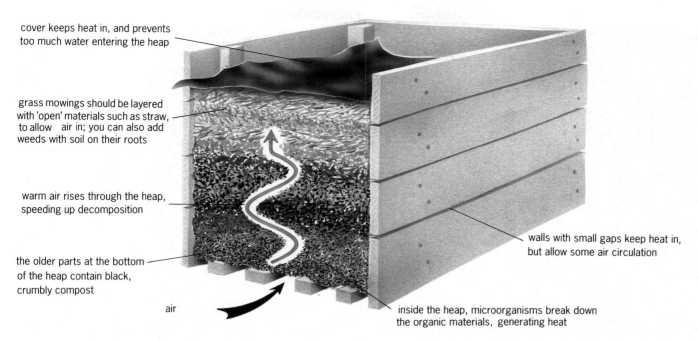

cover keeps heat in, and prevents too much water entering the heap

grass mowings should be layered with 'open' materials such as straw, to allow air in; you can also add weeds with soil on their roots

warm air rises through the heap, speeding up decomposition

the older parts at the bottom of the heap contain black, crumbly compost

air

walls with small gaps keep heat in, but allow some air circulation

inside the heap, microorganisms break down the organic materials, generating heat

19.5 A section through a compost heap

Questions

1 A gardener tells you that she thinks that it is a waste of time to build a compost heap. What could you tell her to persuade her that she is wrong?

2 Suggest how each of the following could help to speed up, or improve, the production of compost:
(a) putting a layer of twigs or tough plant stems in the heap every now and then, instead of just grass mowings
(b) adding horse manure
(c) covering the heap with a tarpaulin
(d) covering the heap with a tarpaulin with some holes in it.

Sewage treatment

19.6 Sewage can be harmful to people and the environment.

Sewage is waste liquid which has come from houses, industry and other parts of villages, towns and cities. Some of it has just run off streets into drains when it rains. Some of it has come from bathrooms and kitchens in people's houses and offices. Some of it has come from factories. Sewage is mostly water, but also contains many other substances. These include urine and faeces, toilet paper, detergents, oil and many other chemicals.

Sewage should not be allowed to run into rivers or the sea before it has been treated. This is because it can harm people and the environment. Untreated sewage is called **raw** sewage.

Raw sewage contains many bacteria and other microorganisms, some of which may be pathogenic. Some examples of these are described in Chapter 18. People who come into contact with raw sewage, especially if it gets into their mouths, may get ill.

Raw sewage contains many substances which provide nutrients for plants and microorganisms. These can cause **eutrophication**. This is described in Section 14.19.

It is therefore very important that sewage is treated to remove any pathogenic organisms, and most of the nutrients, before it is released as **effluent**. Microorganisms play an important part in all the most commonly used methods of sewage treatment.

19.7 Liquids from sewage can be treated by two different methods.

Figure 19.6 shows how sewage is treated to make it safe.

First, the raw sewage is passed through **screens**. These trap large objects such as grit which may have been washed off roads. The screened liquid is then left for a while in **settlement tanks**, where any other insoluble particles drift to the bottom and form a sediment.

There are two different ways in which the resulting liquid can now be treated.

Trickling filters The liquid from the settlement tanks is sprinkled over a trickling filter bed. This is made of small stones and clinker. Many different aerobic microorganisms live on the surface of the stones. Some of them are **aerobic bacteria**, which feed on various

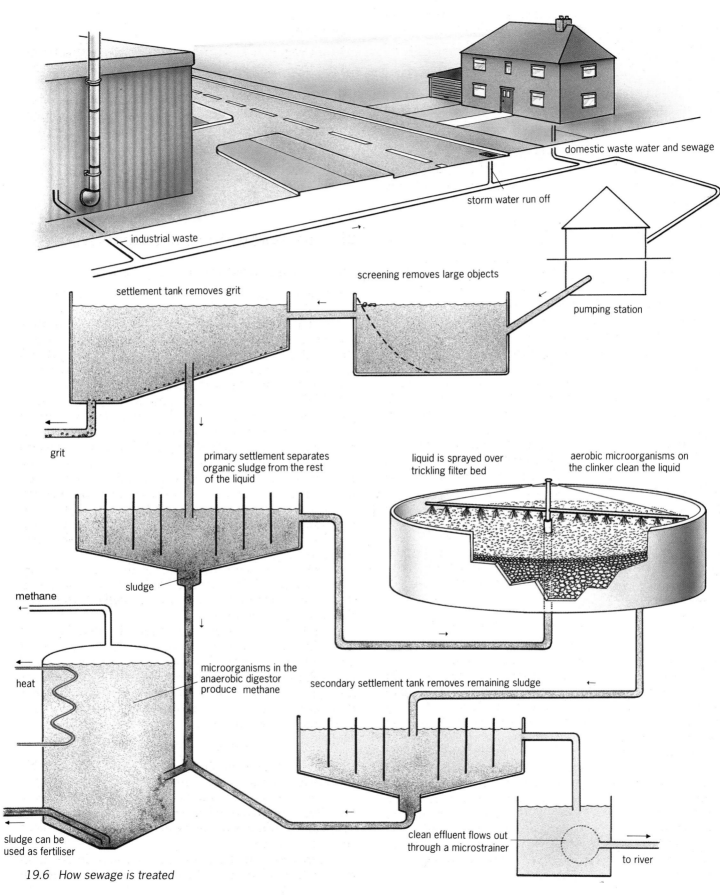

domestic waste water and sewage

storm water run off

industrial waste

screening removes large objects

pumping station

settlement tank removes grit

grit

primary settlement separates organic sludge from the rest of the liquid

liquid is sprayed over trickling filter bed

aerobic microorganisms on the clinker clean the liquid

sludge

methane

heat

microorganisms in the anaerobic digestor produce methane

secondary settlement tank removes remaining sludge

sludge can be used as fertiliser

clean effluent flows out through a microstrainer

to river

19.6 How sewage is treated

288

nutrients in the sewage. **Protoctists** feed on the bacteria. **Fungi** feed saprophytically on soluble nutrients. These microorganisms make up a complex ecosystem in the trickling filter bed.

The liquid is trickled on to the surface of the stones through holes in a rotating pipe. This makes sure that air gets mixed in with the liquid. The liquid trickles quite slowly through the stones, giving the microorganisms plenty of time to work on it. By the time the water drains out of the bottom of the bed, it looks clear, smells clean, contains virtually no pathogenic organisms, and can safely be allowed to run into a river or the sea.

Activated sludge In this method, the liquid from the settlement tanks runs into a tank called an **aeration tank**. Like the trickling filter bed, this contains **aerobic microorganisms**, mostly bacteria and protoctists. Oxygen is provided by bubbling air through the tank. As in the trickling filter bed, these aerobic microorganisms make the sewage harmless.

Why is this method called 'activated sludge'? 'Activated' means that microorganisms are present. Some of the liquid from the tank, containing these microorganisms, is kept to add to the next lot of sewage coming in. 'Sludge' means just what it sounds like! It is a word which describes the semi-solid waste materials in sewage.

Both the trickling filter and the activated sludge methods can run into problems if the sewage contains substances which harm the microorganisms. These include heavy metals such as mercury, disinfectants, or large quantities of detergents. Heavy metals and disinfectants are toxic to many of the microorganisms. Detergents may cause foaming, which stops oxygen getting into the liquid. To solve these problems, the contaminated sewage can be diluted before being allowed to enter the trickling filter bed or the activated sludge tank.

19.8 Sludge can be digested anaerobically.

So far, we have described how the *liquid* part of the sewage is treated. What about the *solid* part?

Solids – sludge – first dropped out of the sewage in the settlement tank. The activated sludge method also produces sludge. This material contains lots of living and dead microorganisms. It contains valuable organic material. It is a pity to waste it.

The sludge can be acted on by **anaerobic bacteria**. The sludge is put into large, closed tanks. Inside the tanks, several different kinds of bacteria act on the sludge. Some of them produce **methane**, which can be used as a fuel. When they have finished, the remaining solid material has to be removed from the tank. It is often used as fertiliser – it is usually quite safe, because it is very unlikely that any pathogenic organisms will have survived all these processes.

Making food with microorganisms

19.9 Yeast is used for making alcohol.

Yeast is a single-celled fungus. Fig 19.7a shows the structure of a yeast cell.

Yeast cells feed **saprophytically**. This means they secrete enzymes from their cells. The enzymes digest the food on which the yeast is living, breaking down large molecules into small ones. The small molecules then diffuse into the yeast cell.

'Wild' yeast grows in many different places. It usually grows on foods which contain sugar, such as fruit. When we grow yeast, we need to provide it with the types of food which it needs. It is usually grown in a solution containing carbohydrate – usually in the form of sugar – and minerals, including ammonium ions. Each yeast cell absorbs the sugar and minerals, and uses some of them to grow. When the cell gets to a certain size, it produces a new cell by budding (Fig 19.7b). Yeast cells reproduce fastest when the temperature is quite warm, around 40 °C.

People have been using yeast for thousands of years to make **alcohol**. If yeast is added to a sugar solution, it absorbs some of the sugar into its cells. It then uses this sugar in respiration.

Usually, the yeast respires **anaerobically**. When it does this, it converts the sugar to ethanol (a type of alcohol) and carbon dioxide. This process is called **alcoholic fermentation**. 'Fermentation' is a name for any type of respiration which makes a product other than carbon dioxide and water. The equation for alcoholic fermentation is:

$$\text{glucose} \rightarrow \text{alcohol} + \text{carbon dioxide} + \text{energy}$$

Many different alcoholic drinks are made in this way. **Beer** is made by providing the yeast with the sugar **maltose**, obtained from germinating barley seeds. Usually, hops are added as well, to give a bitter flavour to the beer. **Wine** is made by providing the yeast with sugar from grapes.

Another use for the alcohol is as a **fuel**. In Brazil in the 1980s and early 1990s, sugar cane was grown

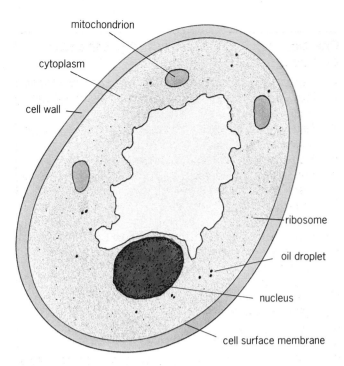

19.7(a) A yeast cell

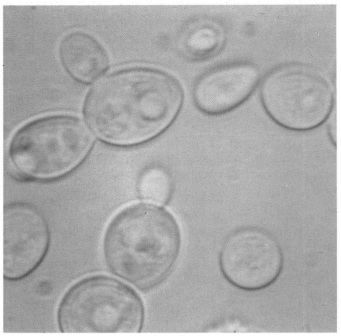

19.7(b) Yeast cells budding

especially for making alcohol. Yeast was grown in sugar solutions made from the cane. The alcohol produced was purified by distillation, and used to fuel motor vehicles. This provides a renewable source of fuel, rather than using fossil fuels which are non-renewable. The alcohol also causes less pollution than fossil fuels, because it does not produce sulphur dioxide and nitrogen oxides when it burns. However, it is an expensive process. In 1994, world fossil fuel prices dropped, making it more economic for Brazil to import fossil fuels rather than to make its own alcohol in this way.

19.10 Yeast is used for making bread.

When yeast respires, it produces carbon dioxide. If this happens inside a dough made from flour and water, the bubbles of carbon dioxide get trapped in the dough, and make it rise. This is how bread is made.

The dough is made using flour made from cereal grains, usually wheat. The flour contains starch, amylase and protein.

The **starch** is the energy source for the yeast. The **amylase** digests the starch to sugar, so that the yeast can absorb it and use it in respiration. Some bread flours have extra amylase added to them to speed up this process. The amylase does not begin acting on the starch until water is mixed with the flour.

The **protein** is important for the texture of the bread. The most important protein in bread flour (apart from the amylase!) is called **gluten**. This forms sticky, stretchy threads as the yeast works on the dough. This helps to trap the bubbles of carbon dioxide, and makes

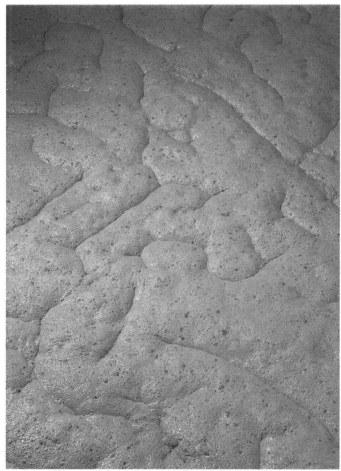

19.8 This is yeast fermenting a maltose solution, to make beer. The froth is formed because the yeast gives off carbon dioxide as it respires.

19.9 *Carbon dioxide produced by respiring yeast caused this bread to rise*

Practical 19.2 What factors affect the way that dough rises?

You can make a 'basic' bread dough in the following way:

1 Mix about 0.5 g of sugar into about 50 cm³ of warm water.
2 Mix about 1 g of dried yeast into the warm sugar solution, and leave for a few minutes.
3 Measure out about 75 g of flour.
4 Add the yeast and sugar mixture to the flour, and pull it around with your hands to make a dough.
5 Leave the dough to rise in a warm place covered with cling film.

There are many factors which affect *how much* the dough rises, and also *how fast* it rises. Choose two factors from the following list to investigate.

(a) temperature
(b) ratio of yeast to flour
(c) addition of salt (sodium chloride)
(d) type of flour used
(e) type of yeast used
(f) addition of 'flour improvers', such as ascorbic acid (vitamin C)
(g) addition of amylase

If you are able to do this practical in a room used for food preparation, then you could bake and eat your bread. However, if you are working in a science laboratory, then it is not safe to do this.

the dough rise well. Farmers who want to sell their wheat for bread making choose varieties which are known to produce grains containing a lot of gluten.

To make bread, yeast, sugar, flour and water are mixed together to make a dough, which is then left in a warm place to rise. The dough is then mixed again, and made into the shapes of the loaves to be made. It is left to rise again, and then baked. The high temperatures kill the yeast, break down the alcohol which it has made, and alter the remaining starch and gluten to make a firm textured bread.

19.11 Bacteria are used to make yoghurt and cheese.

Some bacteria, like yeast, respire anaerobically when provided with a suitable source of sugar. One bacterium which does this is called *Lactobacillus*.

Lactobacillus uses sugar from milk as its energy source. This sugar is called **lactose**. *Lactobacillus* converts the lactose to **lactic acid**.

$$\text{lactose} \rightarrow \text{lactic acid} + \text{energy}$$

Lactic acid, like all acids, tastes sour. However, most people like its taste. The presence of the lactic acid lowers the pH of the milk. This affects the proteins in the milk. They **coagulate**, forming clumps. The milk separates out into these clumps, called **curds**, and a liquid, called **whey**.

All sorts of different foods can be made using *Lactobacillus* and milk. **Yoghurt** is made using a species called *Lactobacillus bulgaricus*. A culture of the bac-

terium is simply added to warm milk, and left for a few hours. Usually, the milk is heated to around 70 °C, and then cooled, before the *L. bulgaricus* is added. This is to kill any other microorganisms in the milk, which might also ferment it, making different, unpleasant-tasting substances.

Other species of *Lactobacillus* are used to make **cheese**. Sometimes, an enzyme called **rennin** is added to the milk along with the *Lactobacillus*. This enzyme acts on the protein in the milk, making it coagulate even more than it would with just the bacterium. The curds and whey are then separated. The whey is used for making sweets, or for animal feeds, or sometimes just thrown away. The curds are pressed and made into cheese. Different kinds of cheeses are made by using different sorts of milk, different mixtures of bacteria, letting the bacteria work at different temperatures, adding different amounts of salt, pressing the curds or leaving them soft, and leaving the cheese to ripen for different lengths of time or in different conditions. No wonder there are so many kinds of cheese!

In some cheeses, **fungi** are added as well. The blue streaks in blue cheeses such as blue Stilton are fungal hyphae. Sometimes, the fungal spores just fall in from the surroundings. This is especially likely if blue cheeses have been made in the same place before – the fungal spores from previous cheeses will be floating around in the air. Usually, though, the spores are intentionally added to the cheese. You can sometimes see that the blue streaks are in straight lines. This is because a thin wire was coated with fungal spores, and then pulled through the curds while they were setting. The fungi need oxygen, so the cheese-maker will also need to make small holes in the cheese to allow air to get into it.

Large holes in cheeses such as Emmenthal are bubbles of carbon dioxide, produced by bacteria.

19.10 *The large cream-coloured lumps in the barrel are curds, which are being made into cheese. The acidity is being checked, to see when the process is ready to move onto the next stage. What makes the curds acid?*

19.12 Bacteria can turn alcohol into vinegar.

A bacterium called *Acetobacter* can convert alcohol into vinegar. Vinegar is a solution of ethanoic acid, which used to be called acetic acid. So you can see how the bacterium got its name.

First, alcohol is made. This is done by letting yeast ferment sugar. The sugar may come from barley; in this case, the sugar is maltose, and the vinegar which will eventually be produced is called malt vinegar. Or it may come from grapes or other fruits, producing wine or cider. The vinegar is then called wine vinegar or cider vinegar.

The *Acetobacter* is then added to the alcohol. A lot of oxygen is needed for it to be able to produce vinegar, so oxygen is bubbled through the liquid. The bacteria are often spread over wood shavings, and the alcohol

Practical 19.3 Making yoghurt

Here is a basic yoghurt recipe. You will need to make sure that all the apparatus you use has been sterilised. If not, then other microorganisms will act on the milk, producing substances which you do not want.

1 Collect some 'live' yoghurt. This is yoghurt which has not been heat treated, so it still contains living *Lactobacillus*. This is your 'starter culture'. You will need roughly 1 cm^3 of starter culture for each sample of yoghurt which you make.
2 Measure 10 cm^3 of milk into a sterile container, such as a test tube.
3 Add the starter culture, and mix gently. Cover the tube with cling film, to stop any other microorganisms getting in.
4 Stand your tube in a water bath or incubator at about 40 °C, and leave for approximately two hours for the bacteria to turn the milk into yoghurt.

Many factors affect the speed at which the yoghurt is formed, and the kind of yoghurt which is made. You can tell what is happening just by looking at your milk/yoghurt, or you could test its pH (because the bacteria are producing lactic acid). Choose two of the following factors, and investigate how they affect the rate of action of the bacteria, and/or the final properties of the yoghurt which is produced.

(a) the type of milk used
(b) the type of starter culture used
(c) whether air can get to the milk or not
(d) the temperature at which the milk is kept
(e) adding lactase to the milk

If you are able to do this practical in a room used for food preparation, then you could taste your yoghurt. However, if you are working in a science laboratory, then it is not safe to do this. You should not eat your yoghurt if you have added anything to your milk and starter culture mixture, such as enzymes, just in case they might make you ill.

trickled over them, rather than just mixing them up in it. This also increases the availability of oxygen to them.

It takes just a few days for the bacteria to convert the alcohol into vinegar. The equation for the reaction is:

$$\text{ethanol} + \text{oxygen} \rightarrow \text{ethanoic acid} + \text{water} + \text{energy}$$

If the bacteria were just given a certain amount of alcohol, and then left until they had turned it all into vinegar, then the whole process would eventually stop. The mixture would have to be removed, the containers cleaned out, and the process begun all over again. To save having to do this, and to speed up the rate at which vinegar is produced, a **continuous culture** process is used. Fig 19.12 shows a continuous culture vessel for

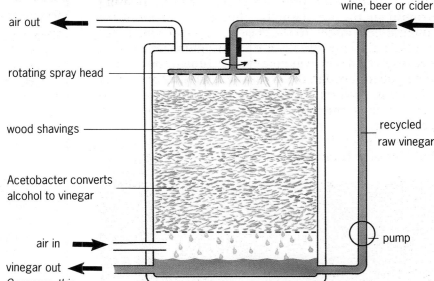

air out

wine, beer or cider

rotating spray head

wood shavings

recycled
raw vinegar

Acetobacter converts
alcohol to vinegar

air in

vinegar out

pump

19.11 This fermenter is used for making vinegar. Compare this picture with Fig 19.12. What goes in through the red pipe which runs up the side of the fermenter and joins the ones at the top? What goes in and out through the other pipes?

19.12 Production of vinegar by continuous culture

the production of vinegar.

To start it off, the bacteria – on their wood shavings – are put into the vessel and given their supply of alcohol. All the time, fresh alcohol is fed into the top of the vessel, and some of the vinegar which the bacteria have made is allowed to run out of the bottom. Some of this 'raw' vinegar is also fed back into the vessel, because it will also contain some unused alcohol. The process can go on for a long time before it needs to be stopped and restarted.

Questions

1 Which of the following processes use **anaerobic fermentation**, and which use **aerobic fermentation**?
   (a) making alcohol from sugar
   (b) making vinegar from alcohol
   (c) making lactic acid from lactose
2 When alcohol, lactic acid or vinegar are being made by microorganisms, the mixture gets hot. Why is this?
3 Look at Fig 19.12. Explain the purpose of each of the following parts of the apparatus:
   (a) the air supply and air vent
   (b) the wood shavings
   (c) the temperature monitors and cooling pipes

19.13 Microorganisms can be used as food.

In the production of alcohol, bread, yoghurt, cheese and vinegar, we use microorganisms to change one substance into another, which we use as food. But we can also use the microorganisms themselves as food.

There are many good arguments for doing this. In many parts of the world, there is a shortage of food, especially protein-rich food. Microorganisms could provide a good source of protein in these areas. Microorganisms do not need soil to grow in. They can use many different substances as food sources, including wastes from other processes – so they could be grown very cheaply. Producing food in this way wastes less energy than producing meat, because it 'taps in' to an earlier stage in the food chain (Section 12.14).

The first attempts to make microorganisms into food used yeast. In Germany during World War I, yeast was cultured in large vats, using molasses as a food source for the yeast, to produce a protein supplement for people. More recently, different kinds of protoctists (usually single-celled photosynthetic ones) and bacteria have been grown for food production. The food made from all of these microorganisms is known as **single cell protein** or **SCP**.

However, there have been big problems in selling SCP as food for people. People are very suspicious of eating microorganisms – even though they like eating yoghurt and cheese! The first SCPs also tasted rather unpleasant, partly because they contained a lot of DNA and RNA, which tastes bitter. Most SCPs are now marketed as animal feed.

One SCP which has found a market as human food, however, is **mycoprotein**. This is made from a fungus. In Britain, the fungus which is used is called *Fusarium*. Its structure is rather like that of *Mucor* (Fig 17.8 on page 258), so it is made of hyphae rather than single cells. But mycoprotein is still often called SCP!

The *Fusarium* is grown in large vats, using carbohydrates as a food source, with other nutrients such as

19.13 *Mycoprotein can be made to look like chunks of meat. It is quite bland in taste, and most people like to cook it with other ingredients, which give it a good flavour.*

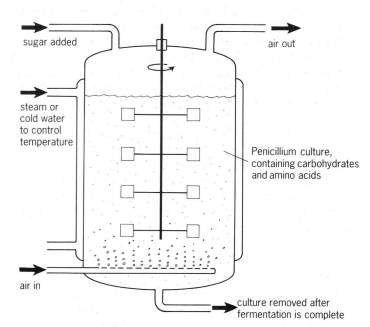

19.14 *A fermenter used for producing penicillin*

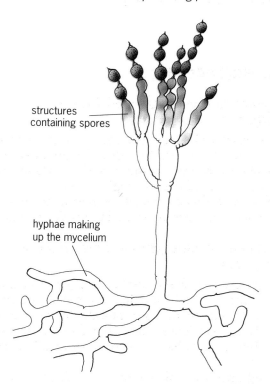

19.15 Penicillium, *the fungus which makes penicillin*

ammonium nitrate added as well. The carbohydrates often come from waste left over from making flour. *Fusarium* reproduces quickly and makes a mass of mycelium, which is harvested and treated to remove a lot of the RNA which it contains. Then it is dried, and shaped into chunks or cakes, ready for eating as it is, or for making into pies or other foods. Some people think that mycoprotein looks and tastes a bit like chicken. If you have not seen any, have a look for some next time you are shopping in a supermarket. It is sold as Quorn®.

Mycoprotein is an excellent food. It has a protein content of 45 %, very little fat, no cholesterol, and a lot of fibre. Because the mycelium of the fungus is made up of long thread-like hyphae, mycoprotein has a fibrous texture which many people like – because it is a bit like meat. It has quite a bland taste, and can easily be flavoured to make a pleasant-tasting food.

Microorganisms and medicine

19.14 Fungi make antibiotics.

Antibiotics are substances which kill bacteria without harming human cells. We take antibiotics to help to cure bacterial infections. You can read about how one of them – penicillin – works, and some of the problems involved with the use of antibiotics, in Section 18.25.

Penicillin is made by growing the fungus *Penicillium* in a large fermenter. It is grown in a culture medium containing carbohydrates and amino acids. The con-

tents of the fermenter look a bit like porridge. They are stirred continuously. This not only keeps the fungus in contact with fresh supplies of nutrients, and mixes oxygen into the culture, but also rolls the fungus up into little pellets. This makes it quite easy to separate the liquid part of the culture – which contains the pencillin – from the fungus, at a later stage.

To begin with, the fungus just grows. This stage takes about 15–24 hours. After that, it begins to secrete penicillin. The rate at which it produces penicillin partly depends on how much sugar it has available. If there is a lot of sugar, then not much penicillin is made. If there is no sugar at all, then no penicillin is made. So small amounts of sugar have to be fed into the fermenter all the time that the fungus is producing penicillin.

The culture is kept going until it is decided that the rate of penicillin production has slowed down so much that it is not worth waiting any longer. This is often after about a week, although the exact time can vary quite a lot on either side of this. Then the culture is filtered, and the liquid treated to concentrate the penicillin which it contains.

Question

1 Penicillin is not produced by a continuous culture method, whereas vinegar is. Look at what happens during the two processes, and explain why penicillin cannot be produced in this way.

Genetic engineering

19.15 Genes can be transferred from one organism to another.

A gene is a length of DNA which codes for the production of a particular protein by a cell. We are now able to take genes from one organism and put them into another. This is called **genetic engineering**.

To explain how this is done, we will look at the way in which genetic engineering is used to produce insulin.

19.16 Human insulin genes are inserted into bacteria.

Some people are not able to make the protein **insulin**. Insulin is a hormone which helps to regulate the concentration of glucose in your blood. People whose bodies cannot make insulin have the disease **diabetes mellitus**. They have to have injections of insulin every day.

For a long time, the only source of insulin was from animals which had been killed for food, such as pigs. Now, genetic engineering has produced bacteria which make human insulin.

The process begins with the extraction of the gene for making insulin from human cells. This is done using enzymes which chop up DNA molecules into short lengths. The particular length of DNA which codes for making insulin is identified, and separated from all the unwanted DNA.

Now the DNA carrying the gene for insulin must be inserted into a bacterium. This is not easy – you cannot just suck up some DNA with a syringe and inject it into a bacterial cell. One way of getting DNA into a bacterium is to use a **plasmid**. A plasmid is a ring of DNA (Fig 19.16), which is able to reproduce itself inside other living cells.

First, some of the DNA in the plasmid is cut out, using enzymes like the ones used for cutting up the human DNA. This leaves a gap in the ring. The human DNA is then mixed up with the plasmid, and a different kind of enzyme added. This enzyme sticks DNA together. It sticks the human DNA into the gap in the plasmid. (You can think of the first kind of enzymes acting like scissors, and this second kind as acting like glue.)

Next, these genetically engineered plasmids are added to a culture of a bacterium. The bacterium most commonly used in genetic engineering is called *Escherichia coli*. A few of the *E. coli* will take up one or more plasmids into their cells. These bacteria now contain the human insulin gene.

The plasmid is behaving as a **vector**. In biology, a vector is something which transfers substances from one kind of organism to another. (Mosquitoes are vectors for the protoctist *Plasmodium*, which causes malaria.)

The bacteria which have taken up the gene are separated from those which have not. These genetically engineered bacteria are now grown in large vats. They follow the instructions on the human DNA, and make insulin. The insulin is secreted into the culture solution in which the bacteria are growing. It can be separated from the solution and purified.

19.17 Many other proteins can be made by genetic engineering.

Several different kinds of proteins are now made by genetically engineered bacteria.

Human growth hormone is now made in this way. This is a hormone normally made by the pituitary gland, which has a wide range of roles in the human body. One of them is, as its name suggests, controlling growth. Children who do not secrete enough growth hormone do not grow properly. For many years, the only treatment for them was injections of growth hormone taken from the pituitary glands of dead people. Not surprisingly, the hormone was in very short supply, and very expensive. There was also the risk of diseases, such as the brain disease Creutzfeld–Jakob disease, being spread from the dead person into the child being given the treatment. Now that genetically engineered human growth hormone is widely available, it is much cheaper and much safer to use.

Factor VIII is also made by genetic engineering. This is a protein normally present in the blood, which helps

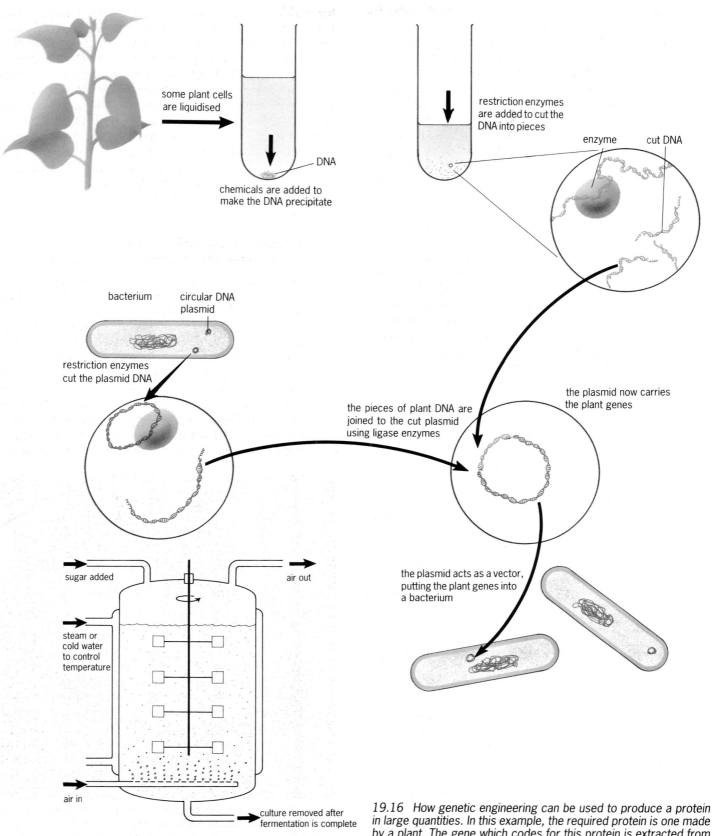

some plant cells are liquidised

chemicals are added to make the DNA precipitate

DNA

restriction enzymes are added to cut the DNA into pieces

enzyme

cut DNA

bacterium

circular DNA plasmid

restriction enzymes cut the plasmid DNA

the pieces of plant DNA are joined to the cut plasmid using ligase enzymes

the plasmid now carries the plant genes

the plasmid acts as a vector, putting the plant genes into a bacterium

sugar added

air out

steam or cold water to control temperature

air in

culture removed after fermentation is complete

the genetically engineered bacteria are grown in a fermenter, where they make the substance coded for by the plant DNA

19.16 How genetic engineering can be used to produce a protein in large quantities. In this example, the required protein is one made by a plant. The gene which codes for this protein is extracted from the plant, and inserted into bacteria, using a plasmid as a vector. This produces genetically engineered bacteria, which can be grown in a fermenter where they synthesise the plant protein.

in clotting. Some people lack the gene which codes for the production of this protein, so their blood cannot clot properly. They have the disease **haemophilia.** (You can read about the inheritance of this disease on page 235.) Until genetic engineering was invented, factor VIII was extracted from donated blood. It was given regularly to people with haemophilia. In the 1970s, when AIDS first appeared and before it was known that it was caused by HIV, many people with haemophilia were given blood containing HIV. They later developed AIDS. (There is no risk of this happening now, because all donated blood is screened to make sure that it does not contain HIV.)

Genetic engineering is also used to produce enzymes used in food manufacture. Enzymes, of course, are proteins, so genes code directly for their production. You may remember that, in cheese making, an enzyme called **rennin** is added to clot the milk. This enzyme was often extracted from the stomachs of calves. Not surprisingly, vegetarians do not want to eat cheese which has been made using this enzyme! However, rennin can now be made by genetically engineered bacteria. Most vegetarians are happy to eat foods such as vegetarian cheese which have been made using this kind of rennin.

19.18 The characteristics of animals and plants can be changed by genetic engineering.

Genetic engineering does not always involve inserting genes into bacteria. It is possible to insert genes into the cells of almost any organism at all.

For example, in tomatoes, there is a gene which controls ripening. Tomatoes with a particular variety of this gene do not go bad so quickly. This makes it easier to transport them from the grower to the shop, and they can be kept on the shelves for longer – they have a longer shelf life. A new variety of tomato has been produced, by genetic engineering, which contains this gene.

Another possible use of genetic engineering in crop plants is to insert genes which give resistance to herbicides (chemicals used to kill weeds). You could then spray your crop with the herbicide, which would kill the weeds and not the crop.

If you look at newspapers and magazines, you will probably find many more examples of genetic engineering being used to produce new varieties of crop plants, because a great deal of money and research is going on in this area at the moment.

We can also insert genes into animal cells, including human cells. Although research is still in its early stages, there are hopes that we may be able to use a technique called **gene therapy** to help people who have genetic diseases like cystic fibrosis. There have been some fairly successful experiments with this so far.

People with cystic fibrosis are lacking a gene needed for making normal mucus in their lungs. This gene has been extracted from human cells, and inserted into a virus. The virus is one which can infect human cells, but it has been damaged in such a way that it should not make you ill. The viruses, containing the human gene, have then been inserted into the air passages of volunteers with cystic fibrosis. The idea is that the viruses – as viruses do – will inject their DNA into the cells lining the respiratory passages. That, of course, will include the human gene which the volunteers are lacking. There are, however, still several problems with this technique, such as the viruses still causing mild illness, or not enough genes getting into the human cells.

19.19 There are social, ethical and moral concerns about genetic engineering.

Genetic engineering, as you have seen, has opened up many possibilities of improving people's lives. It has also opened up many possible dangers.

For example, genetic engineering means producing bacteria and viruses with different genes from their usual ones. This could cause **health hazards.** What if some of these microorganisms were changed in such a way that they became pathogenic? They might cause a new disease, for which there is no cure. To try to make sure that this does not happen, strict regulations are enforced about the kinds of microorganisms which can be used in genetic engineering, the kinds of genes

19.17 *The vessels containing orange liquid are fermenters which are being used to culture genetically engineered mammalian cells. A gene for a particular protein was inserted into a few cells, which were then allowed to multiply. The fermenters provide the cells with perfect conditions for growth and division, and to enable them to produce the protein.*

which can be put into them, and the conditions under which they can be kept. However, what if someone wanted *deliberately* to produce a new pathogen, and release it into the environment?

As well as health hazards, genetic engineering could produce **environmental hazards**. For example, imagine that a new variety of rape is produced, which has been genetically engineered to be resistant to a particular insect which feeds on it. This gene might be passed – perhaps in pollen – to closely related, wild, plants growing nearby. The gene might spread through the population of wild plants. This could upset the food web in the ecosystem, because insects could no longer feed on the wild plants. So far, there have been no instances of this happening, and it is thought to be very unlikely – but it *is* just possible.

Genetic engineering also raises issues about what is morally and ethically acceptable to society. For example, in theory, it will eventually be possible to check the genes in a human zygote, to make sure that there are no major genetic faults. If a fault was found, then the 'right' sort of gene could be inserted into the zygote, so that all the cells in the embryo which developed from it contained this 'right' gene. Should this be allowed? Should it be allowed just for very unpleasant diseases such as cystic fibrosis? Or should it be allowed for things like hair colour or anything else? This is all a long way in the future, but perhaps we should think about it now, before things begin to happen that we are not prepared for.

Like all major new scientific discoveries and inventions, genetic engineering has tremendous potential to provide all sorts of benefits for people, and perhaps also for other living things, as well as equally tremendous potential for harm. Scientists and everyone else must remain well aware of this. If as many people as possible, whether they are scientists or not, try to stay well informed about what developments are taking place, then we can do our best to ensure that the 'good' uses of genetic engineering go ahead, while the potential problems are stopped in their tracks.

Chapter revision questions

1 (a) What is a microorganism?
   (b) describe how one named microorganism is used to make a food eaten by humans.
2 Outline the roles of each of the following in genetic engineering:
   (a) enzymes which cut DNA
   (b) plasmids
   (c) bacteria.
3 Discuss, using particular examples, the possible advantages and disadvantages of being able to transfer DNA from one organism to another.
4 Penicillin is produced by batch culture, whereas vinegar is produced by a continuous culture process. Explain the similarities and differences between these two culture methods.
5 How can microorganisms be used to help to reduce pollution?

Apparatus required for practicals

The apparatus listed is that required for each group performing the experiment.

1.1 Looking at animal cells

section lifter
slide
cover slip
pipette
very small amount of methylene blue (diluted)
filter paper or blotting paper
microscope

1.2 Looking at plant cells

Sections of onion bulb; these can be cut
  beforehand and kept in a beaker of water
slide
cover slip
pipette
filter paper or blotting paper
microscope
seeker or needle

2.1 To show diffusion in a solution

gas jars
crystals of potassium permanganate, copper
  sulphate, potassium dichromate

2.2 To find the effects of different
  solutions on plant cells

solution A – distilled water
solution B – 0.3 M sucrose solution
solution C – 1.0 M sucrose solution
red rhubarb petioles
forceps
scalpel
3 microscope slides
3 cover slips
labels for slides
filter paper or blotting paper
microscope

2.3 To demonstrate osmosis using
  eggs

Session 1:
2 fresh eggs
2 large beakers containing enough dilute HCl to
  cover eggs
Session 2:
deshelled eggs
two large beakers
Chinagraph pencils
distilled water
20% salt solution

2.4 To demonstrate osmosis using
  potatoes

4 petri dishes (lids not needed)
Chinagraph pencil
2 potatoes
apparatus for cooking potatoes
kitchen knife
distilled water
20% salt solution
2 pipettes

3.1 The effect of catalase on
  hydrogen peroxide

safety glasses
raw and boiled potato
yeast suspension, produced by mixing a little
  dried yeast and a little sucrose into warm water
chopped fresh liver
fresh fruit juice
dropper pipettes or other means of transferring
  liquids into tubes
syringe, pipette or measuring cylinder for
  measuring 10 cm^3
about 50 cm^3 of 10 volume or 20 volume
  hydrogen peroxide per group
5 boiling tubes and rack
wooden splint and access to lit Bunsen flame

3.2 Investigating the effect of
  temperature on enzyme activity

four test tubes
beakers
water baths at 35 °C and 80 °C
thermometer
boiling tube
distilled water
10% starch solution
iodine solution
spotting tile
four glass rods
stop watch
Chinagraph pencil
pipette
two syringes to measure 5 cm^3

3.3 Investigating biological washing
  powders

It is not possible to give a detailed apparatus list
  for this practical, as students' designs are likely
  to vary widely.
Notes:
It is easier to obtain quantitative results using
developed film rather than using proteinaceous
stains on cloth. However, students will much
prefer to use 'real' stains on 'real' fabrics. Stains
can be made using egg or 'blood' (in reality
myoglobin) from fresh meat, but teachers would
be well advised to test how such stains perform
beforehand. The best types of fabric to use are
either cotton or polyester cotton.
  For safety reasons, teachers may prefer to use
encapsulated proteases and lipases. These can
be obtained from the:
  National Centre for Biotechnology Education,
  Department of Microbiology,
  University of Reading,
  Whiteknights,
  Reading, RG6 2AJ.
A washing powder enzyme pack, containing five
different enzymes, can be obtained from the
same address.
  Suitable amounts of enzyme to use are in the
range of 1 to 2 g of enzyme for every 100 g of
washing powder. 1 g of this mixture should then
be dissolved in 100 cm^3 of water.

3.4 Investigating the use of pectinase
  in making fruit juice

It is not possible to give a detailed apparatus list
for this practical, as student's designs will vary
widely.
Notes:
The booklet *Practical Biotechnology*, obtainable
from the National Centre for Biotechnology
Education at the address given above in Practical
3.3, gives further details concerning the basis of
these investigations.
  Pectinase and fruit from different sources will
require different proportions of pectinase to fruit.
However, as a general guide, about 1 g of
pectinase to 100 g of crushed fruit will give
reasonably rapid results. This is a much higher
amount than would be used industrially – another
reason why the fruit juice extracted should not be
consumed.

3.5 Using immobilised lactase to make glucose from milk

pasteurised milk
10 cm^3 syringe barrel, fitted with tubing, clamp and nylon gauze as shown in Fig. 3.5
two small beakers
small syringes to measure quantities of 1 to 8 cm^3
small mesh sieve or tea strainer
retort stand, boss and clamp
about 2 cm^3 lactase solution – can be bought as Novo Lactozyme® from the National Centre for Biotechnology Education, see address in Practical 3.3
2% sodium alginate solution
1.5% calcium chloride solution
glucose test strips (e.g. Clinistix or Diastix)

4.1 Testing food for carbohydrates

variety of foods
glucose solution (any strength)
sucrose solution (any strength)
starch power
test tube rack
Bunsen burner
test tube holder
boiling tubes
pipette
tile
scalpel
Benedict's solution
iodine solution
dilute hydrochloric acid
sodium hydrogencarbonate solution

4.2 Testing food for proteins

variety of foods
albumen solution
test tube rack
test tubes
pipettes
tile
scalpel
potassium hydroxide solution
1% copper sulphate solution

4.3 Testing food for fats

variety of foods
cooking oil
test tube rack
clean, dry test tubes
pipette
tile
scalpel
absolute alcohol
distilled water
filter paper

4.4 Testing food for vitamin C

For the basic test:
DCPIP solution. The manufacturers normally recommend working with a solution made by dissolving 1 tablet in 10 cm^3 water, but a less concentrated solution may be preferable – and cheaper. It is well worth trying this out beforehand with the juices to be tested.
test tubes and rack
at least two dropper pipettes
means of measuring 2 cm^3, for example a syringe
fruit juice
Notes:
DCPIP solution should be made up freshly, as prolonged contact with air can affect its performance. Keep it covered while not in immediate use. Some juices, for example lemon juice, do not produce a totally colourless DCPIP solution; it is the loss of the *blue* colour which should be looked for.

This practical suggests adding fruit juice to DCPIP, rather than the other way around, as most students find this easier to understand. However, this can cause problems if students wish to use graduated pipettes or burettes to measure more accurately the volumes of liquid added, because small particles in the juices cause blockages. There is no reason why a standard volume of juice should not be used, and then the amount of DCPIP which can be added, before losing its colour, recorded.

A food processor or blender is very useful for making extracts of fruits or vegetables. Some, such as potatoes, will need to have water added to them.

If students want to make their investigation quantitative, they will need a standard vitamin C solution. Pharmacies sell vitamin C tablets containing stated amounts of ascorbic acid, which can be used to make up such a solution.

5.1 Looking at the epidermis of a leaf

variety of leaves – ivy-leaved toadflax is good
forceps
slides
coverslips
pipette
clear nail varnish

5.2 Using starch phosphorylase to make starch

a small potato
muslin or other cloth for coarse filtration
food blender
centrifuge, preferably one which will spin at around 3000 rpm
at least two dropper pipettes
at least three test tubes, and rack
means of labelling tubes
iodine in potassium iodide solution
white tile or spotting tile
2 cm^3 of 1% glucose-1-phosphate solution

5.3 Testing a leaf for starch

geranium plant which has been photosynthesising
boiling water bath, or beaker etc. as in Fig 5.11
boiling tube
methylated spirits
glass rod
iodine solution
forceps
white tile
pipette

5.4 To see if light is necessary for photosynthesis

Session 1:
geranium plant
Session 2:
destarched plant
apparatus as for 5.3
black paper or aluminium foil
scissors
paperclips
Session 3:
apparatus as for 5.3

5.5 To see if carbon dioxide is necessary for photosynthesis

Session 1:
geranium plant
Session 2:
destarched plant
apparatus as for 5.3
two conical flasks, fitted with split corks
potassium hydroxide solution
distilled water
Vaseline
clamp stands or other means of support for flasks
Session 3:
apparatus as for 5.3

5.6 To see if chlorophyll is necessary for photosynthesis

Session 1:
plant with variegated leaves
Session 2:
destarched plant with variegated leaves
apparatus as for 5.3
Session 3:
apparatus as for 5.3

5.7 To show that oxygen is produced during photosynthesis

Session 1:
large beaker
funnel which fits entirely inside beaker
test tube
Canadian pondweed (*Elodea*) or other water plant
Session 2:
Bunsen burner
splint

6.1 To show that peanuts release energy when they are oxidised

Bunsen burner
heat-proof mat
a peanut
a mounted needle
clamp stand, clamp and boss
boiling or test tube
thermometer

6.2 To show that carbon dioxide is produced in respiration

see Fig 6.3

6.3 To show the uptake of oxygen during respiration

see Fig 6.4

6.4 To show that heat is produced in respiration

Session 1:
pea seeds
beaker
Session 2:
boiled peas
soaked peas from Session 1
mild disinfectant solution
two vacuum flasks
two cotton wool plugs to fit flasks tightly
two thermometers
clamp stands to support flasks

6.5 To show that carbon dioxide is produced when yeast respires anaerobically

four boiling tubes, fitted with bungs and glass
  tubing as in Fig 6.7
boiled, cooled water, or apparatus for boiling it
sucrose or glucose
fresh or dried yeast
boiled yeast solution
glass rod
pipette
lime water or hydrogencarbonate indicator
  solution
two beakers to support boiling tubes
Chinagraph pencil
liquid paraffin

6.6 Examining lungs

set of sheep's or cow's lungs
burette tube

6.7 Using a model to show the action of the diaphragm

see Fig 6.19

6.8 Comparing the carbon dioxide content of inspired and expired air

see Fig 6.20

6.9 Investigating how breathing rate changes with exercise

stop watch
A good exercise in a confined space is stepping
  on and off a chair.

6.10 Investigating the structure of gills

small fish, e.g. sprat
seeker
scissors
petri dish

6.11 To investigate the effect that plants and animals have on the carbon dioxide concentration of water

four boiling or specimen tubes, fitted with bungs
Elodea or other pond weed
snails or other pond animals
hydrogencarbonate indicator solution
(This experiment may also be performed with
terrestrial animals such as woodlice, or leaves of
a terrestrial plant, held above the indicator
solution on a gauze platform.)

7.1 To find the effect of exercise on the rate of heart beat

stop watch

7.2 To see which part of a stem transports water and solutes

Session 1:
freshly-pulled groundsel plant
Eosin solution
beaker
Session 2:
plant from Session 1
slide
cover slip
razor blade
tile
paint brush or section lifter
pipette
microscope

7.3 To see which surface of a leaf loses most water

potted plant with smooth leaves
forceps
cobalt chloride paper in desiccator
self-adhesive book covering film
scissors

7.4 To measure the rate of transpiration of a potted plant

two plants of similar size, in pots of the same size
two large polythene bags
rubber bands
Vaseline
balance

7.5 Using a potometer to compare rates of transpiration under different conditions

a potometer (not necessarily of the type in
  Fig 7.29)
plant with firm stems, such as geranium, which
  will fit tightly into the apparatus
wire
pliers
Vaseline
stop watch
electric fan

8.1 Examining the structure of a hen's egg

hard boiled egg
fresh unfertilised egg
one fertilised egg for demonstration, with a
  window cut in the top of the shell
two petri dishes
paper towel
blunt forceps
binocular microscope
tile
kitchen knife

8.2 Investigating the structure of a wallflower

flower stalk of wallflower (*Cheiranthus*) or other
  simple insect-pollinated flower, with flowers in
  various stages of development
hand lens
razor blade
tile
microscope slide
microscope
seeker

8.3 Growing pollen tubes

four cavity slides
Vaseline
four cover slips
labels for slides
variety of sugar solutions, e.g. distilled water
5% sucrose
10% sucrose
15% sucrose, each with a very small amount of
  boric acid added
four types of flowers, with ripe pollen
seeker
microscope
incubator at 20 °C

8.4 To find the conditions necessary for the germination of mustard seeds

five test tubes, fitted with gauze or perforated
  zinc platforms
pyrogallol in NaOH solution (take care, this is
  very caustic)
cotton wool
one rubber bung to fit test tube
test tube racks
mustard seeds
Chinagraph pencil

9.1 To find which part of the skin contains the most touch receptors

two pins
Plasticene or piece of polystyrene, through which
  pins may be pushed to support them in position
ruler

9.2 To see which parts of the tongue can taste which flavours

solutions of salt, sugar, quinine and lemon juice
4 straws or cotton wool sticks

9.3 Looking at human eyes

small mirror

9.4 Dissecting a sheep's eye

a sheep, bullock, or pig eye
dissecting board or dish
forceps, scalpel and scissors
newspaper
paper towels

9.5 Measuring reaction time

stop watch

9.6 To find out how shoots respond to light

3 petri dishes
Chinagraph pencil
cotton wool or filter paper
mustard seeds
2 light-proof boxes, one with a slit in one end
clinostat

9.7 To find out how roots respond to gravity

Session 1:
broad bean seeds
blotting paper
gas jars
Session 2:
2 clinostats
blotting paper
pins

10.1 Investigating the effect of size and covering on rate of cooling

beaker
Bunsen burner, tripod, heatproof mat and gauze
paper towel or cloth for holding hot beaker
enough cotton wool to cover a boiling tube
one rubber band
test tube rack to hold boiling tubes
one small test tube
two large boiling tubes
Chinagraph pencil or marker pen
thermometer
stop clock
corks to fit each tube

10.2 Investigating the effect of evaporation on rate of cooling

It is quite possible to include this investigation in
Investigation 10.1, simply by adding another
boiling tube which is wrapped in wet cotton wool.
However, this introduces a lot of ideas
simultaneously, and, unless the students are of
high ability or are already familiar with these
ideas, it is probably best to separate them.
2 retort stands, clamps and bosses
2 thermometers
cotton wool
rubber bands
stop clock

11.1 Using a model arm to investigate the action of the biceps muscle

see Fig 11.13
variety of weights
spring balance

12.1 Estimating the size of a bead population, using the mark, release, recapture technique

large tray or bucket
about 1,000 beads of one colour and size
about 50 more beads of the same size, but a
    different colour

13.1 Making a rough estimate of the proportions of particles of different sizes in a soil sample

sample of soil, enough to fill a gas jar
gas jar
large stirring rod

13.2 To estimate the percentage of water in a soil sample

Session 1:
evaporating dish
spatula
balance
soil sample
oven set at about 50 °C
Session 2:
soil sample from Session 1
balance

13.3 To estimate the percentage of humus in a soil sample

Session 1:
dried soil sample from Investigation 13.2
balance
Bunsen etc. and crucible, or oven at very high
    temperature
Session 2:
cooled sample from Session 1
balance

13.4 To find the effect of lime on clay particles

small sample of powdered clay
boiling tube
glass rod
small amount of calcium hydroxide or oxide
spatula

15.1 Breeding beads

two containers
150 beads of one colour
100 beads of a second colour

16.2 The results of artificial selection

A crab-apple fruit, and any variety of cultivated
apple

19.1 Growing bacteria and fungi on agar jelly

sterile Petri dishes, ready poured with nutrient
    agar
glass marking pen
inoculating loop, and access to Bunsen flame
pond water in small container
Sellotape
incubator at about 25 °C

19.2 What factors affect the way that dough rises

For the basic bread dough:
a little sugar
a little dried yeast
about 75 g of strong flour
a beaker or other container for mixing
To measure how fast or how much the dough
    rises, it can be left to rise in a transparent
    measuring cylinder.
For investigating the factors suggested, the
    following materials will be needed:
thermometer
sodium chloride
different types of flour, e.g. plain, strong, white,
    brown, rye, etc.
different types of yeast, e.g. fresh, dried,
    brewers etc.
ascorbic acid (vitamin C)
amylase
The time taken for the dough to rise varies
considerably; this is largely dependent on the
activity of the yeast used, and it is well worth
finding a good source of active yeast in order to
speed up the results from this investigation.
Students will almost certainly need to visit their
dough some time after their lesson has ended, in
order to measure its volume.

19.3 Making yoghurt

a starter culture of 'live' yoghurt – plain live,
    unpasteurised yoghurt can be bought in large
    supermarkets and health food shops
sterile containers in which the yoghurt can be
    made, for example test tubes
sterile syringe or small measuring cylinder for
    measuring 10 cm^3 – alternatively, a line can be
    drawn on the test tubes at a level
    approximating to this volume
pasteurised milk
cling film
water bath or incubator at about 40 °C
For investigating the factors suggested, the
following materials will be needed:
Universal Indicator paper
lactase
different types of milk, e.g. raw, sterilised, UHT,
    goat's
different types of starter culture
water baths or incubators at different
    temperatures

Glossary

abiotic factor: an influence on an organism caused by a non-living feature of its environment.

absorption: the uptake of a substance into the cells of an organism's body.

accommodation: the adjustment of the shape of the lens and eyeball, so that light is focused accurately onto the retina.

acid rain: rain containing above normal amounts of dissolved sulphur oxides and nitrogen oxides.

actin: the protein making up the thin filaments of muscle fibres.

active site: the part of an enzyme molecule in which the substrate binds.

active transport: the movement of substances through cell membranes, using energy. The energy is in the form of ATP, which is first made by respiration. The substances are often moved against their concentration gradient.

adaptation: a feature of an organism which enables it to live successfully in its environment.

ADH: antidiuretic hormone; a hormone secreted by the pituitary gland when the amount of water in the blood is low, which increases the reabsorption of water by the kidneys.

adolescence: the time between childhood and adulthood.

ADP: adenosine diphosphate – a substance found in all living cells, which is converted to ATP during respiration.

adventitious root: a root growing out of a stem.

aerobic respiration: the release of energy from glucose, by combining it with oxygen.

afterbirth: the placenta, which leaves the mother's body through the vagina, just after the baby is born.

age pyramid: a type of graph showing the relative numbers of each age group of a population.

agglutination: the clumping together of cells, due to the action of antibodies.

albumen: a protein which forms a jelly-like substance when dissolved in water, and which is found in egg-white.

alga: a simple plant, with no stems or roots.

alleles: different varieties of a gene, which code for different versions of the same characteristic.

amino acids: molecules containing carbon, hydrogen, oxygen, nitrogen and sometimes sulphur. A long chain of amino acids forms a protein molecule.

amnion: a membrane surrounding a developing fetus.

amniotic fluid: the liquid contained within the amnion, which supports the fetus and protects it.

ampulla: a swelling at one end of each of the semi-circular canals in the ear, containing cells which detect movements of the head.

amylase: an enzyme which digests starch to maltose.

anaemia: a disease caused by lack of haemoglobin, often because of a shortage of iron.

anaerobic respiration: the release of energy from glucose, without combining it with oxygen.

androgen: a hormone which produces male characteristics.

annual: a plant which completes its life cycle within one year or less.

antagonistic: antagonistic muscles work in pairs, one causing the joint to bend, and the other causing it to straighten.

anther: the part of a flower where male gametes are produced.

antibiotic: a drug which kills bacteria without harming other cells.

antibodies: proteins made by white cells which attach to specific foreign cells or other substances (antigens) and help to destroy them.

antigen: a cell or other substance which is recognised as foreign by the body's white cells.

aquatic: living in water.

arachnid: a spider or scorpion; an arthropod with eight or more legs, which breathes by means of book lungs.

arthropod: an invertebrate with jointed legs.

articulation: the movement of two bones at a joint.

artificial selection: the selection and breeding by man of the best varieties of domestic animals and plants, in order to improve the strain.

assimilation: the incorporation of absorbed food into various parts of the body.

atherosclerosis: hardening of the arteries; a disease caused by deposits of cholesterol in artery walls.

ATP: adenosine triphosphate; a high-energy compound, found in all living cells.

atrio-ventricular: between the atria and ventricles of the heart.

atrium: one of the upper chambers of the heart, which receive blood from the veins and pass it on to the ventricles.

autotrophic nutrition: feeding by converting inorganic materials into organic ones.

auxin: a hormone produced in the meristems of plants, which affects cell elongation.

axon: a long process stretching from the cell body of a neuron, which carries impulses away from the cell body.

balanced diet: a daily intake of food containing all types of food in the correct proportions.

ball and socket joint: a joint where a 'ball' on one bone fits into a 'socket' on another, allowing a circular movement.

beri-beri: a disease caused by lack of vitamin B$_1$. The symptoms are weak muscles and tiredness.

bicuspid valve: the valve between the left atrium and ventricle of the heart.

bile: a liquid made by the liver, stored in the gall bladder, and passed into the duodenum along the bile duct.

bile salts: substances found in bile, which emulsify fats in the duodenum.

binary fission: a form of asexual reproduction in which one cell splits into two.

biological control: the use of 'natural' methods, such as parasites or predators, to control a pest population.

biosensor: an instrument which uses enzymes to detect or measure the amounts of a particular substance present in fluids. The reaction catalysed by the enzyme produces a change in the current flowing in the instrument.

biotic factor: an influence on an organism, caused by other organisms.

blind spot: the part of the retina where the optic nerve leaves; it has no receptor cells, and so light falling onto it cannot be sensed.

bolus: a ball of food formed after chewing, which is swallowed.

bone marrow: a cavity of some bones where blood cells are made.

bronchiole: a small tube carrying air to and from the alveoli in the lungs.

bronchitis: an infection in the bronchi, causing coughing.

bronchus: a large tube connecting the trachea to the bronchioles.

bulb: an underground bud, consisting of a short stem and many fleshy leaves tightly packed together.

caecum: part of the alimentary canal next to the appendix, used for cellulose digestion in some herbivores.

cambium: a tissue found in the stems and roots of plants, made of cells which can divide.

cancer: a disease resulting from the uncontrolled division of cells in one or more parts of the body.

canine: a pointed tooth between the incisors and premolars, used by carnivores for killing prey and tearing meat.

carbohydrase: an enzyme which breaks down carbohydrate molecules.

carbohydrate: sugars and starches; a substance made of carbon, hydrogen and oxygen, where the ratio of hydrogen to oxygen atoms is 2:1.

carpel: one of the bones in the wrist.

carnassial teeth: the largest premolars of a carnivore, which slice past each other to crush bones.

carnivore: an animal which feeds on other animals which it kills.

carrier: a heterozygous organism, possessing a recessive gene which does not show in its phenotype.

cartilage: a tissue made of living cells in a matrix of collagen. It is found in several places in the mammalian skeleton, and makes up the entire skeleton of sharks.

casein: a protein found in milk.

catalyst: a substance which alters the rate of a reaction, without being changed itself.

cell sap: a solution of sugars, amino acids and many other substances, found in the vacuoles of plant cells.

cell surface membrane: a very thin layer of protein and fat, which surrounds the protoplasm of every living cell. Membranes are also found inside cells.

cellulase: an enzyme which breaks down cellulose molecules.

cellulose: a polysaccharide (long-chain carbohydrate) with molecules made from glucose molecules linked together in very long chains. Cellulose forms fibres, which make up the cell walls of plants.

cerebellum: an area of the brain which controls muscular co-ordination.

cerebrum: the part of the brain responsible for conscious thought, language and personality. In mammals it is very large and folded, and forms two cerebral hemispheres.

chalaza: a coil of albumen which supports the yolk in the centre of a bird's egg.

chitin: a carbohydrate-like substance which makes up the exoskeleton of insects.

chlorophyll: a green pigment found in all plants and some bacteria and protoctists, which absorbs energy from sunlight to be used in photosynthesis.

chloroplasts: organelles found in many plant cells, which contain chlorophyll, and where photosynthesis takes place.

chordate: an animal with a supporting rod running inside its dorsal surface. Vertebrates are the most familiar chordates.

choroid: a black layer lining the eye, which absorbs light and so cuts down reflections inside the eye.

chromosome: a coiled thread of DNA and protein, found in the nucleus of cells.

chyme: a mixture of partly digested food, enzymes and hydrochloric acid – the result of digestion in the stomach.

cilia: small hair-like structures which project from some cells, and perform waving movements in synchrony with each other.

ciliary muscle: a ring of muscle surrounding the lens in the eye, which can adjust the size of the lens.

climax community: the mixture of species of plants and animals which will finally exist in an environment.

clone: a group of genetically identical organisms.

cochlea: a coiled tube in the inner ear, containing cells which are sensitive to sound waves.

codominance: the existence of two alleles for a characteristic where neither is dominant over the other.

coelomic fluid: the fluid which fills up the space, or coelom, in an earthworm, and also in vertebrates.

coleoptile: a protective sheath which covers the plumule of a seedling of oats, barley, grasses etc.

collagen: a protein which is found in bone and many other tissues.

colon: the part of the alimentary canal between the ileum and the rectum, where water is absorbed.

community: all the organisms which live in a particular habitat.

companion cell: a cell found next to a sieve tube element in phloem tissue.

connective tissue: any tissue which fills in spaces, or connects various parts of the body, e.g. adipose tissue.

conservation: maintaining the environment in a state in which natural wildlife can flourish.

consumer: an organism which consumes other organisms for food; all animals are consumers.

continuous variation: variation in which organisms do not belong to definite categories, but may fit anywhere within a wide range.

contraception: the prevention of fertilisation as a result of sexual intercourse.

contractile vacuole: a vacuole found in *Amoeba* and many other protoctists, in which excess water is collected before being emptied out of the cell.

control: a piece of apparatus identical in every way to the experimental apparatus, except for the one thing whose effect you are investigating.

cork cambium: a layer of meristematic (dividing) cells which produce cork cells.

cornified layer: a layer of dead cells, containing keratin, on the surface of skin. It protects and waterproofs the layers underneath it.

corpus luteum: a structure in a mammalian ovary, formed from a follicle, which secretes the hormone progesterone.

cortex: (a) the part of a stem or root between and around the vascular bundles or stele.
(b) the outer part of a kidney.

cretin: a child whose thyroid gland does not function properly, resulting in retarded mental and physical development.

cupula: a structure inside a semi-circular canal, which moves as the head moves, and stimulates sensory cells embedded in it.

cuticle: a waxy, waterproof covering, found on various parts of various organisms, e.g. leaves of plants and the exoskeleton of insects.

deamination: a reaction which takes place in the liver, where amino acids are converted to urea and carbohydrate.

deciduous tree: a tree which sheds all its leaves in autumn.

deforestation: the removal of forest.

denitrifying bacteria: bacteria which often live in damp soil, and which convert nitrates into nitrogen gas.

dermis: the inner layer of skin, make of connective tissue and containing capillaries, nerve endings etc.

destarching: keeping a plant in the dark, so it cannot photosynthesise and will use up its starch stores.

diabetes: a disease caused by insufficient secretion of insulin by the pancreas, resulting in widely fluctuating blood glucose levels.

dialysis: the separation of a mixture of dissolved solutes by diffusion through a selectively permeable membrane.

diastema: a toothless gap found in many herbivores, between the incisors and premolars.

diastole: the stage in heart beat when muscles are relaxed.

dichotomous key: a way of identifying an organism, in which you are given successive pairs of descriptions to choose between.

diffusion: the movement of particles of gas, solvent or solute, from an area of high concentration to an area of low concentration.

diploid cell: a cell which has two of each kind of chromosome.

disaccharide: a sugar made of molecules which consist of two monosaccharide units joined together, with no intermediates.

DNA: deoxyribonucleic acid; a substance found in chromosomes, which carries a code used by the cell when making proteins.

dominant allele: an allele which has the same effect on the phenotype of an organism, whether the organism is homozygous or heterozygous for that gene.

Down's syndrome: a condition caused by having an extra chromosome, where full mental development does not take place.

duodenum: a short length of alimentary canal between the stomach and the jejunum, into which the bile duct and the pancreatic duct empty bile and pancreatic juice.

ecdysis: moulting; the shedding of the exoskeleton of an insect or other arthropod.

ecosystem: the living organisms and their environment, in a certain area – e.g. a wood, or a pond.

effector: a part of an organism which carries out an action, often in response to a stimulus, e.g. muscles and glands.

egestion: the removal of indigestible food from the body.

embryo: a plant or animal as it develops from a fertilised egg.

emulsification: the breaking up of large droplets of fat into small ones.

endolymph: the fluid contained in the central chamber of the cochlea.

endoplasmic reticulum: a network of membranes in the cytoplasm of cells, where large molecules are built up from small ones.

enzymes: biological catalysts; proteins made by living organisms, which speed up chemical reactions.

epidermis: an outer covering made of one or more layers of cells, found in many parts of many organisms.

epithelium: a tissue which covers surfaces either inside or outside the body.

etiolated plant: a plant which has grown in insufficient light, and is yellow, thin, and taller than normal.

Eustachian tube: an air-filled tube leading from middle ear to the back of the throat.

eutrophication: a process in which extra nutrients are added to water, so increasing the growth of plants and bacteria, and reducing oxygen levels.

extensor: a muscle which straightens a limb when it contracts.

extracellular: outside cells.

faeces: remains of indigestible food, bacteria, mucus etc., which are egested from the alimentary canal.

family: a group of genera with similar characteristics.

fat, saturated: the type of fat found in many animal products such as meat, milk, butter and chocolate.

fat, unsaturated: the type of fat found in many plant products such as olive oil, sunflower oil.

fatty acids: molecules made of long chains of carbon atoms with many hydrogen atoms and some oxygen atoms attached to them. Fatty acids can combine with glycerol to make fats.

fermentation: the conversion of sugar into alcohol and carbon dioxide, often by yeast, by means of anaerobic respiration.

fermenter: a vessel in which microorganisms such as fungi or bacteria are grown under controlled conditions, usually on a large scale, in order to produce substances such as alcohol, antibiotics or food substances.

fertilisation: the joining together of the nucleus of a male gamete with the nucleus of a female gamete.

fetus: a mammalian embryo in a fairly advanced stage of development.

flaccid: a flaccid plant cell is one which has lost water, so that the cytoplasm does not push outward on the cell wall.

flexor: a muscle which bends a limb when it contracts.

flocculation: the clumping of clay particles into larger crumbs, which can be caused by the addition of lime.

fovea: the part of the retina where receptor cells are most densely packed, and onto which light is normally focused.

fruit: a plant's ovary after fertilisation; it contains seeds, and usually helps in their dispersal.

gamete: a sex cell, containing only one of each kind of chromosome (i.e. haploid). Eggs and sperm are gametes.

gene: a length of DNA which codes for the making of a particular protein.

genetic engineering: the manipulation of genetic material to produce new types of organisms.

genotype: the genes possessed by an organism.

genus: a group of species with similar characteristics.

geotropism: the directional response of a plant, by growth, to gravity.

gestation period: the time between fertilisation and birth.

glomerulus: a tangle of blood capillaries inside the cup of a Bowman's capsule in the kidney.

glucagon: a hormone secreted by the islets of Langerhans in the pancreas in response to low concentrations of glucose in the blood. It stimulates the liver to release glucose from its glycogen stores, so raising blood glucose concentration.

glycerol: an organic molecule containing carbon, hydrogen and oxygen, which forms the backbone of many kinds of fat molecules.

glycogen: a polysaccharide used as a storage substance in the cells of many animals and fungi; in humans, it is stored in liver and muscle cells.

graft: a piece of one organism which is attached to another in such a way that it will become part of it.

greenhouse effect: the trapping of heat by a layer of gases in the Earth's atmosphere, especially carbon dioxide, water vapour and methane. Without this effect, the Earth would be too cold to sustain life.

habitat: the place where an organism lives.

haemoglobin: a protein containing iron, found in red blood cells, which carries oxygen.

haploid: having only one of each kind of chromosome.

hepatic: of the liver.

herbaceous: a plant with little or no wood, normally dying back in the winter.

herbivore: an animal which eats plants.

hermaphrodite: able to make both male and female gametes.

heterotrophic: using food made by other organisms; all animals and fungi are heterotrophic.

heterozygous: possessing two different alleles for a certain characteristic.

hinge joint: a joint such as the elbow or knee, where movement is possible in one plane only.

holozoic nutrition: feeding by taking in pieces of food which are digested inside the alimentary canal, as mammals do.

homeostasis: the maintenance of a constant internal environment.

homeothermic: able to maintain a constant body temperature.

homologous chromosomes: chromosomes which carry genes for the same characteristics in the same positions.

homologous structures: structures which are used for different purposes, but which appear to be built to the same basic design, e.g. the limbs of a bat and a horse.

homozygous: possessing two identical alleles for a certain characteristic.

hormone: a chemical which is made in one part of an organism, and travels through it to affect another part.

hypothalamus: a part of the brain to which the pituitary gland is joined, and which is responsible for several aspects of homeostasis, such as temperature regulation.

hypothermia: having a body temperature dangerously below normal.

ileum: the part of the alimentary canal between the duodenum and colon; it is very long, and is lined with villi to help with absorption of digested food.

immunity: the possession of antibodies against a particular disease.

immunosuppressants: drugs which stop a person's immune system from responding to antigens. They are used to prevent the rejection of a transplanted organ.

incisor: a tooth at the front of a mammal's mouth, normally used for biting off pieces of food for chewing.

ingestion: taking food into the alimentary canal.

insecticide: a chemical which kills insects.

insecticide, systemic: an insecticide which is taken into a plant's vascular bundles, and so is carried to all parts of it.

instar: a stage between moults of an insect which has incomplete metamorphosis (e.g. locust), where each stage becomes progressively more like the adult.

integument: a covering.

interferon: a chemical produced by virus-infected cells, which acts locally to inhibit virus infection of other cells.

intracellular: inside cells.

islets of Langerhans: patches of cells in the pancreas which secrete insulin and glucagon.

karyotype: the shapes, sizes and numbers of the chromosomes in a cell.

keratin: the protein which makes up hair, nail, horn and the outer layer of skin.

kwashiorkor: a type of malnutrition caused by a lack of protein in the diet.

lactase: an enzyme which breaks down the disaccharide lactose into monosaccharides.

lactation: the secretion of milk by a female mammal.

lacteal: a lymphatic vessel inside a villus, which looks milky because it contains absorbed fat.

lactic acid: a chemical produced during anaerobic respiration in animals.

lactose: milk sugar; a disaccharide found in milk.

lamina: the blade of a leaf.

larva: a young organism which looks very unlike its parent, e.g. a caterpillar or tadpole.

leaching: the loss of soluble substances from soil, as they are washed out by rain water.

lenticel: an area in a woody stem where the cells are loosely packed, allowing gas exchange to take place.

lignin: the substance present in the walls of xylem vessels; wood contains lignin.

limiting factor: a factor whose supply limits the rate of a metabolic reaction; e.g. low light intensity may limit the rate at which photosynthesis takes place.

lipase: an enzyme which digests fats.

long sight: being unable to focus on nearby objects.

lumen: the space in the middle of a tube.

lymph node: an organ through which lymph flows, containing many white cells, and where antibodies are made.

lysozyme: an enzyme found in tears, which can destroy bacteria.

malnutrition: a condition caused by eating an unbalanced diet, especially if the diet is badly lacking in one or more types of food.

Malpighian layer: a layer of cells at the base of the epidermis in the skin, which divide to provide new cells, and which contain the pigment melanin.

maltase: an enzyme which digests the disaccharide maltose.

maltose: a disaccharide found in germinating seeds, formed from the breakdown of starch.

mechanical digestion: the breakdown of large particles of food into small ones, by teeth and the churning movements produced by muscles.

medulla: the part of a kidney between the cortex and the pelvis.

medulla oblongata: the part of the brain nearest to the spinal cord, responsible for the control of heart-beat, breathing movements etc.

meiosis: a type of cell division in which homologous chromosomes separate, resulting in four haploid cells being produced by one diploid cell.

meninges: membranes surrounding the brain and spinal cord.

menstruation: the breakdown and loss of the soft lining of the uterus.

meristem: a part of a plant which contains cells which can divide.

mesophyll: the central layers of a leaf, where photosynthesis takes place.

metabolism: the chemical reactions taking place in a living organism.

metamorphosis: a change from a larva to an adult organism.

microclimate: the climate in a small area, such as under a log.

micropyle: a small gap in the integuments of an ovule, through which the pollen tube grows. Later, when the ovule becomes a seed, the micropyle remains as a hole through which water enters at germination.

mitosis: a type of cell division in which two identical cells are formed from a parent cell.

mitral valve: the valve between the left atrium and ventricle.

molar: a large tooth near the back of a mammal's mouth, used for chewing, grinding or slicing.

monoclonal antibodies: antibodies all made by the same clone of lymphocytes, and therefore all identical.

monosaccharide: a simple sugar: a sugar whose molecules are made of a single sugar unit.

mucus: a slimy liquid, secreted by goblet cells, used in many parts of the body for lubrication.

mutation: an unpredictable change in an organism's genes or chromosomes.

mycelium: the tangle of threads (hyphae) which makes up the body of a fungus.

myosin: the protein making up the thick filaments of muscle fibres.

natural selection: the selection of only the best adapted organisms for survival and reproduction, by natural factors such as predators or shortage of food supply.

nectar: a sugary liquid secreted by flowers to attract insects for pollination.

nephron: a kidney tubule, where urine is formed.

nerve: a group of nerve fibres, surrounded by connective tissue.

nerve fibre: an axon or dendron; a strand of cytoplasm extending from a nerve cell body.

niche: the role of a living organism in a community.

nitrifying bacteria: bacteria which convert proteins and urea into nitrates.

nitrogen fixation: the conversion of nitrogen gas into some compound of nitrogen, such as ammonia, nitrates or proteins.

nymph: the young stage of an insect, which resembles its parent rather more than a larva does.

obesity: being considerably overweight.

oesophagus: the part of the alimentary canal between the mouth and the stomach.

oestrogen: a hormone secreted by the ovaries which produces female secondary sexual characteristics.

old sight: having an inflexible lens, so that it cannot be adjusted to focus on objects at different distances.

operculum: the covering over the gill openings of a fish.

organelle: a structure inside a cell.

organ: part of an organism; a structure made of several tissues, which performs a particular function, e.g. heart.

osmoregulation: the control of the water content of the body.

osmosis: the movement of water molecules from a dilute solution to a concentrated solution, through a partially permeable membrane.

ovulation: the release of an egg from the ovary.

ovule: a structure inside a plant's ovary which contains a female gamete, and which develops into a seed after fertilisation.

ovum: a female gamete; an egg.

oxidation: the combination of a substance with oxygen.

oxyhaemoglobin: haemoglobin combined with oxygen; it is a brighter red than haemoglobin.

palisade layer: a layer of rectangular cells near the upper surface of a leaf, where photosynthesis takes place.

pancreatic juice: watery fluid secreted by the pancreas, containing various digestive enzymes, which flows into the duodenum along the pancreatic duct.

parasite: an organism which lives in very close association with another, and feeds on it.

parthenogenesis: the production of young from unfertilised eggs.

pathogen: an organism which causes disease.

pepsin: an enzyme secreted by glands in the wall of the stomach, which digests proteins.

perennial: a plant which survives more than one winter.

pericarp: the outer layers of a fruit, developed from the ovary.

perilymph: a fluid found in the semicircular canals in the ear, and also the outer part of the cochlea.

peristalsis: rhythmic contractions of the muscles in the walls of tubes, such as the alimentary canal or oviduct, which squeeze the contents along.

permeable: allowing substances to pass through.

pesticides: chemicals used to kill pests.

pH: a measure of the acidity of a solution; pH 7 is neutral, below 7 acidic, and above 7 alkaline.

phagocytosis: 'cell feeding'; the intake of particles of food by a cell.

phenotype: characteristics shown by an organism, a result of interaction between its genotype and its environment.

phloem: a plant tissue in which substances made by the plant are carried from one part to another.

phylum: a major group of organisms; a subdivision of a kingdom.

pioneer species: a species which colonises new areas while conditions are still not suitable for many other species to live there.

placenta: the organ through which a mammalian embryo is connected to its mother, and through which it obtains food, oxygen etc.

plankton: microscopic organisms which float in water.

plaque: a mixture of food remains and bacteria which builds up on and between teeth.

plasma: the liquid part of blood.

plasmid: a circular piece of DNA found in bacteria, which can be used as a vector to transfer genes from one organism to another in genetic engineering.

plasmolysis: shrinkage of the cytoplasm of a plant cell, so that the cell membrane begins to tear away from the cell wall; caused by loss of water.

pleural membranes: membranes surrounding the lungs and lining the thoracic cavity.

plumule: part of an embryo plant which will develop into the shoot.

poikilothermic: unable to control body temperature accurately.

pollination: the transfer of pollen from an anther to the stigma.

pollution: the addition of substances to the environment which harm life.

polysaccharide: a carbohydrate such as starch or cellulose, whose molecules are made of many sugar units joined together.

population: all the organisms of a particular species living in a certain area.

predator: an animal which hunts and kills other animals (known as its prey) for food.

premolar: large tooth between the canines and molars of mammals; unlike molars, premolars are present in the milk dentition as well as the permanent dentition.

primary consumer: the first consumer in a food chain; a herbivore.

producer: the first organism in a food chain, which produces food, i.e. a green plant.

progesterone: a hormone secreted by the ovary and later the placenta, which maintains the uterus lining during pregnancy.

prokaryotes: organisms such as bacteria, whose cells have no nucleus or other organelles with a membrane round them.

prostate gland: a gland near the junction of the two sperm ducts with the urethra, which secretes a fluid in which sperm swim.

protease: an enzyme which digests protein.

protein: a substance whose molecules are made of long chains of amino acids.

protoctists: unicellular organisms with nuclei.

pseudopodium: 'false foot'; a projection from a moving cell such as *Amoeba* or a white blood cell.

puberty: the age at which secondary sexual characteristics appear, and gametes begin to be produced.

pulmonary embolism: a blockage in a capillary or small artery in the lungs, which may be caused by a blood clot.

pure breeding: producing offspring like themselves; homozygous.

quadrat: a square which is placed over an area so that the numbers of organisms within it may be estimated.

radicle: a young root.

receptor: part of an organism which receives stimuli.

recessive allele: an allele which only shows in the phenotype in a homozygous organism.

rectum: the last part of the alimentary canal, in which faeces are formed before being egested through the anus.

reflex action: an automatic, unchanging response to a stimulus.

reflex arc: the series of neurones and synapses by which an impulse passes from a receptor to an effector in a reflex action.

refraction: the bending of light rays as they pass through materials of different densities.

relay neurone: a neurone in the central nervous system, which passes impulses from one neurone to another.

rennin: enzyme produced in the stomach of young mammals to help them to digest milk; also used in cheese-making.

respiration: the release of energy from carbohydrates; it happens in every living cell.

respiratory surface: the surface of an organism's body across which gas exchange takes place.

rhizome: an underground stem.

ribosomes: very small particles found in all cells, where protein molecules are assembled from amino acids.

rickets: a disease of the bones caused by lack of vitamin D.

RNA: ribonucleic acid; a substance found in all cells, one type of which copies instructions from the DNA in the nucleus and carries them to the ribosomes.

root hair: part of a root cell which projects into the soil, where it absorbs water and mineral salts.

roughage: fibrous, indigestible food, which stimulates the muscles of the alimentary canal to perform peristalsis.

saliva: watery fluid containing salivary amylase and mucus, secreted into the mouth by salivary glands.

saprophyte: an organism which feeds on dead organic material, by secreting enzymes onto it and absorbing it in liquid form.

sclera: the tough outer coat of the eyeball.

secretion: the production and release of a useful substance.

selection pressure: a factor acting on a population which favours certain varieties for survival.

selectively permeable: allowing some substances, but not others, to pass through.

septum: a structure which divides one part of an organism from another; a partition.

sex chromosomes: chromosomes which determine the sex of an organism.

sex linked: sex linked characteristics are determined by genes carried on the sex chromosomes, so that their inheritance is linked with the inheritance of sex.

short sight: being unable to focus on distant objects.

sieve plate: the perforated end wall of a sieve-tube element in phloem tissue.

single cell protein: high protein food made form microorganisms, such as mycoprotein made from fungi.

smooth muscle: muscle found in the walls of the alimentary canal, bladder etc., which contacts slowly and smoothly over long periods of time.

solute: a substance which dissolves in water or another solvent, to form a solution.

solvent: a liquid such as water, in which other substances can dissolve.

species: a group of organisms with similar characteristics, which can breed with each other, but not with organisms of different species.

spermatozoa: sperm; the male gametes of animals.

spermatophyte: a plant which reproduces by means of seeds; conifers and flowering plants.

sphincter muscle: a muscle round a tube, which can close the tube when it contracts.

sphygmomanometer: an instrument used to measure blood pressure.

spinal nerve: a nerve entering or leaving the spinal cord.

spiracle: a hole in the side of an insect, through which air enters the tracheal system.

spongy mesophyll: layer of cells near the underside of a leaf where photosynthesis takes place; they have large air spaces between them.

stabilizing selection: natural selection which acts on a population to keep it very much as it is; the most common form of natural selection.

starch: the polysaccharide storage material of plants, made from molecules of hundreds of glucose units linked together.

stele: xylem and phloem tissue in the centre of a root.

stimulus: a change in an organism's environment which is detected by a receptor.

striated muscle: muscle attached to the skeleton, which contracts when stimulated by a nerve.

stylets: mouthparts of an insect such as an aphid, adapted for piercing and sucking.

suberin: a waterproof substance which forms the cell walls of cork cells.

substrate: (a) a substance which is converted to another during a chemical reaction.

(b) the material on which a bacterium or fungus lives and feeds.

succession: a gradual change in the numbers and variety of organisms living in a habitat, beginning with colonisation and ending with a climax community.

sucrase: an enzyme which digests sucrose.

sucrose: a non-reducing disaccharide sugar.

sugar: a type of carbohydrate made of molecules consisting of one (monosaccharide) or two (disaccharide) sugar units; it tastes sweet, and is soluble.

suture: a join, e.g. between the bones in the cranium.

sweat gland: coiled gland in the dermis, which extracts water, salt and urea from the blood and secretes it as sweat.

swim bladder: an air-filled sac lying just under the backbone of bony fish, which aids buoyancy.

symbiosis: organisms of two different species living together for mutual benefit.

synapse: very small gap between two nerve fibres.

synovial joint: a joint between two bones, where free movement can occur.

synovial membrane: a membrane enclosing a synovial joint, attached to the bones on each side, which secretes and encloses synovial fluid.

systole: the stage in heart-beat when muscle contracts.

tap root: a root system with a main root which grows vertically downwards.

taste bud: a group of cells on the tongue which are sensitive to one or more of the four tastes sweet, sour, salty or bitter.

tendon: tough band of fibres which joins a muscle to a bone.

testa: hard outer covering of a seed.

test cross: breeding an organism showing a dominant characteristic in its phenotype, with one which is homozygous for the recessive characteristic. The offspring from this cross will show you whether the first organism is homozygous or heterozygous.

testosterone: a hormone secreted by the testes, responsible for male secondary sexual characteristics.

thorax: chest; the part of the body containing heart and lungs, separated from the abdomen by the diaphragm.

thrombosis: a blood clot in a vein or artery.

thyroid gland: an endocrine gland in the neck, which secretes thyroxine.

thyroxine: a hormone containing iodine, which speeds up metabolic rate.

tissue: a group of similar cells which together perform a particular function.

tissue fluid: fluid which fills in spaces between cells in the body, formed by plasma which leaks from blood capillaries.

toxin: a poison, especially one produced by pathogens inside the body.

trachea: a strengthened tube in vertebrates or insects, through which air passes on its way to and from the respiratory surface.

tracheole: a small tube branching from the trachea in an insect, with thin walls where gas exchange occurs.

transect: a line along which vegetation or animal life is recorded, usually to investigate changes from one habitat to another.

translocation: the movement of materials within a plant, particularly ones which the plant itself has made, such as sugars.

transmitter substance: a chemical which diffuses across a synapse to transmit an impulse to the other side.

transpiration: the loss of water vapour from a plant, mostly from the leaves.

tricuspid valve: the valve between the right atrium and ventricle.

trophic level: the level in a food chain at which an organism feeds.

tropism: a directional growth response of a plant to a stimulus.

turgid: a turgid plant cell contains plenty of water, so that the cytoplasm pushes outwards on the cell wall.

trypsin: an enzyme secreted by the pancreas, which digests proteins in the duodenum.

umbilical cord: cord containing an artery and vein, which connects a fetus to its placenta.

urea: substance containing nitrogen, made in the liver by the deamination of excess amino acids, and excreted in urine.

ureter: a tube carrying urine from the kidney to the bladder.

urethra: a tube leading from the bladder to the outside; it carries urine, and also semen in males.

uric acid: a semi-solid, nitrogenous excretory product of birds and many insects.

urine: a watery liquid containing urea and other excretory substances, produced by the kidneys.

uterus: womb; muscular organ with a soft lining, where a fetus develops.

vacuole: an organelle containing liquid, and surrounded by a membrane.

vagina: tube leading from the uterus to the outside.

vascular bundle: a group of xylem vessels and phloem tubes.

vas deferens: sperm duct; the tube carrying sperm from the testis to the urethra.

vector: an organism, or part of an organism, which transfers something from one kind of organism to another. Plasmids and viruses can be used as vectors to transfer DNA from one cell to another in genetic engineering. Mosquitoes are vectors for malaria, transferring *Plasmodium* from one person to another.

ventricle: one of the thick-walled lower chambers of the heart, which pumps blood into the arteries.

vestigial: small and useless.

villus: a small 'finger' of tissue, which increases surface area; found e.g. in the ileum and the placenta.

xylem vessel: a long, narrow tube made of many dead, lignified cells arranged end to end; conducts water in plants, and supports them.

yolk: a store of fat and protein food in an egg.

zygote: a cell formed at fertilisation, which will develop into an embryo.

Historical notes

Some landmarks in the study of cells.

Anton van Leeuwenhoek (1632–1723) was a Dutchman, whose hobby was making lenses. Van Leeuwenhoek improved the design of the microscope and made many of them in his lifetime. His microscopes could magnify about 240 times. Van Leeuwenhoek saw things which had never been seen before – tiny living creatures which he called 'little animals'.

Robert Hooke (1635–1703) used a more advanced kind of microscope than van Leeuwenhoek, called a compound microscope – rather like the ones in school laboratories today. He was able to see much smaller things and his drawings and descriptions of a piece of cork are especially famous, because he called the shapes he saw 'cells'. The word was soon being widely used to describe the small units from which all living organisms are made.

Lazaro Spallanzani (1729–1799) was an Italian scientist who was very interested in the 'little animals' which van Leeuwenhoek had described, and in where they came from. Many people thought that they just appeared, by spontaneous generation. Spallanzani carried out many experiments which showed that this was not true – these tiny organisms always appeared from eggs or spores, just as larger ones did.

The electron microscope was invented in 1930. It was not until 1952, however, that it could be used easily with living tissues, because it was so difficult to get suitably thin slices of them. The electron microscope has enabled us to see things 500 times smaller than with the light microscope.

On its own, the electron microscope has enabled us to see what the different parts of a cell probably look like. But by comparing what can be seen with an electron microscope with what can be found out in other ways, a better picture can be built up about what goes on inside cells.

Some landmarks in the history of medicine.

Edward Jenner (1749–1823) was an English country doctor who investigated smallpox, a terrible disease, which often killed the sufferer. In the eighteenth century, it was common practice in England to inoculate children with smallpox germs from a person who had had a mild attack of the disease. The hope was that the child would get a mild form of smallpox, survive, and be immune to the disease for the rest of their lives. Sometimes it worked; sometimes the child died.

Edward Jenner carried out many such inoculations. But he noticed that patients who had had a disease called cowpox – a mild disease caught from cows by people who milked them – did not get smallpox when he inoculated them with smallpox pus.

He tried an experiment. He inoculated a boy with cowpox pus, and later with smallpox pus. The boy did not get smallpox.

This was a much safer method of protection against smallpox. It was called 'vaccination' (Latin 'vacca' means 'cow'). Within a few years, it was being used all over Europe.

Louis Pasteur (1822–1895) lived and worked in France. He was a great thinker, who had a major influence on other scientists of his time. Much of his work was concerned with the causes and prevention of disease.

An industrialist was having trouble with the alcohol he was producing from fermented beet juice; it sometimes went sour. Pasteur proved that the yeast which caused fermentation was a living organism, and that microscopic rod-shaped organisms were responsible for making the alcohol go sour. The science of microbiology had begun.

Several years later, Pasteur showed that the organisms which turned wine sour could be killed by heating the wine gently. The method was called pasteurisation, and is now used all over the world as a way of treating milk to help it to keep longer.

Pasteur's first investigation into disease was with silkworms. He was able to show that a disease of silkworms was caused by a microbe; the first time microbes had been identified as the cause of a disease.

Pasteur firmly believed that each kind of infectious disease was caused by a particular kind of microbe, and he tried, unsuccessfully, to isolate the microorganism that caused cholera in humans. In 1880, Pasteur was working on a disease of chickens, called chicken cholera. He discovered that if his cultures of the microbe were left exposed to the air for some time, they were weakened. If they were then injected into chickens, the chickens became immune to the disease. Like Jenner, Pasteur had discovered a vaccine – and he went on to work out how to make other vaccines. Within a year, he had produced a vaccine for anthrax, and by 1885 a vaccine for rabies.

Pasteur was a great scientist. He worked very hard, was capable of logical thought and deduction, and loved argument. He always liked to show that his intellect was greater than that of the other scientists of his day – and his efforts to prove that his ideas were right and theirs were wrong often led him to great discoveries.

Robert Koch (1843–1910) was a German doctor. Early in his career he began to study anthrax. This was a disease which affected sheep, cattle, horses and sometimes humans. French scientists had shown that the blood of animals with anthrax contained a microorganism. Koch showed that the microorganism actually caused the disease. This was the first time that a particular germ had been proved to cause a particular disease. Koch later went on to identify the microorganisms responsible for many other diseases.

In the course of his experiments, Koch developed many techniques which are now widely used in microbiology – for example, growing microorganisms on a jelly made from agar.

Joseph Lister (1827–1912) was a surgeon in Scotland, at a time when surgery was done with no anaesthetics, and one in three peopled died from infection after major operations. Lister read of Pasteur's work, and realised that the infection was probably caused by microorganisms. In 1865, he tried applying carbolic acid to wounds to kill the microbes, with great success. Gradually, he came to realise the importance of washing his hands and surgical instruments thoroughly before an operation. It was many years, however, before his techniques became widely used by other surgeons.

Elie Metchnikoff (1845–1916) was a Russian scientist. In 1882, he inoculated starfish larvae with microbes and could see, in their transparent bodies, how cells moved towards the infected place and attacked the microbes. He called the cells phagocytes, and suggested that a similar defence system operated in the human body. His discoveries began studies into how immunity works – the science of immunology.

Paul Ehrlich (1854–1915) was interested in the use of chemicals to attack disease. Working in Berlin, he tried out a substance called atoxyl, which contained arsenic, as a treatment for sleeping sickness. The results were hopeful, and he tried making other chemicals from atoxyl. Number 606, which he called salversan, proved particularly effective against syphilis and relapsing fever. Ehrlich's work began a new branch of medicine – chemotherapy.

Alexander Fleming (1881–1955) was born in Scotland, but worked as a bacteriologist in a London hospital. In 1928, while working with Staphylococci which were growing on an agar plate, Fleming saw that a mould had got in by mistake. Around the mould, there was a clear patch, where no bacteria had grown. Fleming suggested that the mould, *Penicillium,* had made a substance which diffused through the agar, and which killed the bacteria.

Howard Florey (1898–1968) isolated the substance made by the *Penicillium* mould, ten years after Fleming's discovery. He called it penicillin. It was the first antibiotic – a substance which kills bacteria but not human cells. Initially there were problems with producing penicillin in large quantities, but by the end of the Second World War it was being manufactured in enormous quantities. Since then, many other antibiotics have been discovered.

Steps in the understanding of evolution and genetics.

Carl Linnaeus (1707–1778) a Swedish naturalist, introduced the idea of classifying living things. He worked with plants, giving each one a Latin name, as described in Chapter 17. His work helped to remove a lot of confusion which had resulted from all the different common names which could be given to one kind of plant.

Jean Baptiste de Lamarck (1744–1829) was a French naturalist and philosopher. He was the first person to put forward a consistent theory of evolution, in 1809. He realised that the earth was extremely old, and that organisms had evolved, so that they became better adapted to their environment. However, Lamarck believed that each organism had a kind of inbuilt 'drive towards perfection', and that characteristics that an organism acquired during its lifetime could be passed on to its offspring. He also believed in spontaneous generation. For Lamarck, each group of organisms began as something created by spontaneous generation, which then gradually became more 'perfect' over a long period of time.

Charles Darwin (1809–1882), like Lamarck, thought that the earth must be very old, and that organisms evolved to become better adapted to their environment. His theory of natural selection, however, which is explained in Chapter 16, has turned out to be much nearer the truth than Lamarck's ideas.

Darwin was a great naturalist, who worked on many biological subjects during his lifetime. His ideas about evolution and natural selection were inspired during a voyage in the *Beagle* to South America from 1831 to 1836. However, it took him many years to sort these ideas out, and he published his most famous book, *The Origin of Species*, in 1859.

Gregor Mendel (1822–1884), an Austrian monk, worked on the inheritance of various characteristics in the garden pea. Other people had previously done experiments like Mendel's, but they did not take as much trouble as he did over accurate recording of results, and were not able to interpret them correctly. Mendel's hypothesis to explain inheritance was that there were particles (we now call them genes) responsible for the appearance of certain characters; that each parent had two of these genes for each characteristic, but only passed on one to its offspring; and that the genes stayed separate in the offspring, so that they would separate again to be passed on to *their* offspring.

Mendel's work was overlooked for 34 years. In 1900, it was rediscovered by several scientists also working on genetics. Once his results were published, they sparked off a tremendous amount of research on the mechanism of heredity, which continues today.

Index